FLAUBERT

FLAUBERT

A BIOGRAPHY

BY
HERBERT LOTTMAN

Fromm International Publishing Corporation
New York

Published in 1990 by Fromm International Publishing Corporation
560 Lexington Avenue, New York, NY 10022 by arrangement with
Little, Brown and Company.

Library of Congress Cataloging-in-Publication Data
Lottman, Herbert R.
    Flaubert : a biography.
    Includes bibliographical references.
    1. Flaubert, Gustave, 1821-1880—Biography.
2. Novelists, French—19th century—Biography.
I. Title.
[PQ2247.L68 1990]   843'.8   [B]   90-2801
ISBN 0-88064-120-7

Designed by Robert G. Lowe

Printed in the United States of America

CONTENTS

PREFACE

THE BIOGRAPHER of a seminal figure such as Gustave Flaubert may on occasion appear to resemble a newspaper editor handling a story. Recent good books about Flaubert were written in the absence of sorely lacking evidence, such as the manuscript of the first version of *A Sentimental Education*, which he was working on at the very moment when he suffered his first attack of epilepsy. Now this document is available. At least one writer was waiting for the notes Flaubert made in preparation for the final version of the same novel, and now those notes have turned up. One biographer, confronted by Flaubert's letters to women, from which all raw language had been censored, as well as by some unexpurgated correspondence with men, came to some erroneous conclusions about Flaubert's sexual preferences. Now we can read uncensored versions of all the letters. Much of the lost material is eventually "found" in auction sales. Sometimes a single sheet of paper comes to the surface this way, shedding new light on an old enigma.

Perhaps each generation needs a new version of the past. What is certain, in every area of study, is that with time more data are uncovered, which when juxtaposed with what we knew or thought we knew require a reordering of events.

Let it be clear that the present writer believes that biography is nothing if it is not history; that is to say, the best arrangement of verifiable fact must precede any attempt to interpret fact. If an author toys with the truth in the interest of making a more coherent story, or to confirm a psychoanalytical or socioeconomic theory, he is betraying history, his subject, and the reader. Some interpreters of Flaubert have been caught in the trap of taking his fiction for reality, assuming that everything he wrote, or nearly everything (including his adolescent sketches), really happened to or was thought or felt by him. People who have fallen into this trap simply do not understand creative writing; they assume that all invention is involuntary and subject to analysis. (The more playful the storyteller, the more troubled he appears to the amateur psychoanalyst.)

We now have a new and careful editing of Flaubert's letters. Two volumes have been published, and two more will be brought out in coming years. Much correspondence from Flaubert's family and friends (or enemies) has recently become available. Flaubert chose to live far from his friends and lovers, so we have an extraordinary written record of his daily existence and his artistic intentions. Some of his contemporaries may have revealed themselves just as eloquently at café tables, but these declarations are mostly lost to us.

Lovers of language carry a biography of Flaubert in their heads. Who does not know about the hermit on the Seine up in Normandy, the man who loved women very well while keeping them at a distance, who was both Madame Bovary the incurable romantic and Saint Anthony the resister of temptation? I shall try not to be unfaithful to the Flaubert legend, where it does not conflict with the evidence.

PROLOGUE

H E HAD REFUSED to heed the suggestion of his editors that he remove those shocking passages from *Madame Bovary*. And even if the Emperor's police had no particular reason to punish the unknown Gustave Flaubert for writing a novel containing suggestive scenes and language, criminal prosecution would nonetheless serve as a lesson to the opposition press by imposing sanctions on the magazine — *La Revue de Paris* — that had published not only *Madame Bovary* but other contributions even more offensive to this timorous Empire. So the trial of Flaubert and of the magazine's editor and its printer would indeed take place. "If I am convicted," Flaubert declared to an influential friend, "it will no longer be possible for me to write a line." And this was his first publishable book, printed in installments in *La Revue de Paris* but still awaiting its appearance between book covers. "They'll keep an eye on me, and a repeat offense will mean five years in prison."[1]

Flaubert was not a Parisian, but he already knew something about how influence was wielded in the capital — whom one had to reach, and what arguments to use. He himself came from another influential place, the rich Norman province whose capital was close enough to the seat of power to matter. What was more, the legislative elections were coming. Hadn't the prefect of Flaubert's district promised to contact the minister of the interior on his behalf? In Paris Flaubert had been moving mountains — at least, he had gotten to some high-placed men and perhaps even more high-placed women, grandes dames who had the ear of Napoleon III.

But in the end he was counting on Normandy. It was essential, he informed his brother — Dr. Achille Flaubert, the respected chief surgeon of Rouen's principal hospital, who had succeeded his respected father in that post — to bring local pressure to bear on Paris. The police investigators who had questioned him had thought at first that he was a nobody, but when they discovered that Gustave Flaubert had independent means, their behavior toward him changed. "They have to learn at the Interior Ministry that we are, in Rouen, what is called a *family*, that we have deep roots in our region, and that in attacking me, especially on a charge of immorality, they will be offending many people."[2]

In truth, he had never left his family, and would never move from his family home. Surely he had the right to invoke them now?

PART I

CHAPTER ONE

CHAMPAGNE AND NORMANDY

HOW FAR BACK need we go to establish the roots of a man? Gustave Flaubert was born and grew up in Normandy and lived most of his life there, and for friends and admirers he was a Norman, even a Viking (the Vikings having settled pre-French Normandy after sacking it). Some have sung Flaubert's Norman heritage to the point of making light of his paternal ancestry, for Flaubert's father came from a reputedly blander region, the disparate Champagne province to the east of Paris, best known for its wine and its battlefields. One authority not only dismisses Flaubert's Champagne antecedents but denies any physical resemblance between Gustave and his father. He is "all Norman," Gustave is.[1]

Misunderstandings such as this one explain why biographers are often obliged to track down and then to repeat boring data on ancestry. We have it from local authorities that the Flauberts were among the oldest families of the Champagne region, where more than sixty towns and villages contained inhabitants bearing that name.[2] The Flauberts who are to help our story begin are first discovered in a village called Bagneux in the Marne district. There, in the seventeenth century, one Michel Flaubert was a *maréchal expert*, a blacksmith who treated horses and other farm animals as well as shoeing them. On Michel's death, his son Jean-Baptiste Constant took over his forge and his veterinary function. (These Flauberts then spelled their name *Flobert*.)[3] The blacksmith-veterinarian Jean-Baptiste Constant Flobert had a son named Nicolas (1754–1814), who in turn was the father of Achille-Cléophas. Achille-Cléophas was Gustave Flaubert's father.

This Nicolas Flobert apparently carried on his family vocation in Bagneux, marrying Marie-Apolline Millon, daughter of a master surgeon — a fair match, for surgeons did not then have the status they enjoy today. Their son Achille-Cléophas was born on November 14, 1784, in Maizières-la-Grande Paroisse, his mother's native village.[4] Nicolas, his bride, and his new son settled in Nogent-sur-Seine, once an imposing fortified village, today a backwater lacking outstanding features.

Indeed, we have hardly made this Champagne region seem attractive. It is a countryside of chalky soil whose perfect grape, when dealt with in a certain way, becomes that fizzy wine. Further south, in true Flaubert country, the land was sown for wheat or utilized for cattle and sheep. It has little to offer the hurried traveler. But Gustave Flaubert was not hurried, and he returned to Champagne and to Nogent again and again, in the days when the trip was a long one; and then, in his most personal, most wistful writing — his novel of apprenticeship, *A Sentimental Education* — he gave Nogent a central role.

Gustave's father was not quite five years old when the Bastille fell to the insurgents of Paris; it would be another three years before the beheading of Louis XVI. Nicolas Flobert was a royalist who did not hide his feelings; the story is that he was hauled off to Paris to be tried by the Revolutionary Tribunal at the time when Robespierre was eliminating the more moderate elements of the Committee for Public Safety. On February 27, 1794, Nicolas was sentenced to a penal colony for his "unpatriotic and counterrevolutionary remarks," but he was freed after Robespierre was deposed.[5] Legend has it that Nicolas's wife was instrumental in effecting his release, thanks to the certificates of honorability she obtained from people back home.[6] One might prefer the version of the story Gustave later told. He said that it was his father, then a child of seven (actually he would have been nine, going on ten), who had saved Nicolas, by delivering a pathetic speech to the magistrate in Nogent.[7]

Everything we can learn about Flaubert's mother is of capital importance. For Gustave lived with his widowed mother until she died, and she survived her husband by a quarter of a century. She was born Anne Justine Caroline Fleuriot on September 7, 1793, in Pont-l'Evêque, in the Auge agricultural country famous for its dairy products since the Middle Ages. Her father, Jean-Baptiste, came from nearby Argences, a village that is hard to locate on a map, which may be why family legend, with the encouragement of Gustave and his niece, confuses Argences with Argentan, a tradition that even lends Flaubert's maternal grandfather a touch of nobility: he was, so Gustave's mother apparently informed her son, Fleuriot d'Argentan, a leader of the Vendean army, which fought a last stand against the French Revolution.[8] Flaubert's niece maintained that Jean-Baptiste was a medical doctor.[9] But someone who took the trouble to look at his marriage certificate found that he was a public health officer, which is not quite the same thing, as readers of *Madame Bovary* will remember. The title was given to would-be practitioners after summary medical training. It is also true that an ancestor of the maternal grandmother of Flaubert's mother, one Jean-François Le Pouterel, went off to French Canada in the seventeenth century and — as impressively thorough research has discovered — claimed to have risked his life trapping beavers.[10] Gustave spiced up the story: "You know that I descend from a Natchez or an Iroquois," he confided to a friend.[11]

Eight days after the birth of Gustave's mother, her mother died. The infant was raised by her father, but he too abandoned her, dying when she was only nine. As an orphan, she was taken under the wing of relatives and family friends, who served as a board of guardians, and was sent to school in the Channel port of Honfleur. Later she was brought to Rouen by her godmother, Marie Thouret, a cousin from Pont-l'Evêque who by then was the wife of Jean-Baptiste Laumonier, the chief surgeon of Rouen's public hospital.[12] This hospital, the Hôtel-Dieu, was to be the scene of Anne Justine Caroline's growing up, of her meeting with a young disciple of Dr. Laumonier's, Achille-Cléophas Flaubert, of her marriage to this young surgeon, and of the birth of Gustave Flaubert.

Rouen in the early nineteenth century was one of France's largest urban centers. Once Normandy's capital, the site of the trial and burning of Joan of Arc, it was a bustling river port, a center for textile manufacturing and the wine trade. As it was a provincial capital, its public buildings were imposing, and its Gothic cathedral was one of the country's leading attractions. All of this is to say that it was hardly a dead end when the young doctor from Champagne, fresh from his Paris training, came up to work alongside Laumonier, the chief surgeon.

Recall his beginnings: his father, Nicolas, had been a veterinarian. The son had an opportunity to aim higher. He attended the lycée in Sens and then found his way to Paris and a proper medical school, where he was remembered as earnest and erudite. During his intern-

ship, he attracted the attention of Guillaume Dupuytren, already a
famous surgeon, a pioneer in this still-primitive discipline who was to
introduce new operating techniques.

Here oral traditions collide. The prevailing story — one told by a
disciple of Achille-Cléophas's, who must have heard it from his master — was that Dupuytren, a jealous man, arranged to send the most
promising of his students far away from Paris. He had a good excuse
in Achille-Cléophas's poor health.[13] (We can document the poor health
with a certificate of exemption from military service, dated 1806, which
describes Gustave's father as five-foot-eight-and-a-half, with brown
eyes and a long chin, and suffering from pulmonary consumption —
which could be tuberculosis of the lungs.)[14] To contradict the story of
Dupuytren's jealousy, it has been argued that Rouen regularly re-
cruited its teachers from among the best students at the Paris Medical
Faculty. Whatever the reason, Achille-Cléophas Flaubert moved up
to Rouen to fill the position of assistant to the anatomy professor, who
happened to be the chief surgeon, Laumonier. He brought along a
warm recommendation from Dupuytren, who pointed out that his
protégé had taken first prizes in all of his classes. "I shall add," said
Dupuytren, "less to praise him than to recommend him to your kind
attention, that he has been one of my pupils and a personal friend for
some years, and that I should be particularly grateful for everything
you do for his training, for his advancement, and for the comfort a
young man as well brought up as he requires."[15] Eventually Achille-
Cléophas was given responsibility for courses in surgery, external pathology, and childbirth, a teaching program that would take on greater
importance when he had his own assistants to share the work load.[16]

In his early years in Rouen Dr. Flaubert was also busy with his
doctoral thesis, which he presented in Paris at the Medical Faculty in
December 1810. In this "Dissertation on the manner of treating patients before and after surgical operations," even a lay reader can see
that its author displays a degree of consideration for patients that was
uncommon in those times. But one may also be struck by the lack of
concern for what we would consider basic hygiene, for sterile conditions in which to handle patients.[17]

And while Achille-Cléophas Flaubert was working for Laumonier,
Laumonier was providing bed and board for Anne Justine Caroline
Fleuriot, the orphan from Pont-l'Evêque. She was thirteen years old
when the intern Flaubert arrived in Rouen, and eighteen when they
decided to marry. The bride's dowry, as her granddaughter Caroline

understood it, was a farm worth four thousand francs* in annual rent; the groom had only his promise.[18] We lack a wedding portrait, though an early, undated likeness of the bride reveals a comely young lady with pleasantly even features and thick tresses parted in the middle. All available portraits of the groom show him clean-shaven and benignly round-faced, not too solemn but not too light-headed, either.[19]

They were married in Rouen's city hall on February 10, 1812. Achille-Cléophas's father had come up from Nogent-sur-Seine to give his consent.[20] The newlyweds lived in the center of old Rouen for the first five years of their marriage, and their first child, baptized Achille, was born there on February 9, 1813; so was their first daughter, Caroline, on February 8, 1816, but she was to die before her second birthday. Later there would be another Caroline, but before her arrival two more male children were born to early deaths, and another son was born to live — Gustave.[21]

In December 1815, when he had just turned thirty-one, Dr. Flaubert was called in to replace Laumonier as the chief surgeon of the Hôtel-Dieu; the older man had apparently suffered several strokes and was incapacitated mentally as well as physically. Flaubert had been earning a living in private practice and could get along without a salary from the hospital or even an official residence, and so the ailing Dr. Laumonier was allowed to keep both until his death. In notifying Dr. Flaubert of his appointment, the chairman of the hospital committee praised his broad knowledge and talent, as well as the deserved reputation he had acquired in private practice. Laumonier's incapacity had encouraged a certain degree of laxity at the hospital, and it was hoped that among other things the new chief surgeon would see to it that his students respected the corpses on which they worked. He was expected, for instance, to make sure that detached limbs and organs were kept together with the bodies they came from, both for sanitary reasons and out of regard for the deceased. Flaubert would have to carry out all major operations personally, or be present if an intern had been authorized to perform one. Either he or an intern surgeon had to be present at all bleedings, then a customary treatment in most illnesses. Only an intern surgeon could bleed a woman in the maternity ward, a place students were not even permitted to enter.[22]

---

*For information on nineteenth-century francs, see the appendix.

CHAPTER TWO

THE HÔTEL-DIEU

THE DEATH of Dr. Laumonier at the beginning of 1818 freed the chief surgeon's quarters for the Flaubert family, which at that point meant Achille-Cléophas, his wife, and five-year-old Achille. This residence was a sturdy stone pavilion occupying a convenient corner on the town side of the hospital. It was here that two other male children were born to the couple, both to die in infancy. Between the birth of the second luckless infant on November 30, 1819, and his death on June 29, 1822, Gustave came into the Flauberts' world.[1]

We can almost seize that instant, we can almost photograph it, so little has the physical environment changed in the 170 years separating us from the birth of Gustave Flaubert. The generously proportioned hospital complex, completed at the end of the reign of Louis XV, resembles, as so many old French hospitals do, a palace and its dependencies. From the main gate on the town side, as one approaches on Rue de Crosne — now Avenue Gustave Flaubert — the visitor confronts an austere facade topped with slate tiles and dominated by the steeples of a chapel and of the Saint Madeleine church, where Gustave received his baptism. From this angle, the chief surgeon's residence stands on the left, its windows facing the main courtyard and the narrow Rue de Lecat. Gustave would have been born in his parents' bedroom, on the second floor; later he was to occupy a room of his own on a still higher, low-ceilinged service floor.[2]

His birth certificate specifies that Gustave joined the world at four A.M. on December 12, 1821.[3] The baptismal certificate adds that the infant's father was absent from the religious ceremony, and at least one writer attributes this to the doctor's anticlericalism.[4] Although they respected custom, Gustave's parents were not practicing Catholics; they have been described as deists, like so many of their bourgeois peers.[5]

One would love to be able to see the world as this child saw it. Lively, industrious Rouen began more or less at the Flauberts' doorstep. Although the hospital is only five hundred yards or so west of the Place du Vieux Marché, it was virtually outside of town when it was built, for its original function was to provide shelter for victims of the plague. The city center owes most of its imposing buildings to the Middle Ages and to the Renaissance, but by the first decades of Flaubert's century, thriving textile factories had caused Rouen to be called the Manchester of France. It contained some 90,000 inhabitants; with surrounding towns and villages, the figure rose to 225,000. The inner city boasted 470 streets, seventeen thousand houses, twenty-nine squares and markets, and fourteen churches (thirteen Catholic and one Protestant). Also "three barracks, three hospitals, two prisons, two theaters," as a local almanac put it.[6] The depth of the river allowed oceangoing vessels to dock in Rouen — up to twenty-five hundred of them each year.[7] In addition to its museums, botanical garden, and learned societies, Rouen also maintained a public library that stored thirty-two thousand books and twelve hundred ancient manuscripts.[8]

Achille was already eight years old when Gustave was born, and he was sent off to high school just as his brother was beginning to take notice of the world outside his nursery. Those were no-nonsense times, when youngsters lived at boarding school even if their parents resided in the same city. But when Gustave was only three, a sister was born, who was named Caroline, just as their parents' firstborn daughter had been. Gustave and Caroline grew up together in a tender relationship interrupted only by her marriage. Then there was Julie, almost the cliché image of a faithful servant. Scholarship has more or less determined that she was born Béatrix Caroline Hébert, in the nearby Eure district; perhaps she was given the name Julie to avoid the confusion of having two Carolines in the same house. She would have been twenty-one when she entered the Flauberts' service in 1825.[9] A family fixture, Julie stayed with the family until her retirement, surviving even Gustave.

When Gustave's niece Caroline first recorded her reminiscences, she was forty years old, and the faithful servant Julie had been dead for four years. In these "Souvenirs Intimes," she describes Gustave as a child, drawing on Julie as her prime source. The servant had grown up in a region "fertile in old stories of love and ghosts," and she would tell them to the boy. Thanks to a year spent in bed with a bad knee, Julie had read more than a young woman of her station normally did; these stories, too, she passed on to little Gustave.

Caroline had also been told a great deal about Gustave by his mother, who had been dead for fourteen years when Caroline set down these recollections. She remembered the description of Gustave as quiet, meditative, and with a naïveté he never shook off. He could spend hours with a finger in his mouth, lost in his thoughts, seeming stupid. Caroline repeats the following unkind anecdote: when Gustave was six an old servant named Pierre used to say to him when he got in the way, "Go look in the garden or the kitchen to see if I'm there." Gustave would obey, telling the cook, "Pierre told me to see if he is here."

There is also the story, again passed on by Caroline, that after teaching her older son to read, Gustave's mother tried to do the same for him, but he only cried. He would say, "Why learn to read, since Papa Mignot reads?" (Mignot was a favorite neighbor.) Gustave was almost nine, says the family legend, before he learned to read.[10]

We need not believe this; in fact the evidence is that it isn't true. But everything about a nineteenth-century childhood is hazy. Take Gustave's favorite neighbor, Papa or *père* Mignot: no one, not even any of his direct descendants, has ever come up with a first name for him. He was a retired farmer living just opposite the chief surgeon's house on Rue de Lecat. One of his sons, Amédée, born in 1801 and later an attorney and law professor, was an early admirer of young Gustave's (who, as we shall see, was more of a prodigy than a slow learner). And his daughter Lucie was the mother of Gustave's best childhood friend, Ernest Chevalier.[11]

Family legend has Gustave dashing across the street to sit on *père* Mignot's knee to hear his favorite stories again and again. The old man read *Don Quixote* to him, and here word of mouth is reinforced by a remark later made by Gustave himself. He knew *Don Quixote* by heart, he said — obviously in a popular abridgment — before he knew how to read.[12]

Then a recollection in a different key. The Place du Vieux Marché, where Joan was burned, was still used for executions in Gustave's time. Once when he was six or seven, on his way home from school, Gustave was passing by the guillotine and saw fresh blood on the paving stones; they were just detaching the basket containing the decapitated head when he got there. Years later, after having a tooth

extracted, he crossed the square and recalled that childhood experience, and that night dreamed of the guillotine.[13]

Surely every child can call up at least one unbearable memory,
even if guillotines and heads in baskets are harder to find now. But
Gustave was in for more. He lived in a hospital, where he could open
a door and find himself in a ward filled with patients; the dissecting
chamber adjoined the family's billiard room. Much later, one of Dr.
Flaubert's students remembered seeing little Gustave inside that dissecting chamber, wearing a white smock and a padded ring around
his head, of the sort children wore to avoid injury when they fell.[14]
Gustave himself recalled it: "The anatomical theater faced our garden. How often my sister and I climbed up the trellis and, suspended
between the vines, looked in at the laid-out corpses. . . . The same
flies that flitted over us and the flowers entered the theater and returned. . . ."[15] Early in our century, a scholar sought to pin a "medical mentality" on Flaubert; it was a well-argued thesis.[16]

In his own version of Gustave's childhood, Jean-Paul Sartre (who
preferred intuitive perception to tangible evidence), in the twenty-eight-
hundred-page, three-volume study of Flaubert he left uncompleted
on his death, paints a grim picture of Gustave's growing-up years.
Sartre cites Flaubert's youthful writings as evidence, and one early
story does present an adolescent who was persecuted, sullen, ferocious, and miserable.[17] But why not prefer Flaubert's "Mémoires d'un
fou" ("Memoirs of a Madman"), written only a year after the story
Sartre quotes? In this partly autobiographical tale, Gustave's hero remembers his childhood: "I was merry and cheerful, loving life and
my mother. . . ." This child also had "moments of sadness and despair," but dare we build on this a hypothesis concerning Flaubert's
childhood?[18]

Sartre paints Flaubert's father as a tyrant, based on analysis of the
son's adolescent writings; his conclusion is that Gustave was rele-
gated to the role of family idiot.[19] In his own diary, probably in the
very period during which he was producing the stories on which Sartre
based his analysis, Gustave wrote: "I loved only one man as a friend
and only one other, my father."[20] (The friend, as we shall see, was
Alfred Le Poittevin.) Later, after expressing scorn for the medical
profession, Flaubert made an exception for his father, recalling how
devoted he had been to his profession and to even the least privileged
of his patients.[21] Flaubert's letters to his parents, and theirs to him,
are further evidence that he was anything but the idiot of the family.

Indeed, we should go back a few years, to deal with a matter that has been questioned but not explained. Family legend dies hard. It was the servant Julie who apparently first told the tale of little Gustave's being unable to read until he was nine years old. She told it to Gustave's niece Caroline, who repeated it to Flaubert's disciple Guy de Maupassant; both he and Caroline published it as fact.[22] This is a piece of nonsense that modern biographers, including Sartre, repeat without questioning. What Flaubert himself would have thought of such a backward child is suggested by his comment on the ignorance of his brother's daughter: because of the abominable way she was being brought up, he complained, she still couldn't read, even though she was six years old.[23]

The truth is that Gustave read early, and well. He seems to have begun writing early, too; later he recalled that he would ask Julie to spell the words he was using in the sentences he invented.[24] The best evidence of Flaubert's capabilities is his own letters, two of them written when he was eight, a year before the legend says he learned to read. Or witness the letter written to his comrade Ernest Chevalier at the end of 1830, when he had just turned nine. He was not only a reader, he was an *author*. He and his friends were writing and performing their own plays. "I'll send you my comedies also," he wrote (true, his spelling is approximative). "If you want to collaborate with me, I will write the comedies and you will write up your dreams. . . ." Soon Gustave told Ernest that he had begun to compose stories in notebooks.

Gustave was all of ten when he informed Ernest that he was now a published writer. He had written a brief paper on Corneille and a still briefer (but funnier) description of constipation, and Ernest's uncle Amédée Mignot had reproduced these pieces in facsimile.[25]

CHAPTER THREE

DR. FLAUBERT

ACHILLE-CLÉOPHAS was a hard-driving man. He created a curriculum of formal medical instruction from what had previously been only an adjunct to the day-to-day operations of the hospital. He instilled discipline, for himself first of all, and managed to have plenty of time for private patients. He was punctual, insisted on detail, and expected others to be like him. He would burst into a hospital ward, followed not only by a flock of students but also by doctors from neighboring towns who wished to learn from his diagnoses. He was known for preferring "surgery that preserves and repairs to surgery that cuts away."[1] It would be another century before historians of medicine began to take a closer look at what surgeons actually did in the days before anesthetics and asepsis, before the very notion of a germ-free environment existed; ignorance of these things, and a liberal recourse to bleeding, resulted in a greater number of dead than live patients after serious operations.[2]

When Dr. Flaubert was nominated as an associate member of the Académie de Médecine in Paris, the police, in that climate of Restoration reaction under Louis XVIII, asked the authorities in Rouen for a report on the candidate. The reply began reassuringly: "His excellent moral qualities and particularly his kindness have earned for him public esteem and consideration." Then the mildest political note one might imagine: "This doctor's political opinions are liberal, but he has never been seen in the role of advocate. His speeches, on the contrary, indicate wisdom and moderation, and his behavior is such that even those who do not share his principals generally accord him their confidence."[3]

Much later, Gustave Flaubert contributed his own recollection: he remembered how, on a pleasant summer day in his last years, his father would announce that he was going to take a walk, and then would rush off to the morgue to find a body to dissect. Or he would spend his own money to travel to a distant corner of the district to perform an interesting operation on a fishmonger who would pay him with a dozen herrings.[4]

His rank and reputation allowed Dr. Flaubert to command respectable fees outside the hospital; not having to pay for his lodgings surely helped him to hold on to his money. But to the charge that the doctor was a "man of money," one of his disciples responded that he treated many patients free of charge.[5]

On their marriage, Achille-Cléophas and Anne Justine Caroline entered into a partnership to control the properties they would acquire during their married life. And then they began to acquire them. The first purchase was in Dr. Flaubert's home province: more than 118 hectares (a hectare being nearly two and a half acres), including a farm called Courtavent. This was in 1819, four years after he took over at the Hôtel-Dieu and two years before Gustave's birth. In 1825, at Pont-sur-Seine, which was also at Dr. Flaubert's end of the Seine valley, they bought woodland and meadows in three lots totaling thirty-four hectares; the next year, in the same region, they acquired another thirty hectares, and two and a half hectares of grazing land was subsequently added to this holding. Turning to Madame Flaubert's native province, they purchased the Ferme de Géfosse at Pont-l'Evêque, more than three hectares with nearby meadows and woodland. In the same region, at Touques — a town near Trouville and the Channel beaches, where Madame Flaubert already owned the Ferme de Beauregard, inherited from her parents — the couple set about adding parcels, several hectares' worth. At Pont-l'Evêque itself they bought a meadow called Parcs et Parquets de Betteville, another eighteen hectares. They added nearly twenty hectares to that in 1842.

Then there was Deauville, an undeveloped stretch of coast contiguous to Trouville. Later the region was to become a resort for millionaires, a center of horse racing and breeding, with a famous beach and casino. Even for that time — 1837 — they paid a considerable sum, eighty thousand francs for a little more than twenty-six hectares. They would add smaller parcels later.[6] The Flaubert properties were inhabited or used by farmers; these investments produced income in the form of annual rentals.

A specialist who set out to study the upper classes of nineteenth-century Rouen happened to stumble upon the case of Achille-Cléo-phas Flaubert. In 1820 only 1,047 Rouen gentlemen paid sufficient taxes to qualify as voters under the existing rules, and Dr. Flaubert was one of them. The Flauberts began their married life with a capital of fifteen thousand francs; at the death of Dr. Flaubert thirty-four years later, his legacy came to eight hundred thousand francs. By that time, this specialist tells us, the good doctor was one of the wealthiest men in Rouen.[7]

The year Gustave was born, the Flauberts decided to take their little family out of the hospital environment, at least on Sundays and holidays. They found a house in the country just outside the city: Déville-lès-Rouen is little more than a mile from the Hôtel-Dieu. It was a pavilion of modest scale, with wing extensions; on the facade, dead center between the upper-floor windows, Dr. Flaubert placed a bust of Hippocrates. We know that the couple paid fifty-two thousand francs for this suburban retreat and kept it until 1844, at which time construction of the railway from Rouen north to Le Havre took a slice of their land, prompting them to look elsewhere for peace.[8]

Dr. Flaubert had a sister, who lived in Nogent-sur-Seine with her husband, François Parain, a goldsmith and jeweler. The Parains had a daughter, Olympiade, called Olympe, who would marry one Louis-Théodore Bonenfant, an attorney; they and their children were also to matter in Gustave's life.[9] With or without his parents, Gustave counted Nogent and, after the death of his aunt, "Uncle Parain" part of his universe. Today the contrast between these towns on the Seine — Rouen the ocean port, Nogent the prairie market town — is perhaps even greater than it was then. Nogent was the last port of call for large vessels from Paris. Today, when river traffic counts for little and Nogent-sur-Seine has all but disappeared from view, that solid stone residence of Flaubert's uncle can still be seen in the town center, though the interior has been converted into the branch office of a bank. It stands on the corner of what is now Rue Gustave Flaubert.

The Flauberts' preferred summer resort was Trouville, only seven miles from Madame Flaubert's birthplace. Later it was to become a fashionable beach and casino town, but when Gustave's parents elected this humble fishing village, it was just barely accessible. In Gustave's fictional confession "Novembre," he describes the journey from Pont-l'Evêque: "I had three leagues to walk, and went off by myself, without a stick, without a dog. First I walked on paths winding through

the wheat; I passed under apple trees, along hedges. . . ." Then he
was on a plateau, in the middle of a hay meadow: "I had the sea
before me. . . ." [10]

And there was Trouville village, "charming with its houses crowded
together, black, gray, red, white, facing in all directions, without
alignment or symmetry." So he described the setting in "Mémoires
d'un fou," that other fictional confession, written in 1838, when he
was not quite seventeen. "Black nets gnawed by the sea were spread
before the doors of houses . . . there were sailors wearing red and
blue." [11]

Inland, at Pont-l'Evêque, we know very well what the Flauberts
could see, for today their Ferme de Géfosse, on a rise about a mile
from the town center, stands as an undeclared monument. The same
cannot be said of Trouville. At first the Flauberts stayed at a humble
inn on the Touques quay; then they rented a house, presumably the
one Gustave's sister referred to as "our cottage." It was torn down
long before our time.

The one thing we are sure of is that Gustave lost his heart in Trouville; perhaps he lost it once and for all. But we are getting ahead of
our story.

CHAPTER FOUR

THE YOUNG WRITER

IT HAS BEEN said that Gustave Flaubert was raised to be a doctor and was educated as a lawyer, until illness led to another change in orientation, making it possible (or necessary) for him to accept a more sedentary existence. But we shall see that Flaubert always intended to become a writer; in secondary school he was already producing work that deserved publication. Surely his vocation began in childhood, when he was writing his own plays and going to grownup theater. In Flaubert's time, as we have seen, Rouen had its own theaters, and actors and actresses with national reputations performed in them; one could see the latest (and often controversial) plays without ever going to Paris.[1]

But Gustave's first theater was the billiard room on the ground floor of the surgeon's residence, where he, his sister, Caroline, and their friends performed. Family legend has it that Caroline, who was only six when Gustave was composing his own plays, was in charge of the stage sets and costumes, making ample use of their mother's wardrobe.[2] In January 1832, when Gustave was ten years old, this theater was already ancient history: in a letter to his friend Ernest Chevalier, Gustave reported that since his departure (Ernest went to school in Les Andelys, twenty-five miles upstream) the billiard room had not been used, because Ernest was not there to help. At the time, Gustave was at work on a new play called "The Miserly Lover" (the hero of which refuses to give his mistress a present). He was also writing histories of three French kings.

At the same time, he sent Ernest a copy of his first published work, the brief pieces Ernest's uncle Amédée had reproduced in facsimile

on lithographic stone, presumably in his law office. In an unsigned
introduction to these "Selected Works of Gustave ∗∗∗," Amédée Mignot
explained that he had come across the works in a school notebook.
The first piece is an "Eloge de Corneille" ("Tribute to Corneille"),
Rouen's native poet; the tone is lighthearted and even intimate, but
with a solemn judgment: "It is you, Corneille, who through your writings corrected your century." The second piece, on constipation, makes
use of pseudomedical terms and some scatological language. The
prefacer also noted that in the same notebook he had found a comedy
in prose and an epitaph in verse; the play, in seven scenes and written
for four actors, is called "The Miser."[3] We can guess that this is the
play Gustave had announced as "The Miserly Lover."

Gustave was only nine when he wrote these pieces — the age at
which family legend has it he was only just learning to read. Early
the following spring, he informed his comrade Ernest that the bil-
liard-table stage had been set up again. Gustave was working with
thirty different plays, performing some of them with Caroline, then
aged seven. Before Ernest joined him for the Easter holidays, Gustave could tell his friend that he had prepared admission tickets for
three rows of seats, and thought they might draw an audience of ten
or twelve persons.[4]

He was eight or nine years old when he posed for the first portrait
we possess, a sketch done by a family friend, the artist E.-H. Lang--
lois. He had an unruly shock of hair, even features, a rigid neck; he
was fitted out as a gentleman with a buttoned-up vest, a cravat, and
a lace collar. Then he was twelve, captured in a sketch by his brother,
Achille. In this full-length portrait, his baggy pants prove that he was
not on show.[5] (This family saved *everything.*)

He was an appealing child. "In my childhood, princesses stopped
their carriages to take me in their arms and kiss me," he would later
tell a friend. "One day when the Duchess of Berry came to Rouen
. . . she noticed me in the crowd, held in my father's arms. She ordered her coach to stop so she could admire and kiss me. My poor
father returned home delighted with this triumph, which was the only
one I ever gave him, of course."[6]

It was customary, we have seen, to put a small child in school and
leave him there. The Collège Royal — Rouen's upper-elementary and
secondary school — was located only twenty to thirty minutes on foot
from the Hôtel-Dieu, but Gustave slept in the dormitory during the
school week. We know something about what this school was like
when Flaubert entered it, thanks to a painstaking memoir by another

of its pupils. Then, as today, a decorative iron gate protected the entrance to the courtyard; once inside, the visitor saw — can still see — a stone-block, three-story structure in Louis XVI style, with a clock in dead center. In practice this clock struck five minutes before each hour to announce the beginning of classes, and a second time to separate the prompt from the tardy.[7]

Shortly before Gustave's arrival, the curriculum changed radically. Until then Latin had been the dominant language, but with the overthrow of the Bourbon monarchy in 1830, modern teaching, in French, came into its own.[8] It is unlikely that the younger children would have been aware of the intellectual agitation of those times. For them the externals could not have changed much, either: the bleakness of the barrackslike buildings, the quasi-military discipline. Judge from this report by an inspector in 1835, during Gustave's third year at the Collège Royal: it was five in the morning. "From the first drumroll, the thirty or forty pupils who were sleeping in the dormitory where I then found myself got out of bed and began to dress; I can only compare the precision and uniformity of this movement to the maneuvers of a regiment of the army. . . ." The pupils marched off to wash, returning in silence to their dormitory. "Then, at a signal, they form ranks; the assistant dean inspects them for cleanliness, and they go downstairs with no sound other than that of their footsteps."[9]

Gustave spent his school days, he would recall in the self-dramatizing "Mémoires d'un fou," "solitary and bored, plagued by my teachers and jeered by my schoolmates." An exaggeration, surely. There may be more truth in the account of his intellectual awakening: he would find a way to go off by himself with a book, devouring not only Byron's poetry, Goethe's *Sorrows of Young Werther*, and Shakespeare's *Hamlet* and *Romeo and Juliet*, but also the controversial books of his own time — which meant the Romantics. In that other unpublished novella, "Novembre," written shortly after he left school, he remembered rushing through his homework in order to be free to daydream. He and his friends were in turn troubadours, insurrectionists, conquerers of the Orient. A more earthy reminiscence: to go to the toilets, the pupils had to cross the courtyard. He remembered the latrines with a certain nostalgia, despite the large puddles of urine. There one could smoke and masturbate, "so poetically, with fingers made rough by the cold."[10]

He was in his second year of the Collège Royal — equivalent to the fifth grade — when he took his first class prizes. We must be grateful for this system of prize giving, as these end-of-term lists of awards,

clearly dated, are often the best record we possess of the school ca-
reers of great men and women. Gustave earned an honorable mention in Latin translation, another in French grammar, and prizes in
geography and for general excellence.[11] A dozen years later, when he
walked by his old school and noticed a crowd on the steps of the
chapel, he remembered the prize ceremonies of his own day, the martial
music, the shouts of "Bravo!," and the prettily dressed women in the
galleries, while he and his schoolmates sat down below, envious of
these splendors. He also recalled the anticipation he had felt, for the
prizes were given on the last day of the school year, followed by two
months of total freedom.[12]

That particular vacation, in August 1833, began with a visit to Nogent-sur-Seine to see the Parains and to inspect the family's local
properties. His uncle's apprentice made up two seals, one for Gustave
and one bearing both his name and that of Ernest Chevalier, "indi-
viduals who will never separate," as Gustave explained to his comrade. On their way home the Flauberts stopped over in Paris, where
the high point was an evening at the popular Porte Saint Martin theater. They saw a "drama in five acts in which seven people die"; the
boy admired a famous actress "who played her part perfectly." At
twelve years of age, Gustave Flaubert was sure of his judgment.[13]

And then when school began that autumn, Gustave sat before a
new French teacher. Under this man, Gustave was to develop his
facility with language and to write some of his first readable stories.
Until now little has been said about this teacher who was so influential in Gustave's growth as a writer; it seemed worth exploring the
murky labyrinth of France's National Archives to look for clues as to
what about him had appealed to Flaubert.

His name was Henry Gourgaud dit Dugazon; he was called Gourgaud-Dugazon. Born in Paris on March 28, 1804, he was a ripe thirty
when he arrived in Rouen for the autumn 1834 school term. His career had a slow start, for after receiving a teaching degree in grammar, he served for four years as a substitute in a Paris secondary
school. When he took up his duties in Rouen, the headmaster seemed
delighted with him: "This young professor shows great promise," he
reported. "He manifests much zeal and devotion." "Zeal and devotion" become a refrain. Following the 1836–1837 school year, an Inspector General also took note of his "capacity" and "method." But
toward the end of his four-year tenure in Rouen, a different tune was
heard. While Gourgaud-Dugazon was held in high esteem, he still
lacked assurance and experience. A report spells this out: "His pupils

seem dissipated, though his class is said to be well run." Yet when he
moved on to the Lycée Impérial in Versailles, he was considered "a
good acquisition" by that school, and at the end of his first year there
was promoted to full professor. He continued to appear indifferent to
discipline, however. His headmaster praised his zeal, his precision,
his methods, but complained: "Unfortunately, he has always lacked
. . . firmness and authority. Pupils acquire or pursue habits of dissi-
pation in his class." This of course was what they had said back in
Rouen: "Families complain, while acknowledging his knowledge and
devotion. . . ."

The Lycée at Versailles tried to get rid of the zealous and devoted
nondisciplinarian. They wished to have him transferred to Paris, but
he protested that his two children had been born in Versailles and
were thriving there. His superiors finally asked for his early retirement. As one chief inspector put it, the professor's good qualities "are
paralyzed by the total absence of discipline." They blamed his shyness, his hesitation, his unwillingness to report problems, "his irremediable weakness, in a word." [14]

It is tempting to look for signs of the influence of this intelligent
but indulgent man on the apprentice writer. Later scholars were to
find, for example, that Flaubert was often scornful of the rules of
grammar, and it is not always clear that he knew what they were. At
the beginning, the bad grammar was only bad grammar, as in the
first version of *A Sentimental Education*, completed in 1845. But then
we find Flaubert cultivating his eccentricity. In the last work of his
published during his lifetime, *Three Tales*, grammatical shortcuts
heighten the effect of his sentences. [15]

During his first term under Gourgaud-Dugazon, Gustave published
his own magazine, a literary journal that he composed in the study
room and titled *Art et Progrès*. It was clearly modeled on the literary
and theatrical journals that then proliferated, and it had the distinction of being hand-printed in a school notebook. Only issue number
2 has been found, with several contributions by its editor, Gustave
Flaubert. The first of these, "Journey into Hell," tells of Satan leading the author on a tour of the world as it is, with its cruelties and
injustices, and pointing out that this world is actually hell. A second
piece is a poetic evocation of love in which the thirteen-year-old author mentions his dancing partner's "swelling breasts" and "burning lips." In a third piece, he notes that all of his teachers have seen
his magazine, and he promises "details" on this "affair" in a subsequent issue. [16] But this "affair" may explain why we don't have any

other issue. Oral tradition has it that Gustave wrote — in issue number 1 — about one of his teachers and his daughters, in not quite
respectable terms; he was nearly expelled from school but was saved
by his eminent father.[17]

His letters to Ernest show that Gustave did not depend on school
for his culture, not even then. He passed on literary gossip, presumably from the magazines and newspapers he picked up at home. He
mentioned new plays he had purchased. (It was then the practice to
publish cheap editions of plays as soon as they were performed.) He
read Beaumarchais and Shakespeare; he expressed anger at reports
that theater censorship was to be reestablished, and that press free-
doms were to be abolished; the measure would pass, he assured his
comrade, for the people's representatives in Parliament were all
corrupt. . . .[18]

At the end of the school year, Gourgaud-Dugazon asked the members of his class to write several stories during the summer vacation.
A notebook exists in Gustave's hand, containing these pieces. He was
not quite fourteen, but he was already composing well-constructed
scenes and lively, if often melodramatic, dialogue; certainly his vo-
cabulary was that of an educated adult today. The first story in this
notebook is called "Matteo Falcone." It is in fact the retelling of a
story by Prosper Mérimée in which a Corsican youth betrays an escaped convict; his father kills the boy before committing suicide. In
"Le Moine des Chartreux" ("The Chartreux Monk"), Friar Bernardo
tries to steal a ring from the dead prior, a ring that has the power to
call up the world outside the monastery, but he dies in the attempt.
There is also a sober portrait of Lord Byron, praising this poet "of
generous and progressive ideas, violent passions, a soul both sensitive
and noble, in a word, bizarre." Byron's works in French translation
were among the best-selling books in the country in the decade preceding Flaubert's schooling.[19]

A scholar who has proven his expertise with regard to Flaubert's
early writings points out that these stories conform to the teaching
curriculum. Each belongs to a different genre, and the topic of one
actually came out of a manual. Presumably Gourgaud-Dugazon as-
signed these themes to all of his pupils. What he obtained from
Flaubert was the revelation of a neo-Romantic writer of considerable
talent.[20] It was the teacher's chief claim to fame.

CHAPTER FIVE

ELISA

In October 1835, when Gustave entered the eighth grade, he found another influential teacher in the person of the young historian Adolphe Chéruel. "His appearance alone imposed silence and respect," a student remembered; he was not another Gourgaud-Dugazon. Himself a former Rouen pupil, he had earned his teaching degree at the Ecole Normale in Paris. In Rouen he taught ancient Roman history, using a book just published by one of his professors, Jules Michelet, who was on his way to becoming one of the most respected historians of his time.

Chéruel took his students from Roman to medieval history — this in the ninth grade — and then to modern times, a course that included literary history. In the next-to-the-last year before graduation, his course was called "Philosophy of History." "His teaching has no equal in the provinces," his superior was to observe. An Inspector General admired the way he utilized geography to explain history, and concluded, "Mr. Chéruel knows how to maintain suspense in his class." [1]

If Gourgaud-Dugazon confirmed Flaubert as a writer, Chéruel gave him his material. All his life long, Gustave was happiest when writing or re-creating history; when necessary (as in the Carthage of *Salammbô*), he reinvented it. When he approached contemporary history, as in *A Sentimental Education*, he undertook research that was as thorough as that for any of his stories of antiquity. His history classes also produced some immediate results: short pieces that dealt with historical events, sometimes in the form of fiction. In exploring the past, he seemed to be testing subjects for his own future, though for the time being he seemed to favor assassins, ghosts, and ravished women, as in his tale called "La Fiancée et la Tombe" ("The Fiancée and the Tomb"), written at fourteen.[2] As he grew older, his taste for "cheap thrills" — eroticism, death and decay — intensified; someone once said that the reticence of the adult Flaubert to publish these adolescent works can be explained by their revelatory nature.[3] On the other hand, he did save them, and no other writer of his time left so much juvenile work. Later Flaubert was to manifest a certain fascination for the Marquis de Sade, but it is clear that his temperament was in place before he discovered that Sade could feed it.

Gustave went to school during the tail end of romanticism, which explains how romanticism was able to enter the classroom. It still needed defending, or so Gustave thought, for in a school paper he explained how difficult it was to win acceptance for the Romantics even now, even though "Victor Hugo has never wished to disown Corneille." He placed Hugo with Chateaubriand, Lamartine, Schiller, Goethe, and Byron as the greats of his time.[4] He would have discovered the classics in Dr. Flaubert's library (whose inventory we possess); at some point he picked up Goethe's *Faust* and gobbled it up while seated under a tree on the banks of the Seine, instead of going home.[5]

If we set aside daydreams, and masturbation in the toilets, schoolboys in Rouen had little time for living. But there were days away from school. In one of his most introspective adolescent pieces, Gustave described one such Thursday holiday during the month of November; he would have been thirteen years old at the time. He hurried from school to the family table to find two English girls already seated there. They were sisters, friends of his own sister, the younger of the two small, slender, with eyes livelier, wider, and more attractive than those of her elder sister. But his heart was won by the older girl all the same, with her round head, pink cheeks, and lovely chestnut hair parted down the middle. He watched her at play in the garden; soon they had reached the kissing stage. He enjoyed listening to her foreign accent. (Two other women who were to count in his life spoke French with English accents.) Research has turned up the identity of this young woman: she was Caroline Anne Heuland, born in London in September 1820, Gustave's senior by a year and then some.[6]

Gustave admired both sisters and liked the kissing of both — so he said in another fictional memoir. During the Easter vacation, he found himself alone with the sister he preferred. The day was hot, and she had been running, so when he kissed her on the neck, his lips "re-

mained stuck on that silken skin. . . ." That afternoon he daydreamed
about her braids, and about her already evident bustline, which he
kissed as much of as her proper clothing allowed. He wrote his first
and only poem for her, with appropriate reference to his bitter pain
and deep melancholy. (Whether it was the real Gustave or merely the
fictional one who wrote the poem is unknown.) She became increasingly provocative; one day she draped herself on his sofa in an inviting manner, but he decided not to take advantage of her, and when
she kissed him, he found that she was crying. But time passed, and
she was married off to her art teacher. (The real Caroline Heuland
married a Rouen painter.)[7]

And then there were the summer holidays. Summer of course meant
Trouville. One summer in that fishing village on the Channel — the
year was most probably 1836, though this has been contested, but the
event will have been no less important if it is found to have taken
place in 1835 or in 1837 — Gustave discovered that yearning could
be as cruel for him as it had been for the English Caroline.

Gustave told the story several times, with variations. The common
elements were a teenage boy and a married woman in her twenties,
with ample breasts and hair parted in the middle. In all versions,
including the historical one, the boy's infatuation remained undeclared.

In the summer of 1836 Gustave had just completed the eighth grade
at the Collège Royal; he was four months from his fifteenth birthday.
One day — this from his "Mémoires d'un fou," written two years later
but not published in his lifetime — the young man went out walking
by himself, as he often did. Beyond the village, on the bathing beach,
he noticed an attractive fur-lined cloak with red and black stripes
lying on the sand. The tide was rising; already one wave had damp-
ened the cloak's silk fringe. He gathered it up and carried it to drier
sand. Then, during lunch at their inn, a woman seated with her husband at the next table addressed him: "Sir, I thank you for your kind
gesture." He was embarrassed, and he lowered his eyes and blushed,
but not before remarking how lovely she was. "She was tall, dark,
with magnificent black hair that fell in tresses on her shoulders; her
nose was Greek, her eyes burning, her eyebrows high and admirably
arched, her skin was ardent and seemed coated with gold; she was
slender and delicate, and there were blue veins climbing her brown
and crimson neck." Had he seen all that with lowered eyes? "She
could have been reproached for a bit of plumpness, or rather, artistic
indifference. . . ." The description has been quoted at length, for it

is the portrait of the amply endowed older woman whom Gustave
Flaubert would seek again and again and sometimes find.

In this early story the boy continues to observe the woman in the
sea each day, envying the waves that strike her thighs and cover her
panting breast with foam. He gazes at the shape of her limbs under
the wet bathing dress. And when she approaches him, his "heart beat[s]
with violence." Maria — he called her Maria in this first memoir —
has an infant daughter. She nurses the baby at her breast, and one
day he is there when it happens. He remarks that her breast is round
and full; he catches sight of the blue veins again. He is troubled;
never before has he seen a woman's nude breast. "It seemed to me
that if I had placed my lips on it, my teeth would have bitten it with
rage."

Gustave's relations with Maria and with her husband were to be
pursued, but more calmly. Her husband was half artist, half traveling
salesman; he sported a mustache, smoked cockily, and was lively,
friendly; he enjoyed food, and young Gustave marveled when he walked
three leagues to buy a melon in the nearest town. Later the real Gustave was to remind the real Maria — whose married name was Elisa
Schlesinger — of the day her husband Maurice walked from Honfleur to Trouville with a gigantesque melon on his shoulder.[8]

She was born Elisa Foucault on September 23, 1810, in Vernon,
another Seine town, this one thirty-five miles upstream from Rouen.
Her father had served under Napoleon and retired a captain. She was
raised in a local convent and at nineteen married a junior officer sta-
tioned in Vernon. Not long after that, her husband, by name Emile-
Jacques Judée, went off for five years' duty in Africa. Somewhere,
perhaps in Vernon, she met Maurice Schlesinger.[9]

But this is already more than Gustave knew, more than he was to
know for a long time, and it is not yet the whole story.

He continued to see the Schlesingers in Trouville, finding ways to
get conversations started, to join them on walks. In the memoir, one
evening the husband suggests a boat ride; as they row, Maria talks,
and Gustave, "intoxicated with love," abandons himself to the sound
of her voice and the rocking of the boat. He accompanies her to her
door, stays behind to look up at her window, and, when the lights are
extinguished, decides that she has gone to sleep. But then, all of a
sudden, he thinks otherwise, in a fit of rage and jealousy. He thinks
of her husband, vulgar and jovial, "and the most hideous of images
came to me": Maria belongs to that man.[10]

In "Mémoires d'un fou," the author says goodbye at the end of the

holidays, and it is an "adieu" forever. But this is because Gustave
himself was still too close to the summer of 1836. In real life he was
to see much more of the Schlesingers. Maurice Schlesinger was a
Prussian from Berlin, born in October 1797, so that he was nearly
thirty-nine when the young writer met him. He was Jewish but apparently converted to Catholicism when he married Elisa — so says
Richard Wagner, who was notoriously sensitive to such things.
Schlesinger's father had been a music publisher and founder of an
influential musical magazine in Berlin. After serving in the Prussian
army, notably in the final campaign against Napoleon, Maurice had
moved to France, begun to sell sheet music and instruments, and
founded a *Gazette et Revue Musicale de Paris*.[11]

If Elisa Schlesinger was Maria in that memoir of adolescence, she
became Emilie in young Flaubert's first attempt at a book-length work,
"A Sentimental Education" — the title used for a better and different
book in his maturity. In the final, published *Sentimental Education*,
which is also a final attempt by Flaubert to exorcise the vision on the
beach at Trouville, Elisa is again called Maria, and the cloak re-
covered from the waves is a shawl that she wears on a boat ride,
which would have blown away had the young man not rushed to save
it. In the novel Elisa's husband, the music publisher, becomes Jacques
Arnoux, an art dealer and the publisher of an art magazine.

Maxime Du Camp was the first to talk about Elisa. In his memoirs,
in which Gustave Flaubert is the central character, Du Camp reproached Gustave for lacking tenderness, but he remembered the beach
at Trouville. He got the dates wrong, he didn't mention Elisa's name,
even though he knew it, but he described her. "She was pretty and
above all curious," he began. He mentioned her headbands, her darkish
complexion, her large, somber eyes.[12] At the beginning of his liaison
with Louise Colet, another older woman with a generous bust, Gustave explained that he had loved one woman from the age of fourteen
to the age of twenty, but without confessing his love.[13] Louise Colet
and Elisa Schlesinger were both born in September 1810, only a week
apart.

Yet no one outside Flaubert's family circle, and only a couple of
his friends, ever got a glimpse of Elisa. One of the mysteries that has
stirred the curiosity of writers closer to our own time is whether Gustave and Elisa consummated their love. In the first version of "A Sentimental Education," written when Flaubert was still in his early
twenties, the character who stands for the author seduces and runs
off with the married woman he desires. But the mature version of *A*

Sentimental Education does not give the lovers a similar license. Had it happened in life, remarked an investigative writer who made Elisa something of a specialty, we should have discovered hints of it in the thousands of pages of Flaubert's correspondence.[14]

She did seem untouchable. But the young woman Gustave encountered in Trouville already had a past, and it is not certain that Gustave ever in his life learned much about it. Even her relationship with Maurice Schlesinger was less conventional than appearances might have suggested. For when Elisa left her first husband, Lieutenant Judée, she didn't divorce him right away. The daughter she nursed on the beach was Maurice's, conceived after the departure of her husband for Algeria, but in the summer of 1836 Elisa and Maurice were not yet legally married. Their child was declared as the daughter of Maurice Schlesinger and "an unnamed mother," for if Elisa had been registered as the mother, the child would have belonged to Lieutenant Judée. Yet there seemed to be nothing to fear from this officer, and even on his return to France he left Elisa in peace.[15]

How explain the passivity of Lieutenant Judée?

Elisa Foucault's marriage to the young officer, we know from the license, was celebrated late one night (at eleven-thirty, then a fashionable hour for a wedding). The groom's witnesses were fellow officers; one of the bride's witnesses was a colonel.[16] A man who made a career of investigating the story of Gustave and Elisa thought that he had discovered the truth about Elisa's marriage. It has not been published before, and is offered here as a possibility. During the wedding banquet — long past midnight — the groom's soldier comrades teased him about his virginity. Surely drunk by then, Lieutenant Judée offered to show what he could do by taking his bride then and there. But he was not up to the effort, and we are asked to believe that his comrades took over the job.

Elisa slipped away before dawn, taking refuge with her sisters in Vernon and then traveling down to Paris. The story is that she became a woman for hire. Schlesinger found her and took her in; when she gave birth, he could not be sure the child was his, but he recognized it all the same. When Gustave encountered Elisa in Trouville soon after that, she was already the good mother and unattainable spouse he could only yearn for.[17]

CHAPTER SIX

REVOLT

Aﬀﬁ FTER THE TROUVILLE SUMMER, after Elisa, there was a new school
year to conquer. Gustave's school days and nights can be followed, perhaps more closely than any other secondary school pupil's
of his day, thanks to the loving conservation of his notebooks. Before
the end of the year — before his fifteenth birthday — he wrote a perfectly turned little essay that was considered worthy of publication in
a journal read by adults. This is "Bibliomanie," the tale of a bookseller who has a passion for books: he steals Spain's first printed volume because he has been unable to acquire it at auction, and is sentenced to death for burning his rival's house in the course of his theft.
When his attorney shows him a second copy of the book, proving that
he had not stolen the unique copy, he tears it up so his will remain
the only one. Scholarship has turned up Gustave's source, the weekly
Gazette des Tribunaux, which reported celebrated or curious cases; in
fact this particular anecdote was probably apocryphal.[1]

The magazine that published Gustave's narrative was called *Le
Colibri*, a recent arrival on Rouen's cultural scene. It was published
twice weekly and subtitled "Journal de la littérature, des théâtres, des
arts et des modes [fashion]," and each issue carried reviews of theater
performances, in Rouen or even in Paris. Gustave's piece appeared in
the February 12, 1837, issue, occupying all of the front page and
most of page two. The signature was simply "F," which explains why
for years it was overlooked, until the original manuscript was discovered.[2]

A letter from Gustave to Ernest Chevalier (of course) gives us some
news of the young writer. It was now late March; he had just been to

see the editor of *Le Colibri,* who would publish a second contribution
from him; he was even going to correct proofs with the editor.[3] This
new piece was "A Lesson in Natural History," focusing on the "genre"
civil servant. Its author — again signing himself simply "F" — posed
as a naturalist describing the species of government clerk whose job
it was to copy. (This of course would also be the employment of the
protagonists of Flaubert's last major work, *Bouvard and Pécuchet.*)[4]

Just about now, Gustave came under the spell of another person
who would confirm his vocation. Alfred Le Poittevin was born in Rouen
on September 29, 1816; his mother had gone to boarding school with
Gustave's mother. He attended the Collège Royal but finished in July
1834, when Gustave was completing the ninth grade. Their parents
remained friends, and Alfred became a kind of elder brother, closer
to Gustave in temperament than his real elder brother. For Alfred
was a declared poet.[5] "We lived in an ideal greenhouse in which
poetry heated up the world's boredom to seventy degrees Réaumur,"
Gustave was to recall, referring to their endless conversations in his
upstairs room at the Hôtel-Dieu.

Surviving work by Le Poittevin does indeed show a love of language. The content reflects the romantic yearnings of his generation — the fascination with the Orient, for example. With one exception, Le Poittevin's works are all in verse and Flaubert's all in prose,
but their themes are not dissimilar. One of Le Poittevin's poems, "To
Goethe," was so much to Gustave's taste that he made a copy of it,
and at least one scholar later assumed that he had written it. The
final stanza hails the great man who abandons his mistress's breast
for the ideal world.[6] In the first letter to Alfred that has come down
to us, written during the 1837–1838 school year, Gustave described
the behavior (real or imaginary) of his friends and himself in a brothel.[7]
Le Poittevin's letters to Flaubert revealed similar preoccupations, and
were written in language that has kept them largely unpublished.

There was also Louis Bouilhet. He was to become essential to the
adult Flaubert, virtually an alter ego. For the moment, however, they
were simply classmates. Bouilhet was born on May 27, 1822, in Cany,
not far from the coast between Fécamp and Dieppe. He, too, was a
romantic poet from his school days, but in his case he remained that.[8]
When Bouilhet took the top class prize in August 1839, Flaubert was
as pleased, he later recalled, as if he had gotten it himself.[9]

Good teachers, classmates and comrades mad for poetry — and then
theater. "I liked nothing so much as the stage," Gustave wrote in his

pseudoconfession "Novembre." He was enamored with theatergoing itself as much as with what was on stage, with the movement and murmuring of the audience. His fascination for the stage led to a wish to have an actress as a mistress.[10] When he was obliged to study more prosaic subjects, he gave his feelings free play in a letter to Ernest Chevalier. He detested criticism, he said, "for the most beautiful woman is not beautiful on the dissecting table, with her bowels thrown over her face, her leg stripped, and a cigar butt perched on her foot."[11] We know what he was sweating over, for the compositions he had to write for the year-end prizes in July 1837 have come down to us; he was asked, for example, to describe "the general character" of the Middle Ages, and to draw up an outline of the state of the world from 1180 to 1215.[12] Of course, he preferred pure poetry. . . .

During the summer holidays that year, the Flauberts returned to Trouville. Gustave's parents looked at some promising land at Deauville, which was then an undeveloped stretch of marshland. Their Ferme de Deauville, located on a rise behind the beach, consisted of twenty-six hectares of good grazing land, and was to cost the Flauberts, as we have seen, eighty thousand francs.[13]

That fall Gustave entered the tenth grade. Early in that term he composed a strange tale entitled "Quidquid Volueris," inspired by the contemporary interest in newly discovered types of apes and the speculation about their relationship to man. In this story we meet Paul, his wife, Adèle, and Paul's curious friend from Brazil, Djalioh. Djalioh desires Adèle, while Paul treats her with indifference. We learn that in Brazil Paul had mated a slave girl with an orangutan, and that Djalioh is the fruit of that liaison. Now we begin to perceive his wild side. Before the tale ends, Djalioh goes on a rampage, kills Adèle's child, and rapes and murders Adèle.[14] Research has uncovered a source for this narrative in *La Revue de Paris*, but Gustave added a twist: while Adèle rots in her tomb, the man-ape is carefully preserved as a skeleton, and the indifferent Paul remarries.[15]

Another story written before the end of that year, "Passion et Vertu," was based on a courtroom report in *La Gazette des Tribunaux*, but once again Gustave went beyond his source. His heroine, Mazza, is married to a banker devoid of feelings, and a seducer, whose name happens to be Ernest, manages to arouse her. Caught up in her new sensuality, she seeks Ernest when he abandons her — he has gone off to America to sleep with slave girls in the land of liberty. After poisoning her husband and her children, Mazza is free to join Ernest, but when he informs her that he is to marry a wealthy girl, she poisons herself, too.[16]

Among his other short pieces of this period, "Agonies" stands out, if only for the prophetic dedication to Le Poittevin: "Perhaps you will laugh later on, when you are married, well ordered, and moral, in casting your eyes on the thoughts of a poor child of sixteen who loved you more than all else, and whose soul was already tormented by stupidities." There follows a collection of "skeptical thoughts" whose message is that all man's actions are based in vanity.[17]

His letters spoke of Rabelais, Corneille, Shakespeare, Montaigne, Byron. In the summer of 1838 his true favorites were Rabelais and Byron, the only authors "who wrote with the intention of doing harm to humankind and of laughing at it to its face."[18] Much has changed since the time of Rabelais, he wrote in a dissertation. We have railroads and chemistry, but has the moral situation changed? A new Rabelais would have a lot to say about that, and his book would be "the most terrifying and sublime ever written."[19]

That autumn Gustave entered the eleventh grade, the next-to-last year of the school program before the crucial baccalaureat examination. He was now free to return home each day, which was as good as things could be until he was quite free of that messy and stinking school (a free translation of Flaubert's prose). He promised Ernest Chevalier that he would smoke on the way to school and back each day and would wait for his classes in a café on the square. He may have been trying to impress his friend, for later he recalled leaving school at four each afternoon to make his dutiful way to the day school where his little sister was waiting to be taken home.[20]

Chevalier had let it be known that he believed in God. Gustave could not understand his friend, for what was consoling about seeing "the dagger that will run through your heart"? Now Chevalier could also believe in "the honesty of cabinet officers, the chastity of whores. . . . So you'll be happy and can consider yourself a believer and three-fourths idiot, but meanwhile stay a man of wit, a skeptic, and a drinker." And what was Gustave up to? "I haven't changed," he said. "I'm more clownish than merry, more puffed-up than truly great." Much later he would add (to his mistress Louise Colet) that he had been a splendid specimen of a man then, "enough to attract the entire audience in a theater, as happened in Rouen for the first performance of *Ruy Blas.*"[21] The reference was to the play by Victor Hugo that opened in January 1839.

Soon he was telling Ernest about a passion play he was trying to write, something "gigantesque" and "absurd," unintelligible both to himself and to everyone else. Satan escorts a mortal through the sky in order to reveal to him the mysteries of creation, and the mortal discovers the absence of God. In addition to Satan, the author introduced Yuk, a god of the grotesque, who provides a note of mocking humor in this universe of anguish and tears.[22] The influence of Byron's mystery plays, of Goethe's *Faust* and the French Romantics, has been noted. And this play, *Smarh,* is a precursor of Flaubert's own *Temptation of Saint Anthony,* a work that he was to write again and again. The image of the hermit in a cave, resisting the world and its temptations, would never leave him.[23]

If the scholars are correct, between the time he began *Smarh* and the time he finished it, he wrote what may be considered his first mature work, the novella "Mémoires d'un fou," completed around his seventeenth birthday. It has been called his only truly autobiographical work.[24] For here is the story of Trouville and Elisa, and the proof that he had not forgotten her.

In February 1839 Ernest Chevalier informed his friend that he was going to study law in Paris, so Gustave felt obliged to announce his own career plan. His choice, he said, was to have none. Of course he would take law courses, he would even work for a doctoral degree to waste another year, but he would not practice. He didn't know if his work would ever be performed or published; such details did not concern him. "Yet," he predicted, "if ever I take an active role in the world, it will be as a thinker and corrupter. I shall only tell the truth, but it will be horrible, cruel and bare."[25] By the end of that school year he was praising the most evil Roman we know of, Nero, and a writer mentioned only in whispers, the Marquis de Sade.[26]

Sartre tells us in his study of Flaubert that the young man ceased to write after finishing *Smarh* in April 1838 (he meant 1839), not to begin again until the fall of 1842; he attributes this silence to neurosis.[27] Perhaps there was a slowing-down, though just at the beginning of that period Gustave started a diary — in the tradition of private journals, with more solemnity than true revelation. "I feel that I shall have an ordinary life, sensible and reasonable, that I shall be a good . . . maker of phrases, a good lawyer, while I should like to have an extraordinary life."[28] In August 1839 — in this period when he was thought by Sartre not to have been writing — he composed what he described as "a rather lively bacchanalian tale," which the best authority on Flaubert's early work has called "the masterpiece" of his youth, both for its style and for its structure.[29] This is "Les Funérailles du Docteur Mathurin" ("Dr. Mathurin's Funeral"), in which a wise man who has avoided excessive passions, now old and ill, decides to die of drinking good Burgundy with his disciples.

And then the school year began, in October 1839, the year that was supposed to be Gustave's final one at the Collège Royal, for the twelfth grade ends with the baccalaureat exams. Gustave was first in his philosophy class; we know this because the French system of record keeping makes it possible to check up on a provincial schoolboy a century and a half after the fact, bridging monarchy, republic, empire, and republic again.

There is a file in the National Archives, for example, that tells us how Gustave led a revolt in class and was expelled from school. It happened because his philosophy teacher was frequently absent for reasons of ill health, and the class did not like the substitute teacher. It all came to a head on Monday, December 9, 1839. As the young men filed into the room, the substitute discovered that they were already quite out of control. He tried to calm them down, but as soon as he began his lesson, Flaubert and two classmates interrupted him; he ordered them to copy lines after class. But the disorder continued: chatter, movement of feet. The hapless teacher attempted to pursue a particularly complicated line of thought, which prevented him from observing the troublemakers, so when the next punishment came, it had to be for the whole class: a thousand lines of poetry. But he offered to suspend the sanction if the guilty parties identified themselves.

And we can actually hold in our hands the petition written (and surely instigated) by Flaubert; his is the first signature. "The Pupils whose names follow refuse to copy lines. . . ." There were thirty-three signatures, including that of Louis Bouilhet, but the vice principal responsible for discipline knew where to look. He called in three members of the class and issued an ultimatum: yield, or face expulsion. Gustave counterattacked with a letter to the headmaster that was cosigned by a dozen classmates (including Bouilhet) and began: "They told us we were children, that we were acting as children; we shall try by our moderation and honesty to convince you of the contrary." Expulsion would mean destroying the futures of the three students involved, the letter said. And why three, since the whole class was involved and was signing this second protest? (In fact, less than half of the class did.) "If the whole philosophy class can be given a thousand lines to copy, the whole class can be expelled."

The headmaster did not see it that way. On December 14 he informed the vice principal for discipline that Flaubert and two other young men had, by their refusal to accept the punishment, closed the doors of the school to themselves.[30] Dr. Flaubert's position on the board of the Academy of Rouen (which supervised the school system) did not help his son. But one could obtain the same secondary-school diploma outside of school.[31]

It was almost as an afterthought that Gustave informed Ernest of his plans. First he was going to get a lot of sleep, and then he would need his comrade's class notes. "If you were a god and could make six months go by in a flash, so that tomorrow I could arrive at August 20 and a diploma, I'd build you a temple of gold," he wrote Ernest, concluding, "Shit on philosophy."[32]

PART II

CHAPTER SEVEN

EULALIE

THEN, AS NOW, the "bac" exam was a ferocious affair, a mountain that had to be conquered before one reached the green fields. Gustave sat down to work on physics, mathematics, Greek.[1] Perhaps as relief he took up his private journal again, jotting down his personal feelings, taking the trouble to write well. "I don't write anymore — in the past I wrote, I felt strongly about ideas, I knew what it was to be a poet. . . ."[2] He sounds as if he is sixty and not eighteen. The same mode is employed when he speaks of having been in love: "And yet I was in love, as anyone might be, and no one knew it! What a pity, how happy I should have been."[3]

There was a respite in April, when he boarded a carriage for Les Andelys to spend some days with Ernest Chevalier, carrying cigars so they could smoke as they roamed the countryside or sat atop the hill at Château-Gaillard, which dominated the Seine valley.[4] Then he was home again, and working. The evidence is that he took it seriously. "I get up every day at three in the morning precisely and go to bed at eight-thirty at night, working all day long," he informed Ernest in July, a month before the exams. He had learned his Greek and could recite Demosthenes by heart, as well as sections of *The Iliad*. Philosophy didn't worry him, but there were physics, math, geometry — and all this was "rough for a man like myself who is rather made to read the Marquis de Sade than like nonsense!"[5]

He passed. His diploma exists, signed by the headmaster who had expelled him and by his former philosophy teacher. His responses were deemed passable in Demosthenes, rather good in Latin (with

Livy), rhetoric, history, and geography, and passable in philosophy, elementary mathematics, and physics.[6]

Now he would make his first long journey, in the company of his father's colleague Jules Cloquet, who after returning to Paris from Rouen's Hôtel-Dieu had a distinguished career as professor of surgical pathology at the Faculty of Paris. Not long before Dr. Cloquet took Gustave on a tour of southern France and the isle of Corsica, he had become a minor celebrity in the United States. He was a friend of the Marquis de Lafayette's and had been at his bedside when he died. A memoir of their relationship was published in the *New York Evening Star*.[7]

In Paris to join Dr. Cloquet, Gustave traveled out to Versailles to call on Henry Gourgaud-Dugazon, the teacher who had guided his first efforts at serious writing. As they walked in the castle gardens, the young man unburdened himself of his doubts concerning his literary career; Gourgaud offered encouragement.[8]

The travelers' first objective was Bordeaux, which they reached via Blois, Tours, and Poitiers; we can imagine what it was like, thanks to *A Sentimental Education*, whose hero, in a horse-drawn carriage, hears the rattling of metal and glass as the heavy vehicle rolls along.[9] We have letters to Gustave from his parents, who were concerned about the effect of the trip on his health; in the first letter from him that has survived, written from Bayonne on August 29, their son assured them that he was ever the robust young man.[10] Thanks to the fame of the surgeon Cloquet, the travelers were received well everywhere. They went through Pau and Toulouse, sailed on the Canal de Midi, visited fortified Carcassonne, Narbonne, Nîmes, Arles. Predictably, the ancient Roman monuments of France's south enchanted the young traveler.

On September 28 they were in Marseilles — with nothing to wear, Gustave reported, for their trunks had not yet caught up with them.[11] Real adventure began in Corsica, where all the roads seemed to lead up (or down) mountains. They followed an itinerary drawn up for them by the prefect in Ajaccio, who promised to put them in touch with friendly bandits. This ten-day expedition offered memorable encounters with natural beauty and with colorful characters bearing tales of violence and vengeance, in an atmosphere of folk belief and superstition. They lived roughly. Gustave filled nineteen notebooks with his observations and saved ten blank ones "for other journeys."

Something happened in Marseilles that did not get into these notebooks, nor into his letters home. It was now late October; "it was cold, everything turned brown and already smelled of return," as Gustave noted in his travel journal. A much older Flaubert recounted what happened then, and the Goncourt brothers, who listened, made a meticulous diary entry of it (as was their practice): "He [Flaubert] falls on a small hotel in Marseilles, run by women who had brought back from Lima a collection of sixteenth-century ebony furniture inlaid with pearls, which was the marvel of the neighborhood." (This, we know, was the Hôtel de Richelieu on Rue de la Darse, close to the old harbor.) There he saw "three women in silk dressing gowns . . . and a pickaninny. . . ." Coming back from swimming in the Mediterranean, the young man was lured into the room of a "magnificent" woman of thirty-five. This was Eulalie, Eulalie Foucaud (née Delanglade), daughter of the hotelkeeper. Gustave kissed her, and that was all, but that night Eulalie came to his room "and began by sucking." [12]

He was not quite a virgin. Apparently he had lost that remaining vestige of innocence simply and handily, thanks to his mother's chambermaid, or so he later claimed. [13] He said it more artfully in "Mémoires d'un fou": "A woman offered herself to me, I took her; and I left her arms full of disgust and bitterness." He was fifteen. [14]

But now he was eighteen, going on nineteen. The new experience was torrid, intensely felt. Several times after that journey, Gustave returned to the scene — ample evidence that it counted for him.

In his travel diary Gustave described their farewell dinner at the home of a Marseilles doctor, a "delicious evening" that concluded with Oriental tobacco, smoked in bamboo pipes, and Rhine white wine. [15] What Gustave did not tell his notebook, he later confided to Alfred Le Poittevin: "I went back to the hotel and came four times." [16] But this was locker-room talk. We also have "Novembre," which Gustave probably began to write as soon as he returned to Rouen, in November 1840. In this fiction the young man sleeps with a prostitute, but she receives him as a prostitute would not. She looks at him with "somber ecstasy"; he is charmed and proud. She sits on his lap, asks him to say that he loves her, calls him handsome, demands a kiss, invites him to stay overnight. She displays her nudity with "a courtesan's pride," and we are able to contemplate "her elastic, convulsive belly, soft enough to lie on like a warm satin pillow. . . ." When they make love, he claims to be a virgin. She cuts off a lock of his hair for a souvenir. [17]

He would confess to Louise Colet that he had written long letters

to Eulalie. "It was to force myself to love her, to practice style."[18] We
do not have these letters, but we have some of those that Eulalie
wrote to him. The first is dated January 16, 1841, ten weeks after
their meeting. She had not heard from her dear angel for a long time,
she wrote; she felt that he no longer loved her, while she thought of
him constantly and would give her life to see him only for a few days.
"Since you left this house, it has become an immense desert for your
lover, this room where we were so happy, these walls that witnessed
our kisses, our burning rapture. . . ."[19] She had asked him to tell
her his plans for the future; was he silent because he loved another
woman?[20]

He replied, and then confided to his diary: "I wrote a love letter, to
write, and not because I love."[21] On February 16 Eulalie advised him
that of the three letters he assured her he had written, only two had
reached her. In the first, he asked her to cease to love him. "Unkind!
cruel friend!" was her expected reply. She closed: "I kiss you all over.
You know, with those intoxicating kisses you loved so much, which
gave you so much pain and so much pleasure."[22]

She was to return to South America — not to Lima, as the Goncourts heard it, but to Guyana on the northeast coast. Was a husband
summoning her? ("If I must leave France another time, my mother
and my cherished daughter, to cross that horrid ocean and again live
in isolation. . . .") She knew one thing: if she left and then came
back again, the first person she would embrace would be Gustave.[23]
In August she still had not sailed, and he was still writing her, and of
love; for her part, she was prepared to give her life "to spend only
one year beside you, loved by you, happy as we were during those
all-too-short days."[24] If she did leave France, she would return to
him, and before her hair turned white, "and I shall be able to hold
you in my arms with the same ardor and the same happiness," for at
her age one knew how to love better than at his.[25]

It should not be a surprise that Gustave, home in Rouen, found it
difficult to settle down. If only he could live in Spain, in Italy, or even
in southern France; now that he had seen something of the world, he
despised the France he knew. He was supposed to be preparing for
law school but in fact was doing little. He had no ambition, he assured Ernest Chevalier. Of course he would attend law school, but
after that he would wander.[26] He spelled this out in his diary: "It's
the East forever. I was born to live there."[27]

It was a year of idleness, before the active life he was soon to begin.
He gained weight; he was "colossal, monumental," he told Ernest.

During the summer he returned to Trouville, for more "crass laziness," as he confessed to his friend. He did nothing but eat, drink, sleep, and smoke.[28] There is a note of reproach in a tender letter from his busy father in Rouen: "Take advantage of your vacation and prove to us, later on, that you are capable of conforming to a new situation, for soon it will be other times, other mores."[29]

In November 1841 Dr. Flaubert's son dutifully traveled to Paris to enroll in the Faculty of Law. But he did not begin to study, and he let Ernest Chevalier know that he despised the very notion of human justice.[30] Still, he was back in Paris the following January. He had not opened his law books. He decided that he would begin to work in the spring, at which time "I shall work for fifteen hours, fail the entrance exam, and call the professors scoundrels. . . ." Or he would pass and then tell everyone how hard he had worked.[31]

Meanwhile, he had something more important on his mind. On January 22, 1842, he wrote to Henry Gourgaud-Dugazon, that wise teacher who did not know how to punish. He confessed his long months of laziness, and his boredom. He was looking forward to another meeting with his teacher; he hoped that it would be during his visit to Paris that spring, and that Gourgaud would give him a full day — "I have so much to tell you, and you listen to me so well!"

He was taking law, he explained; that is, he had purchased the books and signed up for the courses. He pursued his private study of Greek and Latin and enjoyed it. "But what comes back to me at every instant, what takes the pen out of my hand if I make notes, what removes the book if I read, is my old love, the same idée fixe: writing! This is why I am not doing anything." He had arrived at the decisive moment; it was a matter of life and death. Once he had made his decision, nothing would stop him, even if the whole world booed. His teacher knew how stubborn he was. "This is what I have decided. I have in mind three novels, three stories in quite different genres requiring a particular way of being written. This is enough to be able to prove to myself that I have the talent, or don't have it." He would show Gourgaud one of his works, "that sentimental and amorous stew I told you about." (This would be Eulalie's story, "Novembre," then in progress.) Perhaps it was good, but he feared that it might be false and even pretentious.[32]

One of the frequently heard misconceptions about Flaubert's vocation is that it followed a failure at law, followed illness. But of course he was a writer before he was anything else.

CHAPTER EIGHT

PARIS

THERE WERE more wasted weeks in Rouen, during which the new law student finally opened the new books he had acquired but did not do very much with them. The first year of law school required mastery of Justinian's *Institutes* — the basic Roman law — and then France's civil code. He read the opening pages of the code and did not understand them, read the first three articles of Roman law and forgot them at once. Perhaps, he thought, he would suddenly become ambitious, wake early some morning, and try again. Meanwhile, he smoked his pipe and waited for spring. Ernest pursued his law studies, and Gustave teased him: "Instead of doing so much law, do some philosophy, read Rabelais, Montaigne, Horace or some other fellow. . . ."

It would be wrong to say that he was doing nothing, for he was writing "Novembre," which critics see as the most remarkable of his unpublished writings, a coming-to-terms with his childhood, his school, and his discovery of sexual love. And in constant dialogue with Alfred Le Poittevin — now an apprentice attorney in Rouen — he was hammering out his aesthetic positions.[1] He was doing everything but law, even though he was to take his entrance examination at the end of August.[2]

Before that, an obligation. He registered for military service. He described himself, all the same, as "law student," and he was measured at just under six feet, which was quite tall for that time and place. Recruits were chosen by lot; he was lucky, and would not have to serve.[3]

He had his first taste of student life in Paris that summer. "Three hundred young people, bareheaded, filled an amphitheater where an old man in a red robe lectured in a monotonous tone of voice," he was to remember when it came time to write *A Sentimental Education*.[4] He let his family know how bored he was. (They were spending the summer in Trouville.) He moved from a hotel to a room of his own — which had been Ernest's — on Rue de l'Odéon. He attended classes in the morning, studied alone in the afternoons, saw family friends. "I go to sleep every night at one A.M. after having worked steadily since seven that evening," he told Ernest Chevalier.[5] But when we come upon the letters Le Poittevin wrote Gustave during the same period, we hear another story. "I read your letter with admiration," wrote Alfred on July 15, "and in it I found those things you say so well, after having done them so well. . . ." What a picture that is of Léonie on her knees between your legs. . . ." Alfred did have one reproach, for Gustave had been praising a girl named Anna; the only good thing Alfred could say about the wench was that he had not caught the pox after sleeping with her.[6]

Gustave passed the entrance examination all the same, and packed for Trouville. "I arrived from Paris alone," he was to remember. "I left the carriage at Pont-l'Evêque, a three-hour march, and I reached Trouville by moonlight at three in the morning. I still recall the linen jacket and the white stick I carried, and the feeling I had when I picked up from afar the salt smell of the sea."[7] By now the developing resort was something of a family institution. That year the Flauberts had one of the nicer cottages, one that was usually taken for the season by the Schlesingers, who happened to be traveling that summer. Their cousins were invited to join them. Gustave's sister, Caroline, took art lessons from Charles Mozin, Trouville's painter-in-residence. Her parents even had her piano hauled in from Rouen, and then had to bring in a tuner from Honfleur before she could play it.[8]

He described his routine to Ernest: he rose at eight each day, went swimming after breakfast, and then ate again, smoked, stretched out in the sun, dined, and smoked again. He read Ronsard, Rabelais, Horace, "but not too much or too often, as with truffles." He was also thinking about how much he would hate having to return to studying law.[9]

That summer in Trouville he met the Colliers. The dates given for their first encounter, even by the Colliers themselves, are wildly off, but now we have a letter from Caroline to her brother describing their first meeting, in July 1842.[10] Henry Collier, a captain in the Royal

Navy, then lived in Paris with his wife and seven children, among them Herbert, Gertrude, and Harriet. Gertrude, then twenty-two, was the erudite sister; Caroline said she knew all of Shakespeare by heart. Harriet — the Flauberts would Frenchify her name to Henriette — was nineteen and suffered from a spinal disease. As Gertrude later recalled her first contact with a Flaubert: "One day . . . I noticed high up perched on a rock a picturesque chalet and was told it belonged to a marine artist who had built it — Monsieur Mozin. . . . More beautiful than the dark blue sea we saw from the chalet windows or anything in that room was a young girl drawing at one of the tables." This was Caroline. Then Gustave arrived from Paris, and Gertrude discovered a "tall, slender, graceful youth in a red flannel shirt, rough blue cloth trousers, a scarf of the same colour tightly bound around his waist, a soft sort of sombrero hat placed anyhow on his head, which was as often as not bare." By nature "wild and gay and perhaps coquettish," as she was later to confess in a semi-fictional account of that summer, Gertrude flirted with Gustave.[11] But he was more attracted to Harriet. Thinking back on that summer, the young man would say that he had found a family there, and taken away an attachment.[12]

In "Novembre," the novella Gustave was then writing, the young hero's itinerary is summed up: "His natural goodness kept him from medicine; as for business, he was incapable of adding or subtracting. . . . Despite his follies, he had too much good sense to be able to take the noble profession of lawyer seriously." But that was his destiny. "Resigned to be bored everywhere and with everything, he declared himself ready to study law, and went to live in Paris." Back home, he is envied for his life of cafés and theaters, restaurants and beautiful women. "He spent his days working, listening to the rumbling of the streets, watching rain falling on the roofs." The hero of "Novembre" lies down and dies, simply because he wishes it.[13]

He lived — the real Gustave did — close to the Luxembourg Gardens, which also meant close to the law school; his flat was not furnished, so as soon as he moved in, in early November 1842, he began looking for furniture. He sent the measurements of his bed to Rouen so the family could send him a mattress, blankets, and sheets, as well as oil lamps.[14] "I get up at eight, go to classes, come home for a frugal lunch; I work until five in the afternoon and then go out to dinner; before six I am back in my room, where I enjoy myself until midnight or one in the morning." This to his sister, Caroline. He had an arrangement with a neighborhood restaurant for cheap meals, having paid in advance for thirty of them. He was not happy.[15]

"Courage, courage," his father wrote him. "Think that in eighteen or twenty months you can become a lawyer and be done with your hard labor."[16] "I think that I'll even be happy if I am turned down," Gustave wrote his sister; "that's how much the life I've been leading for the past six weeks weighs on me." He thought that he would pass the term, and he did. Before returning to Rouen he attended a Saturday-night party at his "friend Maurice's"; we know that this stands for Elisa's. On that Sunday he went to Versailles for another talk with his old teacher Gourgaud-Dugazon.[17]

Winter holidays at home, with the warmth of the family and the fireplace, made things seem all the more difficult to him on his return to Paris. The days were all right, he told Caroline; it was at night, in his empty room, that he dreamed of home. "Oh, the lovely city, and the wonderful thing it is to be a student," he commented with irony to Ernest. Rich young people on the right bank rode in carriages; students walked in the rain. The rich went to the opera and danced all night. "They make love with noblewomen," while students made do with shopgirls with chilblains or went to brothels — not too often, because when one had paid one's tailor, one's bootmaker, one's café, and one's restaurant, bought books and tobacco, and paid school fees and rent, there was little left for anything, and much torment.[18] There were no girl students for boy students to mix with; when a young man from Rouen was ready to marry, he went back home for a wife.

Still, Gustave was living through the last days of romantic Paris. He simply lived them vicariously, notably in his exchange of feelings with Alfred Le Poittevin. The previous December, when Gustave had returned to Paris, Alfred had recommended that his friend make good use of the whorehouses there but had also advised him to visit the sculptor James Pradier, not for his culture or his social connections, but for useful addresses that Alfred would also be able to use on *his* visits to Paris.[19]

It is only in July 1843 that we hear a different note. "It appears that you are not humping anymore, to judge from your last letter," Alfred wrote.[20] Much later, the Goncourts thought they heard Flaubert say that he had not touched a woman from the age of twenty to the age of twenty-four "because I promised myself not to screw."[21] He said almost the same thing to Louise Colet, and in writing.[22]

*   *   *

Flaubert possessed an antidote to the romanticism of his time. This was his double, known as Le Garçon — call him Big Boy. This Big Boy was a recurring reference not only among Gustave's comrades but within his family, and in her affectionate letters his sister usually found a way to refer to him. The reference was always to affected behavior. Unhappy in Paris, Gustave would write her: "Alone, sometimes, in my room, I make grimaces in the mirror or shout Big Boy's cry, as if you were there to see and to admire me."[23]

Flaubert tried to explain the Big Boy to the Goncourts, but they confessed that they found him difficult to comprehend. Walking by Rouen's cathedral, for example, one of Flaubert's friends would say, "It's a fine thing, Gothic architecture, it elevates the soul." At once another friend would assume the role of Big Boy: "Yes, it's beautiful . . . and the Saint Barthelemy massacre, too. . . ."[24] It was mockery and self-mockery combined.

When the time came for Flaubert to write his first long work (the year was 1843, and the book would be left as an unpublished manuscript entitled "A Sentimental Education" — the first version), he created the character of an author who takes his own times as his subject, but who is determined to write also about the ridiculous side of things, for it was hard to look closely at society without encountering the preposterous and the hypocritical.[25]

CHAPTER NINE

THE FALL

FLAUBERT BEGAN WORKING on his first "Sentimental Education" soon after returning to Paris and law school in February 1843; the nights were long, as we have seen, in his humble dwelling. In this draft there are two heroes: Henry, a student without ambition, and Jules, a would-be writer. Each of his protagonists, he explained later, represented a side of himself.[1] And Elisa Schlesinger is in this book, disguised only slightly as the wife of the director of the boarding-house in which Henry lives. In the novel the young man wins the married woman; she even flees with him to New York.

He wrote this daydream while he was seeing the real Schlesingers; he had found a way to become Maurice's friend. We need not take everything Flaubert later put into fiction as fact, but we can imagine that the situation described in the final, published *Sentimental Education* was based on reality. There the young man invents pretexts for "chance" encounters with the woman he loves, which lead to even more frequent encounters with her husband. Flaubert's letters, over the rest of his life, prove that his friendship with the couple survived these maneuvers. What the novels — both the first and second *Education* — tell us is that his fixation on Elisa continued for long years after their first meeting, and the sight of her bared breast, on the Trouville beach.

The characters who represent Maurice and Elisa in the young man's version of "A Sentimental Education" are vaporous. We have to wait for the published version a quarter of a century later for a credible description of the entrepreneurial Maurice and the adored, if passive, Elisa. Schlesinger was the go-getter Flaubert calls Jacques Arnoux.

He had made his mark in the musical world of Paris; Heinrich Heine marveled at the way illustrious performers fell at his feet for a little bit of praise in his magazine.[2] One of the young composers in his circle was Wagner, who, at his own expense, had Schlesinger publish one of his works; instead of paying Schlesinger, he wrote for his *Gazette Musicale*. Thanks to further assignments, Wagner was able to support himself, until one of his works was performed badly at a concert sponsored by Schlesinger's magazine, and he decided to put Paris out of his mind.[3] Hector Berlioz not only was published by Schlesinger but took care of the *Gazette* when the publisher was away. Schlesinger organized concerts and commissioned articles from the popular authors of the day, including George Sand, Alexandre Dumas, and Balzac. His flamboyant and occasionally expeditious methods got him into trouble, and into the newspapers, more than once.[4]

Gustave was also seeing the Collier family in Paris; indeed, he called on them at the Rond-Point des Champs-Elysées on the very day he returned to Paris for the new school term. Gertrude later recorded her impressions of those years, disguising Gustave as "César." One night at the opera, after *Faust,* he wraps her cloak around her, and they fall into an embrace and kiss rapturously — her first evening of pleasure.[5] But in a letter to his sister, Gustave shows more affection for Gertrude's sister Harriet: she was the good-humored one, while Gertrude always had something new to teach. There were tender teatime encounters, when he could read the dreary afternoon away to an admiring Harriet, condemned to her room by her handicap. Such moments must have shaken the indifference to emotions that he was cultivating.[6]

In March 1843 a singular personage entered his life. Although Flaubert would have rejected the comparison, Maxime Du Camp was to become as instrumental to his career as Alfred Le Poittevin before him or Louis Bouilhet after. It was only that too many things about Du Camp shocked Flaubert; otherwise he was his clone: almost his own age, the son of a surgeon, a law student who preferred writing. "He was charming, though rather ugly, tall, very elegant, slender, with an arrogant posture and abundant brown hair," Flaubert's niece would remember, and he was hardly a young man any longer by the time she could perceive such details.[7]

When they met, Du Camp was sharing an apartment on the Ile de la Cité with Ernest Le Marié, a classmate of Gustave's at the Collège Royal. As Du Camp later re-created the moment, Le Marié was seated at the piano spoiling Beethoven's Funeral March when the doorbell rang imperiously. "I saw a tall young man with a long blond beard and a hat cocked over one ear enter the room." He impressed Du Camp as resembling a young Gallic tribal chief, with "his enormous sea-green eyes under black brows, his trumpetlike voice, his excessive gestures and explosive laugh. . . ." Du Camp quickly found the flaws in the character of his new friend. For instance, Gustave seemed childish in his attempts to be funny, and anyone who failed to appreciate his gross humor was treated as a bourgeois. At the same time, Flaubert was gullible. Since he did not himself lie, he could not imagine that someone might lie to him.[8]

They became friends at once when Gustave confessed his own vocation and read from the manuscript of "Novembre." Thanks to Maxime, we have an outsider's view of Gustave's life as a student; we glimpse his "light-filled little apartment, which overlooked the Luxembourg Garden nursery." We follow him to school. Flaubert dressed in a singular manner: he overdressed, wearing black even in the morning, with white tie and gloves. Du Camp describes a Flaubert in robust health, fit to study at night and wander in the daytime, dining out and going to theater, "mixing pleasure and study, throwing money out the window and bemoaning his poverty. . . ." He sees him "dismissing the women his beauty attracted, coming to wake me up at three in the morning to go out to see an effect of moonlight on the Seine. . . ." Their circle included, when he was in town, Alfred Le Poittevin, "undulating like a woman, uttering shocking statements in a calm voice. . . ."

They talked over their plans for the future — their future as writers, of course. Du Camp did not have his friend's patience. He was already grinding out romantic serial stories and getting them published.[9]

Gustave went home for Easter and then returned to Paris to prepare for the summer examination, "so irritated, so bored, so furious," he described himself, that often he had to talk himself into optimism. In another letter to his sister, which has been dated to May 12, 1843, he mentions an alarming result of this intensive study: "I sometimes suffer twitching and handle my books and notes as if I had Saint Vitus' dance, or as if I were having an epileptic fit."[10] (He uses the conventional expressions *"haut mal"* and *"mal caduc."*)

"I am told, and you tell me, that you are working hard," his father wrote. "This is the way to stand out from the crowd and from all those noisy nobodies who trouble our lives."[11]

But his son was sick of law now, and perhaps truly sick. He was no longer even listening to his professors; he felt in a constant rage. His letters all looked forward to his next trip home.[12] He did return, briefly, by rail, barely six weeks after the first train left on the newly laid tracks from Paris to Rouen. It took four hours and fifteen minutes to cover the eighty-five miles, and what an experience for all but this proud student, who despised the "grocers" who embraced the new means of transportation with such enthusiasm.

His disgust with Paris and with law reached a climax that summer. We learn this not from Gustave but from a letter Alfred Le Poittevin wrote to him: "I would love to see how Father [Flaubert's father] will take the resolution you announce to me, that your active life will end with your law degree."[13] But Achille-Cléophas had another concern. Gustave had presented him with an outrageous bill for five hundred francs, and the good doctor was convinced that his son had "let himself be snared by the knights of industry and the loose ladies. . . ." He instructed Gustave, with resignation, "So pay your tailor, of whom you speak so often and for whom I give you money so often."[14] Perhaps Dr. Flaubert's doubts were unfounded this time. We know from an indiscretion on Alfred's part that Gustave was not touching loose ladies; we also know from Du Camp that he was a clotheshorse even at eight in the morning.

It was decided that Flaubert's parents and sister would join him in Paris immediately after the August exams. They were attempting to help in every way they could; his mother was even hoping to influence the examiners through a mutual acquaintance.[15] It is easy to re-create the atmosphere of that day, if only because the hero of *A Sentimental Education* takes the same examination at the same time and place. In that novel the friend who stands for Maxime Du Camp works with him all the night before, and pursues his questioning as they walk to the school together.[16] "Frédéric [the hero] put on the traditional black robe; then he entered with three other students, followed by the crowd, into a large room lit by curtainless windows and furnished with benches along the walls. In the center, leather chairs encircled a table decorated with a green cloth. It separated the candidates from the examining professors, in red robes, with ermine hoods on their shoulders, caps with gold ribbons on their heads."

"It was lamentable," Du Camp remembered. "The examining professors were not without indulgence." In the novel their first question concerns the difference between an agreement and a contract, and

Frédéric mixes them up. The examiner reassures him, but he is demoralized; his head aches from lack of sleep. He is confused by a question on procedure. When Frédéric hesitates, pulling at his mustache, the examiner snaps: "You won't find the answer in your beard!" The laughter that follows relaxes the atmosphere. But Frédéric fails, as Flaubert did.[17]

He took it as well as he could, joining his family for a holiday at Nogent, swimming in the Seine, reading Ronsard. Back in Rouen, his parents and Caroline left him to travel to their favorite stretch of Channel coast to look for land on which to build a vacation chalet; Gustave returned to Paris, for he was to pursue his studies. He seemed resigned to that, and there is no sign of dissatisfaction in his letters home.[18] His circle of acquaintances was expanding, thanks to his regular visits to the studio-salon of the sculptor James Pradier and his volatile wife. A contemporary described Louise Pradier as "a statue of flesh, beauty in full bloom, voluptuous charm, Parisian wit. . . ."[19] As it happened, Jules Cloquet was her cousin by marriage and had been one of the witnesses at her wedding, so Gustave had easy access to the studio. He took his brother, Achille, along to one of the Pradier receptions, and they found Victor Hugo there! "What can I tell you?" Gustave replied to his sister's curiosity. "He is a man who looks no different from anybody else, with a rather ugly face and ordinary appearance. . . . Yet that was the man who caused my heart to beat faster than anyone else has since I was born." He assured Caroline that he and Hugo had monopolized the conversation that afternoon.

He was also seeing the Schlesingers. "Madame Maurice," as he cautiously called her, invited him to join them in her home village, Vernon, for New Year's Eve. Perhaps Elisa turned his thoughts to Trouville. "I keep thinking about the chalet," he wrote Caroline in early December, meaning the chalet they were planning to put up in Deauville. He intended to go on to Rouen from Vernon after the first of the year, and from there to travel up to the coast to inspect the site of their new seaside home. Then he would return to Paris, and law.

Would Gustave join her at a party given by a friend in Rouen over the holidays? his sister wanted to know. "I don't dance or play games," he responded, "so I have no need to go to a ball. I am a bear and want to remain a bear in my den."[20]

What happened then is crucial to our story, so we must reconstruct the chronology with care. We know that Gustave was in Rouen for his vacation and then, with his brother, Achille, went on to Trouville

and Deauville, that undeveloped stretch across the narrow river, to
see the plot that had been chosen for the family's summer house. For
the return trip they left Pont-l'Evêque in a two-wheeled carriage drawn
by a single horse, with Gustave at the reins, en route to Honfleur. We
can follow their journey, for the road is the same today (though it is
paved now), rising from Pont-l'Evêque, cutting through the Saint Ga-
tien forest. Later Gustave was to recall this itinerary in "A Simple
Heart," in which the old servant Félicité is struck by a mail carriage:
"Leafless apple trees lined the road edge. Ice covered the ditches.
Dogs barked outside the farmhouses. . . ." Suddenly — this is fact,
not fiction — Gustave fell backward into the cab, "as if struck by apoplexy," as he would remember it. He felt "carried away in a sea of
flame."

Achille thought his brother was dead. He managed to get him to a
nearby house, and there applied the standard treatment for most ailments: a bleeding.[21]

CHAPTER TEN

CONSEQUENCES

O UR LANGUAGE has a word to describe the condition whose symptoms duplicate those of epilepsy without necessarily itself being epilepsy: *epileptiform*. The equivalent French term was used to define Flaubert's attack on the road to Honfleur in January 1844, and similar attacks thereafter. During his lifetime Gustave, as well as his friends and family, avoided the more brutal word *epilepsy*, and when, soon after Flaubert's death, Maxime Du Camp chose to utilize it, the writer's other friends were shocked. Epilepsy — grand mal, petit mal — was not to be talked about. When Du Camp sought to find out what had happened, after that first attack, he asked Alfred Le Poittevin, who seemed troubled by the question: "Flaubert's father doesn't want to say anything." Later Du Camp witnessed further attacks. "Suddenly, without apparent cause, Gustave raised his head and became quite pale; he had felt the aura, that mysterious breath which crosses the face like the flight of a spirit; his expression was filled with anguish, and he raised his shoulders in a gesture of heartbreaking discouragement; he would say: 'I have a flame in my left eye. . . .' " Flaubert referred to these incidents only as "my attacks of nerves." [1]

Specialists have diagnosed the disease from the accounts of Du Camp and others, and from Flaubert's own testimony. It has even been remarked that at the time when Du Camp revealed these symptoms, he could not have been inspired by medical literature, since it was not then sufficiently precise. Thanks to the evidence of Flaubert and his friends, doctors today are even prepared to identify the particular kind of epilepsy that afflicted Flaubert. In technical terms, it seems to have been a lesion in the left temporal region, either congenital or caused by an accident at birth or during childhood.[2]

Flaubert's case became a subject of dissertation from the beginning of our century: was it epilepsy? wasn't it rather hysteria? was it both?[3] What is certain is that life for the patient would never again be the same. As time passed, the attacks became less frequent. In 1857, the year *Madame Bovary* was published and some five years after the last attack about which we have detailed evidence, the subject himself explained to a correspondent how he had been cured. "By two means: first, in studying the attacks scientifically — that is, in seeking to identify them — and secondly by will power. I often felt madness coming. There was a whirlpool of ideas and images in my poor brain, during which it seemed that my consciousness, that my *me* sank like a vessel in a storm. But I clutched to my reason."[4] Even if we do not accept his affirmation that he had cured himself or at least mastered his convulsions, we can admire the clinical descriptions Flaubert has left us.

After all this, it may come as a surprise that the medical Flauberts failed to be alarmed. For Dr. Flaubert's son was allowed to return to Paris after the holidays. There is interesting evidence of this relaxed attitude in Achille's letter to Gustave dated January 15, 1844; he asks his brother to pick up some books for him. They will make a hefty parcel "because I think there are seven volumes." Only as an afterthought does Achille advise him, "Stay well and don't worry."[5] In another letter Achille addresses Gustave as *"Mon cher Caduc,"* which literally means "My dear ruin" but which is close enough to *"le mal caduc,"* or epilepsy, to suggest that Achille did not believe his brother was epileptic.[6] In fact, the family did care. When Gustave failed to write home immediately, his sister revealed that if a letter had not arrived from him the previous afternoon, someone from the family would have rushed off to Paris. We also know from Caroline's letter that Gustave suffered from a burn. (As Du Camp tells it, while Dr. Flaubert was bleeding his son soon after his return to Rouen, he poured scalding water over his right hand to activate circulation; it caused a second-degree burn.)[7]

Before the end of January 1844, Gustave returned to Rouen and there suffered a second attack — one that could have been fatal, or so he told Ernest Chevalier. He was given three simultaneous bleedings and put to bed with medication, herbal tea, a diet, and a seton. This was a thread drawn through a fold of the skin to allow an opening for discharges to drain; it was a frequent remedy at the time, as diabolical as bleeding, if less dramatic. The seton was located at Gustave's neck, requiring, as he described it, a stiff collar "less pliable than that of an officer of the national guard."

His morale was excellent, he assured Ernest Chevalier, but "at the slightest stimulation all my nerves quiver like the strings of a violin, and my knees, shoulders, and stomach tremble like a leaf." In a progress report early in February, he told his comrade, "I am purged and bled, they treat me with leeches, and good food and wine are kept away from me; I'm a dead man."[8]

We know something else about Gustave's condition, something we do not find in his correspondence; it is in Maxime Du Camp's letters to *him* that we discover that Gustave was also suffering from venereal infection. *Vérole* is the term the friends used, which then referred to all visible kinds of venereal infection from chancroid (one of the easiest to deal with) to syphilis (the most dangerous). In the early months of 1844, while wearing his seton and being treated in the barbarous way we have seen for his epilepsy, Gustave was also giving himself mercurial massages, then a common treatment for these infections. "And your nervous condition? and your pox, that lovely pox of which you were so proud?" Du Camp would ask Gustave as late as the following January.[9] Was this a souvenir of his student days in Paris? The coexistence of this infection and the preexisting epilepsy makes it difficult to know, for example, whether he had ceased sexual activity in the middle of the previous year because of the one or the other. The kind of epilepsy from which he is believed to have suffered is generally accompanied by a loss of sexual appetite.[10]

Du Camp came up to Rouen to visit his friend, and we have a fresh look at the chief surgeon's residence: "The living quarters were depressing, poorly laid out; everyone was on top of one another." He found Gustave listless, with his arm in a sling for the burn. "Everyone was gloomy, on the alert, and they left him alone as little as possible." Du Camp admired the "maternal love" of Madame Flaubert and the goodness of the doctor, who seemed disturbed by his son's condition: Du Camp perceived his "humiliation, despair, and a kind of resignation in the presence of an act of God that he could not dominate." Gustave? "This poor giant accepted the disaster with a measure of philosophy. He tried to laugh, to make jokes, to reassure the people around him; but then he forgot the part he was playing, he let his head fall, and it was not difficult to understand what was on his mind."[11]

When he could go out and the weather allowed it, Gustave followed his parents to Le Tréport, on the Channel coast north of Rouen. "There are superb rocks, a blue sky that is almost Asiatic in the bright sun," he wrote Achille. "As for me, old man, I'm well. I shaved this morning with my right hand, even though the seton and the fact that I could not close my hand made it difficult." There followed more intimate details concerning which hand he uses for what.[12]

Home in Rouen, early in June, Gustave offered Ernest Chevalier an account of his progress: "No day goes by without my seeing from time to time something like patches of hair or Bengal lights in front of my eyes. . . . Yet my last real attack was milder than the others. I am still wearing the seton, something I would not wish on you any more than the ban on pipe smoking. . . ." He concluded: "I am not ready to navigate alone." One piece of news was cheerful: the family was about to move to a new house at Croisset, acquired after work on the railway line drove them from their Déville weekend home.[13]

The new house was on the Seine, just a couple of miles outside of and downstream from Rouen. Gustave spent much of his summer in a rowboat, reading Shakespeare, and then, back in Rouen, worked on what he liked best, Greek and history. "My illness will have given me the advantage of spending my time as I wish," he wrote a friend.[14]

Gustave's sister, Caroline, was another of the ailing Flauberts. Whatever she had was chronic and apparently serious enough for her parents to keep her under surveillance. Even her piano lessons had to be brief, and it was accepted as a fact of life that she would never go dancing.[15] But if Gustave had by now ruled out marriage for himself, nothing seemed to prevent his sister from marrying. The lucky man was Emile Hamard, a schoolmate of Gustave's but not one of his intimate friends. "He is so dumb that one feels sorry for him," was the way Gustave dismissed Hamard in his private diary.[16]

It was decided that Hamard would first complete his own law studies — that would happen in January 1845 — and then the marriage would take place in March. "Like all newlyweds with some money in our pockets," the bride-to-be explained to her uncle François Parain, "we will make a trip to Italy."[17] Meanwhile, Gustave had taken up the unfinished "Sentimental Education" (the first version, with its two heroes). The manuscript bears a note in his hand indicating that he worked on it in 1843, up to November, and then — following his first attacks — from May 1844 to January 1845. Since it spans his first attacks of epilepsy, we look here for evidence that the words came with more difficulty. In fact, the first half of the text is as heavily edited as the second. If the novel breaks in half, it is due to an artistic defect: it is a young man's book, written too close to the young man's experience. Flaubert himself realized that he had only produced a draft, and never sought to have it published.[18]

The March marriage of Caroline Flaubert and Emile Hamard was uneventful; it is the honeymoon that is worth mentioning, for the bride's father, mother, and brother Gustave were to accompany the wedding couple to Italy. They rode in an open railroad car to Paris, for Gustave's first visit since his convalescence. He was so bold as to call on that wild woman Louise Pradier, who by then had left her husband to live with a younger man.[19] Le Poittevin promptly advised his friend to have lunch with her on his return from Italy. "Ask her, 'Are you the loving kind?' She will reply, 'The way a bad girl should be.' And then take her. You know, that movement you do so well, so rapidly, so often. . . ."[20]

He also called on the Colliers. He mentions this in a wistful passage in his letter to Alfred, but he does not tell the whole story; he was ashamed to tell it. Later he would confess to Louise Colet how he had played a game at the expense of poor Harriet that day. They sat alone together on a canapé; she took his hand and entwined her fingers in his. He let her do it, and she gazed at him with a look . . . that panicked him long after the event. His behavior sickened him; he told Louise Colet that he would have given his life to efface that "look of sad love."[21]

The first stop for the honeymoon caravan was Nogent-sur-Seine. Gustave was already bored. He was again traveling in a group, obliged to conform to other people's desires, and again he would have to see the Mediterranean "as a grocer."[22] In Marseilles he slipped away to visit the Hôtel Richelieu, but the shutters were drawn, the hotel was abandoned, and he could not find out where Eulalie was.[23]

His first aesthetic excitement was in Genoa, where he began to look at paintings seriously. In the Palazzo Balbi, on the street of the same name, he stopped in front of a work attributed to Peter Breughel the Younger, a *Temptation of Saint Anthony*. No other painting ever had so great an effect on him, before or after: "Saint Anthony between three women, turning his head to avoid their caresses." The scene was "swarming, crawling, mocking in a grotesque and wild manner."[24] He quickly reported to Alfred Le Poittevin that this portrayal of the saint's temptations had moved him to consider writing a play on the subject, though he did not see himself as being up to it.[25]

He had an anxious moment when he thought he would have to accompany the family all the way to Naples, but that plan was abandoned. Was it because of Caroline's fragility, or Gustave's? Actually, their father was also having a health problem, a severe eye ache, which was treated with leaches. Caroline had been all right in their succession of carriages until Toulon, and then her back pains had recurred, with an accompanying fatigue. Gustave had two attacks — "nervous attacks" — along the way. The hapless bridegroom could only offer to cut the journey short. From Milan, Gustave wrote Alfred: "As for me, I am really rather well now that I have accepted the idea of always being ill. . . . I have said an irrevocable goodbye to practical life." This Saint Anthony was even prepared to turn down a temptation. Responding to Le Poittevin's suggestion that he go to bed with Louise Pradier, he said that he would definitely call on her, but doubted that he would try anything, unless she invited him to do so *very* ostensibly. He explained: "Humping has nothing more to teach me. My desire is too universal, too permanent, and too intense for me to have desires." [26]

CHAPTER ELEVEN

CROISSET

Gustave's life seemed to be cut out for him, and for years to come. With remarkable lucidity he now told Ernest Chevalier — in a letter dated June 15, 1845 — what this meant. He would live alone with his parents, in summertime in Croisset, in his room, and then in wintertime in Rouen, in his room. He would read, write, daydream, smoke. He even thought of acquiring a painting of a bear, framing it, and hanging it in his room over the title *Portrait of Gustave Flaubert.* (He should have done that; it would have avoided considerable heartache and rage later, on the part of his lovers and even his friends.) Chevalier, meanwhile, was settled in Corsica in his first official post, as deputy crown attorney. "Look at yourself in the mirror at once," Gustave suggested, "and tell me whether you do not have an urge to laugh." Chevalier probably had no desire to laugh at himself, then or later, as he rose in rank.[1]

In a moving letter to Alfred Le Poittevin, Gustave painted a picture of his own — of the hermit he was trying to be: "My sentimental education isn't over, but I'm getting there." In Paris the sculptor Pradier had apparently advised him to take a mistress, but that would mean an active life, and active life had never worked for him.[2]

Croisset was the ideal refuge for a Norman Saint Anthony. (There was no more talk, in any case, of a summer house in Deauville.) The Flauberts had done a considerable amount of work to make their riverside country residence livable year round, by adding fireplaces to the bedrooms, and they did what they could to close off the property to inquisitive riverbank strollers.[3] It was a two-story house, unpretentious to the point of being touching; there were ample grounds, gar-

dens, and then a steep wooded rise to the village of Canteleu. It did
not take Gustave long to feel at home there. "My books are on the
table before me, my windows are open, all is quie:. . . ."[4] This was
Gustave to Alfred in June 1845, but it could have been written a year,
five years, or ten or twenty later.

He rowed. He studied Greek verbs. He forced himself to read the
Greek classics in the original, he worked over Shakespeare's *Life of
Timon of Athens*, and he studied — pen in hand — the plays of Voltaire. Everything he did (everything except taking medicine) seemed
a conscious preparation for his writing.[5]

How close-knit this family was became clear as the Hamards ex-
tended their stay in Paris. Gustave's mother complained that her
daughter was abandoning her; Caroline promised that she would rush
home whenever they needed her. She insisted that she was not so ill
as to require her mother's presence. In a letter to Rouen that he may
have hoped would reassure the family, Hamard said that his wife was
no worse than she had been in Rouen: "She has pains in her kidneys,
abdomen, chest, and heart; she cannot have become ill in Paris because she hasn't even been out on foot, and ever since you left, she
has remained seated. . . ." Hamard knew that he was not loved by
his in-laws, but he tried. "I am sorry that my inclinations keep me
away from Rouen," he wrote them, "but you know that you have your
apartment here, you are at home here. . . ." Caroline begged her
mother to be nice to Emile. "It seems to me that he hasn't done
anything to displease you except to take your daughter away, and any
son-in-law would have done that."[6]

Caroline was pregnant; it had happened during that crowded honeymoon. But by the time she was ready to take to her bed, the family
had a more alarming case to deal with. Dr. Flaubert had developed
an infection (a phlegmon, in medical terminology) on his thigh. His
doctor son called in other doctors, and Jules Cloquet even traveled
up from Paris; they agreed that the abscess had to be opened, and
the patient asked his son to do it.[7] Dr. Flaubert was just celebrating
his sixty-first birthday when he became ill in November 1845; he fought
the infection for two months. Only toward the end did his vomiting
cease, so the quinquina with which he was being treated could be
retained.[8]

He died, the good doctor did, on January 15, 1846. "You knew and
loved the good and intelligent man we have lost," Gustave wrote Ernest Chevalier, "the sweet and lofty soul who has gone."[9] "Never

have more touching signs of regret been manifested, we can report, on the part of an entire city," said the *Journal de Rouen* in describing the funeral. The crowd was dense along the road leading to the cemetery, situated on a rise above the city; the slopes were covered with mourners.[10]

His father's death shook Gustave out of hibernation. He assumed responsibility for raising funds for a suitable monument. And he undertook a more urgent campaign to make certain that his brother would assume his father's place at the hospital, something that was not as simple as the preponderant social position of the Flauberts might have suggested. There was a fight for the succession; Gustave took it upon himself to go to Paris to argue his brother's case. As he later remembered it, he tackled the entire Rouen medical faculty and even managed to obtain a letter from the King to the prefect of Rouen.[11] The fight ended in a compromise: Achille was to share the chief surgeon's job and teaching with one of his father's assistants. He was, however, granted the residence. "There he is," Gustave would be able to announce proudly that June, "and with the finest medical position in Normandy."[12]

Six days after Dr. Flaubert's death, Gustave's sister — now back in Rouen with her husband — gave birth to a daughter, who would be baptized Désirée-Caroline. The new mother showed immediate symptoms of puerperal fever, a frequent danger in the days before antiseptics. Achille, who had been caring for his father, would not have practiced much hygiene before attending his sister. (Across Europe, in Vienna, the Hungarian doctor Ignaz Semmelweis was being laughed out of his hospital for advising interns to wash their hands with caustic soap before delivering infants; he knew that this would reduce the danger of puerperal fever, though he did not know why.)

The fragile Caroline held on until the middle of March, suffering much. "Hamard leaves my room, where he was sobbing, standing near my fireplace," Gustave wrote Maxime Du Camp on March 15. "Caroline speaks, smiles, caresses us. . . . She is losing her memory, everything is confused in her head. . . . The baby sucks and cries. Achille says nothing and does not know what to say. . . ." On the night of her death, they dressed her in her wedding gown, and the next morning Gustave gave his beloved sister "a long and final farewell kiss in her coffin." He had a death mask made, and asked James Pradier to create a marble bust; the sculptor was already working on one of Dr. Flaubert.

Immediately after the funeral, the family rode out to Croisset; no need to stay on at the Hôtel-Dieu now. "Some trip," Gustave wrote Du Camp. "Alone with my mother and the crying baby. . . . Of the four who lived here, two remain. The trees still do not have their leaves, the wind is blowing, the river is high, the rooms are cold and skimpily furnished."

One thing was certain: the surviving Flauberts were prepared to fight to hold on to Caroline's infant, Caroline.[13] It was not going to be easy. Finally a tutor was appointed from Hamard's family, and Hamard himself gave up a civil service job in Paris to set up as a lawyer in Rouen, where he could at least be near his daughter. The Flauberts surely made him out to be worse than he was, "a subject of shame and chagrin for my awakening conscience," as Caroline would recall, "challenging by his manners and opinions all the ideas of order and proper bourgeois life with which I was raised." Hamard was not a libertine, not a crook, his daughter later conceded in an unpublished memoir; rather, he was a "poor deranged personality."[14] Perhaps at the beginning he was only a hapless, unhappy man?

"With her I buried many ambitions, almost all worldly desire for glory," Gustave was to tell Louise Colet half a dozen years later. "I raised her; she had a solid, delicate mind, which charmed me; she married vulgarity incarnate. Such is woman."[15] He told Du Camp that he expected his mother to follow her husband and daughter to the grave soon enough.[16] Meanwhile, there were practical matters to attend to. Since he and his mother had abandoned the hospital residence, they needed another place to live in Rouen, and they found a suitable two-story house on nearby Rue de Crosne.[17] At the same time, Gustave began organizing his room in Croisset for his permanent use.[18]

In April 1846 the family notary, in the presence of the Flauberts and Emile Hamard, drew up an inventory of the deceased Dr. Flaubert's possessions. By the time they finished at Croisset, they were up to 30,760 francs — not counting books. In addition, the partnership set up by Dr. and Madame Flaubert at the time of their marriage had assets worth 207,389 francs.[19] There were three heirs: Achille, Gustave, and the infant daughter of their sister. The widower Hamard would receive half of his daughter's income during his lifetime.[20]

Gustave was certain, now, that his way of life would henceforth remain unalterable. He thanked the heavens for having given him the habit of working. He wrote for eight to ten hours a day, and if disturbed would become upset, even "ill." Days passed without his walking even the length of the garden; the rowboat remained on shore. Perhaps there was bound to be a loss of inspiration, of passion and instinct, in this dogged way of going about work; yet he felt that he needed to learn so much. He was not seeking rewards; he often wondered if he would even publish what he wrote. He thought it might be amusing to wait until the age of fifty and then publish his complete works all at once. But he also dreamed, as Du Camp did, "of long journeys on horseback," and wondered if that might not be preferable to becoming a man of letters in Paris, waiting for a play to be accepted, catering to reviewers, arguing with publishers. Yes, he would travel, and he hoped Maxime would be ready when he was. His health had improved (this in May 1846); he had suffered no attack since the previous October.

Late in May he went to Paris to see about furnishings for his writing room in Croisset, and occasionally he made the short hop to Rouen to assist in the move to the new house, where they were to spend the winter months. Then something important happened: Alfred Le Poittevin announced that he was going to marry. "Since you did not ask for advice, it would be proper on my side not to offer any," he began his letter of noncongratulations. Was Alfred certain that he would not end up a bourgeois? For Gustave, Alfred was a poet, a purer poet than he; he was being abandoned by a fellow artist.[21]

But if Alfred was lost to Flaubert — and he really was — there would soon be Louis Bouilhet. "He is a poor chap who makes a living with private lessons and is a poet," Gustave was to describe him, "a true poet who writes superb and charming things and will remain unknown because he lacks two things: bread and time."[22] The two friends had never lost touch with each other since secondary school. After receiving his baccalaureat diploma, Bouilhet had enrolled as a medical student, and had even had Dr. Flaubert as a professor. He gave lessons on the side and wrote poetry when on night duty at the Hôtel-Dieu. This peaceful arrangement was compromised when Bouilhet joined some fellow interns in demanding wine with their meals and the right to sleep away from the hospital on off-duty nights; they were dismissed before they could resign.

He was Gustave's age — actually, his senior by six months. He looked like Gustave: they were both tall, and later both would be precociously bald. They wore mustaches of the same color and had the same provincial accent — or so Maxime Du Camp remembered. It was even suggested that the two friends were related, the implication being that Bouilhet was Dr. Flaubert's illegitimate son.[23] After Flaubert's death, Guy de Maupassant assured Caroline that the allegation was false but that in any case it could not cast a shadow on Flaubert's mother, though one could always doubt paternity. . . .[24]

Bouilhet was all poetry, Flaubert all prose. Du Camp tells us that though he tried, Flaubert could not write a proper line of verse, and could not even carry a tune.[25] Precisely because he was at home with the logic and the rhythm of poetry, Bouilhet was a good critic of prose that deviated from its purpose. For as long as he lived, he was Flaubert's editor. He was also to keep Flaubert from being lonely. "I think of our Sundays in Croisset," Flaubert would write him later, "when I heard the sound of the iron gate and watched the arrival of the cane, the notebook, and you. . . ."[26]

Perhaps it was inevitable that a scholar, misunderstanding certain humorous gibes in Flaubert's letters to Bouilhet, decided that they signified a homosexual attachment.[27] Looking for psychological flaws, Sartre was convinced that Flaubert's relations with Le Poittevin and Du Camp as well as with Bouilhet were at least platonically homosexual.[28] This *platonically* is disarming. All of these men in fact spent all the time they could sporting with women; to call a friend "old pederast," as Flaubert did Bouilhet,[29] or as Le Poittevin did Flaubert,[30] was a marvelous joke. Thus, when he closed a letter to Bouilhet, Flaubert added a kiss to Bouilhet's mistress and signed off, "I squeeze your rocks."[31] A letter from Maxime Du Camp, filled with talk of his and Gustave's sex adventures with loose women, ended: "I kiss your balls."[32]

PART III

CHAPTER TWELVE

LOUISE

EVEN BEARS, we have seen, come out of hibernation. Gustave went to Paris, and when he was there he dropped in at the Pradier studio on Quai Voltaire. James Pradier was then working on the busts of Dr. Flaubert and his daughter, Caroline. Although he is all but forgotten now, Pradier had the highest of reputations in the middle of his own century. He received prestigious commissions, such as the statue of Jean-Jacques Rousseau in Geneva and sculpture for Napoleon's tomb. He was equally famous for his more intimate marbles — naked women calling for caresses — and his models could be admired in person at his studio. He had even sculpted Louise Pradier pregnant (the child happened not to be his). Louise, of course, was no longer to be seen at the Quai Voltaire studio. She had accumulated lovers and debts; Pradier had had her followed, once by the celebrated detective François Vidocq, but by this time had long since cast his adulterous spouse aside.[1]

Louise Pradier was gone, but another Louise graced the Pradier salon. Louise Colet was both an earnest and prolific woman of letters and a striking beauty; she was sitting for a bust at the time. As Maxime Du Camp (who was not there) later reconstructed the encounter in July 1846, Pradier took Louise Colet aside to say: "You see that big boy over there? He wants to write. You should give him some advice."[2] Gustave's recollection was more incisive: Louise was posing when he fastened his gaze on her, and she stared back. He was struck, he would tell her, by her "ringlets dancing on your white shoulders, your blue dress, your arms, your face, your everything."[3]

Let Louise describe herself (this to her diary, a year before her meeting with Flaubert): "I've gained weight, I no longer have the same willowy figure, but it is still elegant and well shaped. My throat, neck, shoulders, and arms are exceptionally lovely. People still admire the way my neck joins my face, perhaps too well, for it causes my face to appear too round. I correct this defect with my hairstyle, which consists of long curls over my temples, hiding my cheeks, and falling to my shoulders. My abundant hair, done every day by a coiffeur, draws compliments." She was already concerned about her hair turning gray. But she had an expressive forehead, well-shaped brows, and dark blue eyes that were "quite beautiful when they flare up in reaction to a thought or feeling. . . ." Her nose was "charming, fine, distinguished," her mouth "fresh and narrow." Her legs were perfectly shaped, too.[4] Let it be said that extant portraits confirm the honesty of this description. She was a beauty.[5]

So was Gustave, then twenty-four years and seven months of age. It has been noted that the same number of years separated Gustave from Louise Colet and from Elisa Schlesinger; both women were born in September 1810. The day after their meeting at Pradier's studio, Gustave made a surprise visit to Louise's apartment. (It was Wednesday, July 29, as the delighted Louise was to record in her diary.) They dined together on Thursday and hired a carriage to watch the fireworks commemorating the "three glorious days" of July 1830, which had seen the abdication of the ultraroyalist Charles X.[6] They spent that Saturday night together, beginning with a ride in the Bois de Boulogne park; he sent flowers on Sunday and, after waiting for her other guests to leave, stayed overnight.[7] A long time later Flaubert would confess, or boast, that he had seduced Louise Colet in a carriage by playing a role — the man "disgusted with existence" — while inwardly laughing.[8] In fact their first night of love turned out not to be a night of love at all because he was too tense. But she understood, and made it all right. It was the first time anything like that had happened to him, he told her later. So much for inwardly laughing.[9]

Now began one of the most deeply scrutinized collections of love letters in literature, for its span coincided with the conception and then the composition of a masterpiece. "Yesterday at this hour I held you in my arms," Gustave wrote Louise in his very first letter, on his return to Croisset, at midnight on August 4. "I should like to bring you only joy . . . to pay you back a little for everything you gave me in the generosity of your love." That would not be easy, for Gustave was not free. His mother had been waiting for him at the station. "She cried on seeing me come back. You cried when I left. Is our

misery such that we cannot move from anywhere without causing tears
on both sides?" In this first letter we pick up the leitmotif to be heard
over all the years of their love. "I see that you are suffering," he
wrote. "I know I shall cause you to suffer. I wish I had never known
you, for you, and then for me, and yet the thought of you does not go
away."

She feared that he would think badly of her because she had given
herself to him so readily. He promised that this would never happen.
He was hers, yet he dared not say "for always"; he knew the future
too well for that. "I have never looked at a child without thinking that
he will become an old man, nor at a cradle without thinking of a
tomb. The contemplation of a naked woman makes me dream of her
skeleton." If Louise had thought for an instant that she had walked
into a joyous liaison, she quickly learned how wrong she was.

His letters after this first encounter were as long as they were tor-
tured. He feared that they would be discovered, for Louise was married — a fact that concerned her far less than it did him. He needed
a good excuse in order to return to Paris; the excuse would be that
he had to talk to Pradier about his father's bust.

Louise asked to see his writings, but he warned that his manuscripts were unreadable because of the heavy editing he had done on
them. He was not writing now, "because I don't express anything of
what I want to say." He tells her of his desire for the Middle East.
He had loved one woman from the age of fourteen to the age of
twenty without touching her; Louise Colet was the first he had loved
and possessed. "Farewell, farewell, I place my head on your breast.
. . . A thousand kisses, a thousand, everywhere, *everywhere*."[10]

At midnight on Saturday, August 8, he sat down to write: "The sky
is pure, the moon shines, I hear sailors singing as they raise the an-
chor to sail with the coming tide. . . . No cloud, no wind. The river
is white under the moon. . . ." He had waited a whole hour on the
quay for the postman that day. (We can only marvel at the extraordinary speed of the postal service in 1846, when letters were delivered
seven days a week and there was overnight service from Paris to a
small hamlet outside Rouen.)[11]

Flaubert was writing love letters, but in a tone of resignation that
hardly befitted his years. "My youth has passed," he warned her. "The
nervous disease that lasted two years was its conclusion. . . ." Now
Louise had disturbed his tranquillity, had turned him into a beast
lusting for her. He was not made to enjoy life. He would spoil hers.

She spoke again of his work. He doubted that he would publish; if he did, it would not be before at least ten years had passed. She predicted that he would write great things.[12]

Louise was going to find the reluctant writer as difficult to understand as the reluctant lover. She was freer with her body, and with her pen. Born in Aix-en-Provence, she had lived in the south of France until her marriage at twenty-four. She had begun writing poetry in her adolescence; when she followed her husband to Paris — he was a flute teacher at the Conservatory — she began to publish as if her life depended on it, and when she separated from him, her livelihood certainly did. She found a protector in Victor Cousin, an eminent philosopher of the midcentury who was a member of the French Academy and also, starting in 1840, the minister of education. Thanks to Cousin and other influential men, four of Louise's poems won French Academy prizes — prizes that had purses attached to them.

Her relations with Cousin were an open secret. A pamphleteer named Alphonse Karr alleged that when Cousin became a cabinet minister, he raised the government stipend that Louise, thanks to his support, was already receiving; he added that Cousin was taking good care of her during her pregnancy. Louise's husband of record, Hippolyte Colet, prepared himself for a duel, but Louise got to Karr first with a kitchen knife, wounding him only slightly but creating a wonderful scandal.[13] As a matter of fact Hippolyte Colet, and not Cousin, was the father of Henriette, whatever either of these gentlemen may have thought.[14]

It is not hard to make fun of Louise Colet, the poetry hustler, who wrote up her life almost as soon as she lived it. But there were few easy roads for an independent woman in her time; yielding to influential men was expected.

So the first fortnight of their relationship was spent this way: anguished messages came from Louise; Gustave furnished an eloquent defense of his sedentary existence, making uncanny pronouncements on his literary future. And all the while he defended himself as would a maiden.[15] When he was almost ready to go to Paris, disaster. He had developed a common enough ailment in those times of minimal hygiene: a painful boil, an enormous one on his right cheek, which swelled his eye and deformed his face. On August 17 he let Louise know that he would have been in Paris that very evening had it not been for his boils. His head was covered with bandages; his body was covered with boils; he was in bed and could not move. . . . Thanks to his "stubbornness," he got rid of all this and was able to inform Louise on August 18 that he could see her the next day. In Paris they dined alone and returned to his hotel to make love — "with your silk

dress open, and the lace that snaked over your breast. Your whole
expression was a smile, intoxicated with love. How your eyes spar-
kled!" [16] Remember that she knew her eyes were splendid when "they
flare up in reaction to a thought or feeling. . . ."

In Paris he purchased a print by Jacques Callot of *The Temptation
of Saint Anthony;* on his return he hung it at Croisset. [17]

It was becoming a struggle between his duty to his mother and his
desire for his mistress: this was the way he presented the situation to
Louise. The women he cared for most each held a bit in his teeth:
"They pull me one way and the other by love and by pain." It was
Sunday night, the household was asleep, and now he could open a
drawer and take out his "relics." Among these were Louise's slippers,
stained with blood — a true relic of their first night together. There
was also a small bag containing her letters, which he reread, including the latest one, received that morning. In it Louise said that she
suffered; he pointed out that his mother suffered more than she did,
and in silence. "You remember my violent caresses and how my hands
were strong — you almost trembled. I made you cry out two or three
times. So calm yourself, poor child that I love, don't let your imagination upset you!" [18]

In another letter she said something about having a child, having
their love child. Only because he loved her so much could he restrain
his anger at this suggestion "so frightful for my love," he wrote. He
would love any child they had, "but the very idea of this chills me,
and if to prevent one from coming into the world, it became necessary
that I depart it, the Seine is there. . . ." [19]

Then Louise declared that she wished to visit Gustave in Croisset.
This was folly, it was impossible; the whole countryside would know
about it the next day. He had a better idea. Since Maxime Du Camp
was visiting Croisset, Gustave would leave with him on the pretext of
showing him the Château-Gaillard at Les Andelys. But in fact he
would go on to Mantes and stay until the six P.M. train, which would
bring him back to Rouen at eight. Louise would leave Paris at nine
that morning, to be in Mantes at 10:50; he would get there from
Rouen at 11:19, and they would have five "lovely hours" together.
Louise, of course, was dissatisfied with the brevity of the proposed
meeting. "Are you then guarded like a young girl?" [20]

Mantes-la-Jolie, then and now (but then more than now), is a halfway point on the Seine between ancient Normandy and ancient France.

It was a very small town when Flaubert knew it, containing 3,818 inhabitants, according to the railway guide he may have been using. The same guide says this of Mantes: "Pretty little town; post office and coach relay. In a charming site. Possesses two stone bridges and several public fountains. . . . One still sees towers and bulwarks that have withstood the ravages of the ages." By then it was also the eighth station on the rail line from Paris to Rouen.[21]

They spent not five hours together, but twenty. Gustave threw caution to the winds and stayed the night. "We loved each other better than ever, we felt exquisite pleasures," Gustave would declare the very next evening. He had been proud to hear Louise say that she had never "tasted such happiness." He also remembered her crying out "Bite me, bite me!" when he kissed her naked shoulders.[22] But the memorialist of that meeting was Louise, in a poem composed for Gustave alone. We can read it as a diary, for it contains a detailed account of their day in Mantes, even to the menu of the lunch they were served in their room. There was some lovemaking immediately thereafter, followed by a boat ride to watch the sunset. But they were caught in a downpour, and welcomed the fireplace in their bedroom back at the inn. After supper they made love again, their "wild thrusts" recorded by the poetess, who saw her Gustave as

> an untamed buffalo of the American desert,
> Vigorous and superb in your athletic strength.

Her testimony is that both lovers maintained their ardor all night long. At dawn she begged him to stay, but he insisted on leaving; his mother was waiting for him.[23]

He watched her leave for Paris, then waited for his own train. And of course his mother was at the Rouen station; she had also been there the previous evening and, when he had failed to arrive, had spent a sleepless night. "She did not complain," Gustave explained to Louise, "but her face was the greatest reproach one can utter." He did not know when he could see Louise again, but he was convinced that they would love each other longer this way, kept apart as they were by incompletely satisfied desire.[24]

On September 15 he received an important piece of news from his mistress: she had had her period, there would be no palpable souvenir of their meeting in Mantes. Again he reassured her: he would have accepted her child, had there been one. Yet he did not seek an heir. He encouraged her to see Victor Cousin, referred to only by the code name the Philosopher in these letters.[25]

She complained that he did not confide in her. Did she wish to know what was in his heart? "Two or three poor artistic ideas nursed with love; nothing more. The greatest events of my life have been some thoughts, readings, a few sunsets on the sea at Trouville, and conversations lasting five or six hours with a friend who is now married and lost to me." He was a loner. "I had, as I told you, a great passion while still almost a child. When it was over, I divided myself in two, placing on one side the soul I kept for Art, and on the other, my body, which would have to fend for itself. Then you came and upset all that."[26] He took pains to reassure her that he held no other woman in his arms. The days when he would visit a brothel on New Year's Eve were over. Now when he felt desire, a pan of cold water dealt with it, and that was that.[27] He did what he could to arouse Louise's jealousy; he asked her to seek information, through a cousin of hers in the New World, about Eulalie Foucaud, his Marseilles seductress, and then he actually sent her a letter to be forwarded to Eulalie, adding that he wished he could be with Louise to be able to erase with a kiss the sad expression on her face as she read it.[28] We do not have this letter to Eulalie, but we know that Louise was outraged that he mentioned her own breasts after writing Eulalie about hers! Louise warned that this woman might ask him for money. Let her ask, he replied, for he had none. He had already spent three times his income that year.[29]

Poor Louise Colet. She refused to believe that Gustave loved her. Would a lover find an excuse to stay away? If she had not met him, she said, she might have accepted an outstanding position; possibly this meant that she might have married Victor Cousin. She became increasingly exasperated, telling Gustave that he horrified her. She even broke off their daily correspondence. Then, on November 8, 1846, he informed her that although the fund-raising committee for his father's monument had put off its meeting, he was not going to wait; he would come to Paris the next day. He suggested that they meet at the Café de Paris at three, or at his hotel at four.[30]

CHAPTER THIRTEEN

WESTWARD
WITH DU CAMP

THEIR PARIS meeting was stormy. Louise was in tears; Gustave
was not, so she called him selfish. She had suggested that they
meet at Pradier's studio, but he did not appear; there would have
been too many witnesses, he said. When finally they found each other,
days had been lost; they made love, but then the tears began. She
refused his goodbye kiss. At the end of the month he was in Paris
again, but with his mother, which did not facilitate their meetings.
He and Louise rode through the Bois; he read "Novembre" to her.
Another time he slipped out of his hotel on the pretext that he wanted
to see Maxime, but his mother was not well and he could not stay
away from her long.

Maxime accompanied the Flauberts back to Rouen. The two friends
were to visit Alfred Le Poittevin, married and "absent from me," as
Gustave explained it to Louise. He also told her that he talked about
her with Maxime; he was ever fearful that his mother might overhear
them. Apart from that, he and Du Camp spent their time in daydreams. "We traveled in the East with a retinue and then we fell back
on our present existence. . . ." While Du Camp observed surgical
operations at the Hôtel-Dieu, Gustave took sword lessons.[1]

On Du Camp's return to Paris, it was his turn to reassure Louise.
He promised her that Gustave would see her when he could: he was
in good health, but his nerves required calm, and so did his work —
and his work was his whole life. Maxime was later to say that Louise
persecuted Flaubert and even followed him when he was in Paris. He
claimed that once she even burst into a private room in a restaurant,
prepared to murder a rival, only to find Gustave with friends.[2]

Still, so much of what we know about Flaubert before *Madame Bovary* comes from these letters to Louise. We see him reciting Homer, studying La Bruyère ("It's good to dip into these great styles from time to time"). He talked of Shakespeare and then apologized for writing about Shakespeare rather than about himself. "The finest things God created are the sea, *Hamlet,* and Mozart's *Don Juan,*" he told her. An important event: he had ordered a desk chair with a high back, of Louis XIII style and in green leather, from Paris. He wondered what he would write while seated in it. "I am waiting to write a book to discover for myself what I am worth," he said another time, "but perhaps this book won't be written, and it's a pity."[3]

The new year, 1847, saw no improvement in Flaubert's relations with his passionate friend. It began with recriminations. She said that he had treated her like a whore because he had wanted to give her a bracelet after their first night of love; he suggested that they remain friends and write each other occasionally. Then he received two tender letters at once, and promised to come to Paris soon. When there was another angry outburst from Louise, he replied frankly: he loved her, but for him love was not essential. He could not even promise to visit Paris every month.[4]

In February Gustave informed Louise that he would be coming to Paris to see Pradier. Should they meet, or would that make her more unhappy than she already was? Maxime stepped in, advising Louise not to see Gustave if she wished to cure her broken heart. She fired off an angry reply, accusing Du Camp of seeking to hurt her; perhaps Gustave was already with him in Paris. Predictably, the visit led to a flare-up; Gustave saw almost nothing of Louise, and Maxime had to provide her with a day-by-day account of his activities. A childhood friend had died; Gustave called on the parents. Gustave saw Louise at six one evening, and that same night suffered an attack at Maxime's apartment, "due entirely, I am sadly convinced, to what happened between the two of you." Maxime kept his friend under close watch until his departure on Saturday for Rouen — a hurried departure, because Gustave feared that he might have another attack on Sunday.

Louise did not accept that. On Sunday morning she even showed up at Du Camp's, and did not believe the doorkeeper when she said that Du Camp was not there. She even doubted that Gustave had been mourning his dead friend Félix Darcet; she preferred to think that he was sleeping with Darcet's sister, Louise Pradier, the wanton ex-wife of the sculptor, and Pradier himself had hinted as much.

Gustave admitted that there was a time when he had seen the other Louise often, but he had not been particularly attracted to her. He found her interesting as a character study: "The typical woman with all her instincts, an orchestra of female feelings." But to hear an orchestra, one did not get inside it; one went to the rear of the hall![5]

The next time Louise Colet wrote Gustave, she asked him to explain how he had become the way he was. "The hand I burned and whose skin is shriveled like that of a mummy's is less sensitive than the other to cold or heat," he replied. "My soul is the same; it passed through fire." They never could leave each other in good humor; would it be better if they did not meet at all? Then he was in Paris again, in April, prior to his departure with Du Camp on a journey through Brittany. She asked for a "frank explanation": did he love her? If love had to be the only thing in life, the answer was no. But if it meant that one could meet "with charm" and say goodbye "without despair," then yes.

She had asked him to be violent, to take the initiative of breaking with her. "No," came the reply, "I send you good wishes." How did one deal with someone like that?[6]

Stay-at-home though he may have seemed to Louise, Gustave dreamed of travel. He told Ernest Chevalier, for example, that he would like to visit Corsica but did not dare wish it, for he would be free to travel only if the worst happened; Ernest would understand that he meant by this his mother's death.[7] He could not reach the Mediterranean, but he could visit Brittany. As Du Camp remembered it, the voyage was to be a prelude to the longer trips the friends intended to take together. Brittany itself was relatively far-off and remained somewhat removed from civilization, thanks to its peculiar customs and language.[8] One even needed a passport for such domestic travel. We have Gustave's. His profession was now given as landowner, his height as one meter, eighty-three centimeters; his hair and beard were dark chestnut, and he had an oval face, a high forehead, blue eyes, a vivid complexion. It was also noted that he had a scar under his left eye and another, caused by a burn, on his right hand.[9]

They left Paris at dawn on May 1, 1847, walking from Du Camp's apartment near the Place de la Madeleine to the Orléans station, where they would catch the train to Blois.[10] They had decided to write a travel diary; they would make notes and then prepare a final text on their return, with Gustave doing the odd-numbered chapters and Maxime the even.[11] The first chapter alerts the reader to the modest goals of these travelers: "Later on there will be long journeys across the world, on camelback with Turkish saddles." On this trip they sought only fresh air, a bit of wilderness, and vast sandy beaches. All the same, they began with the Loire valley castles, Blois, Chambord, and Amboise (this last owned by the reigning monarchy, with its "nouveau riche bad taste").[12] On their fourth day out, Du Camp revealed in his memoirs, Gustave suffered an attack. They were in Tours, and Du Camp summoned a local doctor of repute, who confessed his helplessness; he could do no more than prescribe a heavy dose of quinine to serve as a stimulant. It was the only such incident during their trip.

Du Camp also let us see the wildness of western Brittany, with its rough roads, its strange tongue, its rudimentary agriculture, humble villages, untidy houses, superstition, misery . . . they went so far out that they became emissaries of civilization and were called upon to treat wounds. Gendarmes who asked for their passports found it hard to believe that they were traveling for pleasure and not on some mission.[13]

Gustave's mother and tiny Caroline — then eighteen months old — joined them in Brest. Gustave and Maxime rode with them part of the way and then walked alone when it pleased them. Saint Malo was a pilgrimage site for these travelers. Although that quintessential romantic Chateaubriand was still alive, he had already built his tomb there. They went on to Chateaubriand's castle at Combourg and sat outdoors that evening reading his *René*.[14]

From Pontorson, near Mont-Saint-Michel, Gustave wrote Louise on July 14 to announce that he was returning to Croisset to prepare himself to write *The Temptation of Saint Anthony*. He would not begin right away, but he expected to work "rather violently" that winter.[15] But it was not going to be that easy. Louise had expected Gustave to come to Paris for the anniversary of their first encounter, and he had not even sent flowers. He told her that he had never promised to come. To her next letter, which was more tender, he replied with the news that he was suffering from his nervous condition, and that Le Poittevin, "whom I loved beyond measure in my youth," was incurably ill. There were family problems, money problems . . . he wished he were somewhere out of France. She offered to help with money, but he assured her that he would get along. One thing was certain: he intended never to work for a living, and certainly not with his pen.

He was then with his mother and niece in La Bouille, a village on the Seine some twelve miles downstream from Rouen; there was an epidemic of children's diseases in Rouen, and they thought it prudent to keep little Caroline out of the city. "If you knew what my life is like!" he wrote Louise at the end of August. "When I go downstairs in the evening after eight hours of work, my head filled with what I have been reading or writing, . . . I sit down to eat opposite my mother, who sighs when she thinks about the empty chairs, and the infant begins to scream or cry!"[16]

Home in Croisset in September, he set to work writing up his Brittany notes. Du Camp joined him in the middle of the month and was present when his friend had still another attack. Gustave thought it was because he was writing, something he had not done for quite a while. Soon he was telling Louise how he went about his work. "Style, which is something I take to heart, agitates my nerves horribly; I become anxious and angry. There are times when it makes me sick, and at night I have a fever." Or again, "I am always disgusted with what I do."[17]

The lovers continued their fruitless dialogue all the while. He warned Louise that he could not make any woman happy; he could not even play with a child. "My mother takes the baby away when I touch it, for I make it shout, and she is like you, she wants to be near me and calls me." In her reply, one of the rare letters of Louise's that has survived (though only in the copy she made), she returned to the more formal *vous* form to conclude with irony: "I cordially kiss your handsome eyes, which are dazzled by all those visions of the East, and to which I must appear rather bourgeois and dull when they deign to look at me. I remain your old, faithful, and platonic friend." He wrote her on his twenty-sixth birthday in December, suggesting that they return to the use of *tu*. Patience; they would meet and kiss again, though it would be worse than ever for her after that.[18]

He and his mother and Caroline took up winter quarters in Rouen. He pursued his sword lessons — three half hours a week. In a rare brush with politics, he accompanied Du Camp and Bouilhet to a banquet sponsored by the bourgeois reformists opposed to the regime of Louis Philippe. The July Monarchy, born of those "three glorious days" in 1830, was living its final hours, challenged by the radical left and by the upper middle class, which in France, as elsewhere in Europe, was demanding a share of the power. Perhaps Gustave and his friends did in fact sympathize with the opposition, but for the moment they professed horror at the political clichés they had to listen to.[19] Yet if the young men in Normandy were unable to take the re-

formist banquets seriously, Parisians felt differently. The banning of
one such assembly on February 22, 1848, provoked demonstrations.
Gustave and Louis Bouilhet rushed to Paris to pick up the thread of
events "from the point of view of art," as they put it, and found themselves at the core of the revolution.

On the afternoon of February 23, after a day of agitation in the
streets, Maxime Du Camp returned to his lodgings to find Gustave
and Louis waiting for him. When the friends went out for dinner, it
appeared as if the protest had died out; the crowd had dispersed,
soldiers were patrolling, and there were even shouts of "Long live the
king!" (By then Louis Philippe had gotten rid of his unpopular minister François Guizot.) But as they approached the Palais-Royal en
route to a favorite restaurant, they passed groups carrying paper lan-
terns and chanting "Long live reform!" Returning to Du Camp's at
nine-thirty that evening, they observed columns of marchers on the
Boulevard des Capucines. Then, as Du Camp knocked on the street
door of his building, they heard a violent explosion. Flaubert said it
sounded like shooting and suggested that they take a look, but Du
Camp laughed it off; he thought it must be children tossing firecrack-
ers. So they went inside to listen to Bouilhet read the first part of a
verse play he was writing on ancient Rome, which was to be *Melaenis*.

What they had turned their backs on was the historic gunning-
down of demonstrators that set off a sequence of events concluding
with the flight of Louis Philippe into exile. The next day Du Camp
was watching the action in the street from his terrace when his Rouen
friends arrived; they had walked from their nearby hotel just as barricades were going up. Du Camp remembered Bouilhet predicting,
"Louis Philippe is lost; he won't sleep at the Tuileries palace tonight." They went out to see it happen. There was fighting around
the Palais-Royal; there the friends lost each other, but Flaubert was
tall and easily found again. He and Du Camp stood with their backs
to a wall and watched a man fall at their feet from a bullet wound.
An officer approached; addressing them as "Citizens," he announced
that "tyranny has been overthrown." The Tuileries palace was open,
he added, and anyone could go inside. So they took up the invitation.
Within the royal dwelling they saw a table set in the state dining
room, with silver coffeepots bearing the king's emblem and even bread
in the breadbaskets. Some of the uninvited guests seated themselves
at the table and said, "This is our reform banquet." The carousing
became violence with the arrival of uniformed troops; by a ruse, Du
Camp and Flaubert were able to save a group of municipal guards

from the mob. Later they would witness scenes of pillage at the Palais-Royal. None of this was lost on Gustave, and the events of 1848
were to provide a story line for the later version of *A Sentimental
Education.*

Exhausted, the two friends returned to Du Camp's place, where
they found Bouilhet waiting. He had been forced to work on the barricades until a paving stone fell on his foot. After dinner they pushed
through the crowd to the Hôtel de Ville and witnessed the reading of
the Provisional Government's decree calling for a republic.[20]

Louise found out that Gustave had been in Paris, and in the thick
of it. She wrote a solicitous note that caught up with him in Croisset.
"I don't know if the new form of government and the social state that
will come out of it will be favorable to Art," he summed up his
impressions of the February revolution. "One could not be more
bourgeois, or more useless."[21] Long after these events Du Camp would
remember the unnecessary violence and the futility of it all, for February 1848 led straight to Napoleon III and the Second Empire.[22]
Flaubert in *A Sentimental Education* stresses the futility.

In her unexpected letter Louise also let drop a bit of news. She was
pregnant, but not by Gustave. In the interregnum created by their
falling-out, she had found other young men to love, and to this day
we are not sure which of them was the father of her second child; the
best scholars come up only with a first name. Gustave told Louise
that she could count on him, whatever happened. He was, he pointed
out, a decent human being; someday she would recognize that.[23] He
was more preoccupied by another event: Alfred Le Poittevin had died
on April 3. "I watched over him for two nights (the last night, all the
night through)," Gustave wrote Du Camp. "I wrapped him in his
sheet, I gave him a farewell kiss, and I watched them seal his coffin."
While seated alongside his dying friend, he read a book for background material to be used in the writing of *The Temptation of Saint
Anthony.*[24]

The revolution reached the provinces. In April Flaubert joined the
local guard, and was part of a formation at a ceremony to plant a
Tree of Liberty.[25] According to Du Camp, Gustave then traveled to
Paris, found a hunting rifle, and enlisted in Du Camp's national guard
company. They were being good citizens, protecting the new republican institutions from the mob. Popular reaction did not manifest
itself until after Gustave left. In June the workers of Paris, disappointed that the new regime was not guaranteeing jobs, challenged

the government. Du Camp served in the guard again, and this time he was shot in the leg while attacking a barricade in the Faubourg Poissonnière neighborhood. He was a hero now.[26]

Gustave and his mother had gone to Forges-les-Eaux, a peaceful village some twenty-five miles east of Rouen, to get away not from revolution but from little Caroline's father, Emile Hamard. Virtually no one knew where they were, not even Gustave's brother, Achille; Bouilhet forwarded their mail. Finally they won a court order that gave Madame Flaubert temporary custody of Caroline; they hoped Hamard would show himself to be totally insane, or be banned from the district, before the order expired.[27]

As soon as he could, Gustave went down to Paris to visit Du Camp, then convalescing. Du Camp remembered that Flaubert was fascinated by a neighborhood street fair, and one day entered the sickroom accompanied by a five-footed sheep, which he and the farmer who owned it had managed to cajole up the stairs. "No bourgeois would have thought of that!" Gustave exclaimed triumphantly. When Du Camp was on his feet — on crutches — he took the train to Rouen to visit Croisset, "where Flaubert was still working mysteriously on *The Temptation of Saint Anthony.*"[28]

CHAPTER FOURTEEN

EASTWARD
WITH DU CAMP

L OUIS BOUILHET was a regular visitor to Croisset. He and Flaubert met several times a week to study the structure of plays and to draft their own scenarios.[1] Early in the new year — the date was February 14, 1849 — we find this entry in Gustave's notebook: "One can do many things in an evening: after dinner I talked with my mother, then thought about travel and dreamed about different existences. I wrote almost a whole chorus of *Saint Anthony*. . . . I read the entire first volume of *Mémoires d'outre-tombe* [by Chateaubriand]. I smoked three pipes and am going to take a pill and then shit, and I am still not asleep."[2]

Much has been said about this *Temptation of Saint Anthony*, the first of three versions only one of which — the last — was published in the author's lifetime. A critic has said that the hermit Anthony is also Gustave Flaubert the hermit.[3] To the classic theme — the expected series of temptations that Anthony is put through, the dialogue with the gods and devils of medieval mystery plays — Flaubert added a private concern. "I have come to the desert in order to avoid the troubles of existence," his Anthony declares.[4]

In writing about Saint Anthony, Flaubert was also dreaming about his own longed-for visit to the Middle East. Du Camp tells us that it was he who asked Gustave's brother to convince Madame Flaubert that a warm climate would do Gustave good. Dr. Cloquet's recommendation, as well as Achille's persuasion, won her over.[5] We now know something more about the motive for the trip, or at least for the consultation with Cloquet. In a long-censored passage of a letter to Ernest Chevalier, written in early May 1849, Gustave confided: "Know that your friend is apparently suffering from a pox whose origin dates from time immemorial. The symptoms seem cured and then re-appear. My nervous illness, from which I still occasionally suffer and which cannot be cured in my present circumstances, may come from this." Cloquet thought warm weather might be the answer, and even placed some urgency on the trip.[6]

Yet Flaubert pursued his writing, with dogged determination. Du Camp wanted him in Paris to help in the preparations for their journey, but "my little book before anything else," said Gustave.[7] This first *Temptation of Saint Anthony* was finished on September 12, 1849, precisely at 3:20 in the afternoon, the author noted on the manuscript. For the next episode we must rely on Du Camp. He said that Flaubert summoned him and he was in Croisset the next day; Bouilhet had preceded him. Gustave began to read his manuscript aloud to his two friends, and kept reading over a period of four days, for a total of thirty-two hours. It was agreed that the listeners would express no opinion until he was finished.

Du Camp recalled those hours as being painful ones. He and Bouilhet listened attentively, waiting for something to happen. His impression was of a rather stupid saint who remained passive as a multitude of temptations were paraded before him, reacting only with "Ah! Ah!" or "My God!" Flaubert became heated as he read, and his friends tried to do the same but remained cold. There were well-made phrases, but there was no progression. Before the last session Bouilhet and Du Camp privately agreed that they would be frank with the author; they felt it their duty to check his slide into romanticism. Bouilhet was the spokesman. When Flaubert asked for an honest reaction, his friend declared: "We think you should throw that into the fire and never talk about it again."

But they did talk about it. "Your subject was vague, and you made it still vaguer": this was the essence of their complaint. Flaubert protested, returning to certain passages that he felt were good, and they agreed. But a succession of good phrases did not make a book. Because Flaubert had a tendency toward lyricism, they felt he should choose subjects that could not be treated lyrically. "Take a down-to-earth subject, one of those incidents bourgeois life is full of . . . and force yourself to treat it in a natural manner. . . ." Did they really say that, then and there? And did Bouilhet in fact immediately suggest a novel based on the story of a public health officer whose second wife had committed adultery, run up debts, and then taken poison?[8] It is more likely that the germ of *Madame Bovary* presented itself a year or even two years later. For one thing, the real health officer died only after Flaubert and Du Camp left for the Middle East.[9]

Even Louise Colet knew that Flaubert was off to the Orient. "He will leave without seeing me, without writing to me! Inexplicable heart! Mine would like to cease to beat and to feel!"[10] In Paris, Du Camp handled most of the preparations. He and Gustave met to purchase clothing and equipment, but Du Camp had it all packed — in two crates, weighing nearly seven hundred pounds — and shipped to Marseilles. They had saddles and other riding equipment, two pairs of boots apiece, kitchen and medical supplies, and a large tent for sleeping and a small one to serve as a darkroom for developing photographs. Du Camp also set about getting the official papers they would need, and he even had Flaubert's pistols cleaned.

All that was lacking was money. Du Camp was expecting a legacy but would get none of it until they were well on their way. Much of the financing had to come from Flaubert's side — from his mother, of course.[11] She recorded the sums that she turned over to her son for the journey: six thousand francs for preparations, another ten thousand at his departure, and three remittances (of six thousand, three thousand, and two thousand francs, respectively) along the way. To this total of twenty-seven thousand francs she added the cost of shipping clothing and equipment, and Customs duty, which came to another five hundred francs.[12]

They were to sail from Marseilles in the last week of October 1849. Gustave first accompanied his mother to Nogent, where she was to spend the first period of his absence with their relatives. In the travel diary he began keeping, he remembered his last day there as the worst of his life until then. When he said farewell, his mother cried out, and he recalled having heard her emit the same cry on the death of his father. He remained calm but then wept in the railway carriage on the way back to Paris. There was time enough at one station for him to get off the train for a glass of rum, and he even thought of returning to his mother then and there.[13]

He made it clear, writing to her, that once he and Du Camp reached Egypt, if they were exhausted or he missed her too badly or she summoned him, he would return.[14]

Bouilhet had come down from Rouen to see his friends off. On their final night in Paris they dined together, joined by Maxime's new friend Théophile Gautier, who was a good ten years older than Flaubert and his comrades and already a well-known author. His first novel,

Mademoiselle de Maupin, had been published in 1835 with a preface announcing the author's dedication to "art for art's sake," and he had invented a battle cry. He was a provocative and influential critic. Flaubert liked what he said, and reported to his mother Gautier's remark that "when you have something in your stomach, you don't die before shitting it out." After dinner — but he did not tell his mother this — Gustave and Bouilhet went to a favorite brothel, and even made a date with one of the girls for March 1851, in front of the Café de Paris. (As it turned out, Flaubert would still be in Italy then.)[15]

"It's the East forever," Flaubert had confided to his diary early in 1841; he was nineteen at the time. "I was born to live there."[16] He had begun to write about the attraction of the Orient in school and was still writing about it (with "Hérodias") in his last years. Romantic writers, the gods of his youth, had to make the voyage, if only in their imagination. He found his Orient in Hugo, Byron, Voltaire.[17] If their trip had a *serious* side, it was thanks to Maxime Du Camp. He had explained to a gathering of the Academy of Inscriptions and Literature his intention to take along a camera in order to collect, "with the aid of this marvelous means of reproduction," views of monuments and the inscriptions found on them.[18] The Foreign Affairs Ministry issued a single passport for the two friends, noting that they were charged with a mission by the ministries of Education and Trade.[19] In applying to the Education Ministry for an assignment, Du Camp had made it clear that he was paying his own way but said that experience acquired during an earlier trip had convinced him that "an official title was indispensable to visit efficiently and without danger the countries he wished to see," as the request explained it. The Ministry complied by issuing an order that entrusted Du Camp with a "scientific mission": he was to explore ancient works of art, record traditions, and take note of inscriptions and sculptures.[20] Du Camp also asked the Ministry of Trade to assign a mission to his friend.[21]

Du Camp's assignment was cultural; Gustave's was to be more down-to-earth, and officials at the ministries of Agriculture and Trade obviously took it seriously. The Office of Commercial Data in the Trade Ministry, for example, expressed interest in Persia and the neighboring region of Turkey, areas that had not been satisfactorily covered in surveys of commercial potential. The friends never got as far as Persia, but the questionnaire this office drew up would also apply to the countries they did visit.[22]

We can follow their journey in the detailed travel log — some of it in the form of notes made on the spot but much of it rewritten — that Flaubert kept in his possession but never published. From his notes we know, for instance, that once again he walked by the hotel on Rue de la Darse — Eulalie's hotel — while in Marseilles.[23] They sailed from that port on November 4, on a ship called *Le Nil*, stopping at Malta and touching African soil at Alexandria, another cosmopolitan port city and the least exotic of all those they were to visit. But as Flaubert wrote his mother, the desert begins at its gates. From the moment when, on November 18, a Sunday, they rode out in the direction of Rosette, armed and on horseback, with their guide on a donkey and four Arabs running behind, they were going to live an adventure.[24] Gustave noted every bit of it, and every oddity. In Cairo they met a hotelkeeper, a certain Monsieur Bouvaret, who had once been an actor in the French provinces; of course everyone later saw "Bovary" in the name. To hear Du Camp tell it, one day on the upper Nile Flaubert cried out: "I've got it! I'll call her Emma Bovary!"[25]

Du Camp also wrote an account of the trip in his *Souvenirs littér-aires*, published after his traveling companion's death. In it he made himself look good, and Flaubert less so: Gustave all but moans as he prepares to leave France, "I'll never see my mother again, I'll never see my country. . . ." Du Camp was often exalted when his friend was pensive; Flaubert detested action. Du Camp said that he never ceased to worry about his friend's health, which was why he brought along his valet, a Corsican and former cavalryman, to keep watch over him.[26]

In his own diary, and in letters to Bouilhet, Gustave spared no detail of their lighter adventures, as when, in a Cairo brothel, they were to "make love through an interpreter."[27] He now wore a large Nubian shirt of white cotton decorated with tassels, and a tarboosh, though (so Gustave told his mother) along the Nile they returned to European clothing, to ensure that they were respected.[28] Years later Du Camp remembered that his traveling companion was soon homesick for Normandy; the temples always seemed to him like other temples.[29] It is true that Flaubert was less interested in archaeology than Du Camp was. For him the little things counted, such as seeing fleas hop over the page as he and Du Camp read over the day's notes. On an outing from Cairo, Gustave watched a dog tearing apart a donkey. "Birds always begin with the eyes, and dogs with the stomach or the anus. . . ." They visited a hospital ward where slaves suffering from venereal disease were treated. On a sign from the doctor, they all stood up on their beds, dropped their pants, and held open their buttocks to show their chancres.[30]

Where was the official mission in all of this? Early in the voyage Gustave noted, "Fruitless attempts to obtain commercial information," indicating that he did remember that he had an assignment, even if he was to do little more about it.[31] On the other hand, Du Camp's contribution cannot be overstated. Using primitive equipment and time-consuming processes, he was putting together what was to be the first comprehensive photographic survey of any region, the first important French book to be illustrated with photographs, the first published work containing photographic coverage of the Middle East. His views of Jerusalem, for example, were among the earliest to be published of that site.[32] He used a technique called calotype, which was an improvement over daguerreotype in that several prints could be made from a single negative. Reproduction was by a process called salt print, in which writing paper was dipped into a salt solution, coated in silver nitrate, and exposed to light during contact with a paper negative.[33] Never the last to call attention to his achievements, Du Camp in his memoirs spelled out the challenge he had confronted. "To learn photography is a simple matter, but to transport the equipment on muleback, on camelback, on the backs of men, that was a difficult problem." Two minutes of exposure were required for an image, forty minutes for a positive print.[34] His photographs are superb, if passive, documents, showing more monuments than people, but that was his mission; in any case the technique he utilized limited spontaneity. One of the few identifiable figures in the two-volume book of 125 photographs that Du Camp published is a bearded man in a white robe and black bonnet walking in Cairo — Gustave Flaubert.[35]

The travelers were in Cairo from December 26, 1849, until February 6, 1850, and then boarded a boat for their journey up the Nile, which was to last until the end of June. Gustave described his life in Cairo to his mother. The Arabs called him Abou-Schenep, the mustached father. He visited the Copt bishop and, over coffee, discussed religious doctrine; the erudition he had acquired for *Saint Anthony* proved useful. Everyone in his party had fleas or lice at one time or another, and he no longer even noticed them.

When he thought of the future, which he did rarely, he wondered what he would do on his return. Would he write? Was *The Temptation of Saint Anthony* really a failure? Who was wrong, he or his friends? [36]

To Bouilhet he was able to describe his experimentation with drugs, with sodomy. "Traveling for our education and charged with a mission by the government," he explained to his friend, "we consider it a duty to test this means of ejaculation. The opportunity has not yet presented itself, yet we are seeking it." Later, in response to Bouilhet's question, he would report that he had indeed consummated one such encounter, in the Turkish baths, with a pockmarked young fellow wearing a white turban.[37]

Getting ready for the river journey up the Nile, he wrote to remind his mother that after they had done with Egypt, she had only to say the word and, after visiting Syria and Palestine, they would return via Constantinople and Athens, cutting five or six months from their itinerary. Then he would take up his good old work habit, close to his mother. He cared only for "the permanent pleasure of my round table, . . . my two hundred pens, and the art of utilizing them."[38]

While on the Nile he drafted a polished version of one section of his travel diary, the only such essay in his notes. He described the crew: the guide, Ibrahim, and his sailors, the second mate at the helm smoking a Turkish pipe. They watched rare birds through field glasses. Two-masted cangias such as the one they sailed in were the usual means of navigation on the Nile, and the Nile was then and is today the way back to Egypt's earliest civilizations, some of them frozen in stone, others still thriving in riverside settlements. Flaubert studied Greek in the morning (Homer), and wrote his log in the evening. They stopped to visit sites; their sailors did obscene dances; naked Copts swam out to their boat to beg and were driven off by blows.

A letter that reached him from his mother raised the question of his future, of a job. "That's the illusion! That's what Bouilhet said when he began studying medicine, what I said in beginning law," he replied at once. "When one does something, one has to do it entirely and do it well."[39]

They sailed by Luxor, Karnak, and the Valley of the Kings, the most extraordinary sites the Nile valley had to offer. But the plan was to proceed upriver as rapidly as they could and then do serious visiting on the return voyage.[40]

Yet there was to be one memorable stopover. Esneh was a town like the others, with houses of dry mud; there were humble shops, a square with a café, a mosque, one ancient temple. But Esneh had something that the other settlements along the river did not: a reputation for its prostitutes. The best-known of these was Safiah, once the mistress of the viceroy Abbas Pasha. Another was called Kuchuk-

Hanem. These *almées* (singing dancers), as they were known, or more accurately *ghawazies* (prostitutes), had been expelled from Cairo. In Esneh they were a tourist attraction, and Gustave even told his mother about them, albeit only about their dancing.[41]

When the friends stepped ashore, they looked in briefly at the temple, walking by houses in front of which the so-called *almées* waited for customers. They were led to a small house with a stairway in a courtyard. "On the steps, in front of us, . . . stood a woman in pink pantaloons, with nothing around her bust except dark violet muslin." She had just come out of her bath, smelling of sweet balsam, and she proceeded to perfume the hands of her guests with rosewater.

In his travel log Gustave took pains to describe Kuchuk-Hanem, "a tall and splendid creature, whiter than an Arab." She had "outsized" black eyes, black brows, wide nostrils, solid shoulders, generous breasts. She wore a large tarboosh, her dark hair divided by headbands; she had on bracelets, a triple necklace, and earrings, and even had a tattoo. Her dance was brutal: "She wears her jacket tight so that her breasts are squeezed together." Before it was over, the girl was wearing Flaubert's tarboosh and dancing on his back and Du Camp's. Then they left her to spend some more time at the temple, to mail a letter, and to dine. When they returned, it was for more serious business. The musicians were blindfolded before Kuchuk-Hanem began the dance of the bee, which ended in total nudity. Then Gustave was alone with her. "I sucked her with rage," he reported to Bouilhet; "her body was covered with sweat, she was exhausted from dancing, she was cold." So he covered her with his fur jacket, and she fell asleep, her fingers entwined in his. During the night they made love several times. "The third time especially was ferocious, and the last was sentimental. We said many tender things to each other, and we held each other toward the end in a sad and amorous way."[42] Du Camp was more detached. He found the girl's dancing unpolished, and his evening had a different conclusion. He slept alone while Gustave sported with Kuchuk-Hanem.[43]

With one of the crew members, the friends went hunting at seven the next morning. Gustave actually believed that a bond had developed between himself and the dancing prostitute. "How sweet it would be for your pride," he told his diary, "if, on departure, you could be sure to leave a memory, and know that she will think of you more than of all the others, that you will remain in her heart!"[44]

CHAPTER FIFTEEN

HOMESICK AND HOME

In a letter to Louis Bouilhet dated March 13, 1850, and written on board the cangia — they were about to cross the Tropic of Cancer; the temperature was thirty degrees centigrade in the shade — Gustave not only spoke of his night with Kuchuk-Hanem; he also wondered what he would do on his return to Normandy. Would he publish? What would he write, and in fact, *would* he write? He had tried to create something during their voyage but had realized that it would be better to use his time for observation. "We are now, my dear sir, in a region where the women are naked. . . . I slept with Nubian girls whose necklaces of golden piasters descended to their thighs. . . ."[1]

On May 2 they arrived, at last, at Luxor. They were to spend a fortnight there, at the site of the Nile's most important cluster of tombs and temples. Flaubert quickly wrote to his mother, his fingers black with silver nitrate from helping Du Camp with his photography.[2] In June, in a letter to Bouilhet, he confessed that he lacked both ideas and ambition; better to work for himself alone. He knew that he would continue, as before, to live in hibernation. This kind of talk, he added, maddened Du Camp, who was ambitious.

On the return sail they stopped again at Esneh. Gustave had a sad reunion with Kuchuk-Hanem, who had been ill; they made love only once. The whole thing left him feeling miserable. But it did not stop him, a fortnight later, in a village called Keneh, from sleeping with "a handsome brute of a woman who liked me a lot and made me understand that I had attractive eyes." And with "another fat pig on whom I came a great deal. . . ."[3] Back in Cairo, they sailed to Alexandria to catch another ship for Beirut.[4] Their stay there was brief, but there was time for a bevy of ladies ordered in by Camille Rogier, the director of the post office and a painter who admired Gautier's "art for art." Flaubert "banged three women and came four times, three before lunch and one after dessert." Du Camp only made love once; he was suffering, we now learn, from a chancroid caught in Alexandria.[5] From Beirut they traveled overland to Jerusalem, a nine-day trek, from four A.M. each day until sundown, with a siesta at mid-day. They slept in caravansaries or outdoors under trees. The party now consisted of eight men and ten animals, four of the latter being the horses of Flaubert, Du Camp, their valet, and their guide.[6]

Jerusalem Flaubert found melancholic. "The curse of God seems to hover over this city where one walks only on shit and sees only ruins."[7] The Jordan river, he noted, was no wider than the Touques at Pont-l'Evêque.[8] Great moments, and deep feelings, alternated with dreadful ones: on one side the "turpitude" and bad taste of the holy places, and on the other, the superb landscapes and ancient sites, the costumes of women, the camel culture. To understand what he was seeing, he advised his mother, she should read the Old Testament. They raced along the Dead Sea, slept in a Turkish fort in Jericho and in the Saint Saba monastery in the desert south of Jerusalem. They bought a lot of rosaries, for Maxime said everyone appreciated them, and they were cheap gifts.[9]

But Gustave could not forget Normandy and what was waiting for him there, what would be expected of him. In a curious letter to Bouilhet written in September 1850, he at once urged his friend to be more audacious — to plunge into work without being excessively critical — and indicated how cautious he himself was. Yet he had re-covered, he said, from the disappointment of his friends' rejection of *The Temptation of Saint Anthony*. He was ready to work again. He mentioned a "Dictionnaire des Idées Reçues" ("Dictionary of Re-ceived Ideas") that would contain popular beliefs and clichés "for the purpose of bringing the public back to tradition, order, and respect, and would be arranged in such a way that the reader would not know whether or not his leg was being pulled." He would work on this project for the rest of his life, and would be only a year away from finishing it when he died.[10]

Du Camp's notes tell us something about the next leg of the trip. "From Damascus to Beirut, September 12–26, 1850: Hours of march: 111¼." Then a steamboat sail to the isle of Rhodes, and on the Turkish mainland another 109½ hours overland to Izmir.[11] What neither Du Camp's notes nor Flaubert's diary reveals is that Gustave picked up another venereal infection in Beirut. It began, he confessed to Bouilhet, with seven chancres, which were later reduced to one; he had to ride horseback through Asia Minor all the same. "I suspect that a Maronite gave me this present, but perhaps it was a little Turkish girl? Was it the Turk or the Christian? . . . This is an aspect of the Oriental question that *La Revue des Deux Mondes* does not even imagine the existence of." Soon after that, in Constantinople, he was about to go to bed with a comely adolescent when she tried to examine him to see if he had a disease. Since he still had a hard sore, he feigned indignation and leapt from the bed. In a letter written to Bouilhet from Athens on December 19, he complained that he had lost a lot of hair.[12]

At that time the identification and treatment of sexual diseases was less sophisticated than it would become later in the century. The familiar term *vérole* — a pox — was widely used, both for relatively benign infections such as chancroids and for the more horrendous syphilis. When a chancre was discovered, whether it was hard or soft, it was *vérole*. Some years would go by before the less consequential chancroid infection was differentiated from syphilis; the hard chancre was later recognized as a primary lesion of syphilis.[13] Before 1850 the best treatment, as prescribed by Dr. Philippe Ricord, one of France's most respected authorities, consisted of applications of or massages with mercury and potassium iodide.[14] The modern reader will be struck by the absence of respect for personal prophylactics (though Ricord himself was an early advocate of condoms), and there seemed to be even less concern for the likelihood of infecting others.

His infection did not prevent Flaubert from enjoying Constantinople. He was amused that after watching a whirling dervish he could spend an evening at the opera and hear the very French *Robert le diable;* only in Constantinople could such a combination be found.[15]

Importantly, he pursued his plans for future writing. He had three ideas, he told Bouilhet. One was "Une Nuit de Don Juan" ("A Night of Don Juan"), in which Sister Anna Maria's divine and sensual desires are seen as identical; the second, "Anubis," whose heroine wishes to be ravished by God; and then there might be a "Flemish novel," about a young woman in a provincial town. He was later to say that this third project was the one that became *Madame Bovary.* At first he thought that the girl would remain a virgin, her desire mystical. In the end he kept the rural background, but to make the story more interesting he invented a more plausible heroine. This was to be Emma Bovary.[16]

If we believe Du Camp, Madame Flaubert wrote him a letter, apparently without Gustave's knowledge, and implored him not to take her son beyond the Euphrates; it was this that changed their course, pointed them homeward. Du Camp remembered that the letter caused him a sleepless night, for to give up Persia was to give up part of his ambition. When he told Gustave of his decision to abridge their journey, he observed his friend's relief.[17]

The news made its way out to the East: Ernest Chevalier was marrying. Flaubert knew that he himself could never do such a thing. "Contact with the world to which I have become enormously close in the past fourteen months makes me want to return to my shell more and more," he told his mother, who wondered when it would be his turn to marry. Marriage would be an "apostasy"; it was not the writer's way. For him the artist was a "monstrosity." He would live alone, with great men to keep him company. He promised his mother that she would not have a rival.[18]

They stopped in Greece on the homeward journey; Flaubert regretted that he would be there for a matter of weeks and not months. Everything excited him — the Parthenon, Thermopylae, Delphi, Corinth, Argos. . . . In Patras, he reported home, they had only five hundred francs left; he hoped that his mother had sent money on to Naples so they could survive until she joined them in Italy. To Bouilhet he confided that his infection seemed to be going away; only the hard sore remained. "But something else is going away, and faster, and that is my hair. You will see me looking like a monk." (He was only twenty-nine.) They sailed from Patras across to Brindisi in southern Italy, and when they reached Naples, they settled in for a long stay.

Day after day they visited the Antiquities Museum, after which they wrote up their notes; at night there was theater. Thanks to the mercury massages, Flaubert's symptoms were less disturbing, and he was, he said, copulating right and left. Pimps offered ten-year-old girls, or boys, but he preferred ripe women, "fat women," as he specified to his new friend and fellow connoisseur Camille Rogier.[19]

The travelers arrived in Rome on March 28, 1851. Gustave's first reaction was disappointment: he sought Nero's Rome, and found the Vatican's. Meanwhile, he told Bouilhet, he was working on his "Nuit de Don Juan."[20] In the company of his mother (Du Camp having returned to Paris), he had a strange experience in the basilica of St. Paul Without the Walls. He saw a pale, obviously ill woman wearing black headbands, with a forehead of ivory, "the corners of her mouth slightly depressed, a touch of blue mustache, the ensemble of her face round!" Hardly the most appetizing woman he had encountered on the trip, and yet he was aroused, and violently so; he wished to throw himself at her feet, to ask her hand in marriage![21] It has been said that he must have been thinking of the only woman he had ever admitted loving, Elisa. Perhaps. But the setting must have brought "Une Nuit de Don Juan" to life. Violent emotions were also to color his visit to Venice. He got into an argument with a Customs official and slapped him; he was nearly arrested but instead had to sign a statement declaring that he had intended no offense to the reigning authority, which happened to be Austria. His mother complained that he had become brutal.[22]

But he seemed gentle to "Lilinne," little Caroline, on his return to Rouen. She was asleep, she would recall, when "a tall strong man seized me in his arms to devour me with kisses." Later she remembered her grandmother as cold, avoiding physical caresses; the little girl received ample compensation from her uncle Gustave.[23]

In a letter from Paris that is of considerable importance because it is the first dated reference to *Madame Bovary* — the date is July 23, 1851 — Maxime Du Camp asked Gustave Flaubert: "What are you doing? What have you decided? What are you writing? Have you made a choice? Is it still 'Don Juan'? Is it the story of Madame Delamarre, which is a pretty one?"[24] The reference is to Delphine Delamare (with one *r*), a Norman spouse who had run her husband, Eugène, ragged, cuckolding and ruining him; then she had drunk poison and left the poor man, a public health officer, alone with their child. Apparently he had killed himself in December 1849, so the event was being talked about during Flaubert's voyage.[25]

Louise Colet had not given up on Gustave. Her very private diary, now open to us, reveals how closely she followed his itinerary. In June 1851, when she discovered that he was home, and even in Paris, she wrote him. She had expected a visit from him, or at least some word; she had tried to reach him through Du Camp, who told her messenger that Gustave would not accept a letter from her. If he would not see her, she wrote, then her letters must be odious to him; she asked that they be returned to her, and offered to return his. Gustave did not reply, and so she resolved to go up to Rouen to meet him.

Thanks to this heartbroken woman's irrepressible need to express herself, we have an account of her trip. She left Paris on Thursday, June 26; she took the train, bearing a packet of bonbons for Flaubert's niece; passing Mantes, she recalled their "day of intoxication" there five years earlier. At the Rouen station she took a cab to the Hôtel d'Angleterre, on the river; when she asked the driver how one got to Croisset, he told her that he had taken Flaubert and his mother there just a week earlier. In her room she composed a letter to Gustave: she had to see him at once, but he need not fear recriminations about the past. It was only that she wished to talk to him before making an important decision.

She found a boatman willing to take her to Croisset and wait for her. Her heart pounded as the sailor pointed out a "charming English-style house of two floors in the middle of a green lawn, with a landscaped flower garden facing the Seine, from which it is separated only by a gate and the road." She asked to be let ashore just beyond the entrance, and walked back to find the gate open. It was then six-thirty in the evening. Her impression as she walked onto the grounds was one of wealth and comfort. She could see through the windows of the Flauberts' house, and thought that the man she perceived was Gustave. She handed her letter to a woman in a nearby farmhouse and stood outdoors waiting for the reply, her heart still beating fast. Finally the woman returned to say that Monsieur Flaubert could not receive her, though he promised to write. She guessed that he had given that order before reading her note, and indeed, a chambermaid then appeared to say that Flaubert was dining with guests; if she left her Rouen address, however, he would go there to see her. She told the chambermaid that she was leaving town that very night and had to talk to him now; the chambermaid came back again to say that this was impossible, but that Flaubert would be at her hotel at eight. Louise was shaken, but as she returned to the boat landing, a door opened to reveal Gustave himself.

His appearance was striking: he was wearing wide trousers and a cotton blouse (surely that was the Nubian shirt); he had dangling mustaches, and his hair had thinned. His voice seemed harsh as he asked what she wanted of him; she thought he was feigning gruffness. He could not talk to her now, he said, but again he promised to take the steamboat to Rouen to see her later that evening. When at

last they met on the Rouen quay, he took her arm and even appeared
moved. Yet he told her that she had gone about this meeting in the
wrong way: Croisset was not *his* home, and he feared that she would
be badly received there — by his mother.

She described her dilemma. On the one hand there was Victor
Cousin and the future of her daughter, Henriette; on the other, there
was Auguste Vetter, the latest man in her life. "Marry the Philosopher," advised Gustave, referring to Cousin. She preferred a third
possibility: to live near Croisset, to work and raise her daughter there.
(Her infant son, born during her rupture with Gustave, had since died.)
She would then be available whenever Gustave wished to see her.
"That would be my happiness, if you loved me," she said through
tears. He was stern: "I can do nothing for your happiness. Neither for
you nor for anyone else; nothing attracts me." She wept and blamed
herself, but also blamed his letters for exciting her feelings without
satisfying them. "So I shall never, never be in your arms!" "Marry
the Philosopher," he said, laughing, "and we will see each other again."
She tried to take that lightly. She gave him two of her plays to read,
and he said that he would return them in Paris that summer, but he
asked that she not write, for her letters would "trouble" him. When
he got up to leave, she burst into tears; perhaps this was their last
meeting? Why should it be, asked he, if he had promised to see her
in Paris? She kissed him with passion, and he returned the kiss, but
she could see that he remained in control of his emotions. There was
a last and better kiss outdoors. She returned to the hotel, managed to
get the midnight train to Paris, and was home at five-thirty the next
morning.[26]

She went to London shortly after that; as she visited the Great Exhibition there, she thought of Gustave and waited for a letter from
him. Her heart stirred when she saw his handwriting. Had he seemed
cold in Rouen? he asked her. He could not be tender, for that would
be hypocrisy and an insult to her feelings. He suggested that she lose
herself in work, as he was trying to do. He could not bring her any
samples, he told her in a subsequent letter, for he had not set pen to
paper for two years.[27] But we know that he was preparing himself.
When Du Camp wrote him on August 2, he promised some ideas for
his "Bovary," which tells us that Flaubert already had his title.[28]

Gustave did finally go to Paris — in September — and he looked
up Louise Colet. He was "handsome, charming," she confided to her
diary. They took a turn in the Bois du Boulogne, dined together, and
"etc." Whatever that meant, she added: "The sadness persists, and I

don't feel loved as I love him." They had another long day together, and he was more than tender, but always in control. She was also disappointed that he seemed not to be concerned about the fact that she did not have a penny to her name.[29]

He wrote to her from Croisset on September 20. He himself was preparing for a visit to London. He had been suffering from a sore throat. And then he announced:

> I began my novel last night. I can already see difficulties of style that make me shudder. It is not a small matter to be simple.[30]

PART IV

CHAPTER SIXTEEN

HESITATIONS

BEFORE FLAUBERT COULD GET VERY FAR with *Madame Bovary*, however, he was off to England with his mother and his niece, crossing the Channel at Boulogne, missing the sunny Mediterranean.[1] The motive for this visit, as for Louise Colet's, was the Great Exhibition of the Works of Industry of All Nations, a world's fair whose exotic touches appealed to Continentals as well as to Britons in 1851.[2] It was Flaubert's first visit to London, and he was not going to miss a thing; the British Museum occupied much of his time. Of course, he saw the Colliers. "I will remember for a long time our walk in Hyde Park," he wrote to Harriet on his return, calling up "that long misty afternoon when I had more fog in my heart than there was over London."[3]

While there he also tried to keep a promise he had made to Louise. In desperate need of cash, she wished to sell an album of letters signed by the great men she had known. During her own visit to London she had left this collection with a bookseller, but he had not yet found a buyer. The evidence is that Flaubert did what he could, but there was still no buyer.[4] His failure was one more source of irritation to her, and later, in her fictional account of Flaubert, she was to have another man mock him for not buying it himself.

During Gustave's absence, Du Camp called on Louise. Perhaps he thought that he could be of assistance to his friend by diminishing him in the eyes of Louise, for he told her that he himself was fed up with Gustave, who lacked both heart and intelligence and, in addition, had no literary future. Louise, to her credit, found that hard to believe. "Perhaps the memory of my love misleads me, but his imagination seems as magnetic as his eyes," as she phrased it in her diary. Thinking of this visit, she wondered whether Du Camp had his own reasons for wishing to poison her relations with Gustave.[5] What we do know is that Du Camp was very much occupied just then with a new magazine, *La Revue de Paris*, which in fact was the revival of a dormant literary journal. The new editorial board included, along with Du Camp, his and Gustave's well-known friend Théophile Gautier. Naturally, Du Camp wanted to publish something by Flaubert. "Novembre" seemed too naive, the early "Sentimental Education" not quite finished, and the first *Temptation of Saint Anthony* too difficult to publish in installments and too long to run in a single issue. Du Camp suggested that his friend write about their travels in Greece, but Flaubert replied that although travel notes were useful for providing style and subject matter, to publish them as such was to promote "low literature."[6]

In the middle of October Flaubert went to Paris. Du Camp later remembered that the purpose of his visit was to consult Théophile Gautier about what he should be doing now. "You believe in the writer's mission, . . . in the divinity of art," Gautier is supposed to have said. "Oh Flaubert, how naive you are. To hold on to a manuscript is an act of folly; as soon as a book is finished, you have to publish it, getting as much money as you can."[7] When Flaubert announced his arrival to Louise, her first reaction was to assume that he must have been in Paris for several days. He informed her that Gautier and Du Camp had suggested that he publish fragments of *The Temptation of Saint Anthony*, but he said he preferred not to do that. (And *she* remembered Du Camp having told her that Gustave wished to publish it in *La Revue de Paris*, while Du Camp considered this the wrong thing to do.) Flaubert added that Du Camp liked the outline of *Madame Bovary*. (Du Camp had warned her, she noted, that it would be a "flop.") She could not repeat all of this to Gustave; he did not love her enough for that. He took her into his arms, but she no longer felt passionate about him, only tender. . . . She also admired his mind. But why had he not mentioned her autograph album, why had he not found a clever way to help her? That was Thursday evening; on Friday afternoon she called at his hotel. "I should like to seem unpleasant to you, so that you would cease to love me, for I can see very well that I make you suffer," he declared. She wept; he wanted to kiss the eyes that he had caused to weep. He would return in three weeks, he said, for a visit of two days. "God, how little that is," she told her diary; "God, how sad my life is!" Yet Gustave was better than any other man she had known.[8]

In a letter to Du Camp written on October 21 from Croisset, Flaubert explained that he could not approve partial publication of *The Temptation of Saint Anthony*. If he were to publish what he wrote, he would want to go all the way, to live in Paris and partake of the literary life and its intrigues. But that would mean action, and he detested action. If he had no mistress and preached chastity, he said, it was not because he could not become sexually aroused; he could be active if he *had* to be.[9]

And he wrote to Louise tenderly, on October 23 at one in the morning, a time that he was often to set aside for letters. He returned to a familiar theme: he wished Louise did not love him, just as he wished his mother did not love him, nor he her. Feelings engendered suffering.

He found it difficult to begin his novel, he reported to Louise. He had spent the day at the open window, with the sun shining on the river. He had written a single page and plotted three more, and he hoped to be under way in a fortnight, but "the color in which I dip my brush" was so new for him that it left him dazzled.[10] So much crossing-out, he reported in his next letter; sentences came hard. "What a crazy style I have taken on." His relaxation consisted of perfecting his Greek and reading Shakespeare.[11]

Du Camp was also hearing about these hesitations. He was not able to reply to Gustave's letter immediately; he was finishing an issue of his magazine and carrying on with four different women. Finally, on October 29, he was ready with some advice. He warned his bearish friend that to "arrive," one had to do more than write and publish; one had to promote oneself, as Du Camp was doing. One had to be as enterprising as Balzac's hero Rastignac in *Le Père Goriot*, an ambitious young man whose behavior indeed resembled Du Camp's in his "desire to arrive," his "thirst for honors" (Balzac's language). Like Du Camp, Rastignac understood how upper-class women could serve as patrons. Du Camp actually cited Rastignac's challenge to Society (with a capital *S*): "Just the two of us now." He explained to Gustave that "in the literary renewal now under way, I must be a captain and not a private." He wished to publish the work of his friend, but he felt that most parts of *Saint Anthony* would bore the reader. "I have made my success, I am going to make Bouilhet's, send me something good and I will make yours."[12]

"Something solemn is occurring inside me at this moment," Gustave announced to Louise. He was going to be thirty years old; he would now have to make a decision. What did he mean? she wondered. And what was her place in all this? The night before his visit, she could not sleep; she even contemplated killing Gustave rather than see him with another woman, if that was the decision he was about to make. Did she have a dagger within reach when he arrived on Monday morning, November 17? Her diary suggests that she did. But it turned out that Gustave's dilemma was whether to publish or not, and whether or not to spend more time in Paris. He seemed demoralized, and Louise tried to help him. On their last evening together he was more affectionate, more passionate than ever. She felt better about everything; moreover, he was going to help her with her own writing. He forgot only to mention money, and she was desperate.[13]

He was in Paris again in early December, and again was fortuitously present at a historical event: the coup d'état of December 2, 1851, which brought the prince-president Louis-Napoleon to power. (In a year he would make himself Emperor Napoleon III.) Once more gunfire could be heard. He escaped blows several times, Gustave was to tell his uncle in Nogent, as well as avoiding being stabbed, shot, and hit by cannon fire.[14] He saw a great deal of Louise now. She told her diary: "Gustave loves me only for himself, as a total egoist, to satisfy his sensual needs and to read me his works. . . . Does he care about my tears?" Other men may have cared more, and we know that at this time Louise was seeing her recent former lovers, but she convinced herself that she still preferred Gustave. He had talent, even if he also had boils, which she was catching from him.[15]

Flaubert, the painstaking chronicler, gave his absent friend Ernest Chevalier an account of his life in the middle of January 1852, a month after his thirtieth birthday. Chevalier had noted that his own hair was growing white. "Mine is disappearing," Gustave told him, "and you will find your friend nearly bald. Heat, a turban, age, worries, and a bitchy pox seem to explain this precocious senility." Gustave was less merry than he had been; his alter ego, Big Boy ("le Garçon"), was no more. In Croisset his niece brought some gaiety into the household, but Gustave's mother was getting old both in body and in mind. Caroline's father, Emile Hamard, was lost in drink. As for Gustave himself, he worked beside the fireplace, not for fame but for himself; if ever he published, it would be as a courtesy to the friends who encouraged him. Bouilhet came out to Croisset on Sundays; thanks to publication of his *Melaenis* in Du Camp's magazine, he was becoming known, and the magazine itself seemed successful. Only Gustave remained unestablished. He had gone through a great deal of money in traveling to the East, and his mother's fortune was not growing.[16]

From now on, the only way to follow the writing of "la *Bovary*" is to read its author's letters to Louise Colet. "Literally speaking, there are two distinct fellows inside me," he wrote her in the middle of January. "One who is taken by roaring, by lyricism . . . [and] another who digs and scratches for truth as well as he can . . . [and] who would like the reader to feel the things he describes almost palpably. . . ." He had let himself go in *The Temptation of Saint Anthony*, while in "A Sentimental Education" he had tried, and failed, to fuse the two approaches. Now he was attempting a third work; it was time either to succeed or to jump out of a window.

"What . . . I should like to write is a book about nothing, a book without exterior attachments, which would hold together by the internal strength of its style," he told Louise. This is not, as one might have thought, a reference to his work-in-progress, *Madame Bovary*, for he made it clear that the ideal book of which he was dreaming "would have almost no subject, or . . . the subject would be almost invisible," which of course is not the case with Emma Bovary's story. "In four days I have done five pages, but so far I am enjoying myself," he reported.[17] Soon he was working with "ardor." He added candidly, "I think that no one ever tried as hard as I am doing, ever since writers began to care about style." A couple of days later the writing was not going so well. "I have sketched out, spoiled, waded through, fumbled," he explained. "As much as I was careless in my other books, to that extent I am trying to be buttoned up in this one, and to follow a straight line. No lyricism, no personal reflection, absence of the personality of the author. It will be sad to read. . . ."[18]

As he warmed up in his writing, his letters to Louise drew off some of the heat. He had begun using the familiar *tu* form again, and in her diary she showed an awareness of his renewed affection. It encouraged her, even helped her writing, she noted, and that might make it possible for her to earn enough to be independent of Victor Cousin.[19]

She had expressed admiration for *The Temptation of Saint Anthony*. He would return to that book at a later time, he told her. "I am now in quite a different world, that of careful observation of quite ordinary details." It was another process: "I desire that there not be in my book a single movement or reflection of the author." He continued to work well, and thought that he could finish the novel in a year, writing eight hours a day. He and Bouilhet were also helping Louise with her poetry; at the moment they had in hand a long narrative poem about an agricultural settlement for young delinquents, which she planned to submit to the French Academy poetry competition. In addition to the editorial help of her Norman friends, she was getting advice and encouragement from a soon-to-be suitor, Alfred de Musset, and a former one, Victor Cousin, who advised her that she would do well to praise the prince-president, Louis-Napoleon, in a closing tribute.[20]

Then, on March 1, Gustave said that he expected to be in Paris the following week; he was waiting to reach a place where he could stop writing. (Timing his trips to coincide with chapter endings was to become a regular practice.)[21] The visit was worth recording — was worth Louise's recording — with "our kisses, his passion, his tender words," for it was like old times. On March 11 she gave a soirée for Louis Bouilhet. Edma Roger des Genettes, a married friend of hers not entirely closed to adventures, read aloud from his *Melaenis* and charmed everyone, including its author. He made that evident in a poem, "To My Lovely Reader," in which Edma's person, more than her reading manner, was appraised.[22] Bouilhet's thank-you letter to Louise was so effusive that one literal-minded scholar assumed that Louise had become Bouilhet's mistress that night.[23] The evidence for this was Bouilhet's exclamation, "Oh, what a fine evening and also what a fine night we spent together!"[24] But the *we* concerns Bouilhet and Flaubert, for after the reading they had gone off to finish the night at the Café Anglais, talking about "art and feeling"; at six in the morning they had watched the sun rise over the Place de la Concorde, and then Bouilhet had taken the morning train. Louise told her diary how pleased Gustave had been with the previous evening's reception; he had thanked her and kissed her. "He loves me; I think he cannot live without me anymore, just as I cannot live without him. . . ." "That will have been poor Bouilhet's first success," Gustave wrote her from Croisset. "He will remember that evening all his life."

On his return Flaubert took a couple of days to collect himself, and then he was back at his writing table. "All the value of my book, if it has one, will be to have been able to walk steadily on a hair suspended between the double abyss of lyricism and vulgarity (which I want to mix in a narrative analysis)," he explained to Louise. It made

him dizzy to think about what this book could become. He had worked
all his life like a mule, so if ever he produced something of value, he
would deserve the credit. If Buffon was correct in saying that genius
was a keen aptitude for patience, then he was sure to be in the first
rank.[25]

CHAPTER SEVENTEEN

MADAME BOVARY

THE NOVEL can be read for the story. Charles Bovary, a luckless child, grows up to become a simple country doctor without talent or ambition. After the death of his first wife, he courts and weds Emma; they settle in Yonville, a village not far from Rouen, and there Emma, imbued with what the author describes as false poetry and false sentiments, seeks solace with a country squire, Rodolphe, and then with the notary's clerk, Léon. Meanwhile, Charles moves from one professional humiliation to another, despite the paternal counseling of the village pharmacist, Homais. Above all, her husband is blind to Emma's infidelities, to her increasing indebtedness, and to her resultant despair, which drives her to suicide.

Reducing Flaubert's achievement to this outline, we can find factual sources (and enough has been written about them) such as the Delamare affair, already mentioned.[1] But surely the most suggestive source is a curious manuscript entitled "Les Mémoires de Madame Ludovica," a naive narrative of the adulterous loves and chilling debts of Louise Pradier, the sculptor's estranged wife. In it there is even a judicial seizure of property, as in *Madame Bovary*; and when Ludovica's confidante threatens to tell her husband about her debts, the erring spouse says she will kill herself. Ludovica's story, put together by an unknown confidante, was among the manuscripts found in Flaubert's possession after his death, together with his own notes on the techniques used by Ludovica to obtain money — many of which in turn became Emma Bovary's techniques. Louise Pradier wrote Flaubert a letter offering information on how the property of an "easy lady" was seized; she signed off with, "I gather up my energy and leap to [kiss] your neck."[2]

All this is far from the "Flemish novel" Flaubert originally intended to write, that story of a young girl who dies "virgin and mystic." He was later to explain that he had retained the entourage — the grim landscapes and personae — but, in order to make the story more understandable, and more readable, had invented a more "human" heroine.[3] The manuscripts testify to Flaubert's labor. After a succession of outlines, there is a first draft covering nearly eighteen hundred large sheets. (He wrote the first draft on one side of the sheet, edited it, and then rewrote it on the reverse side; after consultation with Louis Bouilhet, he then produced a final version that itself would be edited closely.) Important scenes such as the one dealing with the agricultural fair at which Rodolphe seduces Emma were written over and over again.[4] The final manuscript, meaning Flaubert's text before he turned it over to a copyist to produce a clean script for the printer, came to 470 sheets.[5] "He grinds away, gets angry, struggles, feels desperate, swears, shouts, and does beautiful things," Louis Bouilhet reported to Louise Colet after watching his friend at work.[6]

That his meticulous method was deliberate cannot be doubted, for we have the evidence of his intentions in his own hand. And yet there are still doubters who attribute Flaubert's method to illness. The first to say this was his not always reliable or loyal comrade Maxime Du Camp.[7] Closer to our own time, nearly every remarkable characteristic Flaubert had as a writer or as a human being has been explained as resulting from his epilepsy: his reading aloud, his violence, his excesses, even his hypersensitivity, as well as his misanthropy, his disgust with modern life. And of course his writing method, "the panting of his inspiration": "Like all epileptics," one psychiatrist announced, "he shows concern for precise material detail, to the point of absurdity."[8]

Or consider the experts who attribute Flaubert's method not to his illness but to its treatment, notably the use of bromides to calm his nerves.[9]

But was he really a slow writer? In truth he worked quickly when he wished to or had to. At the end of a day spent struggling over a few lines of his novel-in-progress, he could produce a considerable number of pages of correspondence. To his collected fiction, add the mass of drafts, the unpublished writings, and then the beautiful letters. (As for bromides, even if they may have affected his writing in the earliest period, when he still feared further attacks, after the virtual disappearance of his symptoms there was no need for drugs. If the final version of *A Sentimental Education* seemed dosed with bromide, as one writer alleged, it was not because of medication!) [10]

There was a momentous event in April 1852: Louise Colet won the French Academy competition with the poem over which Flaubert and Bouilhet had labored, and that meant some money for her. At the same time, Flaubert could report progress with his own work. He had been writing with rage; one night he went to bed at five in the morning, the next at three. He was working on the eighth chapter (of nine) of the first part of his novel; since his last encounter with Louise, six weeks earlier, he had written twenty-five pages, but he had worked them over so much, recopying, revising, and rearranging them, that he could hardly read them. "I lead a harsh life, removed from all external pleasures, with nothing to sustain me except a kind of permanent rage, which at times weeps over its impotence, but which endures." One can say that this confession betrayed illness; one can also say that it revealed a true writer. "I love my work with a frenzied and perverted love, as an ascetic loves the hair shirt that scratches his belly." [11] Compare this to Henry James's "Now to see deep difficulty braved is at any time, for the really addicted artist, to feel almost even as a pang the beautiful incentive, and to feel it verily in such sort as to wish the danger intensified." [12]

Occasionally his thoughts wandered. He was tempted, he confessed to Louise, to write for the theater. He was also thinking about "a great metaphysical, fantastic, and roaring novel. . . ." At the end of the year — for he continued to think about it — he spelled out its theme: through hallucinations, the hero calls up the ghost of his best friend (in this context, we see that it has to be Alfred Le Poittevin). Later Flaubert would say that the material for his book would be derived from his own "nervous illness"; but it was too early to write it, for the sake of his own health. [13]

Sometimes Gustave's letters to Louise served the function of a diary. May 8, 1852: Bouilhet was beginning to write a play (this would be *Madame de Moniarcy*), and would go to live in Paris that fall; Gustave would be alone, and old age would begin (he was still thirty). May 15: it was Saturday night, an hour after midnight; he had stopped writing in the middle of a page that had taken all day and was far from finished; perhaps it would take until the next night to complete it, since he sometimes spent several hours looking for a single word. He finished this letter as the clock struck three.[14]

Since he did not want to go to Paris before finishing the first section of *Madame Bovary* but had nevertheless promised Louise an early meeting, he suggested that they go to their halfway-point rendezvous again, Mantes. They would have twenty-four hours together, which was better than the five or six times he might have seen her, in a crowd, during a Paris visit. The twenty-four hours stretched to forty-eight (over June 3 and 4), and they were good hours. "I never loved you so much!" he would write her. Then a return to the boring grind. "It's because of the subject and the constant cutting," he explained. "Good or bad, this book will have been a prodigious tour de force, so far are the style, the composition, the characters, and the feeling from my natural manner. In *Saint Anthony* I was at home. Here I am visiting a neighbor."[15] This concise explanation of the Flaubertian method should cancel out the voluminous speculations about illness and drugs.

Once again Du Camp charged in: Flaubert would have to live in Paris to succeed. Gustave's reply was a four-page letter. For Du Camp, Paris contained "the breath of life"; "I find that it often smells like rotten teeth, your breath of life," was Gustave's retort. "To arrive — where?" He scorned fame. Du Camp saw Flaubert's life-style as "neutralizing," but what should a shoemaker do if not make boots? Flaubert would go to Paris when he completed his novel, and he would publish it if it was a good one.[16]

Du Camp also had advice for Louis Bouilhet: he too needed Paris, if he wished to succeed in the theater; he had to be with theater people, with men of letters. "As a general rule," Du Camp explained to Flaubert, "one must associate only with the strong and reject the weak. . . ."[17] Precisely; Flaubert could understand Bouilhet's ambition. A career in theater would be salvation for him: playwrights received up to 10 percent of each day's receipts, which could mean several hundred francs per performance.[18] All his life Flaubert was to help Bouilhet see his plays to the stage. In turn Bouilhet offered his ear for language and his talent as an editor, which seemed more considerable than his creative ability, as all but his friends would say. Bouilhet's job began with *Madame Bovary*.

CHAPTER EIGHTEEN

LOUISE TAKES A RIDE

Louise Colet, as we have seen, could not always wait for Gustave. Sometimes the temptation in other directions was too great, or her material as well as physical needs were too urgent. At other times, however, this was not the case, and she was upset when Flaubert advised her to marry Victor Cousin or at least keep him on the string. Men were always moving in and out of her salon and her private life. She was courted by those whose patronage she solicited; it was up to this sensual and well-endowed woman to cede or not.

The latest suitor was Alfred de Musset, who was her own age, forty-two, but already a superannuated roué. He had been a young star of French letters and a young lover of George Sand, and had celebrated their woeful liaison in an autobiographical novel. That very year, 1852, Musset had been elected to the Academy, a mark of respect that often signified the climax of a career, and in truth his was all but finished. He was to die — one wants to say, of old age — at forty-seven. Louise had approached this new academician with a request that he honor her by reciting her prizewinning poem at the award ceremony. He came to see her, "out of breath, coughing, spitting, seeming tipsy; I offer him a glass of sugared water, he asks for a glass of wine," she recounted in her diary. He could not recite her poem, he informed her, for if he did, the columnists would say that they were intimate. He would not mind their being intimate but did not wish it to be reported in the press. And he proceeded to recite a poem that he had written for her. They went walking, and he bought himself another glass of wine along the way, then a glass of absinthe. She invited him to come and see her again. When she told Flaubert about the en-

counter, he replied with scorn for Musset's person and for his deca-
dent art. "Musset will have been a charming young man and then an
elderly one," he said, in a pithy and not entirely inaccurate ap-
praisal.[1]

It was her turn to call on Musset, and they dined together. He came
to dinner the following day, and on leaving informed her that he was
going to visit "the girls." At the end of the week they took a carriage
ride together, during which he risked his luck and she rebuffed him.
On Saturday, July 3, 1852, he was back; this time she yielded, but he
proved impotent. They went riding in the Bois; he was very drunk by
then, and became furious when she informed him that he could not
see her that evening. She threatened to leap from the carriage, and
he mocked her, comparing this theatrical gesture to her knife attack
on Alphonse Karr. So she did jump, falling backward onto the pave-
ment but then getting to her feet and running to hide in construction
works on the Place de la Concorde. The driver stopped the carriage
to look for her; she asked him to tell Musset that he could not find
her, and he respected her request. "The carriage moves off! What a
coward! or rather, what a brute! He was dead drunk!" She recalled
that it was Saturday night and that Gustave was no doubt writing her
at that very moment; she resolved never to see Musset again.[2]

Indeed, Gustave was writing his letter. Inspired by what she had
written him of Musset, he confessed that he, too, had been like that
once, when he was eighteen. "There are few women who, at least in
my head, I did not undress down to the heels." Love had been the
principal subject of his study, and now *Madame Bovary* would be the
sum of his "psychological science." In another letter, written on
Monday, before he heard about her stormy evening, he derided Musset's writing. Poetry was not simply sensitive nerves, he said; were it
so, he himself would be better than Shakespeare or Homer. One's
personality could not make art; that had been his error in *The Temptation of Saint Anthony*. "In the place of Saint Anthony, for example,
you find me." He would not make that mistake again.[3] (So much for
one remark attributed to Flaubert, that *"Madame Bovary, c'est moi."*)[4]

When Gustave did receive Louise's account of the carriage ride, he
was properly angry with Musset and concerned for her. Was he also
jealous? He himself wondered. Of course Louise did not tell him that
she had been ready to give in to Musset. But before she saw the young-
old poet again, she had to withstand the assault of another distinguished member of the Academy, Professor Abel Villemain, twice the
minister of education, now sixty-two years old. He led her all the way

into his bedroom to reply to her request that he recite her poem at the ceremony, and then he began to kiss her. She slipped away and decided that she would return only in the company of her daughter. Soon Musset was back. She thought him handsome and regretted that he was so ill. He came to dinner with Victor Cousin, and after they left Musset at the Café de la Régence, the Philosopher began to press his attentions on her. When she got rid of him she returned to the Régence to find Musset; he was tipsy again, but she pumped him for information on the next Academy poetry prize. There was another stroll in the Bois, another attempt; she refused; he was angry. They separated, she feeling more pity than bitterness. For she was still under his spell. "It's strange," she confessed to her diary, "I am in love with both, but differently." The next evening Musset walked in, well dressed and looking younger. He kissed her, but she warned that the maid would soon be home. She went to secure the door, and on her return found that he was once again impotent.[5]

On Sunday, August 1, while Gustave was writing to say that he would be in Paris the day after next, she recorded her weekend adventures. "You make fun of Villemain with Cousin, of Cousin with me, and probably of me with someone else," Musset had told her, and she had laughed because what he said was not entirely untrue. She did have another tussle with Villemain, who, "horrible in his ugliness," threw himself on her and recited love poems; then she saw Musset again and recalled his impotence. "Oh! Gustave, Gustave, what a contrast!"[6]

Flaubert had reached the end of the first part of his novel. One momentous night he had gone to bed at two, so full of his work that he had risen an hour later to write until noon. That night he went to bed at one only because he thought it was the right thing to do. "On Friday morning at daybreak," he wrote Louise, "I took a walk in the garden. It had rained; the birds began to sing, and huge slate clouds raced across the sky. I enjoyed some moments of strength and extreme serenity, which one does not ever forget. . . ."[7]

Now began the labor of recopying and editing everything he had written up until then. He read the manuscript to Bouilhet. "What a bitch of a thing prose is," he wrote Louise. "It's never finished; there is always something to redo." For him a good prose sentence had to be like a good line of verse, "unchangeable," and to have as much rhythm. He knew that no writer had ever tried to be so perfect before. He was also trying to do something new with his subject, "to give psychological analysis the rapidity, clarity, and passion of a purely dramatic narration."

It was taking more time than he had expected to revise the novel, for he was constantly finding words he wanted to change, consonances he wanted to remove. Once again he felt the need to tell Louise that *Madame Bovary* was a tour de force, for it was a modern work and he was a man of antiquity. He was like someone playing the piano with weights on his fingers.[8]

He was in Paris from August 3 to August 12. He could not do his own work there, but he helped Louise with her poetry and sought a way to get Bouilhet's published. Louise was with him in his hotel on August 9 when he suffered an attack. She was terrified; he begged her not to call for help, and made an effort to keep himself in control. But she was present when he uttered a rattling cry, and she saw foam at his mouth; he punished her arm with his fingernails. In ten minutes he came out of it, and then he vomited. She hastened to reassure him: his indisposition had lasted only a few seconds; there had been no foam. . . . She felt deep tenderness for him, she admitted to her diary. He spent the whole next day with her, "more amorous, more passionate than ever; broken, but in appearance quite well."

He returned to Paris for the ceremony during which she was to receive the poetry prize. Indeed, August 19 was her day at the Academy: so many of her men, lovers and would-be lovers, were present under that famous roof. Gustave stayed on in Paris, "more and more loving toward me." One day he left her at five in the afternoon, promising to return at six-thirty, and Musset dropped in to complain that she did not love him anymore. She confessed to her diary that this visit troubled her. Then to bed with Gustave, and this despite her having her period. "He was never better," she remembered to note. "He told me that in a year we will be together; patience, courage, pride." He meant that when his book was finished, he would come to live in Paris.[9]

On his return to Normandy, he wrote Louise, he felt sadness; but soon he was working well again. On her side, she spoke of "the miseries of women"; he was dealing with those miseries at that very moment. "If my book is any good," he said, "it will brush gently over many a feminine wound. . . . I will have known your pains, poor obscure souls. . . ."

He wrote Louise one Saturday afternoon when household concerns kept him from his desk. A matter of money, he explained; had he more of it, he would be able to resolve many of his problems. "I will always have enough to live on, but not as I understand it," he told his mistress. "If my good father had invested his fortune in another manner I could have been, if not rich, then at least comfortable." His father had acquired land, but financial investments would have been more profitable. Yet to try to change the nature of those investments now would spell ruin.[10]

When Louise communicated her own sadness to Gustave, he professed not to understand. Complain about solitude? That was just what he needed for his work!

But even with solitude, the novel was not coming easily. How hard it was to write well about trite things! In a book like this, the slightest wrong turn could be fatal. "At the point I have reached, even the simplest sentence has infinite importance for everything else. Which explains all the time I take, the reflections, the disgust, the slowness!" At that moment he was doing the scene in the inn during which the Bovary couple is introduced to Yonville. In a single scene there would be the interplay of all of his chief characters, as well as descriptions of things, of the inn itself, and of the village, and an account of the beginning of the flirtation between Emma and the notary's clerk. The action lasted two hours, and he would need more than two months to write it.[11]

His own Norman surroundings had meanwhile turned to wind and rain; it was late October now. He was reading Shakespeare, had just finished *Pericles, Prince of Tyre*, and would soon return to Sophocles, wishing to know his plays by heart. "The library of a writer should be composed of five or six books, sources that he should reread every day. As for the others, it is good to know them, and that's all." He took up Molière and admired his style. But what a bourgeois Molière was, compared to Shakespeare. "He is always for the majorities, while the great William is for nobody."[12]

The methodical writer now plotted another rendezvous with Louise in Mantes. This time they had nearly a week together and were joined there by Bouilhet. Louise wrote to Victor Hugo, who had only recently settled on the rugged but hospitable isle of Jersey in the Channel, the second stage of his exile after the coup d'état of December 1851. She told Hugo, with exaggeration, that the two young Normans with whom she had been living would defend Hugo's glory unto death. In Mantes she had with her a copy of Hugo's angry pamphlet denouncing the French leader as "Napoléon le Petit," the first of the poet's satirical attacks on the Second Empire. Some months later a friend of the Flauberts' was arrested in Paris for distributing the same work.[13]

Matters of the heart had been dealt with in Mantes; now Gustave's commerce with Louise could revert to literary preoccupations. He was reading Rabelais, he told her; that author was "the great fountain of French letters." In her own work, Flaubert advised, Louise should use her womanhood as an opportunity for knowledge, and not as an excuse for sentiment. There was too much feminity in the novels of George Sand, he felt; "it oozes out," he added unkindly, "and the idea flows between the words, as between thighs without muscle. You write with your head." He himself was about to read *Uncle Tom's Cabin* and was prejudiced before he began, for its success had little to do with its literary merit and much to do with its politics.[14] On December 5 he told Louise that he had begun reading the book. "Speaking of America, what has become of the English?" The reference was to her menstrual cycle, to the redcoats, of course; by December 9 he was alarmed. He found it difficult to think of work while waiting for news from her. "I shall be thirty-one years old Sunday. What a cursed anniversary that could be. . . ." Yet he went on to attack government censorship and then to criticize *Uncle Tom's Cabin* for its moral-religious intentions. One didn't have to talk about slavery, he asserted, only to show it! "The author in his work must be like God in the universe, present everywhere and visible nowhere."

Finally Louise was able to reassure him, and he was overjoyed that no infant was on the way.[15] He began to work with enthusiasm, and the words flowed. He even had time to think ahead. An old idea came back to him, that "Dictionnaire des idées reçues" whose preface alone would make a book. No law would be able to touch him, he explained, for he would glorify everything that was approved, he would show that majorities were always right, that only mediocre books should be praised. He offered Louise some samples from his dictionary: "*France:* needs an iron fist to be ruled. . . . *Negresses:* are warmer than white women. . . . *Erection:* used only when speaking of monuments."[16]

Louise asked for his help. She was going to pursue her correspondence with Victor Hugo, who was now settled in his island retreat. But one could not deal with so conspicuous an enemy of the regime without precautions, and thus Louise wished Gustave to serve as intermediary, receiving letters from Hugo to pass on to her. He consented, asking only that Hugo's letters come to him via London, as the Jersey postmark would be a giveaway.[17]

On one occasion, Flaubert thought it prudent to warn Hugo that a recent letter from Jersey had reached him damaged, the envelope torn in several places so that one could even see the famous man's handwriting. Perhaps the Customs people had been searching for smuggled lace. Or was it the work of the "saviors of society"? Flaubert also assured Hugo that the older man had been more important in his life than any other. . . . But he qualified that praise to Louise. It had not been easy for him to write to Hugo, Flaubert confided, for the great man had too many faults for him to be able to express his admiration with only minor reservations. He blamed Hugo for encouraging mediocre talents, for his membership in the Academy, for his political ambitions. . . .[18]

Soon Hugo was addressing him directly. He sent along his poems attacking Napoleon III, which were to be published as *Les Châtiments*. One day Flaubert received a curious document, consisting of pages from that volume, printed in a tiny three-by-four-inch format for smuggling into France. These poems branded Napoleon III as a murderer who was exploiting the glory of the first Napoleon.

Needless to say, the letters Hugo sent to Louise Colet along with these materials contained advice on her career. The letter that accompanied the pages of *Les Châtiments*, for example, explained how she could go about winning another French Academy prize.[19]

CHAPTER NINETEEN

GUSTAVE AND LOUISE

O N JANUARY 1, 1853, Louise Colet noted in her private journal:
"This past year was the best of my life. Gustave loved me well,
and through him I tasted art and love better than I ever had before."
She attached importance to his literary advice and felt that her work
was going smoothly. He could not say the same for himself. "It is
now impossible for me to write a whole sentence, good or bad," he
complained to her one day. "I have as much trouble placing a word
as if I were writing poetry; there are assonances to avoid, and repetitions of words, and sentence structures to vary." There were times
when all of these problems made him want to . . . drop dead.[1]

Another year of work on *Madame Bovary* had begun. The hermit
of Croisset barely had time to send out New Year's greetings. He told
Louise, on January 15, that he had spent five days writing a single
page, had even given up his readings in English and Greek. Yet he
seemed to relish the difficulty, the challenge of writing well about
mediocrities. He was going his own way, and scorning Maxime Du
Camp, for example, who had just become an officer in the Legion of
Honor. "When he compares himself to me," Gustave wrote Louise,
"it is certain that he must find me far behind him." He offered a
devastating description of his old comrade: "Everything mixes together in his head: women, medals, art, boots, all this whirls around
on the same level; all that counts is what advances his cause."[2]

Flaubert was ready to go to Paris at the beginning of February,
which meant more good lovemaking (it would be even better in Mantes
in the spring, he promised Louise). He returned to Croisset with a
cold, and watched the snow fall. As usual, it took him some time to

settle down to writing. "The erections of the thought are like those of the body; they do not come at will!" Soon the news was better: he had done ten pages between letters to Louise and thought that two and a half pages out of the ten would survive. He believed that his novel would not contain a single "soft" phrase. "God grants genius. But talent is our business."[3]

March 21, 1853, a Monday. It was two A.M. when he sat down to write his mistress: "I am exhausted from having shouted all evening while writing." (A reminder of the peculiar Flaubertian method.) "To try to give prose the rhythm of verse (while keeping it prose, and very much prose) and to write about ordinary life the way one writes history or an epic (without distorting the subject) is perhaps an absurdity," he wrote her on Easter Sunday. "But it is also perhaps a great and original experiment!"[4] On April 26, an hour after midnight, he admitted: "I am exhausted. My throat is raw from having cried out all night while writing, following my exaggerated practice. . . . Let it not be said that I do not exercise. I am so agitated at certain moments that by the time I go to bed it is as if I have walked for two or three hours." He was reading Montaigne in bed, and knew of no other work so soothing.[5]

The only reading that could soothe Louise was a letter from Gustave, but even then . . . she continued to flirt, or to seem to be flirting. On April 25 she sent some of her poems to Musset, noting in her diary, "It's mad; I loved him a little; his memory and his talent move me, and yet it's Gustave that I love!"[6] And then there was another meeting in Mantes, from May 9 to 14; the lovers walked in the sun and talked a good deal, and the rest. Afterward he wrote to tell her how he had watched her train leave for Paris, then lit a cigar — "another cigar" — and dropped in at a café for a kirsch. At Rouen he picked up Bouilhet for the ride out to Croisset, and they spent the weekend working. By Tuesday Flaubert had taken up his routine again: tutoring his little niece, reading Sophocles and Juvenal, and revising "la *Bovary*." An exacting routine, and the last was the most exacting. "I write so slowly that all is of a piece, and when I displace a word I sometimes have to change several pages."[7]

June 14: "Feeling myself in a mood for style this morning, after my niece's geography lesson I grabbed my *Bovary* and roughed out three pages in the afternoon, and rewrote them this evening. It's a full and furious passage. I will surely discover a thousand repetitions of words that I'll have to eliminate. . . . What a miracle it would be for me to write two full pages in a day, now that I barely write three in a week! Yet that is what I did with *Saint Anthony*. . . ."[8] More evidence that his deliberate method had nothing to do with his illness, for of course he had been closer to epilepsy, and to its treatment, while writing *The Temptation of Saint Anthony*.

Late in July he was back in Paris again. Louise was delighted and asked all her friends in, including Charles Leconte de Lisle, who had proved a good and platonic companion; Gustave admired the man and his elegant poems.[9] From Paris he went up to Trouville to be with his mother. "For the past thirty-six hours I have been navigating among the oldest memories of my life," he wrote Louise. He did not mention Elisa Schlesinger; as it happened, she and her husband had moved to Baden-Baden the previous year. He was dismayed to see the extent to which Paris and its chic had invaded the fisherman's port he had once loved.

One day he came upon a picnic exactly like one he had invented for his story "Novembre." "Everything one invents is true," he wrote Louise. "My poor Bovary, without a doubt, suffers and weeps in twenty French villages at the same time, at this very hour."[10]

On her side, Louise was telling him about Leconte de Lisle, for whom she was acting as adviser. Gustave suggested that she serve as procuress for the young poet as well, for if his body was taken care of, his mind would be freed. "Yes, I maintain (and for me this should be a practical dogma in the life of an artist) that one must separate one's life into two parts: one must live as a bourgeois and think as a demigod. The satisfactions of the body and those of the head have nothing in common." Louise could accept that; she had a right to feel that she could give Gustave body and mind both, but separately. "You are and will remain *alone*, and without comparison to anyone else," he wrote her, assuring her that "the ghosts of Trouville" — his early memories of this place — were not a barrier between them.

He had time in Trouville to think about future work, and he informed Louis Bouilhet that he was in a hurry not only to complete his *Bovary* but to write an "Egyptian" tale, about a woman who wanted to sleep with God, and then several critical essays, after which he would plunge into real writing — "gigantic epics."[11] The Flauberts returned to Rouen via steamboat from Honfleur, and Gustave was delighted to take up his work again. He began reading Boileau: "Style is life," he declared, adding that he intended to reread all the classics while making notes for some critical prefaces in which he would demonstrate the inadequacy of literary movements.[12]

He was now writing the agricultural fair scene in *Bovary*. To Louise he described his intention: "Among the details of this rustico-municipal festival (in which all the secondary characters of the book appear, speak, and act), I must pursue, in the foreground, the continual dialogue of a gentleman *warming up* a lady." [13] Bouilhet thought that this would be the best scene in the novel. "What I am sure of," Gustave told Louise, "is that it will be new, and that the intention is valid. If ever the effects of a symphony are invoked by a book, it will be here." *Now* he was writing ten pages at a time, leaping from one sentence to the next. [14]

There was to be a significant change in his writing life now, for Louis Bouilhet was moving to Paris; their Sundays together had come to an end. Gustave reminded Louise that he enjoyed solitude. But he did intend to come to Paris more often now — for one week every second month. As it happened, he could not begin the new schedule right away, for he needed three months to finish the seduction scene. [15]

At one point in this scene, so he told Louise, when he wrote out the phrase "attack of nerves," he was so engrossed in the action, was shouting so loudly, was feeling so vividly what Emma was feeling, that he feared that he, too, was about to have an attack of nerves.

Bouilhet spent considerable time over the New Year's holidays working with his friend, even though the roads were blocked by snow and the Seine was frozen over. On January 2, 1854, Gustave reported on his progress to Louise. While laboring over his phrases, he said, he continued to dream of writing "great sumptuous things, battle scenes, sieges, descriptions of the fabled old East." He had spent two hours, head in hands, dreaming of one such subject. [16]

Louise continued to complain. He had not kept his promise to allow her to meet his mother. He brought up his own financial concerns whenever she mentioned hers. He replied that if his mother were to meet Louise, she would be extremely cool to her. As for money, he was not hiding a treasure, and few people with as little income as he appeared so affluent. Of the two thousand francs he was to receive that year, he already owed twelve hundred. On the happier side, he was still planning to move to Paris. In July or August he would start to look for lodgings, so that they could be furnished by October. [17]

By then Louise had found solace in the person of another romantic poet (also a member of the Academy), Alfred de Vigny, who was then fifty-seven. "May the songs of that old nightingale distract you!" wrote Gustave. Had he known how far her relations with the old nightingale had gone, would he have been upset? His letters display his total absorption in his work. He was even postponing an Easter visit to Paris because Bouilhet was coming back to Rouen and they would be working together there instead.[18] By the first week of April he had copied over everything he had written so far that year: only thirteen usable pages, but they were good ones. He was then studying surgical manuals, reading about club feet in preparation for the operation Charles Bovary was to perform. But he was also reading Greek history for Caroline's lessons. "Yesterday the battle of Thermopylae, in Herodotus, set me dreaming as at the age of twelve. . . ." (At the end of his life he would still be thinking about Thermopylae; it might have been the subject of his last book.)[19]

The battle with Louise continued. On April 12 he protested her claim that he did not love her, though he admitted that sexual gratification was of secondary importance to him; he wished that Louise, too, would live more with her mind and less with her body.[20] The lovers pursued the fight in Paris, and then Gustave walked out. Certainly her affair with Vigny could not have been the motive, and perhaps it happened just as Flaubert himself later explained it: "One evening I arrived at her place at a quarter after nine; she expected me at nine. I sat down opposite her, at the fireplace. 'You are coming from the red-light district,' she said. 'You prefer those women to me. . . .' I apologized as best I could for my involuntary lateness. She would hear none of it. Soon, from the chair in which she was seated, she began kicking me. Exasperated, I measured with my eye the distance between a log that was within reach and her head; I would have killed her, but suddenly I thought of the criminal courtroom, I could see the police, the judges, the public, and myself in the dock. . . . I got up and fled. . . . I never went back."[21] Whether this was true or only partly true, Flaubert liked the story; not once but twice he told the Goncourt brothers that his urge to assassinate Louise had been thwarted by a fear of the criminal courts.[22] The paradox is that it was the placid Norman and not the fiery southern woman who was ready to kill at the climax of a long lovers' quarrel. Louise was to say many things about the affair, as we shall see — but never that.

CHAPTER TWENTY

LAST CHAPTERS

WE SHALL MISS Louise Colet more than Gustave seemed to, for he was never again to express himself so expansively about his work-in-progress. Bouilhet may have been such a confidant, but most of Flaubert's letters to him have disappeared, and the best part of the friends' exchange would have taken place face-to-face.

After the break with Louise, Gustave was soon in Paris again, this time to see Bouilhet. "Not a *word* about my arrival to anyone, of course." He asked Bouilhet to get him rooms at the Hotel du Helder, on the street of that name just off the Boulevard des Italiens, in the theater district. This year, 1854, was to be devoted to contacts — for Bouilhet. "You don't find a place, you make it," Gustave advised, using the kind of language Maxime Du Camp had once used on *him*.[1] For Bouilhet was another placid Norman, and even less at ease with social contacts, with Paris, than Gustave was. One of his biographers, recalling his long relationship with his mistress Léonide Leparfait, called him a family man; he loved Léonie (as she was called) quite maritally.[2] Not that he refused to play games. Thanks to Louise Colet, Bouilhet met and seduced Edma Roger des Genettes, the woman who had recited his *Melaenis* during one of Louise's receptions. "They copulate with rage," Gustave had reported to Louise in January 1854. And before Bouilhet had a play on the stage, he had an actress in his arms.[3]

Gustave did not have Bouilhet's sexual needs. Did he frequent the red-light district, as Louise seems to have accused him of doing? He may have encouraged her to think so. He enjoyed in prostitution the complex combination of lust and bitterness, the denial of human relations, the "frenzy of muscle and clinking of gold"; it made him dizzy to think about all these things at once, "and one learns so much!"[4]

In fact he was again suffering from a venereal infection — this in July 1854, three months after his break with Louise. This would not have been the work of Béatrix Person, an actress he had been seeing, for at this very moment that young woman (then twenty-six) was protesting that being with Gustave had compromised her. Was she chaste, or simply committed to someone else? Whatever or whoever the cause, Gustave was using heavy doses of mercury again; he had fevers, was treated with leeches, and slept badly. But he was in a hurry to complete the second part of his novel, and so could not go back to Paris to consult "the great man Ricord" for another six weeks.[5] This of course was Dr. Ricord, the authority on sexual disease. He was the savior of high society, and the Goncourts were to say of him: "Nothing is less reassuring about the health of today's monarchies than the row of ribbons on Ricord's chest. At one pox per medal, it's frightening for the crowned phalluses!"[6]

Gustave was alone that midsummer; his mother was in Trouville with Caroline. So he could live the kind of writing day he preferred. "Alone like a hermit and tranquil as a god," he rose at noon, took his meals with his dog, smoked fifteen pipes a day, and went to bed at four in the morning. Apparently this life was good for him, for the most unpleasant of his symptoms disappeared.[7]

Louise or no, he fulfilled his promise to spend a season in Paris, taking a flat on Rue de Londres that became available on November 1. One of his missions was to find a theater for Bouilhet's first play. "Finish it," he advised his friend, "and I'll do the rest."[8]

Of course Louise knew that he was in town; of course she attempted to see him. The date was March 5, 1855; on the day following he wrote her:

> Madame,
>
> I learned that you took the trouble to visit me yesterday, three times during the evening.
>
> I was not home. And in fear of the affronts that such persistence on your part might provoke on mine, good manners require that I warn you *that I shall never be here.*[9]

She scribbled a reply on the envelope but kept it to herself; it consisted mostly of epithets such as *coward* and *scoundrel.*[10]

He returned to Croisset in April, and Bouilhet joined him there. Soon he was working "with rage," so he told Bouilhet. (He was writing about the abject Léon, and wondering just how bad he could make him.) He had 120 or 140 pages more to write but feared that they would not suffice, for in real life the end of the story had been the longer part (a further indication that Flaubert was following his sources closely).[11]

Something had changed in Croisset. In a letter to Bouilhet written early in May, Flaubert recalled that his friend had been excited by his niece's new governess, and now so was he. "At the table my eyes are drawn to the soft rise of her breast," he confessed. "I think she realizes this, for she blushes five or six times at each meal."[12] No name here, but persistent and intelligent detective work has established that the new governess was Juliet Herbert, the twenty-six-year-old daughter of an English constructor. In time Gustave would go beyond stares at the dinner table, and Juliet would cease to blush. All her life long, however, and his, the relationship was to remain secret, more secret than any other involving Flaubert. After his death, his niece preserved the secret by excising references to the English governess from letters that were to be published.[13]

But for the moment there were earthier distractions. Bouilhet had written him, for example, about their actress friends, Béatrix Person for Gustave, Marie Durey for himself. Now Gustave imagined himself and Bouilhet, each in his own box at the theater, like two rich men watching their mistresses perform.[14] Then he became serious. On May 30 he dispatched a veritable sermon to Bouilhet, making it clear that his friend had to see more people, influential people. If his play failed to be accepted by a theater, then he must write another and another: *"You have to bother people. . . ."* Even Molière had to try more than once, he argued. Flaubert knew that he was preaching to Bouilhet, just as Du Camp had preached to him, but the earlier situation was different, for Du Camp had taken him for someone he had not wished to be.[15]

The problem was to find a government-subsidized theater for Bouilhet's work. Flaubert even approached his mother's friend Adrienne Stroehlin, the wife of a Rouen cotton merchant, who knew a doctor who had been a prisoner with Louis-Napoleon and was now the Emperor's physician. "Patience," he wrote Bouilhet. "We'll have our day. We'll make our dent. . . . We have to pile works on works, produce like machines, and not deviate from the main road. Everything gives in to stubbornness. I feel the need, now, *to go quickly.*" Was it his acting in Bouilhet's interest that now moved him to act in his own?[16]

And when Bouilhet informed him, at the beginning of a dreary autumn, that the influential Théâtre Français had rejected *Madame de Montarcy*, Flaubert comforted his friend with the thought that all doors open to mediocrity, while originality is despised. "I feel for the stupidity of my era torrents of hate that suffocate me," Flaubert wrote in this letter of consolation. He had the taste of excrement in his mouth, and he wished to coat the nineteenth century with it, the way Indian temples were coated with cow dung.[17]

Soon Flaubert had joined Bouilhet in Paris. He found a new apartment on Boulevard du Temple, a lively thoroughfare lined with informal cafés and theaters whose grisly repertory gave it a nickname, Boulevard du Crime. He had a proper writing room and ample space to receive friends.[18]

One of the more austere of Paris's daily newspapers was *Le Moniteur Universel*, whose masthead proclaimed it the *"Journal officiel de l'Empire Français."* The top of the front page regularly published Imperial decrees, each of which began

NAPOLEON

By the grace of God and the national will, Emperor of the French. . . .

The paper displayed that heading on February 8, 1856, when, at the bottom of the front page — in a space reserved for theater or book reviews or works of fiction — the newspaper published the first installment of *Une Histoire de soldat*, a novel by Louise Colet in which that uncommon woman delivered herself, and the men in her life, unto the newspaper reader. Like much of her prose, it was hastily written, and its story-within-a-story has defeated more than one attentive reader. A waitress talks about her life and describes a lady for whom she once worked as a servant. This lady had been unhappily in love with a man who was always absent. There is even a description of Mantes, their meeting place. The rupture between the Louise Colet character (Caroline) and the Flaubert character (Léonce) occurs when he begins to take his leave and she attempts to detain him. "Then you don't love me! then all is over!" He walks out all the same, without pity. She travels up to his country house. There are tears, pleas, in a house like a cemetery, with Léonce's unsmiling mother close at hand. Caroline goes out into a heavy rain; her maid (the narrator) wonders what kind of mother and son can abandon a desperate woman on such a night. Later, in a theater, Caroline sees her former lover in the company of two vulgar women, and she remarks how he has changed: "his red face was puffed up as if he had drunk too much." Still, the apparition of Léonce brings on Caroline's early death.

Curiously, Louise's publication of *Une Histoire de soldat* has been interpreted as a last appeal to Flaubert.[19] For she seems not to have abandoned hope. We know that she visited Victor Hugo, then on the isle of Guernsey, in August 1856, and that he promised his support. "What good would it do?" she finally wrote Hugo. "I no longer believe in him." She fell ill after that, but as late as March 1857 Hugo was advising her, "Don't waste your time cursing a man, you, priestess of humanity." But she told him that it was not only a matter of losing time; she had almost died as a consequence of her sorrow.[20]

There was no immediate reaction to the publication on Flaubert's part. The evidence is that he was hard at work in Paris, taking advantage of Bouilhet's skills as an editor and making last corrections on his manuscript, for at last *Madame Bovary* was done. He now also took a momentous step, for him. Despite his hesitations about publishing and his misgivings about Du Camp, he agreed to let the latter publish the novel in his magazine. The fee agreed upon was two thousand francs; the novel would appear in *La Revue de Paris* in six parts, after which the author could sell it to a book publisher.[21]

He was a new man. Inviting Bouilhet to dinner at the end of April, shortly before his return to Croisset, Flaubert advised him, "All my other evenings are taken, so much am I a man engaged! well known! entertained by the populace and sought after by important people."[22] This was spoken with irony, but it was clear that he had not wasted his time, the way Bouilhet had wasted his.

CHAPTER TWENTY-ONE

PUBLISHING
MADAME BOVARY

THE IMMENSE LABORS that *Madame Bovary* demanded, however, were hardly behind Flaubert in the spring of 1856. He spent long days revising, which meant cutting unneeded pages; he called himself "heroic." He sent the manuscript to Du Camp on the last day of May, and was anxious to know what he thought of it. "For I won't hide from you, old man," he wrote Bouilhet, "that I *now* have a great desire to see myself in print, and as promptly as possible." Meanwhile, he turned to other projects. He read about medieval life and hunting for a story to be called "The Legend of Saint Julian the Hospitaler," which in fact he would not write for a long, long time. He made deep cuts in the first version of *The Temptation of Saint Anthony*, removing passages that he considered to be excessively lyrical. Then there was an alarm signal: despite all the cutting he had done in *Madame Bovary*, Du Camp felt that he had not cut enough![1]

Du Camp spelled this out on July 14, sending Flaubert a memorandum from his partner at *La Revue de Paris*, Léon Laurent-Pichat, which called for extensive changes. "Let us be *masters* of your novel for publication in *La Revue*," Du Camp urged his friend. "We will make the cuts that we judge to be indispensable; you will then publish it in book form as you see it. . . ." Du Camp coupled his request with a warning: "My very private thought is that if you do not do this, you will compromise yourself and will make your debut with a confused work whose style will not suffice to make it interesting." At issue, of course, was the realistic detail, the frank details, of Flaubert's novel.[2]

Flaubert at once caught a train for Paris. In his confrontation with

Du Camp's magazine, he later told Bouilhet, his legal training came in handy. He won a promise that there would be no cutting — or so he thought. Home in Croisset, he noted that the August 1 issue of *La Revue de Paris* announced the forthcoming publication of his book but spelled his name *Faubet*, which he took as an inauspicious sign. He was alone in Croisset — his mother had gone to Dieppe — alone with his niece's governess, Juliet Herbert. "If I were the way a young man should be! . . . but — " was his comment on this to Bouilhet.[3] He closed another letter: "Laugh: I'm studying English with the governess." "No news from the Reviewers," he informed Bouilhet — in English — on August 31, meaning the editors of *La Revue de Paris*. But soon there was a letter from Du Camp advising him that the first installment of *Madame Bovary* would appear on October 1, "without fail, I hope," a curiously contradictory phrase.[4]

Meanwhile, Bouilhet's play had been accepted by the Second Théâtre Français, as the Odéon was called. "I think of our Sundays so long ago," Gustave wrote his friend. "That goal of which we used to speak will soon be attained — for you, at least."[5]

On September 17 Du Camp informed Flaubert that the first installment of his book had gone to the printers. He would correct the proofs himself in Flaubert's absence, and promised that no changes would be made.[6] Flaubert could therefore apply his mind to other things. He pursued his revision of *Saint Anthony*. He felt that he had made the hermit more central to the story, and it was now possible to perceive a structure. He also toned down the flowery prose. For relaxation he studied English with Juliet Herbert, "which excites me beyond measure," he confessed. "I restrain myself on the staircase so as not to grab her ass." He thought that he would be able to read Shakespeare without a dictionary within six months.[7]

Whatever Flaubert may have thought about Maxime Du Camp, his *Revue de Paris* was thriving. Despite its austere format — customary at that time — it was competing with more affluent magazines for the liveliest new writing, such as Charles Baudelaire's *Les Fleurs du mal*.[8] The October 1, 1856, issue carried, on fifty magazine pages, the first installment of *Madame Bovary*, which takes the novel to Emma's pregnancy and the move to Yonville. To one of his new Paris friends, Jules Duplan, Flaubert complained that he could only see the misprints and the unintended repetitions, such as a page filled with the word *qui* (for "who" or "which"). Yet even if he felt this, he was not going to allow others to criticize his work. When he saw an ironical reference to his work in *Le Figaro*, he told Bouilhet, perhaps seriously, that if he found more of the same he would punch somebody; "The School of Rouen will then become known for its brutality."[9]

At this portentous moment of his life, he found it necessary to write to Elisa. A letter from her, announcing her daughter's marriage to a German architect, had arrived on October 1, "the very day . . . of my debut," he told her, adding that he saw in this coincidence a "curious symbolism." He recalled the early days in Trouville, and promised her the first copy of his novel when it was published.[10]

Flaubert arrived in Paris on October 16, just after publication of the second installment of his novel, to see Bouilhet's play through rehearsals. It was "a question of life or death" for Bouilhet, Flaubert told a friend. We can certainly accept Du Camp's portrait of the "overexcited" Flaubert striding across the stage, making the actors repeat their lines, indicating the proper gestures, moving people around, using the familiar *tu* to prop men, actors, stagehands, the prompter. He took charge of publicity and cajoled the critics.[11] On the eve of the opening on November 6, he distributed complimentary tickets. "In forty-eight hours," he announced to Edma Roger des Genettes, "our fate will be decided."[12] *"Our"* fate.

Madame de Montarcy was a drama in verse, and a well-made one, compounding jealousy and high politics in the court of Louis XIV. "I've just come out of the Odéon," Flaubert wrote their Rouen friend Alfred Baudry, dating his letter "one o'clock in the morning." "My head is still spinning from the sound of applause, and my hand trembles with joy, for our friend has won his place as a major dramatic poet."[13] Paul de Saint-Victor, a well-known critic, wrote in the daily *Presse:* "Since *Ruy Blas* [Hugo's play, performed in 1838] we have not heard so grand a style, so beautiful a tongue, in the theater. . . ."[14]

But while Flaubert was making a success of his comrade, his own career seemed in jeopardy. If we believe Du Camp, subscribers to his magazine were up in arms when Flaubert's first chapters appeared. Could such a woman as Emma Bovary exist in beautiful France? This was the general tone of the protest. Du Camp adds that early in November, which would have been just after the publication of the third of six installments, a friend of his who was close to the government warned him that the magazine was going to be taken to court. For *La Revue de Paris* had also published opponents of the regime. The first evidence of what was at stake is Du Camp's letter to Flaubert dated November 19: "Your carriage scene is impossible — not for us, as we don't give a damn, and not for me, though I must sign off on this issue as the editor responsible, but for the police court. . . . We have had two warnings; they are waiting for us, and they won't miss us when the opportunity arises."[15] Of course the reference was to the scene in which Emma and Léon ride around Rouen in a hired cab; they do not see much of that city, but neither does the reader see what they are doing behind the curtains. Du Camp later remembered Flaubert's verbal reply: "I don't care; if my novel exasperates the bourgeoisie, I don't care; if they take us to trial, I don't care. . . ." Du Camp also recalls going to see Flaubert's mother and getting no help from her, either. So he simply informed Flaubert that the magazine intended to remove the cab scene and to substitute an explanation saying, "The publisher is obliged to remove a passage at this point that is not acceptable to the editors of La Revue de Paris." In a note, possibly to his partner, Laurent-Pichat, Du Camp expressed regret for the trouble Flaubert's novel was causing the magazine: "I was caught up in a very old but already past friendship, and cannot wait until it is done with. . . ."[16]

The December 1 issue appeared without the cab scene, and with the publisher's explanatory note. This time Laurent-Pichat broke the news to the author: more would have to be removed from later chapters. Flaubert fired back a letter to remind the editors that they had held his manuscript for three months before printing a line, time enough to find out what was in it. He had agreed to remove "a very important passage" when they had insisted it could harm them. He had done a great deal but could do no more, "not one correction, not one cut, not one more comma, nothing! nothing! . . . But if La Revue de Paris finds that I am compromising it, if it is afraid, there is a simple thing that it can do, and that is to cease publication of Madame Bovary. This would leave me totally indifferent." The editors, he added, were concerned with details, but it was the whole book that was dangerous; "The brutal element is in the depths and not at the surface." He lost no time in calling on a distinguished attorney from his own province, Jules Sénard, the father-in-law of his friends Frédéric and Alfred Baudry; he would defend his rights in court if necessary.[17]

The final installment of the novel appeared on December 15 with cuts, cuts concerning not sexual transgressions but religious and moral questions — part of the scene involving the last rites for Emma, a dialogue between the pharmacist Homais and the priest Bournisien. The text was preceded by a protest signed Gustave Flaubert:

Considerations that I am not obliged to judge have led *La Revue de Paris* to make a cut in the issue of December 1. These concerns having repeated themselves in connection with the present issue, the magazine has considered it necessary to re- move several more passages. I therefore declare that I am not responsible for the lines that follow; the reader is asked to con- sider them fragments and not finished work.

Despite his precautions, Du Camp's fears were to be realized. If we believe his version of events — and he was still resentful many years later, when he wrote his memoirs — it was Gustave's fault, for he viciously went through earlier issues of *La Revue* to find questionable passages and then gave the collection to a journalist. This convinced the throne that something had to be done about these "disturbers of public morality," and Flaubert's compilation became evidence against them.[18] The recollection of the state prosecutor is simpler: the officer responsible for examining books and magazines called attention to the wicked chapter of *Madame Bovary* and suggested prosecution; the chief prosecutor accepted this finding and sent the case to the police court. Before the final installment had appeared, Flaubert was sum- moned before an investigating magistrate and informed that he was subject to indictment for transgressing against morality and religion. The case seemed to be founded on the scene in which Emma Bovary receives the last sacrament, despite the author's assertion that the de- tails were copied nearly word for word from the official Church rite. The prosecution complained that Flaubert had in fact introduced Emma's sensuality even into this scene, and intended to cite as evi- dence the raucous song of the blind beggar that is heard over the prayers.

Flaubert was ready to believe, however, that the real target was not his novel but *La Revue de Paris* itself.[19] Du Camp made his own con- cerns clear in a note to Flaubert: "Don't make too much noise about the case, but at the same time do everything you can to see that it does not come out too badly. For us it means shutting down, and this is what must be avoided." And Flaubert did throw himself into the fight, as he had for his brother's hospital appointment and for Bouil- het's career in the theater. To his brother, Achille, on New Year's morning, Gustave confided (apparently without foundation) that the investigating magistrate in this affair involving an attack on religion was a Jew.[20] He hoped that their late father's reputation, and Achille's present position, would help him: they thought they were going after a nobody, and they would have to be told, high up in the government, that the Flauberts *counted.*

There was a positive side to all of this. Copies of the magazines containing *Madame Bovary* were being snapped up by buyers curious to read the obscene passages it did not contain. If he could manage to avoid being convicted, Flaubert thought, the book would sell quite well.

He worked for himself and for Du Camp's magazine without respite. On one day in early January, so he told Achille, he spent twenty-one francs on cab rides. In another progress report he announced that the director of the police department was on his side, as were the "great ladies," one of whom had spoken to the Empress on his behalf. The Empress seemed to have been won over, together with Prince Napoleon (who had been, until the birth of the son of Napoleon III the previous year, first in the line of succession).[21]

The expense of energy was fruitless. On January 15, 1857, Flaubert learned from his attorney that he was to stand trial. He wished his defense to be a copy of his novel, with wide margins to allow room for extracts of the classics, to show that for the past three centuries "there hasn't been a line of French literature that is not equally dangerous to morality and to religion."

His stock was rising, he told Achille. He was being asked to write for the quasi-official *Moniteur,* at a fee that would eventually make *Madame Bovary* worth ten thousand francs. "That's where criminal justice leads to. Whether I am convicted or not, I've made my dent."[22]

CHAPTER TWENTY-TWO

FAME

GUSTAVE FLAUBERT was summoned to appear before the sixth division of police court on Saturday, January 24, 1857, but he won a postponement because his attorney would not be available that day. He was joined in the dock on January 29 by Léon Laurent-Pichat, the responsible editor of *La Revue de Paris*, and *La Revue*'s printer, Auguste Pillet. In fact, Laurent-Pichat was the chief defendant; Flaubert and Pillet were regarded as accomplices. The charge was "outrage to public and religious morals and to morality."[1] Thanks to the press, the courtroom was packed.

Achille did not come down from Rouen, so Gustave described the scene for him. He also brought along his own stenographer, at a cost of sixty francs per hour.[2] Thanks to this investment, the proceedings of this most literary trial belong to literary history. The first to address the court was Ernest Pinard, deputy to the Imperial prosecutor, for whom "the entire novel" was on trial; he felt it deserved a subtitle, "The Story of the Adulteries of a Provincial Woman." He recalled that as a child in convent school, Emma had confessed to imaginary sins; was that natural? Flaubert had dared to write that a nobleman at a castle ball was rumored to be the lover of Marie-Antoinette, thereby dishonoring that queen. Pinard read at length from the seduction scene between Emma and Rodolphe, arguing that the glorification of adultery was worse than the act. Emma was more beautiful than ever after her fall? That was "the poetry of adultery."

The prosecutor found it shocking that a blind man's ribald song formed the response to the prayer during the last sacrament; for him the guilty party was Flaubert, while the editor and printer were only "in the second line." It was not sufficient to give a book a moral ending if all the rest was an orgy; one had to think of all the young girls and married women who would read this novel.[3]

Flaubert's attorney, Jules Sénard, was not an insignificant person. This Rouennais of fifty-six had been a president of the National Assembly and a minister of the interior.[4] He spoke for four hours, and from the moment he stood up, he maintained a tone of outrage. Not only had his client written an honest book, a book whose moral and religious message was "the incitement to virtue by the horror of vice," but the man himself was honorable. Sénard had known his illustrious father, and his own children counted Flaubert among their friends. One son, Achille, was a doctor; Gustave, the other, "has devoted his life to study, to literature." He was not the man whom the prosecutor, with fifteen or twenty quotations, had painted as a "maker of lascivious pictures." He noted that the author's realism had been applied not only to scenes of love but to all aspects of Emma's life. Reading out certain passages that the prosecution was objecting to, he stressed their morality in showing how a woman could be led astray by sentimental values. He read a love scene more explicit than any in *Madame Bovary*, and then named the author: His Honor, Justice de Montesquieu! Should he read from Jean-Jacques Rousseau's *Confessions*, too? As for Emma's death, Sénard demonstrated that the respected Sainte-Beuve had dealt in similar terms with the last rites. The beggar's song? Shakespeare and Goethe had used the same kind of irony.

One could not, concluded Sénard, condemn a book on the basis of a few lines. Even if Flaubert had committed occasional errors of taste, he had not offended morality, and in being brought to court "he is already punished too cruelly."[5]

The verdict, delivered on February 7, began with a criticism of those passages — "taken abstractly and in isolation" — that were offensive to taste. In this sense, the book deserved to be reprimanded. Yet it was a serious work; the cited passages, however reprehensible, were brief compared to the novel's dimensions, and they were consistent with the characters. Since the book's main purpose had not been to indulge sensual passion or to mock matters deserving of respect, the court held that the defendants were not guilty.[6]

Flaubert was free, but soon *La Revue de Paris* was suspended for a month because of an article considered to be favorable to the republican opposition to the Empire. A year later the paper was permanently banned, following an unsuccessful assassination attempt on

Napoleon III; the order cited essays and stories published in the *Revue* that allegedly encouraged sedition.[7]

Flaubert came out of the trial, he confided to Louise Pradier, "fatigued, dazed, and with a cold." And what to write in the future that would be less offensive? If he published his *Temptation of Saint Anthony*, he thought, he would soon be back in court. He was advised to make cuts in *Madame Bovary* prior to its publication as a book; because he was uncertain about this, he asked his publisher not to proceed just then.[8]

For he had a publisher. The previous autumn, when the first chapters of the novel were appearing in *La Revue de Paris*, Du Camp had relayed an offer from a well-known Paris book publisher, and Flaubert had been delighted.[9] But then came a more credible offer still, from a young man who was rapidly becoming the sponsor of many of the most promising figures in contemporary letters. The young man was Michel Lévy. He came from eastern France, from a Jewish community only recently emancipated by the revolution; his father, a peddler, had brought his family to Paris when Michel was a child. The Lévys sold theater programs, plays, and sheet music on the sidewalks until Michel's father received permission to open a lending library. Speaking better French than his father, and possessing a more acute comprehension of what he was selling, Michel Lévy was able to become a proper bookseller and then a publisher, first of opera librettos and plays, then of novels and nonfiction. Before he was thirty he was publishing Prosper Mérimée (*Carmen*) and plays by Alexandre Dumas and Victor Hugo.[10]

Lévy followed the daily press and the literary magazines closely. He wasted not a minute after seeing Flaubert's novel in *La Revue de Paris*; he obtained Flaubert's Paris address and called on him personally in December 1856. It did not take long for the two men to come to terms. The sum agreed upon was the same amount that the competing publisher had offered — eight hundred francs — but Lévy offered cash, while Du Camp's candidate wished to pay with promissory notes.[11] Later Flaubert was to give a further reason for his having preferred Lévy. The first publisher had expressed an opinion about the novel, and though it was a favorable one, Flaubert objected; "A publisher exploits you," he told the Goncourts, "but he doesn't have the right to judge you. I have always been grateful to Lévy for never having said a word to me about my book."[12] There was also another, more serious reason for Flaubert's wish to be published by Lévy: this publisher had just signed not one but two contracts with Louis Bouil-het, for *Madame de Montarcy* and *Melaenis*.[13]

We can still read the contract for *Madame Bovary* (and it does not fill a page). For those eight hundred francs, Lévy acquired the pub-lication rights to the novel for a period of five years. He could also sell the translation rights, giving the author 50 percent of the pro-ceeds.[14] Later Flaubert complained about how little money he had obtained for his book, but at the time, the price was considered fair. Lévy had paid five hundred francs for a novel called *Scènes de la vie de bohème*, by the popular Henry Murger, author of the play *La Vie de bohème*, later to become a famous opera.[15]

Of course, Flaubert intended to reestablish, in the book version, the passages that had been censored by *La Revue de Paris*. He gave Michel Lévy the copy of the novel that had been made for Du Camp's mag-azine, indicating in the margin, "Restore everything that is crossed out with a wavy line" — the sign used by the editors in abridging *Madame Bovary*.[16]

Only a year earlier, Michel Lévy had introduced an inexpensive series of contemporary works called the Collection Michel Lévy, bound in soft green jackets and sold at one franc the volume. By the time *Madame Bovary* appeared, the series included works by George Sand, Théophile Gautier, and Stendhal, as well as Baudelaire's translations of Edgar Allan Poe.[17] *Madame Bovary* had a first printing of 6,600 copies in the regular edition and 150 additional copies on fine paper known as vellum.[18] Flaubert made certain that every influential per-son he knew received a copy.[19] He monitored the reactions of review-ers closely, and in the first letter we have from him to Lévy following the book's publication, he asked the question every author asks: "Is it selling?"[20]

In those years, Charles-Augustin Sainte-Beuve was France's most respected critic, upholding tradition and yet accepting the new when he thought it belonged in the company of the traditional. He wrote a column each Monday in *Le Moniteur*, and his "Mondays" were reg-ularly collected into books. On May 4, a little over a fortnight after the appearance of *Madame Bovary* in the bookstores, Sainte-Beuve made it the subject of his column. He reminded readers that the work under review had been taken to court, and he praised the "wisdom" of the judges in acquitting it. The novel "belongs henceforth to art, only to art," said he. The author's portrayal of the provinces was re-markable; Flaubert had not asked whether Emma's story was moral

or consoling, only whether it was true. Something distinguished
Flaubert from other realists: he had style. He even had too much
style, Sainte-Beuve thought, for he sometimes lost himself in description; and because he insisted on telling everything, there were some
unwholesome details. The critic regretted the lack of at least one good
character to provide consolation and repose for the reader.

But if Sainte-Beuve raised these objections, he admired everything
else. Flaubert's book announced a new literature with its "science,
spirit of observation, maturity, strength, a bit of hardness." As the son
and brother of distinguished doctors, concluded Sainte-Beuve, Flaubert held his pen as others did a scalpel.[21]

It was another quarrel of the ancients against the moderns. In the
sober *Journal des Débats*, Alfred Cuvillier-Fleury, a confirmed royalist, explained that he had to deal with *Madame Bovary* only because
Sainte-Beuve, "one of the masters of criticism," had praised it. He
ridiculed the book's popularity and felt the style to be marred by "vulgarity and pretentiousness," but he did concede that Flaubert had
more talent than his fellow materialistic novelists; he even admired
the scene at the agricultural fair.[22] Flaubert followed the negative
reviews with as much curiosity as he did the favorable ones. Noting
that the Catholic *Univers* had been particularly harsh, he complained
that the critics were not doing their job, for there was still more to be
said against his book.[23]

In general, writers were on his side. Even the popular George Sand,
who was not at all like Flaubert, praised his book. Questionable morality? On the contrary, it was for family reading, "good for the
countless Madame Bovarys in flower."[24] Before Baudelaire got around
to writing a review for Gautier's journal, *L'Artiste*, he was taken to
court for a book of his own, and six of the poems from *Les Fleurs du
mal* were banned; he was sure that even if the judges had found
something to condemn in Flaubert's novel, they would have amnes-
tied him because of its beauty.[25]

Fame manifested itself in many ways. In Hamburg, so *Le Figaro*
reported, cabs hired by couples for a particular purpose were being
called Bovarys. Music halls in Paris put Emma on the stage. Flaubert
was tempted by an offer to adapt the novel for the theater; there was
decent money involved. Finally he said no, not wishing to mix art
and money, as he explained to an admirer.[26]

And if the palace had seemed to shy away from Flaubert's version
of provincial morality, the singular Prince Napoleon, the Emperor's
cousin, made it known that he fully agreed with the universal praise

of Flaubert's book, which he thought "remarkable for so many reasons and whose success is so well deserved."[27] But from across the Channel an old friend spoke up: Gertrude Collier, the elder sister who always knew better. She was surprised that Flaubert could have written something as hideous as this book. "I find it all so bad," she wrote in French, "and the talent you applied to it makes the book doubly detestable!!"[28]

Soon after Emma made her first appearance in *La Revue de Paris,* a letter reached Flaubert that comforted him in his conviction that he had not been wrong. A woman in Angers found his novel to be "a masterpiece of simplicity and truth." From her own provincial capital she wrote: "Yes, these are certainly the mores of this province in which I was born and spent my life. This should tell you how much I understood the sadness, the problems, the miseries of that poor Bovary woman. . . ."[29] It was the beginning of a correspondence that was to endure. Marie-Sophie Leroyer de Chantepie was twenty-one years Flaubert's senior, had been raised in a convent, and had never married.[30]

It was not until late in February 1857, after the trial, that he replied. And he replied to each of her subsequent letters. There was never to be anything but letters between Mademoiselle Leroyer de Chantepie and himself; they were never even to meet, and perhaps it was for this reason that he found her an ideal sounding board. "We will talk together like two men," he said, when she told him her age. He said that he was thirty-five, stood five feet, eight inches high, and had the shoulders of a stevedore and the nervous irritability of a kept woman: "I am a bachelor and a recluse."[31]

Quite naturally she became the confidante he needed, now that he was beginning another book. He was in Paris in the middle of March, engaged in archaeological research "on one of the least known periods of antiquity," he revealed. "I am going to write a novel that will take place three centuries before Christ, for I feel the need to escape the modern world, which has kept my pen too busy. . . ." This is the first reliably dated reference to *Salammbô,* in a letter written a month before Michel Lévy published *Madame Bovary.*[32]

He was itching to begin, and there was another reason, which he confided to Maurice Schlesinger — a career reason. He had to write another book now "to sustain my debut. . . ."[33] But not another *Bovary;* he had suffered enough with the minutiae of ordinary life. When he was still only halfway through that first novel, he was already telling Bouilhet how much he wished to deal with "gigantic epics,"[34] dreaming (as he had confessed to Louise Colet) of creating "great sumptuous things, battle scenes, sieges, descriptions of the fabled old East."[35]

"There at least I'll be free," Maxime Du Camp remembered him saying. "Finally I'll be able to shout as I please!"[36]

PART V

CARTHAGE

AFTER THE STORMY WEEKS surrounding the trial of *Madame Bovary*, the "accomplice" Flaubert should have fled to his Normandy retreat, but he did not. He had to see his much-maligned manuscript through book publication in Paris. But we now know that he was equally preoccupied with a new novel, this novel that would allow his imagination to soar. When he settled on Carthage, a city and civilization of the pre-Christian era of which few traces remain, there was more legend than hard fact to guide him. His labors in libraries, his recourse to living scholars, and finally his own field trip were to make him one of the experts on that city. A collection of his notes in the Morgan Library in New York is striking testimony to the efforts he employed to document every trace of his personae and their milieu. There are rough maps, sketches of houses, even floor plans; he was concerned not only about major points, such as the city's defenses, but also about such details as tides and fish.[1]

We know from his letters that Flaubert had his narrative focus from the beginning: the revolt of the mercenaries after the defeat of Carthage by Rome in the third century before Christ, as told by the Greek historian Polybius and others. To this structure he added the passion of a mercenary captain, Mâtho, for Salammbô, the daughter of one of Carthage's rulers. But accounts of ancient history did not contain the quality of detail Flaubert required. A novelist must know what his streets and houses look like, and how to describe the city's walls and the surrounding landscape. He had arduous research ahead of him, he wrote his new Paris friend Jules Duplan from Croisset in May 1857. Later that month he told Duplan: "I have an indigestion from book reading. . . . Since March I have made notes on fifty-three different works; I am now working on the art of war. . . . As for the landscape, it is still quite vague. I still don't have a feeling for the religious side. . . ."[2]

One reason for Flaubert's staying on in Croisset was to save money. He had spent more than ten thousand francs since the first of January, which was too much for the small landowner he was, as he explained to Duplan, who was himself a small businessman. He had another thousand francs' worth of debts, and he realized that he was not going to profit from the success of *Madame Bovary*. By the end of May he understood that fifteen thousand copies of the book had been sold, which signified "thirty thousand francs that slipped from my grasp" (each volume of the two-book set was priced at one franc).[3] In fact, the estimate is that in Michel Lévy's five years of selling the book under the terms of the first contract, twenty-nine thousand copies were printed and sold for sixty-nine thousand francs, leaving some twenty-seven thousand francs in profit. (Lévy offered the author a bonus of five hundred francs, which seems small, and yet the original arrangement, as has been noted, was standard for the time.)[4]

The family fortune still consisted entirely of farmland that produced income in the form of rent — when the farmers paid it. So Flaubert reminded his cousin Olympe Bonenfant, whose husband collected for the Flauberts in the Nogent region. Madame Flaubert did not like to complain, said Gustave, "but I assure you without the slightest exaggeration that these continual uncertainties about money make life disagreeable." In order to pay the bills on time, his mother deprived herself of many things; she was selling her carriage and letting Caroline's governess go.[5]

Losing the governess would be too bad. Juliet Herbert was now collaborating with him, as Flaubert informed Michel Lévy: "An English translation of *Bovary* that satisfies me fully is being put together under my roof. If the book is to appear in England, I desire that it be this one and not another." It would not cost too much, and besides, it was "a real masterpiece."[6] Alas, no trace has been found of this second masterpiece. An English version of his novel was published only after Flaubert's death, translated by the daughter of Karl Marx, who later committed suicide just as Emma Bovary had.

Thanks to his new friends, and his reputation, Flaubert was now in a position to invite his literary colleagues to Croisset. At this first Norman salon the participants would be Théophile Gautier, the critic Paul de Saint-Victor, and Ernest Feydeau, a writer of Flaubert's own age who had also had a recent debut. We have a letter from Feydeau to Saint-Victor concerning this visit in early June: "One has the right to dress as a peasant," Feydeau informed him. "One is asked — by Flaubert — to bring one's own metaphors."[7] Metaphors, but not hiking shoes: "I do hope," Flaubert had told Feydeau, "that you are not going to make me live the life of a galley slave, nor oblige us to get up at strange hours. We'll leave the doors open, and you'll be able to wander around the countryside from dawn on." To Gautier he announced that his guests would have works by the Marquis de Sade on their night tables. At least one of the guests was more interested in a living specimen, Juliet Herbert. Flaubert told Feydeau later in June: "If you wish, oh lewd lover of nature and the arts, to see the governess again, you have to come before September 1, for that is when the young lady returns to Albion."[8] There is no hint of Flaubert's own interest in her.

Bouilhet arrived at the beginning of July. "We spent our time trembling like two cowards," Flaubert reported to their mutual friend Jules Duplan. "He's afraid for his play, and I for my novel." (Bouilhet was writing a play to be called *Hélène Peyron.*) The friends separated without reaching any useful conclusions, but from Mantes, where he was now living, Bouilhet summed up his feelings: *Salammbô* could be written, but he was appalled at the difficulties it presented.[9]

Of course it would be difficult, but Flaubert loved difficulty. He had now read one hundred books for his research, and still needed to know so much. "I'd pay a lot to have the reproduction of a simple mosaic that was really Punic!" he wrote a friend at the end of July. Even so, a month later he thought he was ready to begin writing.[10] Early in October he had reached the point where he could introduce Salammbô, the daughter of Carthage's general Hamilcar. (Hamilcar had actually existed, but Salammbô was the author's creation.) "I'm polishing up her clothing, which amuses me," he told Duplan. "I think I use the word *purple* or *diamond* in every sentence of my book."[11] He was obviously on to something; Salammbô's costumes, as we shall see, were to take Paris by storm.

This novel — and it was well for him that he did not realize this — was going to be five years in the making. That autumn he was ill — psychologically, he told his Paris friends, though to Bouilhet he described a medical symptom, pain at the back of his head. Bouilhet turned this back into a psychological problem, telling Gustave that it would all go away with the first good sentence he managed to get out. Can we connect this depression to the departure of the delicious

Juliet Herbert? Flaubert did regret losing her, as did Bouilhet, and Bouilhet thought that Flaubert's mother would also miss her.[12] In a better mood, Flaubert declared to Feydeau: "I have undertaken a brave thing, to try to resuscitate an entire civilization about which we know nothing!" He offered a theory: "Books are made not like children, but like pyramids, with a well-thought-out plan, and by placing large stone blocks one atop the next. . . ."[13]

In mid-December Bouilhet joined him in Croisset to "shout for a week."[14] Then Flaubert was off to Paris for his second winter season.

It began badly. There was talk about producing *Madame Bovary* at the Porte Saint Martin theater, but Flaubert began to worry about what commercial considerations might do to the novel. Then he came down with influenza, which took three weeks out of his season. When Mademoiselle Leroyer de Chantepie reported from Angers that a Paris friend had described Flaubert to her as "one of the boulevard dandies and the most sought-after man of fashion in Paris," he had to laugh; on the contrary, he assured his provincial friend, he was what they called a bear. Even in Paris he lived like a monk, often not going out for a week at a time. He had not been to the opera in four years; the year before, he had had a pass for the Opéra-Comique and had never attended, and the same was true this year for the Porte Saint Martin. Indeed, "I don't know how to dance or play any card game, or even how to make conversation in a drawing room. . . ."[15]

But when he began to move, he could be very visible. He took Bouilhet's new play in hand; he was, he boasted to Alfred Baudry, "the absolute master" of its fate.[16] He had also begun seeing the actress Marie-Jeanne Detourbay — or Jeanne de Tourbey, as she then called herself — who would eventually rise to become mistress to the Second Empire, though for the moment she was only mistress to Marc Fournier, director of the Porte Saint Martin theater. The Goncourts sized her up: "a brunette with beautiful eyes . . . a beauty that a bell summons to the salon" — this latter a reference to a brothel.[17] She was just twenty-one when Flaubert met her. Perhaps it was on this or a later birthday that he wrote her, "I kiss your lovely hands and your feet as well, and everything else that you would like. . . ."[18]

One of those who admired the bear in Flaubert was Baudelaire. "I should really like to lead the hermit's existence of one of my friends whose name I won't mention," the poet wrote a confidant, "and who, living quietly with his mother, found sufficient tranquillity of mind to achieve a fine recent work and become famous overnight."[19]

The paradox is that the man who for the most part could not be dragged from his study for anything less than an emergency now undertook a field trip to Carthage, which at that time was a wild place; the very site was only just being positively identified. "I'm very happy about it," he admitted to Mademoiselle Leroyer de Chantepie. "I'm going to be able to live on horseback again and sleep in a tent."[20] He left Paris on April 12, 1858, alone this time. In Marseilles he did not forget to look for "the famous house where — eighteen years ago! — I humped Madame Foucaud, née Eulalie de Langlade [sic]." (This he disclosed not to his Angers pen friend but to Louis Bouilhet.) Everything had changed at the hotel on Rue de la Darse. The ground floor was now a shop; upstairs, where the bedroom had been, he discovered a barbershop, and he got himself shaved.[21]

Once again he kept a travel log — his last, for this was to be his last long trip. So we know that he sailed on April 17, disembarking at Stora on the Algerian coast for an overland trip to Philippeville (now Skikda), then heading inland to Constantine. From Stora again, he continued the sea journey east along the coast of North Africa, reaching the Gulf of Tunis on April 24. Before he set out to explore Carthage, he had time for distraction, as indicated by his log entry for May 1: he slept with a Jewess, in a bed totally enclosed by curtains.[22]

His first objective was Utica, the ruins of an ancient city that had been Rome's base in Africa. He noted details of the landscape, reveled in the hunt for scorpions, and slept on boards, to the roar of dogs barking to keep the jackals away. He killed a snake with a whip. He spent four days in and around Carthage, riding between eight and fourteen hours each day, walking through ruins and trying to guess what they had been, following walls, and looking for roadways, all in a landscape of red rock and red earth, ravines and slopes, and cliffs along the sea edge. He made notes by moonlight and got to know Carthage quite thoroughly, at every hour of day and night.[23] One day he went out to the site with the French consul, the Count de Saint Foix, who was impressed. Thanks to Flaubert's "vast historical knowledge," the count declared in a letter he sent to France, "I know this site perfectly and without doubt better than many Tunisians do."[24]

Before leaving Tunisia Flaubert wrote Jeanne de Tourbey, "How my heart will beat when I ring your doorbell." He had been thinking of her all during his voyage, living with a memory of her, "which is a desire."[25] More prosaic was his mother's letter to him from Croisset, dated May 3: if he was a man of his word, he was halfway through his trip; his niece was sad that he did not mention her in his letters; she herself was waiting for mail and hoped he would make no stops on the way back, for "we have had enough separations, and you will end up not finding the old woman at home."[26] One remembers *A Sentimental Education* and Frédéric Moreau's mother, with the sentimental blackmail she uses to keep her son at home, calling attention to her solitude, her age, the sacrifices she has made. "A little patience, my goodness!" the fictional mother tells her son; "Soon you will be free!"[27]

CHAPTER TWENTY-FOUR

"HIM"

NOT LONG AFTER Flaubert's return to Croisset, Bouilhet arrived for a fortnight of work. Their conclusion was that *Salammbô* had to be rewritten from scratch. Everything he had done so far was "false," Flaubert explained to Ernest Feydeau, and yet he was sure that he could attain "the proper tone." It would take time; the public would have to wait (and the press as well, for *Salammbô* had been promised to a newspaper).[1] Feydeau traveled up to Croisset with his wife. He had just written *Fanny*, a frank portrait of a married woman and her affair with a younger man; it was creating a minor scandal and selling better than *Madame Bovary*. On the Feydeaus' departure Flaubert took up *Salammbô* and wrote a whole chapter in a fortnight, "in a continual bad humor," he told Feydeau. "Which does not prevent me from shouting from morning to night enough to break my chest. Then the next day, when I read over what I have done, I often cross it out and begin again." In October he went to bed with aches all over his body and pain at the back of his head; it was a "black illness" similar to the one he had almost died of as a young man, so he told Feydeau. By then he had written three chapters of his mad enterprise — "To give people a language in which they did not think. We know nothing of Carthage."[2]

And then to Paris to help Bouilhet with his new play. *Hélène Peyron* opened at the Odéon on November 11, 1858, and this time the reviewers were not indulgent. But Flaubert went to work on the critics and later was able to tell Marie-Sophie Leroyer de Chantepie that the play was a great success.[3] He returned to Croisset, leaving his mother and Caroline at Boulevard du Temple, where they had a separate flat in the same building, so he could live alone in that "wild and extravagant" manner he preferred. He rose each day at noon and went to bed three or four hours after midnight, falling asleep only at five; he no longer knew whether it was night or day, nor what day it was. He did accomplish something: ten pages in eighteen days.[4] He spent his Christmas reading the manuscript of Feydeau's next novel and making suggestions; New Year's was devoted to *Salammbô*, and only then was he ready to join his family in Paris.

During that stay he became closer to the Goncourt brothers, that singular writing team, social historians by day and private diarists by night. Of course it is their diary, recording the foibles and the wit of the elite of their era, that we read now. The brothers had first taken notice of Flaubert at the time *Madame Bovary* was published, at the offices of Gautier's magazine, *L'Artiste*; that day the talk had been of metaphors and assonances.[5] "Jules was blond and Edmond dark; both wore their hair artistically wavy, both wore monocles, and both smoked madly," as a biographer was to seize their images. They were exemplary brothers; it was said that they even shared a mistress, an indication also of their scorn for sentimental love.[6] In writing their diary one of the brothers, usually Jules, sat at the writing table while the other stood by to offer a picturesque detail or to sharpen a phrase.[7]

Now, in May 1859, they had an opportunity for a close-up view of Gustave Flaubert. He appeared at their door, for he had heard that these avid collectors had come across a mace that might have come from Carthage. Then the visitor began to look around, amused at the Goncourts' collections of almost anything. And they looked at him: "Very tall, very strong, with large protruding eyes, puffed lids, full cheeks, rough falling mustaches, a worn, red-splotched complexion." They identified with their new friend, for were they not also bears?[8] Soon the brothers were to publish their first novel, containing another portrait of this "big boy, ravaged but powerful, with a nature that can support anything, twenty-seven hours on horseback or seven months of forced labor in his room; the eyes blue, deep, penetrating; the Manchurian mustaches worn aggressively; a strong voice, a military and high voice. He is a man who saw something killed before his eyes in his lifetime: an illusion, a dream, I cannot tell which."[9]

Before returning to Normandy, Flaubert cemented another friendship that had begun with *Madame Bovary*. In April 1857 he had met George Sand, the celebrated novelist with whose legend he had grown up, even if he had not always approved of her down-to-earth rationalism or her unbridled sentimentality. An outspoken republican, she was considered licentious and even dangerous by proper society and the Church. She had heart, but her conception of her artistic mission differed from the younger writer's sense of his own. She also produced a great deal of work, and had seventy-five books in print by the time she sent a set of them to Flaubert in 1866.[10]

Their first meeting had been a brief encounter at the theater. Now, two years later, he called on her. We have a portrait of Sand as she would have appeared to Flaubert just then: "Her fifty-seven years have left their mark . . . , extinguishing that young and passionate grace, that striking countenance which, through the heaviness of certain of her features, had been her chief attraction. Her figure had filled out; her eyes remained handsome but seemed drowned in the waves. . . ."[11]

Flaubert went home with four completed chapters of *Salammbô*, notes for a fifth, and a clear idea of what it was going to cost him to complete this book. In the middle of July 1859 he was at work on chapter five: the mercenary captain Mâtho has violated the temple and taken the sacred veil, and he presents it to Salammbô while declaring his love for her. As for love, Flaubert himself had Juliet Herbert beside him now; she was in Croisset not for work but for her own pleasure, and presumably also for his.[12]

Ernest Feydeau wrote and told Flaubert that Louise Colet had been saying nice things about his novel *Fanny*. Flaubert warned him that she would soon invite Feydeau to visit her; if he went, he must be on his guard: "She is a pernicious creature." He suggested that Feydeau read *Une Histoire de soldat* for amusement. He had served as the model for this story, he said, as well as for "an unpublished comedy and a quantity of detached pieces. All that because my piece detached itself from her."[13] What he did not know was that Louise was preparing a still more formidable piece — of artillery this time. Her novel *Lui* ("Him") began to appear in installments in the summer of 1859. It introduced the marquise Stéphanie de Rostan, a still-beautiful blonde of forty, her neck of white marble resembling Pradier's *Sappho*, her arms "of a perfect model and a dazzling whiteness." She divides her time between two lovers, the poet Albert de Lincel (Alfred de Musset, of course) and a man the author again calls Léonce. The latter lives in the country, working like "an art fanatic" on a great book. Stéphanie is the confidante of this unknown genius; she has a letter from him daily and a rendezvous every two months. For Léonce's sake she has turned away the poet, not realizing that it is he who really understands love, who knows that one cannot set aside a few days for it and then forget it for the rest of the year. Yet the marquise is saddened when Léonce encourages her to pursue her affair with Albert.

Not only does *Lui* describe the Colet-Musset affair, but its very title calls up Musset's liaison with George Sand in Venice, which Sand herself had described in *Elle et lui*, only to be followed by Paul de Musset's counterattack in defense of his brother, *Lui et elle*. In Louise Colet's *Lui* the woman who stands for Louise (Stéphanie) shows the man who stands for Alfred de Musset (Albert) the letters she receives from the man who stands for Flaubert (Léonce). Albert concludes that Léonce loves her with his head, not with his heart. Léonce's letters describing the writing of his masterpiece are ridiculed by Albert — "as if writing was a work of symmetry, inlay, and polish." Léonce is dismissed as a pedant; his book must be "a heavy and flagrant anthology of Balzac." To show how heartless his rival is, Albert points out that Léonce is rich and could have given money to Stéphanie and attributed it to the sale of her autograph album. As she listens to the poet, her love for the novelist seems to dissolve.

Everything is in the book, even Musset's attempt to ravish Louise in the carriage (here we learn that he had used his teeth to tear her neck scarf). Still, in *Lui* the poet seems closer to the woman than the novelist. Two years pass; Stéphanie comes upon Albert in the Tuileries and invites him to her home. But it is too late: he resists, and not long after, he dies. She resolves to live for her child's sake and to love Albert de Lincel even in death.

Did *Lui* create a scandal? The author claimed that the literary pension she had been receiving for twenty years, thanks to her influential protectors, was canceled.[14] Surely the general reader would have been more likely to be able to identify Musset than Flaubert in this roman à clef. Flaubert noticed it, of course; he felt that though the book might have been designed to rehabilitate Musset, it made him appear even more outmoded than George Sand's account had. He himself, he thought, came out of Louise Colet's book "white as snow, but as an insensitive, miserly person, in other words a dismal imbecile. That's what comes of copulating with the Muses."[15] His revenge was that the book did its author no honor and was soon forgotten.[16]

Flaubert's own book was getting written, despite his doubts and summer visits from friends. Perhaps Maxime Du Camp was right to take the long view, as he did in a letter to his old comrade in September 1859: "Carthage moves forward; so much the better; you will have much satisfaction and great sadness at finishing this one; you'll begin another that will cause you as much pain, and so on and on. . . ."[17] At the beginning of autumn Bouilhet wrote to ask Gustave whether he would soon be going to Paris to see his girlfriends.[18] Perhaps it was that very day that Flaubert wrote to Jeanne de Tourbey. He had nothing to say, he reported, except that he missed her, "beyond measure." He thought of her adorable person "with all kinds of deep melancholies." He imagined her now, surrounded by men. He was planning to be in Paris in December, at which time he would be at her knees, ready for talk of "sentimental philosophy, while looking into your eyes. . . ."[19] Before the autumn was over he was having lascivious dreams, he confessed — this to his confessor Bouilhet, who attributed them to his long working days.[20]

He did visit Paris, briefly, to accompany his mother and Caroline to their Boulevard du Temple lodgings. The Goncourts ran into him at the station, and he proceeded to complain of the difficulties he was facing in the re-creation of Carthage.[21] Alone now in Croisset, he spoke of his trials to Feydeau: "Sometimes I feel empty and exhausted down to the marrow of my bones, and I think of death with eagerness, as an end to all this anguish. Then things gradually get better. . . . When *Salammbô* is read, I hope that [the reader] won't think of the author! Few will guess how sad I had to be to undertake the resuscitation of Carthage!"[22]

It was not too late for New Year's visits when he returned to Paris again. The Goncourts invited him over on January 12, 1860, and set the scene in their diary: they were in their dining room, a "pretty box" of a room covered in rep and filled with works of art, including a recently acquired Gustave Moreau. Along with Flaubert, they had invited Paul de Saint-Victor, Charles-Edmond, Aurélien Scholl — writers and critics all — and two young ladies. The talk was of Colet's *Lui*, of the theater, of theater managers and their exasperating ways — and of women. "I have found a simple way of doing without them," confided Flaubert. "I sleep on my stomach, and during the night . . . It's infallible." (The ellipsis is the work of the Goncourts.) Then the brothers were alone with Gustave, in the salon filled with cigar smoke; as he strode back and forth, striking the chandelier with his head in passing, their guest unburdened himself. The pains he took, Flaubert complained, were hardly appreciated. He spent his time removing assonances, but what made *Madame Bovary* popular was its bedroom comedy. His masters in style were La Bruyère, Montesquieu, and Chateaubriand; he proceeded to recite his favorite passages. Of *Sa-*

lammbô he said: "Do you know what I ask? I only want the intelligent reader to shut himself up for four hours with my book, and I'll
give him a dose of historical hashish."[23]

On his way home from a reception — it was Sunday, January 15 —
Gustave collapsed on the street in front of his door on Boulevard du
Temple. "I nearly killed myself," he would say; in any case, the cuts
on his forehead and nose made him "hideous."[24] Thanks to a letter
written by his brother to Dr. Cloquet, we know that the family considered the attack to be "epileptiform," even though for a long period
he had seemed to be quite cured. Achille added that Gustave did
everything he could, in his manner of living, to provoke further attacks — "he makes night into day, works to excess, and is continually
overexcited."[25]

SOMETHING PURPLE

A WEEK after his fall, Flaubert still had "a horrible gash on the nose and eyebrows that prevents me from showing my face to the populace," as he informed the Goncourts.[1] So they came to see him at Boulevard du Temple, and as a result gave posterity a description of his writing room, with his window on the boulevard. The centerpiece was a gilded Indian idol, a Buddha; on the desk, they saw pages of his manuscript that seemed to consist entirely of crossings-out. Then at last he could go out again, and he called on them. Familiarity bred reservations on their part. "At bottom he is provincial and affected," they confided to their diary. "One feels vaguely that he made all those great journeys in part to astonish the people of Rouen. His mind is as heavy and as bloated as his body. . . . He is mainly concerned with the drumbeat of his sentences. There are few ideas in his conversation. . . . His stories have an odor of small-town fossils. . . ." His indignation toward the Academy and toward the Pope seemed excessive and outdated. "He is clumsy, excessive, without a light touch," they concluded.[2]

After convalescing Flaubert returned to his feverish activity, devouring books he could not find in Rouen (he "swallowed" some fifty of them between February 1 and March 30, so he told Mademoiselle Leroyer de Chantepie).[3] The notebook he used that year has survived, and through those winter months in Paris we can follow his research on plants and herbs, on coins from Carthage and elsewhere in the ancient world, even on antique rites as described in a Latin translation of the Talmud.[4] "At last!" he exclaimed to Bouilhet at the end of March. "Two more weeks and I go home to Croisset." He let

Bouilhet know that he was not doing much lovemaking these days; when he did, though, he "frankly" believed that it was good for his health.[5] Yet when the Goncourts saw him the following Sunday, April 1, they noted: "We find Flaubert tired, lost, almost stupefied by work. Nothing but work in this life of his. . . ."[6]

Back in Croisset that month, he pursued his writing, interrupted only by Bouilhet's visits. In moments of despair he again dreamed of travel. To Ernest Feydeau he revealed that he was in the middle of chapter eight but wished he were writing the tenth, because that was where his lovers were to consummate their affair.[7]

His own relief appeared in the person of Juliet Herbert, who had again crossed the Channel to spend her holidays in the home where she had been employed. (The evidence of this discreet visit has come down to us not in Flaubert's hand but in surviving letters from Bouilhet.)[8] Then he joined his mother and Caroline at Fécamp on the Channel coast, where Madame Flaubert's boarding-school friend Marie Le Poittevin lived. There he could think only of Alfred Le Poittevin: "I was almost afraid that I might see him appear before me," he later told Bouilhet.[9] At nearby Etretat they visited Madame Le Poittevin's daughter, Laure, Gustave's own childhood friend, who was then married to another Gustave, de Maupassant. Certainly ten-year-old Guy would have been home from school then.[10]

And so to Croisset. He told Ernest Feydeau that he was almost done with his research, and with chapter nine, "after which I enter into the part where my hero enters into my heroine." He was smoking a great deal. "I roar like a madman, I drink gallons of water, I am forlorn every morning and full of enthusiasm every night. . . ." Soon he was able to say that he had finished the ninth chapter and was preparing two more, which he would finish that winter in Croisset, where he would be "all alone, like a bear." Again he announced the coming sex scene: "It must be at once dirty, chaste, mystical, and realistic!"[11]

Bouilhet had news. His play L'Oncle Million was going into rehearsal in Paris. But for this once Flaubert could not spare the time. Bouilhet promised that he would need him for only the three days preceding the opening of his play, during which time he would be able to read the latest chapter of Salammbô.[12] So Flaubert went down to Paris at the end of November to stir up the literary and journalistic community on his friend's behalf. A verbal snapshot of opening night: the Goncourts watched Flaubert and Bouilhet come out of the theater surrounded by "men wearing caps, to whom they give handshakes" — this of course being the claque brought in to applaud loudly.[13] But this time the claque could not help. The reviews were negative; even Flaubert's friend Gautier, though he admired the use of verse in a modern comedy, thought that the action was "a bit frail" for five acts: the son of a provincial businessman wishes to write rather than make money, and he almost loses his fiancée, until the girl's uncle sees to it that the poet wins her. "After the fall of the curtain," said Gautier, "Mr. Bouilhet's name was greeted by long bursts of applause."[14] But we know why.

Flaubert returned to Croisset at once but engaged their friend Jules Duplan to watch over Bouilhet, whose morale was so low that he had gone into hiding and whose lack of funds prevented him from staying on in Paris.[15]

Each thus retreated to his lair. "I become more and more bearish and gloomy," was Flaubert's New Year's message to Feydeau. He had finished his tenth chapter and was well into the following one. "I read Virgil every afternoon and gasp at the style and at the precision of the language."[16] He did not turn his back on poor Bouilhet; indeed, he invited him to stay in Croisset for two months while his mother and Caroline were in Paris. A grateful Bouilhet declined, pointing out that he could not abandon the woman with whom he was living in Mantes; moreover, he had to stay put in order to give unity to a new play he was writing. Flaubert himself stayed in Croisset until he had finished his chapter and was ready for his spring in Paris.[17]

The Goncourt brothers ran into him on a Saturday evening in the middle of March at a café. The next day he read them the very first chapter of *Salammbô*, "with his resounding voice that has the snarl of a beast, mixed with the dramatic purring of an actor's speech. . . ." They heard him say: "The story, the plot of a novel does not matter to me. When I write a novel I try to render a color, a tone. For example, in my Carthage novel, I want to do something purple." *Madame Bovary*, he added, had a "gray tone."[18]

Henceforth the Goncourts, for all their preciosity, become the richest source of information on Flaubert in Paris. Comparing their diary entries with other evidence, such as letters, we find them to be uncannily accurate, and sometimes their dating is better than anything else we have. We first meet the uninhibited Suzanne Lagier, an actress then twenty-seven years old, in their company (actually she is in Flaubert's, for Sunday lunch) on March 31. A week later — for Flaubert's Sundays had again become a habit — the Goncourts spent an afternoon at his apartment. They looked more closely at his study, which was "gaily lit by the daylight of Boulevard du Temple and whose main attraction is a Brahma in gilt wood. . . ." His writing desk was a large round table, with a manuscript conspicuous on top of it; at the back of the room there was a large leather sofa, with a plaster of a Greek statue above (the deminude Psyche of Naples).

After the other guests left, the Goncourts were alone with their host, and they learned still more about this curious provincial, who this time revealed his idiosyncrasy of acting out and declaiming his novel as he wrote, screaming so loudly that he had to drink buckets of water afterward. On the following Tuesday it was Flaubert's turn to call on the brothers, and they took note of his obsession with Sade. When he next showed them a chapter, a battle scene — "enumerated horror," they called it — they were reminded both of Sade and of Chateaubriand, whose *Les Martyrs* describes a battle and ends with the Christian heroes being devoured by animals. For the Goncourts rhythm was an enhancement, while for Flaubert it was everything: a work not conceived for speech was worthless.[19]

Then it was time for a less private reading of his work-in-progress. The event was scheduled for May 6, 1861, a Monday; as announced by Flaubert to the Goncourts,

1) I shall begin to howl at four o'clock precisely. So come around three.

2) Oriental dinner at seven. You will be served human flesh, bourgeois brains, and clitorises of tigress fried in rhinoceros butter.

3) After coffee, a return to the Punic shouting until the audience collapses.[20]

In fact he did not stop reading until two in the morning. Whatever they may have told the author, Edmond and Jules de Goncourt were disappointed, and confided as much to their diary. For if Flaubert had kept his personality out of *Madame Bovary*, he was all too present in the new work. They found "childish effects, and others that were ridiculous." The long descriptions bored them.[21] Literal, fussy, good mostly at surfaces, the brothers could get nothing from this book that was so different from anything anyone else was writing.

Flaubert returned to Croisset and from there accompanied his mother to Trouville for some family business involving their local landholdings. Once home, he swore that he would not leave again until his novel was finished. By the middle of July he had completed the thirteenth chapter of the fifteen the book was to contain. "It seems to me that *Salammbô* is deathly boring," he told the Goncourts, who did not argue with him.[22] His adviser Bouilhet encouraged him to keep on the way he was going. "Don't drown yourself in too many psychological analyses," he wrote, "but stick to images, massacres, contortions, *naive things* — which is to say, *epic things.* . . ."[23]

Before saying that, Bouilhet had been with his friend in Croisset over an August weekend, and had arrived only to find that he had another visitor, "Miss Juliet" — a nonexistent guest, for Gustave was to tell even intimate friends that he had seen no one except relatives all summer. No need to wonder why: Juliet Herbert was not an actress, not a courtesan, not even a woman of letters; she was a governess, and her good name was her stock-in-trade.[24]

At the end of summer Flaubert was exhausted. "The poisoning of la Bovary caused me to throw up in my chamber pot," he wrote Jules Duplan. "The attack on Carthage gives me aching arms. . . ."[25] He already knew that even if he finished on schedule, he would need three months to read over his manuscript, have it copied, and then correct the copy. Since summer was a bad time to publish, that would put the book off until the autumn of 1862. He was concerned about the excitement that would inevitably accompany the publication of Victor Hugo's mammoth novel *Les Misérables*, which would begin appearing in February 1862 at the rate of two volumes a month for four months; it would be presumptuous and even stupid to try to fight *that* tide. In any event he was expecting severe criticism: "*Salammbô* will 1) irritate the bourgeois — which is to say, everybody; 2) upset the nerves and hearts of sensitive readers; 3) anger the archaeologists; 4) seem unintelligible to ladies; 5) give me the reputation of being a pederast and a cannibal. Let's hope so!" (He was not without a comic appreciation of his audience.) Or again: "I'm getting to the dark parts. They are beginning to march over entrails and to burn little children. Baudelaire will be content!"[26]

CHAPTER TWENTY-SIX

TEN THOUSAND FRANCS

SALAMMBÔ was not finished by New Year's Day 1862, as its creator had hoped. But he was halfway through the final chapter. As he described it to the Goncourts: "I pile horror upon horror. Twenty thousand of my chaps have just died of hunger and of eating each other up; the rest of them will end under elephant paws or in the jaws of lions." He now expected that finishing the manuscript and revising it would take him until the end of April, and in any event he continued to feel that his novel should not appear in bookstores until the excitement over *Les Misérables* had died down.[1]

When he was ready to join his family circle in Paris, he advised Alfred Baudry, who was planning to visit Croisset, to come either on Saturday, February 8, or on the following Tuesday, for on Sunday he would be occupied with recopying and on Monday "I purge myself, sir," so as to arrive in Paris "fresh."[2] On Wednesday he left Croisset, stopping over at Mantes to submit his latest pages to Bouilhet. He had alerted the Goncourts to his arrival and had set February 16 as the date of his first Sunday reception.[3]

We get a good helping of news about Flaubert at this time from the Goncourts. Flaubert brought the irrepressible Suzanne Lagier to their home. She wore mourning dress, the brothers observed, and "talks to us for two hours about her mother, whom she has just lost, and about her ass, which she still has — she and many others. Her mother or her ass, her ass or her mother, her mother and her ass: these are her successive subjects of emotion and vulgarity." They saw it all as "an incredible profanation"; they recorded these things but hardly approved of them. At lunch at Flaubert's they heard Suzanne

Lagier say to their host: "You are the garbage pail of my heart, I confide everything to you. . . ."[4]

At this point we have another view of Flaubert in Paris, from the young historian Hippolyte Taine. He had already published his *Essais de critique et d'histoire*, in which he proposed that a person, a body of literature, a century, or a civilization could be broken down in a scientific way such that one would find that "all the parts depend on one another like the organs of a plant or an animal. . . ."[5] Taine described Flaubert, who called on him at the beginning of March, as "a large, vigorous man, square-shouldered, with large mustaches and . . . the look of a cavalry captain who is already used up and who has been a drinker." Taine followed up with a visit to Flaubert at Boulevard du Temple, where "I was struck again by the brutal energy of his face, and with his heavy bull eyes." He found him in a loose jacket and open shirt, his hairy chest visible. Flaubert's face was blotched with red, and of course he was nearly bald by then: "One sees the excess of work, and the imagination whipped into line."[6]

"Courage, confidence," Bouilhet urged him on, from Mantes at the end of March, "especially for the ten pages still to be written." Bouilhet pointed out that nothing "pushed you from behind," especially since Flaubert did not wish to publish immediately.[7] A few days after that, though he had still not reached the last page of *Salammbô*, Flaubert was seated on his large sofa, his legs crossed Oriental-style, telling the Goncourts what he would like to write in the future. He had long desired to concern himself with the contemporary Middle East, where the natives were becoming civilized and the Europeans falling back into savagery. Another project was a novel he identified only as "the husband, the wife, the lover," which was the way he was to begin one of the early outlines for the second version of *A Sentimental Education*.[8]

And then on Sunday, April 20, 1862, at seven in the morning, *Salammbô* was finished. So was Flaubert, almost. "I have a fever every evening and I can barely hold a pen in my hand," he wrote Marie-Sophie Leroyer de Chantepie. He began rereading and correcting at once, until the very sight of his own handwriting disgusted him. He needed Bouilhet, but Bouilhet was holding back; he did not join Flaubert in Paris until May 10, when he had finished writing his latest play, *Faustine*.[9]

When he returned home at last, Normandy seemed an anticlimax. Flaubert stalked his riverside domain like a beast in a cage. Bouilhet sought to be reassuring: he had all the time in the world to find another subject. But everything seemed to be going wrong. Flaubert had an outbreak of boils. There was talk of building a road across their land.[10] (Nothing came of it.) It was in this mood that he took up his next major preoccupation: finding a publisher and getting the best possible terms from him. Why not Michel Lévy? He decided to ask his Paris friend Jules Duplan if his brother Ernest, a notary, would agree to serve as intermediary. At the same time he informed Lévy that although other publishers wished to have his new novel, he would prefer to stay with him. He had no complaints with him, he added; on the contrary. But as he wished not to have to say or to hear disagreeable things, he was engaging a third party to make the necessary arrangements. "I warn you, dear Michel, that you are going to find my demands exorbitant. But I beg you to consider that this work has taken me five years and has cost me in travel and other expenses at least four thousand francs."[11]

So Lévy sat down with Ernest Duplan to hear a singular set of demands. Not only was Flaubert asking for a considerable sum of money, but he was insisting that the novel be accepted by the publisher sight unseen. Lévy objected; he had never published a book without examining it first, and that was also the only way he could judge its monetary value. For Flaubert was asking for twenty-five thousand francs, which was indeed an exorbitant sum; not even Hugo or George Sand got that much. The notary informed his client: "Michel Lévy admires your kind of talent; he believes in the influence of your name; with this favorable attitude, he will most likely be more positive when he has read your book."[12]

But Flaubert would not have it that way. If Lévy had a chance to look at the manuscript, he would surely find fault with it. "He must buy my name and nothing but that," Flaubert insisted to Jules Duplan. He authorized Ernest Duplan to find out from the publisher how much he *would* be willing to pay for a manuscript he would not be allowed to read. For Flaubert said he found it repugnant to be judged by Lévy. "One is compensated in two ways: in pride or in money. . . ."

It became a complicated, four-way negotiation. Flaubert submitted his demands to Jules Duplan, who turned them over to his brother the notary; Bouilhet was also brought in as an adviser, and suggested as a compromise that Flaubert himself read selections of the manuscript to the publisher, an idea Flaubert did not appreciate. He was also insisting that his book be published without illustrations, for who was going to be able to do a portrait of Hannibal, or even a sketch of a Carthaginian armchair? Had they existed, he said, he himself could have used them. Nor did he appreciate Lévy's apparent concern that the novel might contain obscenities, for "if my immorality has benefited anyone, it is he, I think!" Flaubert summed up: concessions on money if necessary; concessions on art, not a single one![13]

His intermediaries showed themselves to be reasonable when Flaubert was not. Ernest Duplan, for example, let it be known that he fully comprehended the publisher's wish to see the manuscript before purchasing it, not in order to weigh its literary value but to be sure that it could pass the censor.[14] But another tone colored these negotiations. In Ernest Duplan's report on his first meeting with the publisher, he complained of Lévy's "Judaic jeremiads."[15] "Let us hope that the Israelite will fork up his piasters," Flaubert wrote Jules Duplan.[16] Henceforth, when things were going wrong, the Jewishness of Michel Lévy would run as a leitmotif through Flaubert's letters.

Clearly this age-old prejudice came easily to Flaubert and his friends — to some of them, at least. It was part of the bourgeois mind-set; it was a seldom-questioned tenet of the land-rich. Sartre called it a defensive reflex of a society that refused to assimilate, or assimilated with reluctance, those new members that the French Revolution had given it.[17] Perhaps the most extreme example among Flaubert's friends was the Goncourt team, in whom superior talents of observation were accompanied by an absence of charity. At the other extreme would be Flaubert's disciple Guy de Maupassant, in the next generation; he had Jewish friends and Jewish mistresses, and the anti-Semites — including Edmond de Goncourt — knew this and deplored it.[18]

In his work Flaubert was cautious, at least in the beginning. In *Madame Bovary* the usurious merchant is a Christian who makes it clear that "We aren't Jews!"[19] But in the final *Sentimental Education* there is a slighting reference to "the Jew Isaac,"[20] and in the manuscript that remained unedited at Flaubert's death, *Bouvard and Pécuchet*, a character named Goutman is a cheat and is called a "dirty Jew."[21] If one bothers to look, one finds similar sentiments in the correspondence. Flaubert also warned Louise Colet to be cautious about an Armenian she had encountered: "I believe in race more than in education," he explained.[22]

The evidence is that there was nothing unusual about the operations of Michel Lévy's publishing house. A scholar's history of his company describes the parallel development of a music publisher of Catholic origin, suggesting that his business methods were similar to

Lévy's. These two entrepreneurs were in fact partners in a theatrical venture; both eventually acquired castles, wore the Legion of Honor medal, and became pillars of the Orleans dynasty.[23]

So it should be clear that the climate was not propitious for an early resolution of the differences between Flaubert's demands and Lévy's concessions. What is more, the negotiations got under way during that difficult period when an author is still feeling not quite satisfied with the book he has just finished and is exploring the field before settling on a new project. Flaubert had been thinking of writing for the theater, for instance. As early as September 1860 he had received encouragement in this vein from Bouilhet: "I am persuaded that you will enjoy it more than I do, because you were born a ham actor. . . ."[24] The following year he had begun to look into a particular form of theater that seemed likely to provide a vehicle for his ideas, the *féerie*, a fantasy genre that had once been the rage in Paris. As with *A Midsummer Night's Dream*, the fairy play allowed for transformations, the appearance of witches and good fairies, and ample use of song and dance.[25] The plan was to enlist the collaboration both of the experienced playwright Bouilhet now was and of a third author, Charles d'Osmoy, a landed aristocrat in Normandy, a wit and occasional playwright in Paris.[26]

Walking on the boulevard the previous winter, Flaubert had told Edmond and Jules de Goncourt that his next project would be a fairy play, for which he first intended to read all the similar plays written until that time. The brothers thought this "a singular process of imagination."[27] In May 1862, when he was home in Croisset, Flaubert turned to his dependable Parisian friend Jules Duplan, asking him to round up all the fairy plays performed in Paris over the past thirty years. Duplan did what he could, and Flaubert quickly gobbled up fourteen of these plays, joking that it was the worst classroom punishment he had ever had.[28] By the end of June he had read thirty-three such plays, as well as Hugo's mammoth *Les Misérables*. This last he found lacking in truth and in grandeur; the style seemed intentionally incorrect and "low." Hugo was not a thinker, he concluded, but was simply capable of summing up the banal ideas of his time.[29]

On July 5 Flaubert reported to Jules Duplan that he had just finished an eighth reading of the manuscript of *Salammbô*, having found still more errors in the final copy. Then the enormous packet was dispatched to Jules's brother, with a reminder of the terms the notary was to request: "I ask for 125 author's copies, *no illustrations*, and as much money as possible, of course."[30] Then he was off to Vichy, the famous health resort. For his mother, he told friends. He stopped in Paris on the way, partly because Bouilhet was there, but also because he wished to see the faithful Jules Duplan, who was in worse trouble than Flaubert had ever been. He was a partner in a shop that sold Oriental silks and rugs, and the business was failing.[31]

Going to Vichy for his mother? More than a century later, someone turned up a brochure entitled *Clinique médicale de Vichy pendant la saison de 1862*. It describes a patient of forty who was "tall, of a solid constitution" but who, on his return from a trip to the Middle East, had been affected by a jaundice that would not go away. The patient had no pain, but his swollen liver was all too apparent; the local doctor prescribed five half glasses of a water called Grande-Grille daily, and mineral baths. Twenty days later the patient returned, assuring the doctor that he had followed the treatment to the letter — and "the character of this distinguished man is a certain guarantee of his truthfulness," the doctor's report added. The jaundice had been conquered.[32]

While drinking the waters, and bathing in them, Flaubert followed the negotiations over *Salammbô*. Bouilhet called on Lévy, and after an hour and a half of discussion was able to relay a new set of proposals to the author. Lévy agreed to read the manuscript only in the office of the notary, but also made another offer: if Flaubert promised to sell Lévy the next modern novel he wrote for ten thousand francs, then the publisher would pay ten thousand for *Salammbô* sight unseen, and the two contracts could be signed the same day. Bouilhet recommended that Flaubert accept, for who could match those terms? Lévy would promote the book well. For example, Flaubert had at one point asked for thirty thousand francs; well, Lévy would be willing to spread the story that he had really paid out that sum, thereby contributing to the excitement surrounding the book.

Lévy's offer was "superb," Bouilhet assured his friend, if only in comparison with what other writers got for their work. "Ask Gautier, who receives a thousand or two thousand francs maximum for a book."[33] On August 15 Bouilhet went to see the publisher again and won a new concession: if Flaubert's next novel after *Salammbô* did not have a modern subject, Lévy would read it and decide whether or not to publish it for ten thousand francs, but in either case would still pay ten thousand for the first modern novel after that, even if he had to wait ten years for it.[34] But Lévy was demanding an answer right away, for he did not wish his high offer to serve as bait for other publishers. Or, as the notary put it, "The circumcised one seems to make this a matter of pride and of principle."[35]

From Vichy Flaubert wired Bouilhet: "I accept." What had decided him, he told the notary, was the assurance that he did not have to write a modern novel within a given period.[36] "So we are married, or rather remarried, for another decade," Michel Lévy wrote his author, "and past experience makes me feel that neither of us will wish a divorce."[37] "We will make a good couple, let us hope so!" Flaubert replied. He promised to be in Paris soon for a final look at the manuscript, so they could give it to the printer on September 20 for publication a month later.[38]

It was to be a busy autumn. In Paris Flaubert got to work removing all the superfluous *and*'s from the manuscript. Bouilhet's new play, called *Dolorès*, was scheduled for staging that same September, yet he was giving Flaubert hours of his time. Flaubert confessed that he lacked an idea for a future work; he was "dumb and empty like a jug without beer," he told the Goncourts. He wasn't even making love.[39]

The proofs exasperated him. He found errors in every sentence, he complained. Early in October he spent a week in bed with a boil that almost became a carbuncle; it went away, but then other boils appeared. He told his niece that in a month's time he had gone out only twice, once for a bath and once to see the printer; he spent another week in bed, "so ravaged by rheumatism that I could not move without crying out."[40] He asked Lévy for further sets of proof because of all the errors he was finding; he wanted each chapter to begin on a right-hand page, the way Alexis de Tocqueville's work had done when Lévy published it. He wanted there to be one less line per page, one less letter per line.[41] Taking note of his labors, Jules de Goncourt wrote, "You, my dear Flaubert, would have created the world better than it was done; you would not have stopped on the seventh day." Goncourt promised that they would stir up Paris when the book came out.[42] But in the privacy of their study, he and his brother told their diary, "Something dubious has appeared in Flaubert now that he has agreed with Lévy to spread the story of receiving thirty thousand francs for *Salammbô*." Flaubert had seemed so frank, and now the brothers were finding him to be less honest than he appeared.[43]

CHAPTER TWENTY-SEVEN

THE EMPRESS'S GOWN

SEEING FLAUBERT at the home of the critic Paul de Saint-Victor a few days before the publication of *Salammbô*, the Goncourt brothers allowed themselves another ironic judgment about this author who on the one hand pretended not to care about success and on the other, "works on it more than anyone else does": he even saw himself as competing with Victor Hugo! In the view of the Goncourts all Normans were sly, but Flaubert was more than sly. They saw him again on Sunday, November 23, and again noted with distaste how he worked at making influential friends even while affecting indifference to such considerations.[1]

Certainly Flaubert cared a great deal about what Sainte-Beuve was going to write about *Salammbô*. He made sure that a copy was delivered to the critic, and enclosed a letter to say that he was submitting it "with trembling."[2] (On November 28 Sainte-Beuve advised his protectress, Princess Mathilde, "I am up to my neck in *Salammbô*. *Ouf!*"[3] What did *ouf* mean?) The Goncourts found Sainte-Beuve "exasperated" by this novel; he told the brothers it was "unreadable," an anthology of brilliant excerpts. When they repeated this to Flaubert, he was indignant. The next day all the parties concerned found themselves at what was to become a regular literary dinner at the Magny restaurant, located on the tiniest of streets near the Seine, just off the Rue Dauphine. When the Goncourts arrived, in fact, they found that Flaubert was already deep in conversation with Sainte-Beuve. Flaubert told them in an aside that the critic had calmed down considerably. He would write three articles on *Salammbô*, Flaubert said, and would "apologize" in the third of them. Flaubert added, speaking of Sainte-Beuve, "He's a charming man."[4]

But the first blow came from an unexpected direction. In *Le Figaro*, on December 4, a columnist published an unusually violent attack on Flaubert, ending with the witty judgment that his style belonged in *"le genre epileptique."*[5] (The Goncourts saw a connection with the "widespread rumor" that their friend was indeed an epileptic.)[6]

On the more serious side, and as he had promised, Sainte-Beuve set aside three successive Monday columns in *Le Constitutionnel*, for which he was then writing, for his evaluation of *Salammbô*. The first, on December 8, covered more than four columns out of a six-column page, in a newspaper that contained only four pages. Sainte-Beuve introduced his criticism with a warning that he was setting friendship to one side in order to be impartial, which was the greatest compliment he could pay. It had been hoped, he pursued, that Gustave Flaubert would create another *Madame Bovary*, for the century needed a major realist. Instead, he had withdrawn from the world to deal with a place whose very location had long been uncertain. With a sigh, the critic was nevertheless prepared to respect the author's caprice.

Certain elements of the story disturbed Sainte-Beuve. He found Mâtho's desire for Salammbô "artificial"; he objected to the sadism of the battle scenes. In his third and final article, he went further: the basic concept of Flaubert's novel was erroneous, he declared, for a historical novel could not be placed so far out of time. It could only be a tour de force, and in this critic's opinion it had failed. He could only marvel at the strength and the skill Flaubert had deployed in the execution of "an impossible enterprise."[7]

Of course Théophile Gautier's review was favorable. It appeared in another establishment newspaper, *Le Moniteur Universel*, on December 22, the same day Sainte-Beuve's third and final article was published. "Without doubt the study of present-day reality has merit," wrote Gautier, as if replying to Sainte-Beuve. But was it not tempting for an artiste to reconstruct "a vanished civilization"? He found the reading of *Salammbô* "one of the most violent intellectual sensations one can experience." Flaubert was a master, and his book would remain "one of the greatest literary monuments of this century."[8] In a letter, Sainte-Beuve grumpily cited Gautier's column as proof that criticism was far from being an exact science.[9]

Taking as much care as he had when writing his novel, Flaubert composed a detailed reply to Sainte-Beuve. Was Sainte-Beuve so certain that his Carthage was false? For he had employed accepted rules of evidence, just as if he had been creating a modern novel. And he had been hurt by the reference to his sadism, for had he not been taken to court for his "outrage to morality"?[10]

Would their friendship suffer? They would be *better* friends than ever, Flaubert assured Sainte-Beuve in a note sent on Christmas day. Privately Sainte-Beuve offered his opinion that Flaubert's book would be admired first by those who sought, like George Sand, something new or, like Hector Berlioz, something musical, and then by "a great lady" for whom *Salammbô* "would accord with the search for the latest French fashions and the inventions with which her pretty head is sometimes taken . . ." — a clear reference to the Empress![11]

The second printing of the book was sold out before the end of January 1863, and a third was ordered. Michel Lévy informed the author that the comedy writers at the Théâtre du Palais-Royal wanted to stage a parody of *Salammbô*, though he advised against it because there was talk of a serious adaptation for the Opera. The parody was performed all the same; as for the opera version, the press reported that its music would be composed by none other than Giuseppe Verdi. (In fact this project was never to see the light.) Flaubert was delighted to hear that sermons delivered in two Paris churches had attacked his book as a return to paganism.[12]

Sainte-Beuve's patroness, Mathilde, was the cultivated member of the ruling dynasty; she had the critic make up the guest list for her Wednesday dinners at the Rue de Courcelles town house that had been given to her as an official residence by her cousin the Emperor. Early in January 1863, Flaubert was invited there for the first time, and he lost no time in seeking advice on protocol. The Goncourts were also invited, and once again found themselves in Flaubert's company. They had expected a small party, but when they arrived, the mansion was lit up for a very formal reception, with a uniformed guard standing in the entrance hall. After greeting the Princess, they entered an elegant room to find women wearing diamonds and men decorations — and there was the Emperor himself. The Goncourts saw themselves and Flaubert as the odd men out, practically the only guests who were not covered with medals.

Nevertheless the Empress Eugénie turned to Flaubert the undecorated to ask if he could provide details of a costume worn by Salammbô, since she would like to wear it at a ball. When the Goncourts heard that, they knew their country cousin was going to be "more swollen up than ever." There was indeed irony in the scene:

the bear out of hibernation was in private conversation with Eugenia María de Montijo de Guzmán, countess of Teba, Empress Eugénie. "*Salammbô* is our great event," Sainte-Beuve had informed the English critic Matthew Arnold. "The Empress was so impressed by it that she wishes to dress as Salammbô in a masquerade ball, and has asked to meet the author."[13]

Flaubert was even more insufferable to the Goncourts after that conversation. They heard him say that he expected to order special trousers for formal occasions. At one point in their evening at Rue de Courcelles, this man from the Seine valley suggested to them that they stand so as not to turn their backs on Prince Napoleon. . . .[14]

Flaubert took the Empress's request to heart. He asked an authority on things Oriental for a copy or a description of a small portrait of a woman in embossed gold that he had used as a model for one of the four costumes worn by Salammbô in his novel. For the sketch that he would present to the Empress, he addressed a painter who specialized in Middle Eastern themes, Alexandre Bida. Bida was to be told by Princess Mathilde, however, that Her Catholic Majesty could not go out in a skin-tight dress.[15]

In the end it would seem that not Eugénie but a certain Countess Virginie di Castiglione wore a Salammbô gown at the Tuileries palace on February 9; she was known as the Emperor's mistress, which made her a good second choice. A similar gown was also seen on Madame Barbe Rimsky-Korsakov, a stunning lady, if we accept the portrait by F. X. Winterhalter in the Orsay Museum as a good likeness; she was known for her lack of inhibitions as well as her beauty. Prosper Mérimée, who saw Madame di Castiglione in a Carthaginian gown, described her as "bare-legged, with rings on her toes and disheveled hair floating over the world's most beautiful shoulders."[16] Were there two gowns? In any case, there were two stories.

If Flaubert forbade illustrations in his book, he contributed his expertise to a woman's magazine called *L'Illustrateur des Dames*, which published sketches of all four of Salammbô's dresses. They were ample from the waist down, even bouffant; only the bodices explained the fear that they would prove too tight-fitting for the Empress.[17] The story does not end here. Some months later, when Hector Berlioz was preparing the staging of his opera *Les Troyens à Carthage*, he called on Flaubert for help with the costumes.[18]

After the reference to Flaubert's epileptic style in *Le Figaro*, one might have predicted that the full review of the novel, when it appeared, would be negative. Nearly all of the front page of the January 8 issue of that paper was devoted to Flaubert. The writer, Théophile Silvestre, dismissed the novel as a mystification and Michel Lévy as a Barnum, a circus manager exploiting a curious animal. Then the author turned to Flaubert's own personality, even his physique. He was "robust but with a tendency to softness"; he was wealthy, and so worked without effort or problems. Silvestre even found a way to tell the world that Flaubert "had no wit or conversation, even with women." He predicted a future "without glory" for Gustave Flaubert.

Du Camp and Bouilhet had all they could do to calm Flaubert down. His mother feared that he would challenge the *Figaro* writer to a duel. Bouilhet wrote to reassure him, "I declare that your physique is superb!"[19]

In a popular daily, *La Presse*, George Sand rose to the defense of Flaubert, her article taking the form of a letter that began, "Yes, my dear friend, I like *Salammbô*, because I like experiments and because . . . I like *Salammbô*." She was willing to concede that the author's colors were too bright, and his battle scenes hard to take seriously. But these artistic defects were amply compensated by the book's "grandiose qualities."[20] Sand meant every word of this, for we can find the same enthusiasm in a letter she wrote to her friend Juliette Adam: "You must read it; it is a superb work of the kind that leaves a permanent stamp on its times. I tell everybody: it's a book of the century."[21] After obtaining Sand's address from Levy, their mutual publisher, Flaubert thanked her, and she replied that she had only done her duty: "I should have considered silence as cowardice, or as laziness. . . ."[22] Their friendship could only grow.

In one of the few personal asides in a notebook devoted almost exclusively to literary references and aphorisms, we can read: "Today, December 12, 1862, my forty-first birthday, went to Monsieur de Lesseps to leave a copy of *Salammbô* for the Bey of Tunis. . . . To see Hector Berlioz. To the Palais-Royal to leave my card at the Prince's [Napoleon]. Purchased two oil lamps. Received a letter from B." Then an important final line: "And took up seriously the plan for the first part of my modern Parisian novel."[23] The reference is to *A Sentimental Education*; "B." — Bouilhet — was helping him to map it out. "We will talk about it at length," Bouilhet promised.[24]

In truth Flaubert had not quite made a definitive choice of subject for this "modern" novel. He wavered between two themes: on one hand, a young man's wandering through his times, especially through the ferment of Paris in 1848; on the other, the tale of two copy clerks who, after experiencing the stupidities of their century, set out to compile a record of them. (This latter would become *Bouvard and Pécuchet*.) When he submitted his dilemma to Bouilhet, the poet seemed to prefer the satire because he thought Flaubert's mood was more suited to it.[25] Yet Flaubert himself seemed to be leaning the other way. He dined with Princess Mathilde and at the end of the evening left with the Goncourts. Before they got into a carriage, he had time to tell them that his modern novel would encompass the Romantic movement of 1830, the events of 1848, and the Empire. "I want to hold the ocean in a carafe," he explained.[26]

Henceforth the Rue de Courcelles — the home of Princess Math- ilde — was to be the setting for encounters both invigorating and dig- nified, under the intellectual chairmanship of Sainte-Beuve; more in- formal dinners continued to be held at the Magny restaurant. Flaubert seemed equally at home at both. But he also tolerated a still lower order of society, as the Goncourts noted with distaste. "Flaubert has a certain obscene way of talking to women that disgusts the women, and even the men a little," reads a fastidious entry dated Saturday, January 21; the next day the brothers went to Flaubert's regular Sun- day open house, only to find Suzanne Lagier there. "That woman is mixed in with everything dirty, doubtful, suspect, and sinister Paris has to offer," they declared to their diary. Yet they did not refuse an invitation to the actress's home on the following Friday, and dined there in the company of Flaubert, Saint-Victor, and Gautier. The building in which she lived, they observed, was largely occupied by kept women.[27]

So back to Mathilde. She was born in May 1820 in Trieste, the second child of King Jerome of Westphalia, who had lived in exile since the fall of his brother, Napoleon Bonaparte. Raised in Tuscany in comfortable and even princely surroundings, Mathilde married a wealthy Russian nobleman, Anatole Demidoff, and they settled in Paris. But Demidoff, it turned out, had another woman in Italy, so Mathilde sought consolation in the arts and among artists (her husband dared to be upset when she bared her breast for a statue). Thanks to the intervention of the Czar, the couple were separated. When Mathilde's father died, her brother, Prince Napoleon, received the lion's share of the inheritance, but by that time her cousin was Emperor, and she received a royal stipend.

There was a time when marriage seemed likely between Mathilde and this man who was to become Napoleon III, when she was sixteen and he twenty-eight. Instead, she became his confidante. There is a portrait of Mathilde in which she is shown wearing a crown; she has a full face and strong limbs, as well as a low neckline. This is the mature woman Flaubert would have known.[28]

Mathilde's salon tolerated unorthodox behavior and religious dissent, during a reign that was often hostile to free expression; the Goncourts heard her say on one occasion that she talked differently when a woman was present. In appropriate weather her salon was transferred to her suburban villa at Saint Gratien, north of Paris, close to Lake Enghien.[29]

Flaubert might have been surprised to discover how the Princess viewed him: she thought he lacked what Parisians called wit; he was the typical bourgeois! She also seemed to understand Flaubert's political views better than those who later strung together his offhand remarks to form what they presented as his political philosophy. "Both absolute and inconstant," she judged him, "wishing to die for his country yet living quite well with everybody, victors and vanquished, he had no political convictions. At times he called for all possible repressions, at others he objected to any restriction of freedom whatsoever."[30]

PART VI

COMMANVILLE

CHOOSING A SUBJECT seemed as much of an ordeal to Flaubert as writing the book. He utilized and then stored a number of sketchbooks filled with ideas for novels. Some of the themes recurred again and again, such as a plan for a novel on the contemporary Middle East and another concerned with hallucinations.[1] "General rule: one must never do a thing without pleasure," Louis Bouilhet advised his friend, who was still uncertain as to whether he should proceed with *A Sentimental Education* or with *Bouvard and Pécuchet*.[2] Flaubert was home in Croisset at the beginning of spring, working on the outlines of both novels, hoping that by the time Bouilhet came for a visit he would be ready to choose. "I wasn't born to write about modern things," he explained to Jules Duplan. "They take too much out of me."[3]

His publisher, of course, thought he was made for modern novels. "It will be modern," Flaubert assured him.[4] But finding a way to make his own first years in Paris interesting seemed to him beyond his grasp. So he spent his time reading English and Greek, particularly the poet Theocritus. "Nice preparation for dealing with life in Paris!" he joked to Duplan.[5]

Even worse, spring brought him a fierce desire to travel — to China, to India; the green fields of Normandy set his teeth on edge, he told the Goncourts.[6] He did not go to China or to India; he went back down to Vichy, with his niece Caroline and his mother. In the month he spent in the spa, from June 8 to July 5, he did much reading — Goethe, Balzac, Alexander Herzen's memoirs of Russia. He professed to find his fellow bourgeois vacationers insufferable, and claimed that, unlike most watering places, this one seemed to lack easy women; it was said that they were waiting for the visit of the Emperor and his court.[7]

But Caroline remembered that visit to Vichy, and her uncle, with tenderness. He strolled with her, even accompanied her to church on Sunday. She sketched on the banks of the Allier river while he read; from time to time he would stop reading to talk to her or to recite a poem.[8] The Vichy interlude did serve a purpose: it brought Flaubert to the point of decision. For better or for worse, he would do the fairy play now, postponing both novel alternatives. "You will be quite surprised," Maxime Du Camp wrote encouragingly (for Gustave had brought many friends into his decision-making process), "that when you finish your play, the novel will have ripened all by itself."[9] Bouilhet arranged to spend time with Charles d'Osmoy in Trouville, where the latter happened to have a summer residence, to write the verse passages of the play. Flaubert would write the prose dialogue.

There was a temporary setback in August, when Bouilhet saw Marc Fournier at the Porte Saint Martin theater. Fournier had taken a look at their scenario and the first four scenes, and objected to the very idea of putting another fairy play on the stage; he felt that the public had had enough of them. But the authors were not going to stop now. If no theater would have their play, then Flaubert was determined to write a preface for it and publish it in book form.[10]

In *Le Château des Coeurs* ("The Castle of Hearts"), gnomes steal the hearts of men and replace them with machines. The Fairy Queen orders her people to retrieve the hearts before the gnomes take over the world, but in order to do that they must first find a pair of true lovers. So we meet Paul, a once-wealthy young man who is now ruined, his valet, and the valet's pretty sister, Jeanne, who has been sent to Paris by her parents to earn her living with her charms. Paul goes to Paris to regain his fortune but finds his bourgeois peers selfish. He contemplates suicide, but the Fairy Queen sends him to deliver the hearts of men from the black castle where the gnomes have stored them. He resists the temptations put before him by the gnomes and, armed with Jeanne's love, attains the "Castle of Hearts." Finally he restores the hearts to their rightful owners and wins Jeanne and immortality. The Goncourts, for whom Flaubert outlined his plot, warned their friend that the theme of a missing heart had been used before. He knew that, he said, but insisted that this play would be different because it dealt not with one heart but with everybody's.[11]

Still, when he finished writing, on October 19, he was dissatisfied. It was a well-made play, he confessed to a friend, but so empty! If he knew it was not very good, why then did he expect it to be taken by a theater? Because he did not think a play had to be better than that to be successful! [12]

Now there was a visit by the Goncourts to Croisset, their very first, and once more one has to be grateful to them for looking around. Gustave was at the Rouen station on Thursday, October 29, 1863, to welcome them, accompanied by his brother, Achille, "a tall and Mephistophelian lad, thin, with a large black beard, his profile chiseled like a silhouette. . . ." They boarded a carriage for the journey to Croisset, where they saw "a pretty dwelling with a Louis XVI facade set at the bottom of a slope on the edge of the Seine, which here seems to be the end of a lake. . . ."

The scene switches to Flaubert's writing room, with its two windows giving onto the Seine and its river traffic, three more onto the garden. Large bookcases of oakwood stood between the garden windows, and the rear of the room was covered with bookshelves. There was a fireplace, a bronze bust of Hippocrates; on the wall they spotted the Jacques Callot engraving *The Temptation of Saint Anthony*. They also saw Pradier's bust of Gustave's dead sister, and were reminded of a Greek statuette. Then in the center of the room they looked at the desk, a large round table covered with green cloth; the inkwell was in the shape of a toad.

The next day Edmond and Jules sat for a reading of *Le Château des Coeurs*. "To have read all those fairy plays, only to write the most vulgar of them all!" They observed Flaubert's mother, with her "dignity of a great former beauty." They saw Caroline as a poor thing, caught between the "studiousness of her uncle and the old age of her grandmother." She offered them friendly words, a "pretty blue expression and a pretty pout of regret" as she accompanied her grandmother upstairs at seven in the evening.

By now they were ready to sum up their observations. They found the household austere; the fire was inadequate in the fireplaces, the rugs were as short as they could be. There was Norman money saving to be seen even in what provincials were usually generous with, food. And by the next day they realized that they would never get outdoors if it were left to their host. He read "Novembre" to them, and they liked it; he dragged out the clothes he had brought back from the Middle East and dressed himself and his guests in them. The next day, at their request, he read from his Eastern travel log; they found it just the thing to astonish the bourgeoisie of Rouen.[13]

He soon followed his friends to Paris, for he had a mission — finishing the fairy play and finding a theater for it. Writing his niece, he admitted that this was not really his kind of literature. Instead of wasting time on intrigues to get it on the stage, he would rather be working on a novel "alone, like a bear," back home in Croisset. But he must tell her about his social success. The previous evening he had dined at the home of Jeanne de Tourbey, whose guests had included Sainte-Beuve, the newspaper publisher Emile Girardin, a deputy, and a prefect. "Prince Napoleon now calls me his dear friend," he was proud to tell his niece.[14]

Then it was her turn to astonish. Caroline — his Lilinne, the little girl whose pout as she accompanied her grandma to bed at seven had been remarked by the Goncourts — Caroline had received a marriage proposal. Flaubert dropped everything to rush home for an assessment of the situation. The suitor seemed a respectable man, and Flaubert's mother felt that his prospects spoke well for him; she herself wanted to see her granddaughter married while she was still alive. But it was not as simple as that, for Caroline did not love this stranger, and he did not seem the sort of person her education had prepared her for. She wept, talked to her suitor, and wept some more.

She was infatuated, it turned out, with her art teacher, a young painter who had taken her on because she was the niece of the author. She had learned to love art with this teacher, and he was also the first man she thought she was in love with. (She was then almost eighteen.) As for this Monsieur Ernest Commanville, he had first spied her at the marriage of her cousin Juliette, Achille's daughter. He was a dealer in timber, the son of a dealer in timber. His father had left debts, but he was understood to have paid them back, and he now prospered. He was tall, handsome, and twenty-nine.[15]

Her uncle was prepared to see Caroline refuse a man whom she did not care for. "When I saw you crying so abundantly the other night," he wrote her, "your grief wrenched my heart." Commanville had good references. She could find a more brilliant person, but then he would be a bohemian, and Flaubert could not accept the idea that his Caroline would marry someone without money. Better "a millionaire grocer than a great man who is poor" — these are his words — "for the great man will have, besides his misery, brutal and tryannical manners that will drive you mad. . . ." In any case, he warned her, she would have trouble finding anyone above her in education or in intelligence.[16]

After a third meeting with Commanville, poor Caroline still could not decide. She did discover that he liked music. And he had taken private tutoring from Louis Bouilhet; could Bouilhet tell them what he thought of his former pupil? "It is ridiculous for me to be seeking information from everyone," she admitted, "but I am so afraid, so afraid of making a mistake."[17]

But the wheels were turning now. "He is a businessman in a fine financial position," Madame Flaubert wrote to her Paris notary, explaining that Commanville had a fully equipped sawmill in Dieppe that was quite profitable. She asked the notary to announce the marriage to Caroline's father, Emile Hamard, but to see that he stayed away from Rouen for the time being. They would use money from Caroline's inheritance to dress poor Hamard properly and to find a room for him in a respectable hotel before Commanville called to ask for the hand of his daughter. Madame Flaubert also hoped that the notary would stress to Hamard the advantage for Caroline of marrying a rich man who loved her, "and who accepts her without a penny."[18]

For Caroline had at last said yes, even if, for a long while after that, she felt that she had been "abducted." Then she began to enjoy the excitement. She liked having to find and to furnish a home; she liked being loved. The marriage was scheduled for early spring 1864.[19] Flaubert could now turn to other concerns.

Bouilhet's new play, for one thing, was in difficulty with the Imperial censors, so Flaubert took up the cause and made it what he called "an Imperial affair."[20] Of course Flaubert participated in its staging and attended all the rehearsals. *Faustine* is a historical play, dealing with events in ancient Rome during the reign of Marcus Aurelius. It was well received, and the present Emperor and his Empress attended it and seemed to enjoy it, which helped draw an audience.[21]

Flaubert could also now return to the Magny dinners. One of them, in the third week of January, was attended by Sainte-Beuve and Hippolyte Taine as well as Théophile Gautier and the Goncourts, and the talk was of women — "the usual subject of conversation," the Goncourts noted. "On this Flaubert, his face afire, his voice bellowing, rolling his big eyes, starts off by saying that beauty is not erotic, that beautiful women are not made to be laid. . . ." His ideal sex partner, he told the assembly, was both ugly and unclean. He went on to declare that sex was not even necessary for health; it was a need created by the imagination. At this point Taine (then thirty-six years old and a teacher at the Saint Cyr military academy) objected: if he delivered himself to coitus every two or three weeks, he said, he felt relieved of tension, and he worked better afterward. Flaubert replied that it was not the seminal emission that counted, but the emotion.[22]

In the middle of March he was back in Normandy, to be with his niece in the days preceding her marriage. "Poor old man," Du Camp wrote on April 5, "I don't think you'll be very merry tomorrow." He was referring to his friend's return to the house the evening after the wedding — alone and face-to-face with his mother.[23]

Nor was Caroline particularly merry. Some time earlier, she had announced to her grandmother that though she would marry Ernest Commanville, she was determined not to have children and felt that her future husband should be so informed. Her grandmother smiled, obviously hearing the child in Caroline talking. On their wedding day, which came all too quickly as far as the bride was concerned, the new husband and wife celebrated at lunch with family and friends. Before they dressed to leave for their honeymoon trip, the newlyweds walked in the Croisset garden and sat down together in the summer house. Ernest took her hand and she said, "So you were willing to marry me despite . . ." He seemed not to understand; *she* realized that Madame Flaubert had not delivered her message and had not cared that she did not love her husband-to-be. Indeed, Caroline did not even comprehend the role of sex in marriage. All of this made for a sad honeymoon; the physical problem only served to magnify the intellectual one. Venice, with its invitation to romance, seemed torture to the overeducated, undersophisticated young woman.[24] She made it a point to let her uncle and her grandmother know that she was getting along well with her new husband, but whether it was because she had given in or because he was resigned, we will never know. She never did have children, though she had admirers and perhaps even lovers and married a second time after being widowed.[25]

Alone in Croisset with his mother, Flaubert now got to work on his new novel — *A Sentimental Education*, it was to be. In May he went back to Paris to consult Bouilhet about his outline. He spent long days at the Bibliothèque Impériale, and he borrowed books and shipped them to Croisset for summer reading.[26] Although he had chosen a "modern" subject, the events he wished to dramatize were twenty years behind him. In his usual way, he set to work overresearching them. "It seems to me that you are reading a lot of Socialists, when the question will take up so little place in your book?" Bouilhet posed it as a question.[27]

Flaubert accompanied his mother on summer trips to Trouville and to Etretat, returning to Croisset to receive Juliet Herbert. He also made his first field trip for his new novel, visiting Montereau at the junction of the Seine and Yonne rivers, for his father's province was to be the site of his hero's childhood.[28] He explained to his pen friend Marie-Sophie Leroyer de Chantepie, "I wish to do the moral history of the men of my generation — *sentimental* would be more accurate." He described his unwritten book more or less the way some critics did when it was finished and published: "It is a book of love and passion, but of passion as it might exist today, which means inactively." He admitted that the story, though true, would not be very amusing; for one thing, it lacked drama, and the action was spread over too long a time span.[29] "I'm working like a slave," he told Jules Duplan. "I go to bed every night at three. As for the work itself, I don't know what it's worth; the enthusiasm hasn't come yet."[30] Yet he pushed ahead so he would have a substantial segment of manuscript to show Bouilhet when they next met.[31]

And yet when the Emperor summoned him, he heard the call. In November he was invited to the palace of Compiegne, and he promptly dispatched his exact address there to Jules Duplan — Room 85, second floor, corridor of La Pompe — since he wished Duplan to buy and send him a bouquet of white camellias, "the prettiest available," for it had to be fit to present at a formal reception there. He enjoyed himself at court, though he claimed to find all the changing of clothing and the punctuality of the ceremonies a bit tiring. The bourgeoisie of Rouen would have been "astonished" to see him, for he was a celebrity, as he informed Caroline.[32]

Back in Croisset he was now alone. His mother had taken up her winter quarters in Rouen, on the Quai du Havre near the new residence of the Commanvilles. Caroline was later to remember herself as being an efficient housewife; her husband was then doing well in business, and he seemed happy with her. In Rouen they received the best people: successful businessmen, army officers, government officials; the Flaubert name gave Caroline entry everywhere. One of the high officials whose company she particularly enjoyed was dashing Ernest Le Roy, baron and prefect of their district and thus the representative of the Empire in Rouen. The baron enjoyed her company, too.[33]

THE LEGION OF HONOR

IN Croisset, in Paris, and then in Croisset again, Flaubert had a bad winter. He missed Lilinne, had just begun a book, and suffered in the frightful weather. "Rheumatism, neuralgia, and an abominable depression; this has been my fate for the past three months," he summed up for a friend.[1] His condition alarmed him sufficiently that he consulted Dr. Cloquet during a stay in Paris in February 1865. The verdict was that his neuralgia, though painful, was not dangerous. "Rub yourself, masturbate your whole body," Bouilhet advised, "and try to ejaculate your dissatisfaction."[2] For his condition was at least in part mental. He lacked money, for instance, and both his mother and their Paris notary, Frédéric Fovard, were keeping him on a tight rein.

There is a revealing letter, dated February 10, from Madame Flaubert to Fovard. Gustave's position, she explained, caused her much chagrin about the present and concern for the future. For if he was unable to get along on seven thousand francs a year when he spent most of his time in Croisset, how would he manage later on? She did not think that her children would agree to divide up their property now. She was trying to sell a large farm near Nogent, but she feared that if Gustave were given his share of that, he would quickly spend it all. She hoped that Fovard's friendly advice would put her son back on the right track.

Madame Flaubert intended to go to Paris herself to sit down with Fovard and examine all of her son's bills, in the hope that they could obtain reductions in some of them, "but Gustave must be very frank, for I do not believe that he owes as much as he says he does, and it is to have money in his pocket that he is asking for 7,000 francs. I must tell you that I won't pay before seeing the bills."[3] In a letter summing up her possibilities, Flaubert's mother offered her difficult son 700 francs a month for the four months he spent in Paris each year — and she would also pay his Paris rent, which came to 1,050 francs a year — and then another 1,200 francs total in pocket money for the eight months he spent in Croisset. She pointed out that of the 16,337 francs that she had received in rent from their tenant farmers the previous year, she had given him 9,000 francs, leaving only 7,377 for her.[4]

Her son also appealed to their notary: "Nothing is more painful for me than to ask my mother continually for money. Try to persuade her that I don't live a wild life!" If she was going to pay his debts, then let her do it without all of this complaining. He did owe money to his upholsterer, to his tailor, to a haberdasher (the upholsterer had redecorated his writing room in Croisset; the bills for clothing covered a period of two years). In all, his debts — including bills owed in Rouen — came to 5,609 francs; his mother turned over 3,000 francs to Fovard, all she could afford until their Courtavent farm near Nogent was liquidated.[5]

Flaubert was upset and irritated, but he was working. He took advantage of his stay in Paris to read old newspapers that covered events of the period about which he would be writing; he visited art dealers and learned about engraving techniques. In the novel, the husband of Madame Arnoux — his re-creation of his adolescent love Elisa Schlesinger — was to be a dealer in art (not in music, as Elisa's husband Maurice was). After a slow start, Flaubert's social life picked up. Among other events, he attended a ball given by Prince Napoleon at his Palais-Royal, later describing for Caroline a succession of twenty-three drawing rooms. He had, he added, spoken to at least two hundred guests during the course of that soirée.[6]

On her side, Caroline could talk about her own social life now. The great event seemed to be the ball given by Monsieur the Prefect, after which she could tell her uncle that Baron Le Roy had taken a liking to her. He was soon to adore her: Caroline became the object of the baron's pressing attentions. She would find flowers at her pew in the Rouen cathedral, and he would arrange brief encounters when she was in Paris. Soon there were incendiary letters between them. Caroline later insisted that this liaison remained "on the heights." She committed all manner of imprudences but did not fall. Concern for her family restrained her, she said; otherwise she would have flown

off with the handsome baron. We are also told that Ernest Commanville knew nothing about all of this but still thought it wise to settle
Caroline in Paris and to take her with him on long trips.[7]

One night that spring, after a soirée at Mathilde's, Flaubert took
the Goncourts to Jeanne de Tourbey's. The brothers had seen "that
former brothel girl from Rheims" before, but this was their first visit
to her home, which they pronounced "an apartment for a stage courtesan, with gilded stage props" (of course she was both a courtesan
and an actress).[8] The scene switches to the Rue de Courcelles home
of Princess Mathilde, on April 26, 1865, a Wednesday — the day of
her weekly soirée. Observing their hostess, the Goncourts noted: "She
has eyes, she has a place alongside herself, she has attention and
interest only for Flaubert, who tells us as we leave that she did a
couple of turns in the garden alone with him, in the shadow and the
night. . . ." They wondered if she saw Flaubert as a potential lover,
and decided not; they preferred to believe that she was using Flaubert
to challenge the rumor that she was overly interested in the Goncourts themselves![9] It is certainly true that Mathilde was not a statue
but a woman who had lovers. She enjoyed the company of outspoken
men; Flaubert, that of princesses. Were they flirting? No correspondence between Flaubert and Mathilde has been found for 1864 and
the early months of 1865, the period in which the princess seemed to
have eyes only for him; it has been suggested that Mathilde's heirs
destroyed that particular batch of letters.[10]

On the surface, surely, Flaubert's Paris season was rewarding, with
Mathilde's receptions, the Magny dinners, and his own Sundays at
home. But then came Croisset, in the spring, and a letdown. "What
do I have exactly?" he asked, writing Mathilde in a moment of
depression. "What is certain is that I am becoming hypochondriacal,
my poor brain is exhausted. . . ." Caroline was with him, to try to
cheer him up. "Is it the beginning of the end, or a temporary condition?" Meanwhile, he had given up smoking.[11]

It *was* a temporary condition, as it turned out. Soon he was settled
in with his novel. But at the beginning of summer he allowed himself
a change of scene; this time it was he who crossed the Channel for a
meeting with Juliet Herbert. We owe what we know about this visit
to the remarkable scholarship of an English writer who even compared official London weather reports of the day with notations in
Flaubert's diary. It was his first visit to Juliet. With her, and perhaps
at times without her, he went to the British Museum, the Royal Gallery, the National Gallery, and Hampton Court. At one point in his

notes he mentions a "delicious return trip," which, as our source says, implies that he was not alone. We know that he visited Juliet at home, saw her mother, and even dined there. On Sunday, July 2, for instance, he spent all day at the Herberts' house on Milman Row, sitting in their garden and drinking champagne with lunch. He took moonlight walks — surely not alone.[12]

Immediately after that he made another long-postponed trip, this one to Baden-Baden, where Maxime Du Camp spent summers with his mistress Adèle Husson, often in the company of her husband, Emile. Did Flaubert see the Schlesingers while he was there? Three years earlier Elisa had suffered a breakdown so serious that she was taken off to a nursing home, and even her husband was not allowed to see her for over a year.[13] Now would have been the time for Flaubert to meet her again, when he was writing the story of his long love for her. This encounter between them seems so called-for that it has even been written about.[14] But we now know that Elisa was in Normandy when Flaubert was in Germany; she was even in Mantes, where Bouilhet then lived.[15]

Gustave returned to visit his mother's sickbed: she was suffering from shingles and what was diagnosed as a generalized neuralgia. He became her nurse, though at night her complaints kept him awake and he had to sleep in his writing room. And yet he was working. "I went to bed last night at four," he reported to Caroline, "and I'm beginning to shout again, in the silence of my writing room. . . ."[16]

He now shared a secret with the Goncourts. Princess Mathilde had learned from the brothers that Flaubert had never received the Legion of Honor medal, so she got to work on that. Soon there was a press report to the effect that the Goncourts and Taine, as well as Flaubert, would be decorated on New Year's Day, and Sainte-Beuve confirmed to the Goncourts that the Princess had intervened with the Emperor.[17] Surely Edmond and Jules must by now have realized that it paid to be on good terms with their burly Norman friend. Hadn't Flaubert told them, after his visit to Compiegne, that the Empress Eugénie had asked a confidante (who repeated it to Flaubert), "How does he find me?" The Empress wished to know what Flaubert thought of her![18]

In an early outline of *A Sentimental Education*, the very first phrase seems to open the door to a secret room: "The husband, the wife, the lover all loving each other, all cowards." The next line describes what would in fact become the opening scene: "Voyage on the Montereau boat: a high-school pupil." This would be his hero, Frédéric Moreau, who has just graduated. The third line is a moving one, and the most direct identification we can find of Flaubert with a work he was writing:

Me Sch. —— Mr Sch.   moi

No key is necessary to identify Madame and Monsieur Schlesinger, and of course the *moi* is the young Gustave. This scenario concludes: "She loves him when he no longer loves her, it's at this moment [that he takes her] — or that she offers herself." The last phrase is penciled in as an afterthought. Indeed, in the final, published version of the novel, Flaubert would prefer the true state of affairs: he never slept with Elisa.[19]

There were to be many more pages of scenario, but the essence is here. With Flaubert's one, unconsummated love as its framework, *A Sentimental Education* is the story of a young man's apprenticeship to society. In Flaubert's first, unpublished novel, also called "A Sentimental Education," there is a married woman who looks and perhaps talks the way Elisa did, and there is a young man, but that young man cannot know much about the world because the author didn't know much when he wrote this draft. Still, many scenes first tried out in the early novel were to be repeated in the final version, as were many devices, such as the use of a confidant.[20]

At least one history textbook recommended *A Sentimental Education* for a better understanding of the political and social climate of the mid–nineteenth century.[21] Flaubert not only made use of concrete events, he also used people he knew — such as Maxime Du Camp and Du Camp's most conspicuous mistress, Valentine Delessert, who becomes Madame Dambreuse in the novel. We find not only Elisa, but a little of the actress Suzanne Lagier, a bit of Louise Pradier. And just as Flaubert was partly Jules and partly Henry in the first version of this book, his Frédéric Moreau in the final version contains a little of Du Camp and a great deal of himself.[22]

He did not appear on the Legion of Honor list, not that time. Early in January 1866 the Goncourts (who had also been forgotten) stopped at Croisset on their way to a holiday in Le Havre. After dinner and talk, they had time to note in their journal: "He does indeed work fourteen hours a day."[23] By then it was time for Flaubert to think of moving to winter quarters in Paris, where he had another kind of hard work cut out for him. "Like you, I lead an agitated life," he wrote his niece, "but not in society; I am lost in porcelain workshops. Yesterday I spent all afternoon with the workers of Faubourg Saint Antoine and the Barrière du Trône. In the morning a coach driver came to see me. Today I am going to the Ivry station. When I return home, I read treatises on earthenware. . . ." He told Caroline that he had been too busy even to attend the Tuileries ball (though one can guess that he may have been sulking because of his failure to receive his medal). He hoped that his niece would write him, "if the flirting of Monsieur the Prefect gives you any free time."[24]

There is a fresh witness to the life Flaubert led in Paris in the person of George Sand. She of course belonged to an older generation, and when she attended her first Magny dinner in February 1866, she found herself among a group of men most of whom were younger than she — "my little comrades," she called them. Only Sainte-Beuve was over sixty, as she was. "One pays ten francs per head; the food is mediocre," she noted in her journal. "One smokes a lot; one speaks by shouting at the top of one's lungs, and everyone leaves when he feels like it." She offers succinct judgments on her "little comrades" (with Sand, they made an even dozen that evening). "Flaubert, impassioned, seems more sympathetic than the others. Why? I don't know yet." (Was it because Flaubert, like herself, came from the country and lived in the country?) "The Goncourts are too lively, especially the younger one, who has a lot of wit but talks back too much to his old uncles." Louis Bouilhet was present, and she noted his resemblance to Flaubert; she found him "modest." The most talkative, and one of the smartest, was Uncle Beuve, as they called him. The Goncourts did not forget to mention Sand's presence in that day's entry in their journal, where they used the first person singular in their customary way: "She is seated next to me, with her fine and charming head, which with age resembles more and more that of a mulatress. She seems intimidated as she looks about her, whispering to Flaubert, 'You're the only one I feel comfortable with.' "[25]

Living in Paris, as Flaubert was now quite aware, was expensive, and having sufficient cash to pay for his clothing and his cabs and his dinners was a challenge he had not quite resolved. Sometime that winter he conceived a solution that would involve neither his mother nor the family's remaining fortune. He asked their notary, Fovard, to see if his publisher, Michel Lévy, might be willing to give him a bonus.[26] "Did you see the infant of Israel?" he reminds Fovard. In fact he was ready to accept either a bonus or an advance payment for future work. The evidence is that Fovard pointed out that there were no grounds for asking Lévy for more money. "Now that you have recalled me to decency, I thank you for not having done anything," Flaubert wrote to the notary. "Better to tighten one's belt than to show oneself weak before the infants of Israel." Still, he wondered, was there no way, "while behaving properly," to obtain a bonus for *Salammbô*, which had made even more money than *Madame Bovary* because of the higher price per copy?[27]

He was also suffering from his usual ailments. "At the moment I have a boil on my right cheek, another on my left kneecap, and a third in the middle of my right thigh that is as big as a small chicken egg," he complained to Caroline in the middle of March. "Not only am I unable to walk, I can't stand up, and I am enveloped with bandages and buried under poultices." He took baths and drank bitter beverages. When Bouilhet came down for a visit, Flaubert had a boil at the temple; by the time the poet returned to Mantes, his companion had sprouted two new ones, on his left shoulder and on his thigh. Then the boils disappeared, and he rushed to the library to read old newspapers. One day he spent seven and a half hours reading news of 1847, the year before the revolution broke out.[28]

One Sunday in May he described the scene at Boulevard du Temple to his niece. It was nine in the morning, and he was already at his desk; Bouilhet was stretched out on his bed reading Michelet's latest work, *Louis XV*. They were expecting the usual Sunday visitors, after which they would dine at Adèle Husson's.[29]

His friendship with George Sand was flowering. She asked if she could dedicate her next novel to him, for each of her books bore the name of a friend. "I kiss the two big diamonds that decorate your trumpet," she wrote him. "You are right to love me," replied he, "for it is an exchange."[30] When she appeared at the next Magny dinner, on May 21, the Goncourts cackled: "Madame Sand makes her entry in a peach-blossom dress, a romantic ensemble that I suspect was put on with the intention of raping Flaubert."[31] When her next novel was published, with its dedication to Flaubert, he discovered that it bore the title *Dernier amour* ("Last Love"), which inspired some gentle ribbing from his friends.[32]

Before he returned to Croisset later in May, Flaubert appealed again to his family's notary: "If the Israelite refuses to give me a bonus of three thousand francs, try to find six thousand for me among the capitalists of your acquaintance, to be paid back in several years (choose the date yourself) with cumulative interest."[33]

* * *

In Normandy he settled down for a long, uninterrupted bout of writing. Did he doubt the basic premise of *A Sentimental Education* even as he was working away on it? Bouilhet assured him that it was a good one. "What must be watched is the interest of details . . . ; the details of your book are and must be more and more amusing. . . . We'll cut them later if it proves necessary."[34] Then it was time for distraction again: Flaubert was going over to England. "Please give my regards in London to whom it may concern," wrote Bouilhet, and we can guess the name of the person concerned.[35]

The cross-Channel voyage was only the beginning of a summer marathon: two weeks in England with Juliet, then to Saint Gratien to visit the Princess, to Chartres for research, to Ouville in Normandy to visit Achille's daughter, with whom his mother was staying, and to Dieppe, where the Commanvilles had their summer home. We know little about his stay in London, only that he lived at the Herberts', spending his evenings with Juliet, while finding time to pursue his research, notably at the South Kensington Museum, where he indulged his curiosity about ceramics, acquiring information to be used for the factory that his character Jacques Arnoux was to manage.[36]

It was while he was in Dieppe with Caroline that he learned he had been accepted into the Legion of Honor, which gave him the right to wear the five-pointed badge that at the time bore the likeness of Napoleon I, the founder of this order of merit. (He was then one of some seventy thousand persons who had received this distinction.) In France's National Archives one can see the letter written by Sainte-Beuve to the minister of education, Victor Duruy, in July 1866; the critic asked the minister how it could have happened that this distinguished writer — who had been personally received by the Chief of State and the Empress at Compiegne — had not been honored.[37] "Do I find the hand of a friend in this?" Flaubert asked Sainte-Beuve. Did he mean a man or a woman friend? For Mathilde had been the first to inform him that he was to receive the decoration.

To the Goncourts, whose names did not appear on the list of new knights of the Order, he expressed regret that they had not been cited while a best-selling writer of adventure stories, Pierre-Alexis Ponson du Terrail, had.[38]

CHAPTER THIRTY

GEORGE SAND

A FRIEND wrote to congratulate him on his decoration, and Flaubert seized the occasion of his reply to talk about his work-in-progress. (The friend was Alfred Maury, but it could have been anyone; Flaubert needed to get these things said.) He was pessimistic about his novel; it seemed mediocre because its very conception was defective. "I want to represent a psychological condition that has never been described before. But the milieu in which my characters act is so rich and swarming with life that they are in constant danger of being swallowed up. I am therefore obliged to place on a secondary plane those things that are actually the most interesting."[1] Once again, when *A Sentimental Education* was finally published, some critics sought to make the same point, though few proved as articulate about it as the author had been.

He decided to stay in Croisset to work, and not to budge until the opening of Bouilhet's next play, *La Conjuration d'Amboise*. At the end of August 1866 George Sand, returning from a visit to Alexandre Dumas on the Channel coast, accepted Flaubert's longstanding invitation to come to Croisset. Once more we see the bear's cave as a first-time visitor did, for Sand put it all in her diary. This visitor found Flaubert's mother a charming old lady, the site calm, and the house comfortable. The service was good, everything was clean, and there was water — "everything one can desire." On her first evening there, her host read *The Temptation of Saint Anthony* to her, and they talked in his writing room until two. The next day they toured the countryside with Madame Flaubert, Caroline, and some friends, and in the afternoon Sand and Flaubert walked around the family property. She told her diary: "Flaubert sweeps me off my feet." [2]

Flaubert's friendship with Sand now assumed the tangible form of correspondence — letters of growing length in which they recorded the quotidian events of their separate lives and their feelings about things that mattered to them. They remained as unlike as ever in their art, she the chronicler of sentiments, he the artist who placed sentiment rather low on his list. But in talk, and in the written conversation of their letters, they were not so opposite as all that. "You are a being quite apart from the ordinary, very mysterious, but sweet as a lamb all the same," wrote Sand. She added that Sainte-Beuve, who admired Flaubert, also thought him to be wicked. He replied that he was neither mysterious nor wicked; on the contrary, he felt himself to be a bourgeois beneath the skin. [3]

His notary surely would have agreed. His appeal to Fovard for money had come to nothing, and now he turned to Jules Duplan, cautioning him that he did not wish his family — especially his mother — to know about his "excesses." He hoped that Jules's brother Ernest, who of course was also a notary, might help. He required six or seven thousand francs, to be paid back in three years, after the publication of his new novel. Duplan suggested that he rely on his family notary; Flaubert replied that Fovard was not answering his letters.

So he returned to the other scheme: "All writers receive money in advance," he affirmed; why could he not get six thousand francs from Michel Lévy as an advance on the ten thousand Lévy was to give him for *A Sentimental Education*? Surely such a request would not dishonor him? "If Lévy refuses, I shall hold a grudge against him eternally. . . ." [4]

Lévy made a counteroffer, not of an advance but of a simple loan; he would hold on to the promissory notes and not let them circulate. Flaubert did not believe that assurance. He was certain that if he signed the notes, his nephew Commanville and his brother, Achille, would find out. He would rather stay in Croisset indefinitely and hold down his expenses. But he had a memory, and Lévy would regret not having honored his request. Oh, why had Jules Duplan's brother let him promise his next novel to that publisher! To this Jules objected that Ernest had only followed Flaubert's instructions that Lévy must take *Salammbô* sight unseen; to cover himself, Lévy had demanded an option on the "modern" novel to follow.

Flaubert insisted on firmness. He begged Ernest Duplan to be "very insolent" with Lévy. He thought it would be a good joke to lead Lévy to believe that he had asked for the money only to show him up. (The reader may be reminded of Antonio in Shakespeare's *Merchant of Venice*, who berates Shylock even as he seeks to borrow from him.)

All the while, he worked. He told Jules Duplan that he was now engaged in the most difficult part of his novel. By New Year's he hoped to be halfway through. On October 1 he wrote, "I struggle with abominable doubts."[5] By the middle of that month he had a new concern. Bouilhet's play was scheduled to open at the Odéon, and once again Flaubert was enlisted to drum up support among his influential friends. That meant going to Paris. George Sand suggested that Bouilhet and Flaubert dine with her before the opening, but Flaubert had to tell her, "*One does not dine* the day of a premiere, when one is very nervous and has to take care of another nervous person." The play opened on October 29. In her diary Sand noted: "Great success. Pretty play, exquisite verse, well played. . . . Flaubert and Bouilhet are happy and charming in their contentment — well deserved."[6]

The Goncourts had attended a rehearsal, and had not been impressed. "The play designed to succeed," they dismissed it, "with false history, false poetry. Not one true note, not one true feeling. . . ."[7] Certainly they were right about its being a play designed to succeed, for it went on and on, with more than a hundred consecutive performances, full houses, and an invitation for Bouilhet from the Emperor in Compiegne.[8]

On the Saturday following the opening, November 3, George Sand took the Rouen train with Flaubert. They were met at the station by both Dr. Achille Flaubert and Madame Flaubert; Sand was of course a celebrity. There was much conversation in Croisset, and much reading. After Flaubert read his fairy play to her, Sand noted in her diary: "It is full of admirable and charming things, too long, too rich, too full." At two-thirty in the morning she was hungry, so they went down to the kitchen for cold chicken and then outside to get water from the pump. After that they smoked and talked until four. The next day she managed to get her host to take a walk with her, which for him was "heroic." They climbed the hill to Canteleu for the view. Then, after dinner that night, *she* read to *him*. The following day it rained, but they were committed to taking a steamboat trip to Rouen for a long day's tour of the city followed by dinner at Caroline's and a visit to the Saint Romain Fair to watch a pantomime. In gray, cold weather the next day, Flaubert read *A Sentimental Education* to her, from ten in the evening until two the following morning. She found it quite good, she told her diary.[9] "Although too kindly and too ready with compliments," her host wrote Edma Roger des Genettes, "she shows acuteness in her perceptions, as long as they do not disturb her socialist hobbyhorse."[10]

"I don't know what sort of sentiment I have for you," he wrote Sand after she left Croisset, "but I am experiencing a kind of tenderness that I have felt for no one else until now." "Age does not matter," she replied, "for I feel in you a protection of infinite goodness, and one evening when you called your mother 'my girl,' I had tears in my eyes." She made an interesting observation about *A Sentimental Education:* "It's exquisite, but it's curious — there is a whole side of you that isn't revealed and isn't betrayed in what you write." They begin to refer to each other as old troubadours. "They were most pleasant, those late-night talks of ours," he wrote her. "There were moments when I had to restrain myself from pecking at you like a big baby."[11]

In their work, in their approach to art, they remained as far apart as ever. Sand, for example, could not understand why writing had to be so difficult, so painful for him. And he had to tell her that he did not believe that a novelist had any right to express an opinion: did God express an opinion?[12]

He now lived in total solitude, he reported to Edma Roger des Genettes in December. "I hear no sound other than the crackling of my fire and the ticktock of my clock. I work by lamplight for ten hours out of every twenty-four."[13] He was still in hibernation in the early weeks of January 1867, when he wrote Jules and Edmond de Goncourt. He was bored and working too hard, and yet he was not sure what he was accomplishing. "No matter. I think I have gone beyond the emptiest part of my interminable novel. . . . By the light of my lamp I roar out my sentences in the silence of my office. I go to bed at four and wake at noon." He confided to the brothers that he was chaste, and didn't even feel like masturbating. "Which does not prevent Madame Sand from thinking that from time to time 'a beautiful lady comes to see me,' so little do women understand that one can live without them."[14] He explained to Sand: "Beautiful ladies have occupied my mind a great deal, but have taken little of my time. To call me an anchorite is a more just comparison than you think. . . ."[15]

And yet he was to live an extraordinary moment this very month of January. Elisa Schlesinger — the Elisa of Trouville but also the Madame Arnoux of *A Sentimental Education* — Elisa was in Mantes. It was time not to ignore her. What Bouilhet jokingly referred to as Flaubert's "romantic rendezvous" would furnish a useful case study for his novel.[16] We honestly know nothing about their meeting in Mantes, but this has not stopped writers from imagining the scene. The next-to-last chapter of *A Sentimental Education* provides a logical account of this final meeting between Frédéric and Madame Arnoux; the date is given as March 1867, which is close enough to Flaubert's real-life rendezvous with Elisa. In the novel, as in reality, the woman he loves resides far from Paris, and is chaste; her husband is old and ill. Her daughter is married; her son in the army. "But we meet again!" she exclaims. "I am so happy!" She confesses that she had been afraid of him in the past, and afraid for herself. They recall old times. After a sigh she says, "In any case, we have loved each other so much." "Yet without belonging to each other," he replies. "It was probably better that way," says she. He disagrees: "No! no! how happy we would have been!" "Oh I believe that, with a love like yours!" she cries.

She removes her hat, and in the light he sees her white hair. He is shocked but proceeds to tell her how much she has meant to him over the years. They embrace; he says he has never married because of her; they are now close to consummation. But Frédéric breaks away; it would be almost incestuous to go further, and he also fears that the memory would disgust him later on. She admires his restraint. She kisses his forehead as a mother would. They would not meet again.[17]

Back in Croisset, there was a duty to perform. Michel Lévy was lending Flaubert five thousand francs; should he thank him? Jules Duplan thought he should. So he wrote Lévy on January 27: "As I have the habit of not forgetting either good or bad deeds, I shall always remember yours with pleasure. . . . I shake your hand and am more than ever your devoted Gve Flaubert." Then he informed Duplan of his intention to begin his Paris season in the latter half of February. He had worked well, he said, but confessed that he did not know what his writing was worth. "This is what is atrocious in my book, that it has to be all written before one can judge it. No major scene, no piece of fine writing, not even a metaphor, for the slightest embroidery will mar the texture."[18]

Bouilhet's play had reached its hundredth performance, and there was to be a celebration. Flaubert accompanied his friend to Paris on February 19, and while there learned that his family's Courtavent farm near Nogent had been sold. His mother promised to share the proceeds with her children, which meant that Gustave would receive ten thousand francs. Half of that would be used to reimburse Michel Lévy's loan, or as Flaubert explained it to Duplan, "I'll spit up half of it for the Israelite."[19]

In Paris he worked — this time on the revolution of 1848, making use of the library of Parliament. He eschewed society, he told Caroline;[20] yet he took up his seat at the Magny restaurant. This time he was to meet a new face, an American friend of George Sand's named Henry Harrisse. The Goncourts dismissed him at first sight as a "kind of Yankee journalist," and judged him an idiot, but he happened to be an attorney and a historian; born of American parents in Paris, he had published works of criticism and history. He had done an English translation of Ernest Renan's *Life of Jesus*, and was introduced into the Magny circle by Renan. "The American in question is charming," Sand assured Flaubert. "He literally has a passion for you, and he writes me that after having seen you he likes you more than ever."

Writing from her country home in Nohant, in the far-off Indre district, Sand informed Flaubert that she would soon be in Paris again. "You will tell me at what hours you do not receive the fair sex, and when sixtyish troubadours will not be disturbing you." He hastened to reassure her that neither she nor anyone else would find the fair sex at his Boulevard du Temple lodgings.[21] In fact Flaubert had himself examined by Dr. Cloquet — that is, had his testicles examined — and was informed that he suffered from a condition "frequent among ecclesiastics": he did not ejaculate often enough (so Flaubert confided to Bouilhet).[22] At the same time, their friend Sainte-Beuve was really ill, with a genital disorder that restricted his movements. This had not prevented him, however, from getting up in the Senate chamber (his services to the Empire had won him appointment to that body) to defend freedom of thought against certain Church authorities who sought to reduce Ernest Renan to silence because Renan's best-selling *Life of Jesus* had taken a rational approach to a mystical subject. It was a courageous position to take in those days — Renan himself lost his professorship at the Collège de France — and Flaubert hastened to tell Sainte-Beuve: "Thanks for all of us."[23]

Flaubert received George Sand and her son, Maurice, at Boulevard du Temple; he in turn was invited to dine with Prince Napoleon at Jeanne de Tourbey's home, and also dined with Princess Mathilde on Rue de Courcelles. Despite all that, he suffered from a bad cold that kept him from making field trips out of Paris to visit earthenware workshops, and he could not finish his novel before doing that. "I'm laboring away at the 1848 revolution with fury," he told Bouilhet. "Do you know how many books I've read and made notes on in six weeks? Twenty-seven, good friend. Which didn't prevent me from writing ten pages." [24] When at last he could go out, he rushed off to Creil, in the countryside north of Paris, which was to be the site of Jacques Arnoux's pottery factory. He returned there twice, the last time standing in the rain for two hours while taking notes.

Again he was without funds (the sale of the Courtavent farm had not yet been finalized), but he didn't dare tell that to his mother. He did say so to Caroline, though, and her husband advanced five hundred francs on Gustave's share of the farm. When the sale was final, his share came to 15,566 francs, so he asked Commanville to keep the five hundred francs he had advanced and to send him an additional five thousand to cover his debts, and not to say anything about all of this to Madame Flaubert. Commanville remained his banker for the balance. There was also a significant change in Bouilhet's fortunes now. The curator of Rouen's municipal library had died. Bouilhet rushed up to submit his candidacy for the job, and of course received the support of Flaubert's brother as well as of the Flauberts' well-placed friends. So Bouilhet would now have a guaranteed income of four thousand francs per year. [25]

On his return to Croisset late in May, Flaubert found his mother looking older, older even than her seventy-three years. She had been ill while he was in Paris, but it was agreed that it would only have frightened her if he had returned earlier than planned. [26] Living in hibernation was not going to keep him from pursuing his research, and now that Bouilhet was in charge at the Rouen library, he could get whatever he needed from there with a minimum of difficulty. [27] But his hibernation — or rather, his estivation — was hardly impenetrable. There was an irresistible invitation from Paris. Several foreign monarchs, including Alexander II of Russia, had come to Paris to visit the Exposition Universelle, an ambitious fair with fifty thousand exhibitors and palatial, if temporary, pavilions designed to display the glories of the Empire. Napoleon III planned a reception for his distinguished guests at the Tuileries on June 10, and as Flaubert explained the matter to his niece, these sovereigns wished to see him as "one of the most splendid curiosities of France." It was quite an affair; he compared himself, in a letter to Mathilde, to Madame Bovary impressed by her first ball. During his thirty-six hours in the capital, he also managed to do more field research, at the Jockey Club, at the Café Anglais, and in an attorney's office. He calculated that he had spent twenty hours in cabs; so he told Jules Duplan when asking him to drop in at the Café Anglais to pick up an 1847 menu that had been promised him.[28]

The month of July was devoted to writing, partly at his mother's apartment in Rouen, as the house in Croisset was being painted. Indeed, for a week he lived in a small pavilion at the bottom of the garden, which survives today. His mother continued to decline. To cheer her up he took her to Paris in August to visit the Exposition.[29]

We now know something that Flaubert all but kept to himself that summer. His intention had been to go on from Paris to London — to see Juliet, of course. He did not go because he was struck by violent diarrhea — he thought it was due to the heat. This "grotesque indisposition" even kept him from a promised visit to Mathilde at her Saint Gratien villa outside Paris; he thought that he might actually have "a touch" of cholera.[30] Back in Croisset, he got to work again, and then in mid-September went up to Dieppe to see his niece. If he was to finish his novel in two years, he could no longer budge from his armchair — so he explained to George Sand, who was hoping to lure him to Nohant that autumn. His next travel would be to Paris, again for research; he was there from November 7 to November 11, returning to an empty house in Croisset. This is how he described his daily existence to Ernest Feydeau: "I sit down to work around twelve-thirty; at five I doze off, sometimes until seven, and then I dine; then I plunge back into work until three-thirty or four in the morning, and I try to get some sleep after reading a chapter of the sacrosanct, immense, and extra-fine Rabelais."

He was still alone on his forty-sixth birthday, which gave him the leisure and the inspiration for some "philosophical reflections." "Looking back," he wrote Jules Duplan, "I do not see that I have wasted my life, but what have I actually done! It's time to produce something decent."[31]

CHAPTER THIRTY-ONE

TURGENEV

FLAUBERT was back in Paris at the end of January, and his first encounter with friends and fellow writers at the Magny was something of a celebration, with eighteen at the table, including Louis Bouilhet, the Goncourt brothers, Théophile Gautier, and George Sand, who was escorted by Henry Harrisse. Four nights later he was again in this restaurant; he had invited George Sand to his home for dinner, but Prince Napoleon had also asked her, so Flaubert joined them at their favorite meeting place. "Charming dinner during which the Prince is splendid and the brightest of us all, as always," Sand told her diary.[1]

One of those rare family documents dates from this point. It is a letter from Madame Flaubert to her second son, written from her winter quarters in Rouen on February 10; she dates the letter as "anniversary of my marriage in 1812, birth of Achille, February 10, 1813" (in fact the official marriage and birth certificates show both events as falling on February 9). She complains about her financial problems, the bills for firewood, wine, and taxes, but this time she does not blame Gustave. They are both responsible, she declares, "for I am convinced that you and I are robbed more than anyone else because of our carelessness and extreme negligence."[2] By the beginning of spring, Gustave made a shy approach to his niece and her husband, who of course was his banker now. "Do me the favor of asking your spouse how much I can expect from him on April 1," he asked Caroline. "For since the first of January my vast capital, deposited in his hands, has grown by . . . is it one or two thousand francs? I don't remember."[3]

Being in Paris allowed him to do more of the rigorous fieldwork on which he insisted. Now, for example, in order to guarantee the authenticity of a scene in which Madame Arnoux's child struggles for life in the throes of a severe croup, he had to see a case of that disease firsthand. "It was abominable, and I came out of it heartbroken," he told his niece, "but Art obliges."[4] For this episode we have a witness, a young intern at the Sainte Eugénie hospital in Paris. His professor informed him that a friend wished to observe "the symptoms of croup when they have reached the stage of suffocation"; when the intern came upon such a case, he was to call on Gustave Flaubert at Boulevard du Temple. The young man liked that idea, for Flaubert had a certain reputation among medical students, many of whom knew by heart Homais's letter to a Rouen newspaper in *Madame Bovary*. On the first appearance of a child with advanced croup, he rushed to Flaubert's apartment, finding the writer wearing golden slippers, trousers of an incredible girth, a large robe in bright colors, and an Oriental hat he could not identify — a tarboosh? In any case, Flaubert changed in haste and accompanied the young man to the hospital, bombarding him with questions along the way. At the hospital he was taken to see the little patient, who showed "premonitory signs of asphyxia" and was about to be operated on. "I've seen enough," Flaubert told the intern, after only two or three minutes of observation. "I beg you, deliver him of that." The operation got under way, but when the intern was able to look around, he discovered that Flaubert had left. "A tracheotomy was much too much for him," the professor explained to his assistant. "He is extremely sensitive."[5]

The Goncourts manifested their impatience with Flaubert at this time. Calling off a dinner he was to have given his friends on a Monday night, Flaubert told the brothers: "I am invited to a concert by the Emperor. And since I already refused an invitation to a ball . . ."[6] But he saw his friends the following Wednesday at the regular soirée of the Princess, and in the privacy of their midnight jottings, they took revenge. Flaubert had turned Mathilde's gatherings into a provincial drawing room: "Whatever story is told, one can be certain in advance that he will say when it is over, or even before it is over, 'Oh! I know a better one,' and whichever person is mentioned: 'I know him better than you do.' " (Later they would call Flaubert "a Norman savage," but that diary entry was subsequently crossed out.)[7]

We also have an extraordinary testimonial to his impatience with Paris during this period. For suddenly the construction going on at Boulevard du Temple, the late-night merriment of neighboring cab-

arets, seemed too much for him. On Sunday, May 17, he told the
Goncourts, he returned home at eleven-thirty, prepared for a good
night's sleep. He blew out the candle and at once heard the blast of
a trombone and the beating of drums. A wedding party was in full
swing downstairs; it was hot, and all the windows were open. At six
the next morning, the masons took over, so an hour later he was on
his way to check in at the Grand Hotel. There he was told that he
would have to wait until a room was ready. As soon as he got into it,
someone began hammering nails into a crate nearby. He tried to
change his room and finally went off to his old favorite, the Hotel du
Helder. There the room was as dark as a tomb but hardly as quiet —
guests were shouting, carriages were rumbling along outside, iron pails
were being moved about in the courtyard. At one in the afternoon, he
was back at Boulevard du Temple, packing. He went to Du Camp's
apartment, hoping to sleep there that night, but masons were putting
up a wall at the rear of the garden. So he tried a public bath: sounds
of children playing in the courtyard, and a piano. He returned to the
Helder, where he found the clothing his servant had laid out for him
for the Tuileries ball that evening. But he had not eaten; thinking
hunger might be responsible for his nervousness, he went off to the
Café de Paris. As soon as he was seated there, a fellow diner vomited
alongside him. He left to go back to his hotel, looked again at his
formal clothing, and ordered his servant to pack up. He hailed a cab
for the station to catch the night train to Rouen; on the way, his trunk
fell off the top deck and struck his shoulder.[8] Even in Croisset it took
some days before he could sleep through the night; at thirty-three
leagues' distance, he still heard the masons at work.[9]

George Sand gave him time to recover, and then she joined him in
his retreat. "Flaubert is waiting at the station and obliges me to go
pee so that I don't become like Sainte-Beuve. [It was known that the
critic urinated with extreme discomfort now.] It is raining in Rouen,
as always. I find Mama less deaf, but alas without legs! I have lunch;
I talk while walking under the arbor, which the rain does not pene-
trate. I sleep an hour and a half on a chair, and Flaubert on a sofa.
We talk again. We dine with his niece and her husband. . . . I go to
bed at midnight." The next day was "superb," and they visited a Romanesque abbey church; that night Flaubert read her three hundred
pages of his work-in-progress, to her delight. She retired at two. On
Tuesday Flaubert took her back to Rouen, where they called on
Bouilhet at the library, and so to the station.[10]

He worked hard, but in July he was ready to travel again. First to the Channel coast to visit his nieces, then south to Fontainebleau to explore the famous forest for an important scene in his novel. Of course he had to be in Paris, too, and worried about that; he asked Jules Duplan to find out whether the masons were still making an infernal racket. They were, so he got the faithful Duplan to book him a hotel on the boulevard — anything except the Grand, he said.[11]

From Paris he visited Mathilde's summer drawing room at Saint Gratien. The Goncourts were also on hand to report on their fellow guest. "The Princess yesterday [August 6] delivered a terrible scolding to Flaubert concerning his visits to the Tourbey woman. In the dignified manner of a princess and of a woman of the world, she complained this morning, almost humorously, of having to share with such women the company and thoughts of men like Taine, Renan, and Sainte-Beuve, who stole twenty minutes from her, when dining at her home, to go off to see that tramp."[12] Despite the scolding, Flaubert enjoyed Saint Gratien and the company of the Princess, and was sorry when it was time to go. "I was so troubled Thursday evening in leaving you that I did not have my head on my shoulders," he wrote her. "One will never know all the softness there is beneath my heavy gendarme's skin."[13]

He went back to Fontainebleau to do more exploring. We know how thorough he was because we can follow his itinerary — along the paths, up the slopes, on foot or in a carriage — in his notebook, where he described the scenery and even individual species of trees, jotted down the characteristics of the surrounding villages, and looked into an inn where his Frédéric was to sup with his Rosanette. And so on to Dieppe to see Caroline (and Alexandre Dumas), then home to Croisset to begin writing the Fontainebleau episode.[14]

His next obligation was the opening of the play made from George Sand's novel *Cadio*. It disturbed and annoyed him to have to make a trip to Paris that October, but he knew that he had no choice.[15] Sand thanked him, "you who move about so little," for coming down to be with her. Her letter is worth reading because it shows how different the friends really were. He had teased her for liking her actors and actresses; she replied, "I like them as I like the woods and fields, all things, all beings that I know a little and study always." This grand lady who had been a fiery young woman open to everything and everyone — to revolutions, to young and seductive men, to everyone's books and music — overwhelmed her friend the hermit. He was at a loss for words; in any case, he felt empty. "Since my return, my longest nights have not exceeded five hours, and now that my chapter is done I desperately need sleep," he wrote from Croisset.[16]

He told Ernest Feydeau that he was becoming more and more irritable and unsociable; he thought he would end up resembling Marat, the angry, diseased revolutionary leader.[17] Sand, for example, pressed him to come to Nohant for the baptism of her granddaughters. He was unhappy to have been asked. Three weeks earlier he had made a brief trip for dinner and had lost four days because of it. If he went to Nohant, he would lose a month: "Real images would replace in my poor brain the fictive images that I compose with such difficulty; my whole house of cards would come tumbling down."[18]

But if he would not go out into the world, the world might come to see him — at least the world as personified by Ivan Sergeyevich Turgenev, one of Russia's best living writers. The son of landowners, he could travel when and where he wished, and he did wish. He was born on October 28, 1818. In 1843, on his twenty-fifth birthday, he met the French critic Louis Viardot during a hunting party in Russia, and some days later heard Viardot's wife, Pauline, sing at the St. Petersburg Opera. She was then twenty-two, a renowned performer also known for her singular lack of beauty. But Turgenev was soon infatuated with her, and somehow Louis Viardot accepted this *amitié amoureuse*, which by the time of the revolution of 1848 had become simple *amour*. Indeed, Turgenev may have been the father of Pauline's fourth child.[19]

In 1862, the Russian published *Fathers and Sons*, whose most memorable character was a young nihilist. The novel aroused both student radicals, who thought the author was mocking them, and the conservative establishment; from then on, Turgenev no longer felt quite at home in mother Russia. Guy de Maupassant, who met Turgenev some years later at Flaubert's, marveled that he was even taller than Flaubert. By then Turgenev had long white hair, white brows, a large white beard, strong features, and a reassuringly friendly face. For Maupassant this "colossus" had timid, even childlike gestures; he spoke in a soft voice. With his artistic judgments, he broke the narrow mold of Parisian literary men, for he could compare all of the world's literatures.[20]

Flaubert had been seeing Turgenev on and off since 1863. Not long after their first meeting, Turgenev sent Flaubert two of his books. "For a long time," replied Flaubert, "you have been a master for me. But the more I study you, the more your talent overwhelms me." Just as reading *Don Quixote* made him wish to ride horseback "along a road white with dust" and to eat olives and raw onions, so Turgenev's work made him long for the snowy fields of Russia.[21]

"Since I saw you for the first time (in a kind of tavern across the Seine [the Magny restaurant]), I have felt a great sympathy for you," Turgenev wrote him now, in 1868. "There are few men, especially among Frenchmen, with whom I feel so tranquilly at ease and so wide awake at the same time; I have the feeling that I could talk with you for weeks at a time. . . ."[22]

Unfortunately for the continuity of their relationship, they were not often in the same place at the same time. Now, for example, Turgenev was off to Russia, but said that he would be in Baden-Baden in July and from there would visit Paris.[23] Flaubert was in Paris in July and reminded Turgenev of his promise, but the Russian was handicapped with what would be a frequent ailment — gout.[24] Finally they did meet, that autumn in Croisset; the happy day was Sunday, November 22, 1868. "There are few men whose company is better and whose minds are more seductive," Flaubert exclaimed to Mathilde.[25] On his return to Paris, Turgenev found a cheese Flaubert had shipped to him, together with some passages copied out of his novel-in-progress. If the whole book was as good as the fragments, Flaubert would have a masterpiece, he commented. He asked for Flaubert's photograph and — surprise — the camera-shy Flaubert sent him one.[26]

In a progress report to George Sand in December, Flaubert wrote: "I am working excessively and am at bottom overjoyed at the prospect of the *End*, which is approaching." He was doing nothing else, not even reading. "I'll return to Beauty when I am delivered of my hateful bourgeois characters."[27]

There was one ominous sign in this final month of the year. Louis Bouilhet was ill, with a mysterious ailment that could not be treated. He complained of anguish, spasms, moral as well as physical anxiety, and insomnia.[28] This refrain was to be heard regularly in the coming months, crescendo.

CHAPTER THIRTY-TWO

BOUILHET

EARLY IN JANUARY 1869, from Croisset, Flaubert wrote to his publisher, Michel Lévy: he expected to have *A Sentimental Education* done by May so that it could be at the printers in September.[1] "I see no one, I know nothing, I live like a stuffed bear": this to George Sand in the middle of the same month.[2] But before the end of January he was in Paris for an intense week of work — seven to nine hours in a carriage each day, so he said, to visit sites he would be writing about: funeral parlors, the Père Lachaise cemetery, the countryside of Montmorency, and shops that sold holy objects.[3]

On his first day home in Croisset, February 2, he wrote to Turgenev. He was anxious to finish his book and to have Turgenev's critique, "because yours will be that of a practician. . . ."[4] Until then he had counted on Louis Bouilhet for a friendly ear, but now their regular Sunday sessions seemed to be compromised. One such visit to Croisset was canceled because Bouilhet had symptoms of a cold. On the following Sunday he was still confined to his home, but now the cold had turned into something more like nerves. The week after that, he could not speak without coughing, so he felt it useless to go to see his friend in Croisset.[5]

Flaubert was finding it hard to end his novel, to conclude his vast panorama of his times, to make sense of the political, social, and personal history he was recording.[6] Still, at the end of March he felt ready to begin his Paris season; he intended to cloister himself *there* during the final days of writing.[7] When the cloister opened up, in May, it was to George Sand, who came to dinner at his lodgings to hear the next-to-last pages of the novel read by their author; she told her private diary that she liked what she had heard.[8] Flaubert and Sand were together again at the Wednesday reception given by Princess Mathilde, where the watchful Goncourts remarked that Flaubert used the polite *vous* with Sand while she let slip a more intimate *tu* in her response, upon which the Princess looked toward the Goncourts meaningfully. "Is it a lover's *tu*?" they wondered. "Or that of a second-string actress?"[9]

One of the things that came out of their meeting at Mathilde's was an offer by Sand to serve as an intermediary with their mutual publisher, Michel Lévy, who was doing her complete works at the time. Flaubert was hoping for an improvement in his contract with Lévy, and he sent a copy of it to Sand. She kept her promise. Lévy confirmed that he would pay ten thousand francs for Flaubert's modern novel; if it ran to two volumes, the sum would be doubled. Furthermore, if the book was successful, Flaubert would earn even more than that.[10]

Then on Sunday morning, May 16, 1869, at four minutes before five A.M. — so he dated his letter to Jules Duplan — he was able to say:

FINISHED! old man! yes, my book is finished!

He had not left his writing table since the previous day at eight in the morning; his head was spinning. A week later he was still feeling the effects. He had already recited the first three chapters to Mathilde and her circle, and they were demanding more; along with everything else he had to do, and his exhaustion, he was going to have to devote four sessions of four hours each to that. He later told Caroline that much of his success was due to the *way* he read rather than *what* he read.[11]

On the same Sunday that he wrote Caroline, the Goncourts came to Flaubert's and spied the finished manuscript on the green writing table; it reposed in a box specially made for this purpose, on which they could read the book's title. They decided that their friend "employed a solemnity that was slightly ridiculous" for the slightest thing he produced. They were not sure which was more lamentable, his vanity or his pride.[12] It is a pity that they could not see inside the elegant box. Pages covered — blanketed — with meticulous changes and scratchings-out: it was hardly the work of a dandy.[13]

Another piece of business occupied him in the final days of this Paris season. His apartment on Boulevard du Temple had proved to be too expensive. It was far from the places he needed to go and thus cost too much in carriages; and then the Commanvilles had a new house on the other side of town. Fovard, the notary, informed Flaubert that he had found a reasonable apartment for him (for fifteen hundred francs' annual rent) on Rue Murillo, facing the elegant Parc Monceau. If it was not far from the Commanvilles, it was even closer to Princess Mathilde's town house. Gustave lost no time before visiting what turned out to be a fourth-floor walk-up, with a succession of small rooms high above the fantasy landscape of the park. He took an immediate liking to it, signed a lease as soon as he could, and began choosing material to cover the walls, and to use for curtains.[14]

When he returned to Croisset early in June, he felt exhausted, suffered from a flu, and coughed and spat; he felt, he said, as if he had been beaten with a club. But this did not stop him from picking up the notes he had made for a final revision of *The Temptation of Saint Anthony*. Once again he was reading religious dogma.[15] He waited for Bouilhet to return from Paris so they could begin to correct the copy that had been made of his novel.

It was to be the last service Bouilhet could render. In his latest letter, dated June 2, he had described his condition: a depression he could no longer fight off. "I assure you that I am very sick, at times; I feel bested by things that in the past would not have touched me."[16] When they finally did get together later that month, Flaubert found his friend "fragile and sad."[17] All the doctors could say was that he needed to get away from Rouen. They suggested the inevitable Vichy.

Bouilhet was not the only one who been put to work on *A Sentimental Education*; Flaubert had also left a copy with the man who had shared his experience of Paris in 1848, and who had had more vivid adventures. Maxime Du Camp took the assignment seriously. He turned in twelve pages of detailed notes and offered frank observations of a kind Flaubert could not always get from closer friends. "You accomplished a tour de force in writing such a book, on a subject that is not a subject, without a plot and without striking characters," Du Camp wrote him on June 8. He liked some of the scenes and some of the personae, but he felt that the manuscript needed considerable cutting. He deplored certain elements of Flaubert's style, of his grammar; even the title of the book came in for criticism. Rather than "Story of a Young Man" for the subtitle, he suggested "Story of a Simpleton." (He was not the only one to question the title, but could Flaubert have *accepted* that?) For him, the best title would be "Mediocre People."[18]

Flaubert even asked Du Camp's compliant mistress Adèle Husson for help, and received another detailed report. She warned that the verb *coucher* — literally, "to go to bed with" — would upset women readers. Du Camp seconded that; it was true that men talked that way, he admitted, but in *Madame Bovary* Flaubert had been pleased with himself for having his peasants speak proper French. So Flaubert changed "goes to bed with" to "becomes her lover." [19]

Now he put aside *A Sentimental Education* for *Saint Anthony*. He thought he could link his saint's hallucinations together by some logical connection, and thus heighten the dramatic interest of the work. By the end of June he was working on the new-old project "like a madman." [20] "The joy of not having to depict and dramatize bourgeois people delights me despite everything," he explained to George Sand. "Everything" included the health of Louis Bouilhet, who was being treated in Vichy — still with no clear notion of the nature of his illness. Flaubert confessed to his niece that Bouilhet's illness was affecting him in a very practical way just then, for he needed his friend for that final run-through of *A Sentimental Education*.[21]

It is now thought that Bouilhet suffered from a severe kidney deficiency, diagnosed at the time as albuminous nephritis, perhaps complicated toward the end by uremia, a case of Bright's disease that had probably begun over a year earlier.[22] Even the best mineral water was not going to help.

The Vichy doctor realized this and sent the sick man back to Rouen. Earlier, when a group of doctors, including one brought up from Paris, had examined Bouilhet in Rouen, he had refused to see Achille Flaubert, afraid (Gustave thought) to learn the truth. But when Bouilhet returned from Vichy, Dr. Flaubert did examine him, confirming the diagnosis of the Vichy doctor: he was incurable. There was an unpleasant incident when Bouilhet's two sisters came down from Cany, their hometown, to create what Flaubert described as "religious scenes." Bouilhet coolly sent them away. (Of course, he lived with his mistress Léonie and her son.) Flaubert felt that Bouilhet's anger was helping keep him strong, and he went off on a planned visit to Paris on July 17, a Saturday. He was to learn that on the following morning at five, Bouilhet had become delirious. He died in his Léonie's arms. He was forty-seven. On Monday morning, Flaubert was awakened by the doorkeeper, bearing a telegram. He packed hurriedly, wrote a note to Du Camp, went out to inform Duplan, and then walked the streets until the next train left for Rouen. "In seeing the steeples of Mantes," he was to tell Du Camp, "I thought I would go mad, and I am sure that I wasn't very far from that."

He led the funeral service with Charles d'Osmoy. From Léonie he learned that in his final hours, the free spirit Bouilhet had wanted to marry her; she had refused, to show him that he was not going to die, and her son had approved of her refusal. Following the coffin up the slope to the hilltop cemetery, with a crowd he estimated at some two thousand mourners, Flaubert had the feeling that Bouilhet was walking alongside him at the funeral of someone else, and that they were talking about it. It was very hot, and he had difficulty breathing; finally he was led away by his brother and an unknown bystander.

Bouilhet had left his books and papers to Léonie's son, Philippe Leparfait. He had requested that four of his friends, Flaubert among them, decide what to do with his unpublished works, which included a volume of poems, four plays in prose, and a verse drama called *Mademoiselle Aïssé*.[23] In fact Flaubert was treated as if he were the surviving heir, for he received letters of sympathy from all over.

His actions from that moment on were to show what it had meant for him to lose "my counselor, my guide, my companion of thirty-seven years," as he expressed it. Within a matter of days he had set up a committee to raise funds for a suitable monument to the dead poet. Was Bouilhet worth a monument? The point would be debated. Already there was the cruel comment of Jules Barbey d'Aurevilly: "Monsieur Bouilhet, who has just died, will occupy our attention this week, but I do not believe he will have more than a week's time, like domestic servants who are discharged. After that week, and despite the fact that a play has been accepted by the Odéon for which the author's death will serve as a come-on, and which will be performed like a symphonic Requiem, this poor Bouilhet will be definitively sent to oblivion."[24]

At the end of the first week of August, Flaubert was in Paris again, bearing the copied and corrected manuscript of *A Sentimental Education*. He also wanted to hasten preparations at the new flat at Rue Murillo so he could begin to use it that autumn. And of course he was taking his role as Bouilhet's literary executor seriously.[25] Getting *Mademoiselle Aïssé* into a theater would require governmental intervention, so he began by calling on the appropriate officials, and soon the director of the Odéon theater was promising that the play would be presented without changes.[26] "I am prepared to be mean, vicious, and unsociable," he promised Bouilhet's heir, Philippe Leparfait. "I shall avenge our poor old man, who took so much from those dogs."[27]

Later in August he began to receive proofs of *A Sentimental Education*. Reading them, and commuting between Boulevard du Temple and Rue Murillo, filled his days. He took up temporary quarters at Saint Gratien and even corrected his proofs there; his valet acted as courier. Flaubert reported to Caroline, obviously with pleasure, that the gossip columns were talking about his forthcoming novel. Four different articles had described the famous box in which he carried his manuscript. He had other concerns: the Odéon was unhappy with the second act of Bouilhet's play, so he agreed to revise it; he was also working on Bouilhet's last poems, and thought he might have to finance their publication himself.[28]

As usual, he showed himself to be a demanding author. His correspondence with his publisher tells us that he considered sentence rhythm more important than grammar, and he waged continual war against word repetition. He urged the printer to whip up his workers so the novel could be in bookstores early in November, leaving time for it to be read and talked about before the opening of Parliament, at which point politics would crowd out everything else.[29]

Then Sainte-Beuve, who had been so ill for so long, died without giving his friends an opportunity to say goodbye. We know from George Sand's diary that Flaubert's grief was genuine, for she watched him at the funeral. (Everyone who counted in letters, arts, and science was there, along with very young and very common people — but no senators and no priests, Sand was delighted to observe.)[30]

Charles d'Osmoy joined Flaubert for another revision of the fairy play they had written with Bouilhet, *Le Château des Coeurs*.[31] On November 5, Sarah Bernhardt played the fourth act of Bouilhet's *La Conjuration d'Amboise* as part of a benefit performance.[32] And then Flaubert found a new recruit to Bouilhet's cause in Edgar Raoul-Duval, one of the first guests at his new lodgings on Rue Murillo. Raoul-Duval, who had come to Rouen as state prosecutor with a fine reputation as an orator, was not a Norman, but his wife was, and he was to make his name in his adopted province. His choice of the unconventional Flaubert as a friend suggests how unlike the Rouen bourgeoisie he was.[33]

Soon it was time for *A Sentimental Education* to appear on bookshop counters. Would the political agitation of the moment affect its reception? The last legislative elections had given the opposition a majority in the largest cities, but the Emperor had not convened Parliament as he should have, and some deputies were threatening to take matters into their own hands.[34]

PART VII

CHAPTER THIRTY-THREE

FAILURE

THERE WAS NO REVOLUTION, no fighting in the streets, not even a palace coup. And still *A Sentimental Education* failed to excite the book-buying public in the way Flaubert (and his publisher) had hoped it would. The complaint of establishment critics was summed up cruelly by Barbey d'Aurevilly, in the space once filled by Sainte-Beuve's column, in *Le Constitutionnel* of November 19, 1869, two days after the publication of Flaubert's book: "*A Sentimental Education* was a famous book, like *Salammbô*, before publication; for ever since *Madame Bovary*, the press does not fail to play the trumpet in advance in honor of Flaubert and his works." Barbey said that *Salammbô* had not lived up to its advance publicity, and so the sycophants had employed a similar tactic with the present work, kneeling, like the Wise Men at the cradle of the Christ child, before "the box that contained Flaubert's manuscript. . . ."

Barbey d'Aurevilly characterized the author as "a man of rare ideas who, when he has one, cooks and recooks it. . . ." The new novel showed this "empty head." The mediocre young man who served as the hero of *A Sentimental Education* was quite common, and everything around him was the same — friends, mistresses, society, feelings, passions. . . . Barbey blamed it all on the "vile school" of Realism, which obliged Flaubert to portray vulgarity as he found it.

"We protest as we read the book," wrote Edmond Schérer in *Le Temps* on December 7, "but we read it." This was the best Flaubert could hope for from the influential press. Even friends and acquaintances who received autographed copies were afraid to compromise themselves; they simply changed the subject. "Brave men are rare,"

Flaubert complained to George Sand. (One of these few brave men was Emile Zola, who liked what Flaubert had done and told him so.)[1]

He was hardly indifferent to criticism; had he ever really been? Finally he swallowed his pride and appealed to Sand: would she be his spokesman? She had already told him that she loved his book, which she felt displayed the energy of the best of Balzac but with more truth. "If they do not treat you fairly," she had promised, "I'll get angry and say what I think." Two days after his appeal, Sand wrote from Nohant to inform him that she had written a review (it was then two A.M.) and was waiting for a telegram from Flaubert indicating to which newspaper she should send it. He replied the next evening (the mail service was also excellent between the village of Nohant and Paris) to confirm what he said in a telegram he had sent her: his choice was Emile de Girardin's *La Liberté*, a widely read afternoon daily. (He had already made sure that the paper would publish her article as soon as it was received.)[2] In her review, Sand explained that Flaubert had sought to offer examples of the many kinds of people to be found in modern society, when novels usually depicted only two or three types. But the novel must be in constant movement, she insisted, and in *A Sentimental Education,* Flaubert had succeeded in presenting a new feeling: indignant laughter at the perversity and cowardice of the works of man. . . .[3]

Soon enough, however, Flaubert himself was acknowledging the defects of his book, even expounding on them. To a critic in *Le Journal de Rouen* he expressed his gratitude that at last someone had understood what was really wrong with the book: its repetitions, the artifice of its composition.[4] A decade later, he was still explaining why the novel had failed. It had been too true, he announced to Edma Roger des Genettes; it lacked "the falsity of perspective." "Every work of art must have a pivot, a summit, it has to make a pyramid. . . ."[5]

Was the novel selling? At first it seemed so. Lévy had printed three thousand copies, and the first batch quickly disappeared. But then sales slowed, and eventually stopped. In 1873, four years after publication, the original printing had yet to be sold out, so Lévy did a cheaper edition in order to earn his money back. Flaubert had received sixteen thousand francs as an advance, which sum took into account the fact that *A Sentimental Education* was longer than *Salammbô* but not quite twice as long. Lévy had published the new book at twelve francs for the two volumes, a high price for the time.

This fact, compounded by poor reviews and perhaps also political unrest, seemed sufficient to explain the poor sales.[6]

All the same, Flaubert gave himself a Christmas present. For the first time, he would visit George Sand in Nohant, the family estate in the Indre valley where she had been raised and had lived the many lives she wrote about, the Nohant of Franz Liszt and Chopin, the Nohant that already seemed the shrine it was to become after her death. In renewing her invitation, Sand reminded him that her village was "a hundred thousand leagues from literary life and Paris society." He took a morning train on December 23 and arrived in Nohant at five-thirty that afternoon, following a two-and-a-half-hour coach ride from the Châteauroux railroad station. There were parlor games and singing that first evening, and bedtime was at one, as Sand noted in her ever-ready diary. On Friday, the day before Christmas, it rained and snowed, but the assembly was merry all the same. Flaubert had presents for the grandchildren of his hostess. During the afternoon she "received" in her bedroom — Flaubert, but also her longtime friend Edmond Plauchut, whom she had first met when he was a young journalist. After dinner there were marionettes and a raffle, all among appropriate holiday decorations. "Flaubert enjoys himself like a child," she observed. They went to bed at three. Lunch was served late on Christmas day. In the afternoon Flaubert read *Le Château des Coeurs* to the company; Sand told her diary that it was pleasant enough but not "destined to succeed." They spent another merry evening, with Flaubert the life of the party. On December 27, the snow fell continuously; to entertain his fellow guests, Flaubert dressed in women's clothing and did a Spanish dance with Plauchut. Some neighbors arrived, and that calmed them down. Flaubert said his goodbyes that evening, for he was to leave at dawn.[7]

Back in Paris, he sat down with the old manuscript of *The Temptation of Saint Anthony*. He missed his "midwife," he told Sand, "he who read my thoughts more clearly than I": Bouilhet. He decided that he had more reading to do for this book.[8]

Perhaps it was now that he heard the rumor — something was said about it at a dinner attended by the Goncourts — that Louise Colet was about to publish his letters. He wrote Edmond a worried note asking for details.[9] We do not know what Goncourt told him, but we do know that Flaubert was still very much in Louise Colet's thoughts. She had been to Egypt, along with Gautier and other celebrities in-

vited to the inauguration of the Suez Canal, and had composed the
expected poems dealing with her first experience of that civilization.
But she also wrote an account of the trip that was not published until
after her death. From this we learn that she actually sought to find
Flaubert's dancing prostitutes, or as she put it, "to discover as a living
mummy one of those seductive *almées* who helped him tear and revolt my heart in his travel journal." For twenty years had passed since
Flaubert had destroyed their love.

She went on to describe a dream — a hallucination — she had experienced on the Nile: Flaubert appeared, and she told him that he
no longer had a hold on her. "But, opaque and heavy as an animal
mass, the obstinate larva sat itself on my burning chest." It seemed
to be strangling her, then began biting her; in fact, there were roaches
about. Then she was awake, and realized that she need not fear him;
it was he who should be afraid that she would trouble his conscience.
"Death is in him," her curse continues. "The sympathy he inspires
in putrid newspapers will have no echo in the future. . . . He will
not escape punishment." [10]

From Baden-Baden, Ivan Turgenev informed Flaubert that a new
Russian literary magazine, *Vestnik Evropy* — the title can be translated as "The European Messenger" — had published a long and favorable essay on *A Sentimental Education.* "You are so good to point
out a journal that praises my unfortunate book!" Flaubert replied.
"Yes, of course they were unjust to you," Turgenev wrote back, "but
that is the moment to stiffen and to toss a masterpiece to your readers. Your *Anthony* can be that projectile." [11]

It was not to be as simple as that. First there was the organization
of an evening performance at the Odéon for the benefit of the Bouilhet monument. Then Gustave developed an uncomfortable boil just
under his right eye, which became a generalized eczema. And Jules
Duplan, the faithful Duplan on whom he leaned so often when he
was in Croisset, Duplan was gravely ill. Flaubert watched over him,
missing the opening of a new play by Sand so he could be at his
bedside. Duplan died on March 1, 1870. To Sand, who suggested
that he join her in Nohant for fresh air, Flaubert explained that what
he needed was work, not the country. For the first ten days after Duplan's passing, he opened his door to no one. Then he attacked *Saint
Anthony,* reading "grim things" — religious works. [12]

Yet he had to respond to a summons from Hortense Cornu, a confidante of the Tuileries palace: "Come to see me, urgent matter."

Indeed it did seem of consequence. George Sand had just published a novel called *Malgrétout* in installments in *La Revue des Deux Mondes*, and it was being said that the adventuress portrayed was modeled on none other than the Empress Eugénie. Both the Emperor and his lady were upset. Madame Cornu was not supposed to tell Flaubert that Eugénie had empowered her with the mission, but she did tell him, and she hoped he could get Sand to write a letter declaring that she had not intended any slur on the Empress. She could do what she liked, Flaubert assured Sand when he relayed the request. "The Empress has always been very friendly to me, and I would not mind being helpful to her."

In *Malgrétout* the adventuress is out to marry a wealthy and influential man, an emperor if possible, in order to make her mark on history. Sand swore to Flaubert that she had invented the character, and she said that those who claimed to recognize the Empress were "bad servitors and bad friends." Flaubert simply sent her letter on to Madame Cornu, and the Empress, through Flaubert, conveyed her apologies to the novelist. The Empress "had never intended to insult genius."

By now George Sand had replaced all of Flaubert's earlier confidants, especially when it came to deeply personal matters. "Everything irritates and wounds me," he complained to her a fortnight after the death of Jules Duplan. "And since I control myself in front of people, I am taken by fits of weeping during which I think I am just going to die. I am beginning to feel something quite new for me: the approach of old age."[13] This to a woman so much older, and never without one manuscript in progress, another in proof. But by early April, Flaubert's work was going better. He spent his days at the Bibliothèque de l'Institut de France, and at night at Rue Murillo read books borrowed from the Bibliothèque de l'Arsenal.[14]

He was using a class notebook to record his private feelings, and gave this particular one a title: "Expansions 1870." The opening entry was a meditation on suicide: it was consoling to think that one could always end one's pain by killing oneself, but then one went on living. He noted that Le Poittevin, Bouilhet, and Du Camp had left him for women. "Am I then a monster?" He was the one who never changed; he was the absurdity. "Poor old madman, who at fifty carries the devotion that they had (perhaps) at eighteen." (He was eighteen months short of his fiftieth birthday.)[15] Writing Sand, he complained of physical as well as moral hurts — a bad cold, a bloodshot eye, he reported on April 14. "I am submerged by a black melancholy that comes on several times a day for any reason or no reason. . . . Perhaps it is because I haven't *written* anything for so long."

She could at least help him materially. He wanted more money from his publisher but found himself simply unable to raise the subject with Lévy — he had "an invincible shyness," he said. So of course she offered her help. He explained that he had received sixteen thousand francs for *A Sentimental Education*, though based on its length he should not have gotten more than fourteen thousand. When he had feigned surprise that Lévy was not giving him twenty thousand francs (as he had at one point promised), the publisher had assured him, "Don't worry! We'll see about that later!" Flaubert hardly dared ask for the four thousand francs now, but his financial situation was disastrous: "If Lévy isn't very polite with me, if he plays hard-to-get, if he doesn't cough up the bank notes, I'll get ugly and violent." Yet he also knew that this would only be an act on his part, for "Lévy certainly has the right to hold back, since my book did not succeed as we had hoped it would. . . ."

She tried; Lévy told her that he would do what he could. On April 29, Lévy called at Rue Murillo and explained his own financial problems to Flaubert. Although he had not earned back his investment on Flaubert's novel, he offered an advance of three or four thousand francs on the following book; it would be a loan without interest. Flaubert refused. "What do you expect?" Sand consoled him. "A Jew will always be a Jew." She promised to pursue the matter, reminding her friend that in the present state of political confusion, Lévy was "the most solid publisher, perhaps the only one." She herself had been offered more money to publish elsewhere but had decided to stay with him.[16]

Flaubert wrote Turgenev at the end of April about his season of sad news. Bouilhet, Duplan; now Ernest Feydeau was paralyzed, and Jules de Goncourt insane.[17] We now know that the younger Goncourt was in the final stage of syphilis — what was diagnosed as the tertiary phase, a general paralysis leading inevitably to death. We have a striking self-portrait of Jules during what must have been an early phase of his final illness. The scene was Saint Gratien, where the Goncourts were irritated by the presence of a Jew among the guests — Adolphe Franck, a professor at the Collège de France, who the brothers said had "a face one sees behind the counter of a usurer's office." One morning Jules de Goncourt, annoyed by what he saw as Princess Mathilde's "eulogy of Franck and of Jewry," burst out — "in a moment of morbid irritation that I can no longer control," he confessed to his diary — "In that case, Princess, become Jewish!" There was silence; the other guests turned pale. Jules understood that he had been impolite and tried to apologize to Mathilde, bursting into tears as he kissed her hand.[18]

At the end of the first week of May, Flaubert was at his desk in Croisset with a clearly defined agenda. First he would write a preface for the last poems of Bouilhet; then he would take up *The Temptation of Saint Anthony*, which he would have to put aside when rehearsals began for Bouilhet's *Mademoiselle Aïssé*. It took some time for him to settle down, for he felt no desire to write — yet he would continue to write, he promised George Sand. His existence was hardly joyous: his niece was away, his mother so old that talk about anything except her health was difficult; and of course he had no female companions in the vicinity.[19] Writing about Bouilhet caused him pain, he told Du Camp: he felt a perpetual sob in his throat, and his head ached continually.[20]

Jules de Goncourt died on June 20; he was thirty-nine. Edmond wrote Flaubert to say that he hoped that "the man whose talent he esteemed so highly, whom he loved so much" would be at the funeral.[21] Flaubert would tell his niece that he had seldom witnessed a sadder one. Of the seven friends who had gathered at the early Magny dinners, only three remained: Gautier, Edmond de Goncourt, and himself.[22]

He was in the proper mood for writing his preface to Bouilhet's poems. In it he admitted that his personal relationship with the poet made objective criticism impossible, and said that it was impossible to know which writers would survive their times. Analyzing the nature of Bouilhet's genius, he did not fail to point out his weaknesses — his plots, for example. Bouilhet thought in verse, which meant going against his age.

He concluded with a portrait of two young men who spent their Sundays reading poetry and talking about the books they would write. Then they did write them. One friend died, and the other treasured his memory as "a rampart against all that is mean and low. . . ." The dead friend would serve as a guide, and keep him company in his solitude.[23]

CHAPTER THIRTY-FOUR

DEFEAT

Bathing in the cold Seine was doing him good, Flaubert reported at the beginning of July 1870, after the funeral of Jules de Goncourt, after weeks of living with the papers and the memories of Louis Bouilhet. Still, when he walked in the evening in his garden, the sadness remained. "My life was turned upside down by the death of Bouilhet," he wrote Caroline — this a year after the loss of his friend. "I have *no one* I can talk to!"

This was only a manner of speaking, for there was a certain amount of movement right there in Croisset. He announced in the same letter that he was dining that Sunday with "the terrible Raoul-Duval" — terrible because he had fought a duel the previous week. Then Charles d'Osmoy came for a visit, to work with him on a play they had found among Bouilhet's papers, *Le Sexe faible* ("The Weak Sex").[1] But all the same . . . "Apart from you and Turgenev," Flaubert wrote George Sand, "I don't know a human being with whom I can open up on the things that I hold closest to my heart, and both of you live so far away!"[2]

On the night of July 14, in a letter written at two A.M., he told his niece: "I have rarely seen so lovely a night. . . . The moon shines through the tulip tree, the passing boats cast black shadows on the sleeping Seine. . . . The calmness is incomparable. . . ."[3] That same night in Paris, the streets were filled with crowds shouting "To Berlin!"; through an improbable, somewhat operatic sequence of events, the French Empire was moving toward war.

The chief cause was serious enough. Maneuvered by a strong man, Otto von Bismarck, Prussia had been building an empire from what had formerly been a loose confederation of states. In 1870 it became known that Spain was planning to offer its throne to a relative of King Wilhelm of Prussia; if this came to pass, France would be virtually surrounded by potential enemies. Emotions were aroused, and to assuage them Napoleon III moved firmly. Wilhelm was apparently willing to be reasonable, but Bismarck, perceiving a means to achieve German unity, added fuel to the fire in the form of an insulting statement, the famous Ems dispatch, which the French could not accept. On July 19, France declared war on Prussia, with manifest enthusiasm. Flaubert was "nauseated, grieved by the stupidity of my countrymen," as he let George Sand know. This time, from his retreat, he had sized up the situation accurately. He predicted "frightful butchery . . . bridges cut, tunnels destroyed, all this human effort lost. . . ."[4]

Visitors to Croisset talked war. "The public anguish has touched me," Gustave confessed to Caroline. He wondered if her husband's business would be hurt. (Commanville brought in wood from the north of Germany.)[5] In letters to Commanville, he spelled out his personal needs: there were bills to pay, and he needed fifteen hundred francs right away and another fifteen hundred in August, to be drawn on the funds Commanville was banking for him. Commanville advised his wife: "Reply to your uncle that the money he asks for will be sent if necessary, but that at the present time the businessman's skill consists in collecting moneys due to him while postponing paying the money he owes."[6]

"What gnaws at me," Flaubert told Caroline, "is my forced inactivity."[7] For news was coming in now, but not of victories. The fighting was bloody on the eastern frontiers. By the middle of August Flaubert had put his work aside; not knowing what else to do, he told Sand, he had volunteered as a nurse at the Hôtel-Dieu, for his brother no longer had any students. "If Paris is besieged, I'll go there to fight," he promised. "My rifle is ready."

He was convinced that the war would end in revolution. He blamed it on the introduction of universal suffrage, a remark that moved George Sand to draft an open letter in which she defended the right to vote: "The day when it functions properly, the errors of public authorities, whoever they are, will become impossible." However much she loved Flaubert, she was not about to abandon her principles. On his side, he was asking himself whether the French did not deserve to be punished.[8]

Meanwhile, a citizens' defense committee had been formed in Paris,

as Marshal Maurice de Mac-Mahon led an army to the northeast
frontier to reinforce Marshal Achille Bazaine; the Emperor himself
decided to accompany his troops. Writing Du Camp, Flaubert said
that his sadness was turning itself into a desire to take part in the
war. He swore that if he could be sure he wouldn't kill his mother by
doing it, he would join up with his friend d'Osmoy, who was march-
ing to the front at the head of a company of riflemen.[9] Two days after
that, Flaubert informed Caroline that his mother was resigned to his
departure "because, if Paris is surrounded, as I think it will be, I am
determined to move off with a rifle on my back. This idea almost
makes me merry."[10] He noted with approval that on the initiative of
his brother and Raoul-Duval, Rouen was raising a battalion of five
hundred men.[11]

Late in August, their Nogent relatives turned up, fearing the arrival
of the Prussians in their region. Croisset was now quite congested,
and the comings and goings were driving him mad, complained
Flaubert. "I have stomach cramps and a permanent headache," he
wrote Caroline on August 31. There was news: the national guard of
Croisset — "an important affair," he noted with irony — was about
to be called up.[12]

He could not know it then, but the decisive battle of the war was
about to begin. In Sedan, on September 1, the army that had marched
to defend the frontier was crushed, and Mac-Mahon was wounded.
The Emperor offered his sword to Wilhelm of Prussia and next day
was a prisoner, along with eighty-three thousand French soldiers. On
September 4, the Empire evaporated. The Empress fled to England,
and Paris got its republic — without a shot being fired, noted Sand
in her journal. "An immense and unique event in the history of
humanity!"[13]

The new republic — France's third — intended to pursue the war,
defending Paris and other territory not yet in enemy hands, rejecting
Bismarck's demand for the cession of Alsace-Lorraine. On September 4, the day the republic was instituted, Flaubert became a lieutenant in the local company of the national guard, a citizen's army that
had only recently been formed. He began at once to drill his men,
and he in turn went to Rouen for training, which incidentally enabled
him to escape the crowd — they were now fourteen in all — in the
Croisset house.

He had another concern. He had talked to Alexandre Dumas during a visit to Dieppe, and they agreed something would have to be
done for Mathilde, the victim of an "idiotic calumny" that she had

escaped to England with a fortune in gold. Her baggage had in fact been opened and found to contain no treasure, but still she had not been permitted to sail across the Channel from Dieppe. She did get to Belgium without difficulty, joining other high-ranking personalities of the Second Empire in exile.[14]

When it became clear that the war would go on, and that the Prussians would sweep across France even if Paris resisted, her husband decided that Caroline Commanville, a young and comely woman, should not be around when the enemy soldiers arrived. She sailed to England and found a bed in the tiny Chelsea house of Juliet Herbert's family. Juliet herself was serving as governess on a seventeenth-century country estate called Lyndon Hall, in Rutland. Caroline was invited there for a taste of the English countryside and of a proper English country house with a domestic staff of thirty. In all, Flaubert's niece spent four months in that friendly place of exile. While she was away, Baron Le Roy, the handsome prefect who had wooed her, took part in the war and at the fall of the Empire joined the colony of exiles in Belgium.[15]

The siege of Paris, when it began, was almost a relief; at last there seemed to be something one could rise up against. At the end of September, Flaubert wrote his niece that he was beginning night patrols. "I have just made a paternal speech to 'my men,' in which I announced that I'll run my sword through the belly of the first one to retreat, and told them to shoot away if they see me deserting. . . . Can you believe it, I feel almost merry. Yesterday I began to work again, and I've got my appetite back!"

He wrote Du Camp in the same vein. It was a duel unto the death, and all of France was prepared to fight. News arrived from Paris by balloon and by pigeon, and it did seem as if the French had the upper hand. Flaubert himself felt that they could win over the "marvelous precision machine" of the Prussian army, for "sentiment, inspiration, despair" also counted.[16] In a letter to Sand, he recalled his ancestors' (imagined) American Indian blood, and added, "I seriously, stupidly, animalistically feel like fighting." But in the same letter he also said that he had returned to the manuscript of *The Temptation of Saint Anthony*.[17]

His gloomiest thoughts were reserved for Mathilde in Belgium. (As a precaution, he mailed his letter to her via England.) He complained of the inertia of the provinces, the rough behavior of volunteers billeted in private homes, the manifest poverty. "Whatever happens,"

he told her, "everything we loved has gone forever." But at roughly
the same time, he was telling Caroline that he was writing, and not
badly. "One gets used to everything, and then I think that I have
come full circle, for I was close to going crazy or dying of sorrow and
anger." In a second letter to Mathilde, he described living in Croisset
with his mother, in the middle of "a stupid population," while wandering bands of impoverished people threatened anyone who happened to cross their path; the shutters had to be kept closed even in
midday. The militia he was in charge of had proved so undisciplined
that he had resigned from it.[18]

Commanville visited Croisset on Sundays, the day on which Flaubert always felt particularly demoralized, for it had been Bouilhet's
day in Croisset and the day he had dined at the Princess's in Paris.
He reported to his niece that the Prussians had not crossed the
boundary of their district, and said he was still hoping for a turnabout
in the military situation and counting on Paris, on Marshal Bazaine.
But when a change came, it was for the worse, with the surrender of
the French under siege at Metz — "something inexplicable," Flaubert wrote a friend. "Did Bazaine betray us?"[19] The French in fact
decided that he had, and he was found guilty of betraying the republic. Now the Prussians were free to pursue their march across France.

The snow came early. His mother moved to the Commanville
apartment in Rouen, "and I am here, all alone, at the fireplace, to
immerse myself in my sadness," Gustave wrote Caroline. By the end
of November he had established a routine: he slept in Rouen from
Monday to Thursday to escape the solitude of the countryside, then
spent the rest of the week in Croisset.[20] And then at last they came.
A part of the enemy army that had laid siege to Metz had moved
north, driving the French from Amiens and swinging west to the Seine
valley. The Prussians entered a disarmed Rouen, cutting it off from
the rest of the world. The house in Croisset received a contingent of
ten enemy soldiers, three of whom were officers, and six horses. When
the soldiers turned up, Gustave and his mother took refuge in the
Hôtel-Dieu, but soon they were back at the Commanville apartment
on the waterfront; there, too, they had Prussians as guests — two at
first, and later two more.

A letter to his dear Caroline, still in England, described her uncle's
state of mind, and the state of their Normandy, at that moment; it
has since been given the date of December 18. They were isolated
from the rest of France, even from the rest of Normandy, and were

at the mercy of the invaders. He felt deep humiliation as well as grief. On the previous day, he had walked for three hours looking for hay and straw for his uninvited guests.

He rose late, read a lot, and dined at the fireside with his mother in Rouen; two or three times a week he went to call at the Hôtel-Dieu, or to see friends.[21] Charles Lapierre, the publisher of the daily *Nouvelliste de Rouen* (which, like the other papers, had suspended publication), remembered Flaubert's visiting him at his home or his office, "troubled, anxious, and at the same time obsessed with historical memories that led him to find parallel situations." He paints a Flaubert prepared to believe all rumors and to repeat them despite his friends' teasing. Thus one day Gustave insisted that an army corps had gotten clear of Paris and was in Vernon, on its way to free Rouen; his milkman had told him that.[22]

Commanville had offered to bring Flaubert and his mother to Dieppe, but there she would have no friends, and of course Achille was in Rouen. Nor did Flaubert want to be any farther from Croisset than he was; already he worried about what would become of his writing room, his books and notes and manuscripts. He had only been able to hide his notes for and manuscript of *The Temptation of Saint Anthony*.[23] Late in January, a new Prussian corps took over the city, seemingly rougher and more demanding than the previous one. The weather grew colder, and the snow refused to melt. Just keeping the fires going at Croisset was costing a fortune.[24]

The surrender of Paris, an armistice that was to hold until a peace treaty could be signed, brought new gloom. France was now so dishonored that Flaubert could only wish for its total disappearance. He hoped that civil war would kill many people, himself included; he no longer wore his Legion of Honor medal, for "the word *honor* is no longer French." He planned to ask Turgenev how one could become a Russian citizen.[25]

France did not disappear; Bismarck, like Hitler in 1940, needed a government with which to negotiate. On February 8, 1871, the French elected a national assembly. The mood was conservative, and the new legislative body that met in Bordeaux chose as its chief of government the veteran politician and historian Adolphe Thiers; it was he who negotiated the treaty ceding Alsace-Lorraine as well as a huge indemnity to the victors.

Then the Channel steamers were operating again. Flaubert and his mother rushed to Neuville, the Commanville home outside Dieppe, where they found more occupation troops. There was pillaging, and once again, as at Croisset, they had to hide precious objects. But Caroline's return from England made everything more acceptable. Her uncle began to work again, or tried to. "But the noodle is still pretty weak," he wrote his friend Léonie Brainne.[26]

CHAPTER THIRTY-FIVE

SAINT ANTHONY

IN EXPLAINING to George Sand why the Prussian occupation had been the worst experience of his whole life, Flaubert reminded her that he had never been progressive, or humanitarian. But he did have illusions, and these illusions had been punctured by the barbarity of the civilized Germans, those gentlemen "who know Sanskrit and who guzzle your champagne, who steal your watch and then send you their visiting card." Now, he declared, he had only one desire: "to live in the sun in some quiet country."[1]

Pending the realization of that dream, he would go to Belgium. It was a scheme he had cooked up with Dumas, a fellow partisan of Princess Mathilde, to express their solidarity. But preparing such an expedition was not simple, and for a while Flaubert thought he would have to let Dumas go without him. There were now forty Prussian soldiers at Croisset, and he would have to go there to get what he needed for his voyage. Finally Dumas joined him in Rouen, and they traveled together on March 16, 1871 — not the direct way, via Amiens, for the rail line was encumbered by occupation troops, but through Paris. They left Paris the next morning, reaching the Belgian capital that night.[2]

On the following day, March 18, Paris ignited. This time it was the city against the rest of France — the Paris of ordinary citizens, workers, and craftsmen, who felt betrayed by the bourgeoisie of their city as well as by the new government. This Paris declared its independence, organizing itself as an autonomous Commune. When Flaubert heard that there was fighting in the streets, he immediately pan-

icked — was Caroline in Paris? Was his mother being cared for? He
needed to know before he moved on.

For Brussels had not been his only destination, we now know. His
correspondence is circumspect, since he takes pains to avoid any reference to Mathilde, but he made sure not to tell even his intimate
friends where he was going *after* Belgium. By prearrangement, he
was sailing to England to see Juliet Herbert; he had promised that to
her. (If he had not promised, he assured Caroline, he would be rushing back to France.) He stayed in a hotel in London — Hatchett's, on
Dover Street — bombarded his family with questions, and for his niece
added, "Juliet sends you a kiss." He sailed back to the French coast
from Newhaven on Monday night, March 27, arriving in Dieppe the
following morning.[3]

While he was away, his mother, then in Rouen with Caroline,
stopped in at her notary's to write out a will. She gave Croisset to her
granddaughter Caroline, "in recognition of the good care that she has
always given me, and to avoid the sale of property, which would have
been sad for me." She signed the document and dated it March 20,
1871. Then on June 18, at the bottom of the same sheet of paper, she
added a codicil:

> I desire that my son Gustave Flaubert have lifelong use of the
> office, bedroom, and dressing room that he occupies in the
> dwelling house located in Croisset that I have willed to Madame
> Commanville. . . .
>
> In consequence, I give and bequeath this lifetime use to him
> personally, and as long as he does not marry.[4]

Like so many of his fellows — fellow writers and thinkers — Flaubert
tried to understand the Paris revolt, and could not. "Pure Middle
Ages," he called it in a letter to George Sand. What, he asked her,
did she think of these socialists — the insurrectionists of Paris — who
employed the same methods the Empire had used, and what of the
Prussians, with their house searches, their shutting down the press,
their executions without trial? We know that the socialist Sand was
no less depressed, and the feeling was shared by even the most republican of their peers, not excluding Hugo.[5] In truth, the Commune
had been born of the violence of war and siege; the first blood spilled
was that of guardsmen drawn from the ranks of the little people. When
Thiers sought to recover the guard's artillery, his officers were captured and killed; he set up his government in Versailles, leaving Paris
to the national guard and to the workers' movements. On March 26,

the rebel Parisians elected their own assembly, which ruled Paris as a state in revolt against Versailles. In a succession of decrees both practical and idealistic, the Commune took up the cause of the dispossessed, encouraged the blossoming of innumerable social ideologies, and rendered rough and ready justice. It was put down ferociously. The end, in May, became known as the Bloody Week, but in fact there were many bloody weeks, and long years of penal servitude for the insurgents.

Considering what was going on in Paris, Croisset seemed a haven of calm. Flaubert was back at his desk on April 1, finding the mass of notes for *Saint Anthony* and a box of letters just where he had hidden them. Soon he was working "violently." If nothing else interfered, he notified Sand, he expected to complete his book the following winter. He tried not to be distressed by the news from Paris; the invasion had been worse. He hated democracy, he said, because it was based on "the morality of the Gospel," which for him meant "the exaltation of Grace to the detriment of Justice." But he also had angry words for the late Second Empire. "Everything was false: false realism, false army, false credit, and even false whores."[6]

Yet he had only tenderness for one particular member of the Imperial family. He wrote Mathilde on May 30. Since some of his letters had already gone astray, intercepted either by the government or by the Commune, he saw no reason to hold back any longer, "so I shall return to my regular practice and call you as I used to, by your real name, since for me you are still a Highness. . . ." He described his life, alone in Croisset with his mother, who could no longer walk and was weaker every day. His sole distraction was watching Prussian soldiers march by from time to time, his sole occupation his *Saint Anthony.* "This extravagant work keeps me from thinking of the horrors of Paris. When we find that this world is too evil, we must take refuge in another."

To Caroline, he described his timid return to social life — a visit, for example, from the philosopher Frédéric Baudry, who helped him with Indian philosophy, something he needed for his book. There had also been a visit from "three angels," which is how he described three women friends — Charles Lapierre's wife, Marie-Valérie, her sister, Léonie Brainne, and her friend Marie-Angèle Pasquier, an actress who used the name Madame Pasca. Léonie and Madame Pasca were widows, and all three angels either were or had been beauties.[7]

With Léonie Brainne he had at least an *amitié amoureuse* — a flirtation, that is, pursued in letters and in banter; Flaubert finally had a

feminine companion nearby again. (Marie-Valérie and Léonie had
been born and raised in Rouen.) Léonie was thirty-five and had been
a widow since 1864.

The conservative government — the men of Versailles — had begun their sweep into Paris by taking the exterior forts, and had then
entered the capital by the undefended Porte de Saint-Cloud; the
Commune barricades went up too late. The fighting was fierce, but
Paris was taken, street by street. "Well, Princess, your sinister predic-
tions were unfounded," Flaubert wrote Mathilde. "Far from spread-
ing all over France, the Paris Commune is in its last convulsions.
. . ." And yet he was not anxious to return to the capital. He even
considered giving up his apartment on Rue Murillo, for it would be
too painful to be so close to Mathilde's house on Rue de Courcelles,
now state property. He was concerned about the probable reaction to
the Commune; the fear of socialism would lead to a conservative regime "more stupid than ever."[8]

But he did go to Paris in June; he had essential research to do for
The Temptation of Saint Anthony. The city made him nauseous, he
was to tell George Sand. "Half of the population wants to strangle
the other half, which feels the same. . . . And the Prussians do not
exist; they are excused and *admired.*"[9] Edmond de Goncourt, who
had not seen Flaubert since the death of Jules a year earlier, dined
with him on June 10. "He has not changed," the surviving Goncourt
confided to his diary. "Man of letters before anything else. The catas-
trophe seems to have passed over him without having the slightest
effect on the impassive composition of his little book."[10]

The impassive composition was pursued back in Croisset. Then
Turgenev announced a visit for August. In his reply, Flaubert warned
that the Russian might find him excessive in his hatred of Prussia;
what he resented most was that the enemy had turned him into a
brute of the Dark Ages.[11] Before the end of July, he was back in Paris
and back at the library he continued to call the Bibliothèque Impériale, for he could not get all the books he needed in Rouen. While
there, he began working for Bouilhet, trying to find a theater for *Mademoiselle Aïssé.*[12] At the beginning of August, he wrote a letter that —
though he could not have imagined this — was to be the opening gun
in a new crusade. The letter was addressed to Etienne Nétien, the
mayor of Rouen, and was a reminder that Flaubert was the chairman
of a committee set up to build a monument to Louis Bouilhet. They
now had twelve thousand francs at their disposal, and could pay for

a small fountain decorated with a bust; the mayor would of course have the opportunity to approve the design. They needed to know where the city would place it, in order to obtain an estimate of the costs involved.[13]

He pursued his library work, but the evenings were long. He missed his ever-ready companion for nights on the town, Jules Duplan. So he sat at his window on the park, reading, and went to bed early. He complained to Caroline that his mother, who was staying at the Commanville home on the Channel coast during his absence, was badgering him to return to Croisset. "It seems to me that *at my age* I have the right, once a year, to do what pleases me." He had not accomplished all he had hoped to on his earlier trip to Paris, he told Caroline, because of his habit of setting a date in advance for his return, "as if that were so important!" [14]

But by the middle of August he was home, ready for Turgenev. The Russian was to disappoint him, but he promised to visit in October. Flaubert hoped that he would stay several days at that time, for he needed his friend. "To whom can I talk now? Who in this lamentable country 'busies himself with literature'? A single person, perhaps? Me! Debris of a vanished world, old fossil of romanticism. . . ." [15]

He in turn had an unexpected invitation. Elisa Schlesinger, now sixty-one and a widow, was in France, even in Trouville. Would he come to see her there? He explained, as he did to everyone else, that he could not leave his mother unless Caroline was available to replace him. "This is why, dear old friend, eternal tenderness, I shall not join you on that Trouville beach where we first met, and which, for me, still bears your footprints." Could she not come to Croisset? She never did.[16]

To George Sand, who in a letter had lamented, "I am sick of my nation and of my race," he replied with an even deeper pessimism: "I believe that the mob, the mass, the herd will always be despicable." He wished to compliment her on an article she had published on the corruption of the working class by the industrial revolution. But Sand decided that things had gone too far. She was not going to be pushed into a corner by her disillusioned friend, or made to sound like the reactionary she was not. Her response soon took on the proportions of a manifesto; she submitted it to the newspaper *Le Temps*, which published it as "Reply to a Friend." To Gustave, she summed it up in more personal terms: she did not repudiate her belief in progress. Her open letter moved him, and he confessed that he had shed a tear — without being converted, of course. He felt that she was overlooking the notion of justice. He believed in a natural aristocracy; one could not elevate the masses even if one tried, which meant that universal suffrage was even stupider than the divine right of kings. "Yet we must respect the mass, however incapable it is," he conceded, "for it contains the seeds of an incalculable fecundity. Give it liberty, but not power." He added a gem: "The whole dream of democracy is to raise the proletariat to the level of stupidity of the middle class."[17]

There was a necessary trip to Paris that autumn to make arrangements for Bouilhet's play and for his posthumous poems. Flaubert arrived in Paris in the second week of October and once again immersed himself in the politics of the stage. "I am involved in the blackest of intrigues," he reported to Caroline. "It is probably the first time I have ever lied with so much insolence!" (It was a matter of getting the right theater, and the right cast.)[18] When it was time to go home, on October 18, he ran into Edmond de Goncourt on the way to the station. Goncourt noted: "He holds under his arm, closed with a triple lock, a minister's portfolio in which he keeps *The Temptation.*" The two men shared a carriage, and on the way Flaubert revealed the theme of his story: Anthony faces one trial after another and conquers them all, but he is defeated in the end by life cells. Flaubert seemed astonished at Goncourt's astonishment at this.[19] Indeed, in the novel, after resisting all the sensual and intellectual temptations thrust before him, Anthony perceives "tiny globular masses, small as pinheads and covered with hairs." The book closes with Anthony's fervent wish to "exist in everything . . . , to run like water, vibrate like sound, shine like light . . . to be matter!"

From Croisset, Flaubert used the mails to pursue Bouilhet's theater business. We know from what he told his niece that he performed this extra work on Sundays, Bouilhet's day, in order to keep it separate from his daily routine. In a letter written at the end of October 1871, he reported "an extraordinary event": he had actually gone out of the house, and as far as the vegetable garden. He had stood there contemplating nature, and had felt so moved by the sight of a small calf lying next to its mother that he had kissed it on the forehead.

His next letter raised a new concern. "Are Ernest's affairs worrying you more than you say?" he asked his niece. He happened to need some of the money her husband was banking for the family.[20] We do not have Caroline's reply, but we know that Flaubert was right to worry. Commanville had made some wrong decisions before the outbreak of the war. Convinced that the price of timber was going to rise, he had acquired large tracts of forest in Scandinavia; the war had depressed the market, however, and he lacked the capital to withstand the shock.[21] The story was to come out slowly, and Gustave would not be the first to hear it.

When he returned to Paris in the middle of November, he brought his mother along; she was to stay with the Commanvilles, who had a room for her in their home on Rue de Clichy.[22] On Flaubert's first Sunday at Rue Murillo, Edmond de Goncourt came to visit and got an earful of *The Temptation of Saint Anthony*. He saved his honest opinion for his diary, expressing dismay at the excessive Orientalism of Flaubert's book, and its use of "the half-witted tricks of a fairy play." Worse, the work simply lacked originality. Flaubert had employed the most colorful and eccentric settings, but he lacked true fantasy, personal invention — so thought Goncourt.[23]

Now there were to be daily and painful negotiations at the Odéon theater, a fight for the right actors and actresses and for approval of his revisions of Bouilhet's text. Publishing Bouilhet's last poems was a further hassle, for publishers could not make money with poetry, and few, if any, were prepared to assume the expense Flaubert insisted on — for he wished to choose the quality of paper, the format, and even the printer. Finally he suggested that the book be published at the expense of Bouilhet's literary heir, Philippe Leparfait, believing that the money advanced would be quickly covered by sales.

On December 1, following custom, Bouilhet's play was read aloud to the newly selected cast, by Flaubert, "to keen enthusiasm," he reported to Leparfait. Rehearsals began the following week, with Flaubert directing; he had also done the research for the costumes. He was proud to be able to say that the theater manager admired his staging.[24]

MADAME FLAUBERT

W HEN HE WAS NOT at the theater, Flaubert was with the printer. He read the preface he had written for Bouilhet's poems to Goncourt, who "broke into tears," and then he went back to work on it the same night, stopping only at three.[1] In the midst of these occupations, a new challenge came to him from an unexpected quarter. Rouen did not wish to have a monument in honor of Louis Bouilhet. The problem, Flaubert was to learn, was that in the opinion of the city fathers, his friend had died without achieving incontestable success. And he had not even been born in Rouen. Despite a strong appeal by Raoul-Duval and other Bouilhet supporters, the city council had voted 13 to 11 against a monument. Mayor Nétien and six of his deputies were in that majority.[2]

Flaubert was, predictably, furious. "I want to whip the asses of the city council until they bleed." He would do that, he decided, in the form of a statement. Assembling the facts, including any information that would embarrass individual councilmen who had opposed the monument, became a priority; that and rehearsals (daily and Sunday) took up all of his time. One of the actresses proved inadequate, so he undertook to give her private coaching. He almost killed the prompter, he boasted to his friends. In the final days before the opening, he slogged across Paris in the snow because the cabs were not circulating; he was sometimes so exhausted on his return to Rue Murillo that he "cried like a baby."[3]

And as if all this were not enough, he received a singular Christmas greeting. Caroline announced, at last, that her husband's business was in peril. And her uncle Gustave, the least business-minded of the family, was called upon to save the situation. Commanville needed a considerable sum of money; on Christmas Day, Flaubert appealed to Raoul-Duval for a loan of fifty thousand francs, which was only part of the required sum.[4] Swallowing his pride, he also turned to the Princess, who was now back in France from her Belgian refuge. She did not have enough cash on hand, but she offered to mortgage her Saint Gratien estate. He refused to allow her to do that. She suggested that he see Alphonse Rothschild, grandson of the founder of the banking dynasty. "But if he refuses?" Flaubert asked her. "Then we will try elsewhere!" replied Mathilde; "Count on me." Flaubert reported this conversation to Commanville in a letter written on December 27 at one in the morning, before he turned to the proofs of Bouilhet's book. The previous night he had worked until three, and had risen at eight for rehearsal.

He thought he had established a new record in the final week of the year: one night he didn't go to bed at all. His time was then divided between finding money for Commanville and designing a new set for *Aïssé*.[5]

The play opened on January 6, 1872, with Flaubert in the wings, for he was handling props as well as directing the cast.[6] But nothing could help — not even his influential friends, not even Sarah Bernhardt in the title role. When Michel Lévy published the play as a book two weeks later, Flaubert took pains to see that the unfavorable reviews were quoted in it.[7] One of the roughest was by Francisque Sarcey, writing in *Le Temps:* "Mr. Bouilhet has the worst of defects: he is boring. . . ." In a reference to Flaubert, Benoit Jouvin in *La Presse* criticized Bouilhet's "pitiless admirers," who, at the risk of discrediting his reputation definitively, "are auctioning scraps of paper that he had perhaps intended to burn." If this was how they admired Bouilhet, then what did one have to do to betray him?[8]

The reviews were a "death blow," as Flaubert reported sadly to Philippe Leparfait.[9] But there was still *Dernières Chansons*, Bouilhet's last poems, published in the handsome edition over which Flaubert had labored so long. The volume included as a frontispiece a portrait of Bouilhet, who had the receding hairline, the lock of hair falling over the collar, and even the mustache of Flaubert, with a goatee into the bargain.

Round three would be Flaubert's open letter to the Rouen municipal council. Charles Lapierre promised to publish it in *Le Nouvelliste de Rouen*, and with his permission *Le Temps* in Paris also planned to use it, but in the end it proved to be too much for Lapierre's readers, and he backed out, though he did print the full text as a pamphlet on his presses.[10] Flaubert's letter began with a list of the reasons given by Rouen for refusing the monument to Bouilhet — a monument, he made it clear, that would have cost the city nothing. Dealing with the objection that his friend's literary merit was insufficient, he pointed out that French cities often overlooked distinguished citizens while honoring lesser persons; he had done considerable research on this. After predicting that Bouilhet's poetry and plays would continue to be heard and read after a hundred years and more, Flaubert mentioned some of the things Rouen should be preoccupied with instead of literary criticism, such as building a new bridge. His final paragraph blasted the decadence, the impotence, of his bourgeois peers, whose only intellectual effort "consists of trembling before the future."

It was only on January 21 that he could sit down to tell George Sand some of the things that had been happening. He had never worked so hard, he said, and yet he had never felt so robust. "Explain that to me!"[11] But he also suffered his usual winter ills. A throat infection he had been complaining of since the beginning of the year took a "rather violent" turn; he spoke only with difficulty, complaining to Léonie Brainne of swollen glands that made him appear "ignoble."[12] Reactions to his pamphlet began to come in. The press treated him kindly, and off the record Emile Zola told him, "You should have used an even heavier stick."[13] Zola was a new friend, a writer of the next generation, nearly twenty years Flaubert's junior; the first works that would mark him as a master of an even starker realism than Flaubert's began to appear twenty years after *Madame Bovary*. For Zola, Flaubert's first published novel had changed literature overnight; its perfection made it the "definitive model" of the modern novel, lighting the way for the naturalists of Zola's generation.[14]

But Zola later confessed that his first encounter with the master was "a great disillusionment, almost painful." He had started out with the image of a Flaubert of his own making — Flaubert the resolute realist — and instead found a "hale and hearty fellow" who favored paradox, an unreconstructed romantic who actually derided his own masterpiece. For he told Zola that he had written *Madame Bovary* to "annoy" the realists, wishing to prove that one could paint the world as it is and still be a great stylist.[15] The would-be disciple sent Flaubert his books as they were published, and when he gave Flaubert a copy of *La Fortune des Rougon*, the first of a series of twenty novels describing the "natural and social history" of a Second Empire family, the older writer acknowledged it as being "atrocious and beautiful," regretting only that in his preface the novelist had expressed an opinion, "a thing that, in my personal poetics, a novelist does not have the right to do."[16]

By the middle of February 1872, the nature of Flaubert's ailment had changed somewhat. "I have rheumatism in my back, and my long daily sessions at the library aren't doing me any good," he reported to his niece. He asked that her husband send him some cash. "I really don't like to be always asking him for money. But I don't see who else can give me any, since he is holding everything, or almost everything, that I possess." He was then getting a thousand francs a month from Commanville, the income from his own funds.[17] He expected to be able to finish his readings for *Saint Anthony* by the end of March, after which he would return to Croisset to relieve his niece of the duty of watching over his mother. His social life in the last days of his Paris season was lively enough. He was invited to dine by Victor Hugo, now home from exile and a hero; Flaubert found him friendlier than ever.[18] In his business life, there was a significant change: he broke with his publisher.

From the beginning there had been a misunderstanding about the publication of Bouilhet's last poems. Flaubert's naïveté about costs had led him to think that he could carry the issue by the force of his own enthusiasm. He not only chose the printer, but also increased the expense by insisting that there be a blank page facing each poem, to make the book appear to be of customary length. He had expected Michel Lévy to advance the cost of publication and then to reimburse himself as copies of *Dernières Chansons* were sold. But on March 19, the printer, Jules Claye, informed Flaubert that Lévy had refused to pay the bill. The next day, a stormy meeting took place. Lévy denied that he had ever agreed to finance the book, and complained that Flaubert had never even shown him proofs, and had never warned him that he would be receiving a stock of two thousand copies. "I have broken forever with gentleman Lévy," Flaubert informed Philippe Leparfait.[19] Jules Troubat, who had once been Sainte-Beuve's secretary and now worked as an editor for Lévy, offered to act as an intermediary. He passed on an offer of compromise from his employer, who was ready to advance the cost of printing on the condition that Leparfait reimburse the deficit in a year's time. Leparfait agreed, and even ventured to tell Flaubert that he had been wrong to blow up in front of the publisher, who happened to have all of Bouilhet's books in print.[20]

And so to Croisset, where Flaubert discovered a houseful of painters, and his mother in rapid decline. He found that he could not get back to writing, could not even understand what he was reading; his break with Lévy, he thought, had something to do with the state of his morale. "I was brave this winter, until my fight with Lévy," he admitted.[21]

"Why did I meet you too late!" he wrote to Léonie Brainne, who was now the object of his most tender feelings. " 'To have a little place in my life,' you say. No! It isn't little at all. . . . I've drained from your lips, my lovely, something that will remain in my heart. . . . I am going to return to reading Hegel while trying not to think of that beautiful face I would like to cover with kisses."[22]

This was written on a Sunday evening. The next day, his mother's condition worsened dramatically. It was the beginning of the end, and her son's vigil began. He would tell Du Camp that from Monday night until his mother's death the following Saturday, April 6, he did not close an eye.[23]

Madame Flaubert had willed Croisset to her granddaughter Caroline, but could she really do that? For the property had belonged not to her alone but to the partnership formed by Dr. and Madame Flaubert upon their marriage; Achille and Gustave each had a share of that legacy. The brothers agreed that their mother's intentions were to be respected: Caroline would receive the property intact, and the original purchase price of ninety thousand francs would simply be deducted from her part of the final settlement.[24]

All this deciding took time, however. Gustave's letters in the days following the death of his mother betrayed his uneasiness. "How and where will I live?" he wondered aloud to Frédéric Fovard.[25] In Rouen, the family notary drew up an inventory of the contents of the Flaubert residence, all but the "books and brochures claimed by Mr. Gustave Flaubert and recognized as his property." Everything was counted, including sixteen hens and three roosters, three ducks and twenty-two ducklings, a cow about to give birth, an oak billiard table. . . .[26] "It was sinister," Flaubert described the experience. "It seemed to me that my mother was dying all over again and that we were stealing from her."[27]

He found his way back to his writing table at the end of April, for "life is tolerable only if one forgets one's miserable person," he explained to George Sand.[28] "Tomorrow, for certain, I begin making sentences," he promised his niece on April 29. "You cannot imagine how *your* Croisset is calm and lovely!" he added, underlining the possessive. He confessed that he could not stop thinking of his mother.

It was a new life; he was more alone than he had ever been. "Meals in my own company, at that empty table, are hard," he wrote Caroline on May 5. "Finally this evening, for the first time, I had my dessert without tears. I'll probably get used to this wild and solitary existence. I don't see that I have the *means* to lead any other kind." Actually he was seeing friends, including his "angels" — Léonie Brainne, her sister, and their actress friend. And he had a new male friend in his neighbor Edmond Laporte, whom he had first met half a dozen years earlier through Jules Duplan.[29] Laporte was a Parisian, ten years Flaubert's junior, who lived and worked a few miles downstream from Croisset. He managed a factory that turned out lace and netting, and was then a bachelor, marrying only after Flaubert's death. Although Laporte had not the slightest connection with the literary or theatrical or social circles of Gustave Flaubert, he would prove good company, a loyal friend and helper, almost to the end.[30]

Yet Flaubert's misanthropy, which may have seemed exaggerated when he expressed it in his letters, came to life in face-to-face meetings. "We dine, of course, in a private room," Edmond de Goncourt told his diary during a visit Flaubert paid to Paris in June, "because Flaubert wants no noise, wants no other diners nearby, and also wants to take off his jacket and boots when he eats." Flaubert had been planning a trip to Vendôme, a hundred miles southwest of Paris, for the inauguration of a statue of Ronsard, on the invitation of the mayor of the town. Then he learned that Paul de Saint-Victor was also going; on the spot, Flaubert decided that he would not make the trip. He had become so sensitive, he told Goncourt, that the idea of sitting opposite an unpleasant person on the train was insupportable. He led Goncourt into a café so that he could write his valet to tell him he was returning to Croisset the following day. Signing and sealing the letter obviously pleased him; the two friends went to the station so Flaubert could buy his ticket for Rouen. As they waited in line, Flaubert expressed a desire to be dead and gone, dead without resurrection.[31]

CHAPTER THIRTY-SEVEN

VENTING SPLEEN

For the summer of 1872, Flaubert had two irrevocable commitments. He had to accompany his niece — always a little bit ill but now suffering from exhaustion, migraine headaches, and a sore throat — to the watering station of Bagnères-de-Luchon in the Pyrenees. And then he had to be in Paris to meet Juliet Herbert, for when he had told her that he was going to stay in Luchon until early August, she had replied, so Flaubert reported to Caroline, with "an indignant letter."[1] So there was to be another of those very secret encounters with the English governess; theirs had now become the longest-lasting romantic relationship of his life. How secret it still was is suggested by the vague way he wrote about his stay in the Pyrenees to George Sand, telling her that he would be there for five or six weeks when he was actually planning to hurry back to Paris to greet Juliet.[2] In the end, though, Juliet's visit was postponed until September.

On July 1, still in Croisset, he was able to announce that he had finished *The Temptation of Saint Anthony*. Now he was ready to work on a manuscript left by Bouilhet, a play called *Le Sexe faible*. Then, he told Sand, he would get to work on a modern novel that was to be the "counterpart" of *Saint Anthony*, with "the pretension of being comical." This was *Bouvard and Pécuchet*, which he then thought would take "at least" two or three years to write.[3]

There was more paperwork in connection with his mother's succession. He asked Commanville to send him some cash so he could pay his bills and leave some money with the Croisset house staff when he went off to Luchon. "For as long as my income is not assured," he explained, "I simply have to eat up my capital, which is not amusing."[4] The evidence is that Commanville served as banker not only for Gustave but for other family members, including the deceased Madame Flaubert. He used their money and paid them interest.[5]

It would have been surprising had the old Croisset bear found his paradise in Bagnères-de-Luchon. He and Caroline arrived on July 7 and took rooms in a private home, but there was so much noise that he could not work. He decided that the local bourgeoisie was despicable; the town physician in turn attributed his susceptibility to the abuse of tobacco. He picked up Charles Dickens's *Pickwick Papers* and read it through, enjoying parts of it immensely but finding the composition "defective." All English writers except Walter Scott were like that, he commented to George Sand; they lacked a central plan.[6]

He slept. He tried the famous baths and drank spring water. He began to worry about that irritability of his, fearing, he confessed to Princess Mathilde, that he might become like Jules de Goncourt. He picked up the Bouilhet play, thinking he could make it clearer; he had to write a first act and five or six additional scenes.[7] One day he and his niece went up into the mountains as far as the Spanish border. He felt, he told Léonie Brainne, that he had rid himself of the bourgeois at last, of everything that was false; this made him think that he should go traveling again.[8]

He explained to Caroline how he saw *Bouvard and Pécuchet*. It would be the story of two quite ordinary copy clerks who decide to try out every science and art, and who then record the disastrous consequences. Later he wondered if his niece had understood much of what he had in mind, and he regretted having attempted to describe the book at such an early stage.[9] Caroline also took advantage of their stay in Luchon, and the distance from her husband, to reveal some secrets of her married life — her lack of compatibility with her husband, his inability to comprehend either her mind or her heart. She apparently also made it clear to her uncle that her present condition of moral and physical disarray was due to the loss of the man she really loved, Ernest Le Roy, the handsome baron.[10] He had died on July 5.

Preparing for their return, Flaubert alerted Turgenev: he would be in Paris for a few days before going home to Croisset, where he expected the Russian's visit. He wished to read *Saint Anthony* to him, and to talk to him about "a lot of things."[11] Back in Croisset, he picked up his notes for *Bouvard and Pécuchet,* announcing to Edma Roger des Genettes: "I am going to begin a book that will occupy me for several years. . . . It is the story of these two fellows who copy a kind of critical encyclopedia in farce. . . . For this I shall have to study many things about which I am ignorant: chemistry, medicine, agriculture. I am now in medicine. But one has to be crazy and triply mad to undertake a thing like this!" Once again he showed a remarkable perspicacity concerning a project that he had not yet begun, and that would be unlike any other book written by himself or anyone else.[12]

Meanwhile, he waited for Turgenev, waited and waited. The lackadaisical Russian did not even write with an excuse. So Flaubert sent a letter to warn him that he himself would be traveling — "roving" — for his "affairs," for three weeks beginning at the end of August.[13] He used the same language in writing Sand: "I must rove about for my affairs."[14]

Actually there was only one affair: Juliet. She was to meet him in Paris at the beginning of September, as Gustave informed Caroline. (Caroline was very much his confidante where Juliet was concerned, just as he had been hers with Ernest Le Roy.)[15] On his first Sunday with Juliet Herbert, he took time out to write his new friend Edmond Laporte, who had decided to help him come to terms with his solitude by giving him a dog. It was a greyhound, steel-gray in color, still a puppy but likely to grow quite big. In Paris, Flaubert made the decision to accept the gift, asking Laporte to hold the animal until he returned and to call it Julio. He did not say why, but simply attributed his choice to "a number of mystical reasons."[16] He and Juliet must have had a good laugh over that.

He was in excellent health, he told his niece. He ascribed this to the weeks he had spent with her in the Pyrenees, but this was said after a week spent with Juliet Herbert.[17] While he was still in Paris, the publisher Georges Charpentier, the son of the founder of the firm of that name, informed him that he wanted to purchase the rights to his books, all of which originally had been published by Michel Lévy.[18] Then Juliet left; Gustave was so sad that he arranged to go back to Croisset the same day, September 21. It was not a merry return. "I delivered myself to thoughts about earlier times so heavy that I felt crushed under them," he wrote Caroline. But he shook them off and got to work, correcting the clear copy that had been made of *The Temptation of Saint Anthony* and doing his reading for *Bouvard and Pécuchet*.[19]

The beginning of autumn brought foul weather. His only distraction was to kiss his new dog, to whom he made speeches. "What a happy mortal! His quietude and beauty make me jealous."

But if he admired Julio's insouciance, it was not his own way. If his own morale was acceptable, he explained to his pen friend Edma Roger des Genettes, it was because "I am meditating a work in which I shall vent my anger. Yes, I will finally be able to rid myself of the things that are suffocating me. I will vomit over my fellows the disgust that they cause me, and even if it breaks my chest, it will be immense and violent. . . ."[20] Yet on the same day, if the dating can be trusted, he wrote one of his most feeling letters to Elisa Schlesinger, "my old friend, my old tenderness." He could not see her handwriting without being stirred, he said. When he opened her letter, he thought that she would be announcing a visit. "I should so much like to receive you in my home," he pursued, "to have you sleep in my mother's bedroom." He described his retreat, his happiness in solitude. "The future for me contains no more dreams, but the past comes back as if bathed in a golden mist." And the face that stood out most splendidly from this past was hers. Yes, hers. "Oh poor Trouville!" This is the last letter to Elisa that has survived, and it may be the last he wrote.[21]

Some vignettes of Flaubert's first months alone, truly alone: "Sunday I went to dinner at the Lapierres' [in Rouen], and I went on foot along the river to enjoy nature. My heroism did not do me any good. A boat filled with loudmouths that was sailing upstream alongside me spoiled the view."[22] There were visits from neighbors such as Dr. Charles Fortin, Raoul-Duval, and even Caroline. Then it rained, rained without stop. "Despite my love for Croisset, I find that its climate lacks charm," he wrote his niece after her departure. "This is why more than ever I plunge into the silence of my office, my only distraction being to contemplate my dog as he yawns."[23]

A telegram informed him that Théophile Gautier had died, at sixty-one, from a heart ailment. The news arrived too late to allow Flaubert to go to the funeral. He had appointments in Rouen that day, October 25, and decided to keep them. The spectacle of his townsmen — their vulgarity, the things they said, and the way they said them — made him want to vomit and weep both, so he told his niece. "For he died, I am sure, of being suffocated for too long by the stupidity of his times." Flaubert's disgust with the people of Rouen did not extend to all their ladies, and he made his visit to Charles Lapierre's wife and her sister Léonie. They accompanied him not to the Saint Romain Fair that was then taking place, but up the hill to the cemetery.[24]

"I am disappointed in you for becoming savage and unhappy with life," George Sand reproached her troubadour. She suggested that he marry; he ought to be able to find a woman he could love, or whose love would make him happy. But he objected that he was not cut out for such an existence. He could not afford a wife, and he was too old. And too decent to inflict his personality on another being. When she persisted, suggesting that the feminine element might have been lacking in his life, he confided to her: "I loved more than anyone ever did. And then chance and the nature of things led to the fact that I was gradually surrounded by solitude."[25]

Turgenev sought to cheer him up, but Flaubert made it clear that his condition was incurable. Yet he was not going to be beaten down, for he was working on a book in which he would vent his spleen. He softened his language in explaining his mood to Léonie Brainne: "All the friends who have gone, public idiocy, being fifty, solitude, and some money worries — surely these are the causes?"[26]

George Sand made a timid attempt to effect a reconciliation between him and Michel Lévy, who was better than Flaubert thought he was; if he had made mistakes, she would try to repair them. But Flaubert did not think she could help. Lévy had hurt him in a sensitive place, the memory of his poor Bouilhet. He was not Christian, he added, and the hypocrisy of pardon was impossible for him.[27]

As for his money worries: he himself confessed to being appalled by his household expenses, by what he was spending for cider alone! But when the Commanvilles reproached him for wasting money, he was upset. "Do you think that I can watch over the expenses of my servant! Suicide would be sweet compared to such a life. . . ." (The unconscious echo is of King Lear's reply to his ungrateful daughters about the cost of his retinue.) "My life is abominably barren, without pleasure or distraction, without emotions," he concluded. "But I won't push asceticism to the point of prying into my kitchen." In a letter to Edma Roger des Genettes on December 12, 1872, his fifty-first birthday, he told her that he hoped he would not have as many more years to endure. He was not so free in his movements as she might think. "Feel sorry for a man who is exceedingly harassed by business matters!"[28]

On December 23, the surviving Flauberts were assembled in Rouen in the study of the family notary Gustave Bidault. Gustave and Achille were present, Ernest Commanville spoke for Caroline, and Emile Hamard was represented by a proxy. It was time for the division of property following the death of Madame Flaubert. According to her wish, Croisset would go to Caroline. Gifts made during her lifetime were also taken into account, such as a sum of 105,000 francs turned over to Achille on his marriage and an identical sum constituting the dowry of Madame Flaubert's deceased daughter Caroline. Just as carefully, it was noted that Gustave's mother had made cash donations to him equivalent to the sums given to her other children. He had in fact received 47,076.50 francs of his 105,000-franc share.

In all, the legacy amounted to 701,365.55 francs, of which sum 528,500 francs was in property owned by the partnership set up by Dr. Flaubert and his wife after their marriage. In the end, each heir was to receive about 210,000 francs, with Gustave's share to be augmented by the amount still owed to him, plus 1,686.37 francs in interest. Part of this would be given to him in cash, part in property. He received the Deauville farm, which then consisted of twenty-four and a half hectares of land with a meadow of nearly five hectares in nearby Tourgeville, property valued at 130,000 francs.[29]

PART VIII

CHAPTER THIRTY-EIGHT

GUY

As soon as the division of his mother's legacy was settled, Flaubert packed for Paris. The beginning of 1873 found him settled in the capital but "not very merry," he complained to George Sand. In his first days in Paris, he walked "like a rural postman," which helped him sleep. But then he caught cold and could not go out at all — "I am suffering too much, in addition to which I'm hideous, with my coughing and my pocket handkerchiefs," he explained to Sand, who was hoping that he would visit her in Nohant.[1]

One of the things he wished to do was to put some order in his professional life. As of January 1, 1873, the rights for both *Madame Bovary* and *Salammbô* had reverted to him, while Lévy still had seven years to go as publisher of *A Sentimental Education*. But Bouilhet's contracts seemed destined to tie him to Lévy indefinitely. Flaubert was to pay the balance of the printing bill for Bouilhet's last poems, and he grumbled that he was so disgusted with the publishing business that he had turned away both Georges Charpentier and a Belgian publisher. "I could sell *Bovary* and *Salammbô* now," he told Philippe Leparfait, "but the nausea that such negotiations cause is too much! I desire only one thing, to drop dead. I lack the energy to kick the bucket myself. That's the secret of my existence."

In the end, he paid out twenty-one hundred francs to finance the book of Bouilhet's poems, and was negotiating either to buy back the rights to *Melaenis* or to sell the last poems to Lévy, so that one way or another a complete works of Bouilhet could see the light of day.[2] Clearly he was delighted to use his inheritance in this manner. Lévy had thought he was poor, Flaubert told George Sand, and that was why the publisher had treated him badly. "Well, I'm taking revenge for the poor."[3]

He was still feeling ill in February, complaining of fever and chest pain. Every time he had gone out for air over the past month, he told Léonie Brainne, the cold or flu had come back stronger. But he did manage to get together with "good Turgenev" and to read *Saint Anthony* to him, to their mutual satisfaction.[4]

He declared to Edmond de Goncourt, who recorded it under the date of February 26, that "indignation alone keeps me going. Indignation for me is the pin that dolls have up their ass, the pin that keeps them standing up. When I cease to be indignant, I'll keel over."[5]

But to believe this was to overlook that other trait, the one that helped to explain the attachment of his friends: his irremediable sentimentality. It now seemed that he was going to have a new outlet for his need for intense relationships in Guy de Maupassant, the son of his childhood comrade Laure, who of course was Alfred Le Poittevin's sister. In a letter to Laure, by then Madame Gustave de Maupassant, he began with what he called a "declaration of tenderness" for her son. For he found Guy charming, intelligent, of good sense, and witty. "Despite the difference in our ages, I consider him 'a friend,' and then he reminds me so much of Alfred! I am even frightened by the resemblance at times, especially when he lowers his head while reciting poetry. . . ." He felt that Guy should be encouraged in his poetry, "because it is a noble passion, because literature consoles for so many things, and because he may develop talent — who knows?" He found the boy a bit lazy but thought he could learn to work, to be original — and lofty.[6]

Friends, as we have seen, since they played together in the garden of the chief surgeon's residence, Laure Le Poittevin and Gustave Flaubert had never been totally out of touch. She lived on the Channel coast at Etretat and, after separating from her husband, raised her sons, Guy and Hervé, alone. When Flaubert sent her a copy of *Salammbô* on its publication in 1862, she informed him that she was reading it aloud after dinner. "My son Guy is not the least attentive," said she (he was then twelve years old); "your descriptions, so lovely sometimes, so terrible at other times, make his dark eyes shine. . . ."[7] In March 1866, when Flaubert sent his condolences on the death of her mother, Laure described her humble existence, devoted to her sons. "The younger one is only a good little peasant up to now, but the older boy [Guy] is a young man, already quite serious. The poor

lad has seen and understood so many things. . . ." Surely she was
alluding to the scenes between herself and her estranged husband
prior to their separation.[8]

As Guy grew up, and after his military service, he began to see
more of Flaubert; he was proud, Laure told Flaubert, that the older
man sometimes consulted him.[9] (When Guy began to work at the
Ministry of the Navy in Paris as a clerk, Flaubert asked for information on copy clerks, for he was then beginning to work on *Bouvard
and Pécuchet*.) We have a portrait of Guy at the time he began to see
Flaubert regularly, from a near-contemporary, Flaubert's niece Caroline. "At twenty, Guy de Maupassant was a handsome boy of average height, somewhat square-shouldered, but his head was a solid
bust resembling that of a young Roman emperor. Active in physical
exercises, a bit in love with himself, or in any case paying more than
usual attention to his personal appearance. . . ."[10]

"I don't know whether you have talent," Maupassant remembered
Flaubert saying the first time he submitted his work to the master.
"The work you have brought me shows a certain degree of intelligence, but don't forget this, young man: talent, as Buffon said, is
nothing but exceeding patience." This apprenticeship, Maupassant
recalled, was to last seven years, during which time he brought Flaubert
poems and stories, even a play, none of which survive. Above all
Flaubert demanded originality. "The slightest object contains something unknown. Find it. To describe a fire and a tree in a field, stand
in front of that fire and that tree until they look like no other tree and
no other fire."[11]

"To Guy de Maupassant whom I love like a son," read the inscrip-
tion on a photograph of himself that the master gave to the disciple.
So it was not very difficult to bridge the gap, and some writers put
forward the hypothesis that Guy was Flaubert's son. The legend was
helped along by an inconsistency in the documentation of Maupassant's birth. His death certificate gave his place of birth as Sotteville,
and some say he was born in Fécamp, but official records list him as
having been born in the castle of Miromesnil in Tourville-sur-Arques.
(All three are in the district now known as Seine-Maritime.) It has
been suggested that Laure Le Poittevin, after convincing her fiancé
to obtain the right to call himself *de* Maupassant, also arranged
for her first son to be born in a castle, or to appear to have been born
in one.[12]

Could Gustave Flaubert have been Guy's father? He sailed to Egypt
with Maxime Du Camp a little more than nine months before Guy

was born, but the counterargument holds that if a place of birth can be altered, so can a date. Yet nothing we know about Laure's relations with Flaubert, no scrap of evidence, suggests that there was then, before, or later, any touch of guilt or regret. And a batch of letters between the two is available for our examination, letters not written to be published. Surely a simple woman would have betrayed herself in some line of some letter, had there been something to betray.

Thirteen years after Flaubert's death, Paul Alexis, a disciple and biographer of Zola, confided to Edmond de Goncourt that after a visit to Laure he was convinced that Guy was Flaubert's son. For one thing, Laure had insisted that "physically and morally" her son did not resemble his legal father. Referring to Guy's burial, she said that he had not wished to have a lead coffin, but wanted to be closer to the earth. "He was always preoccupied with this idea," she said, "and when he presided over the burial of his dear father in Rouen — " She stopped short, Alexis remembered, and corrected herself: " — of poor Flaubert . . ."[13]

There is also an argument based on literary evidence: the persistence of the theme of illegitimacy in Maupassant's work. A scholar found that thirty-two of his stories contain variations on the problem of uncertain parentage.[14] The possibility has also been suggested that Maupassant was Flaubert's son but that Flaubert himself never knew it, and neither did Maupassant until after Flaubert's death.[15]

We can visit Flaubert's lodgings on Rue Murillo with Maupassant, on one of those Sundays when Flaubert was in town and received friends from one to seven: "a bachelor flat, quite simple," Maupassant remembered it. "The walls were bare and the furnishings modest, for he had a horror of arty curios." When the bell rang to announce the first visitor, Flaubert threw a light red silk cloth over his desk, covering both the manuscript on which he had been working and his writing tools. As the valet had Sundays off, Flaubert himself opened the door for his guests. Often the first to arrive would be Turgenev, whom Flaubert "kissed like a brother." Then Hippolyte Taine, "his eyes hidden behind glasses, his manner shy," and Alphonse Daudet, "who brings the atmosphere of Paris, a lively Paris, sophisticated, active and merry." And Zola, out of breath from the climb upstairs, followed by the faithful Paul Alexis. Zola spoke little but listened well, putting in a word when the conversation faded. "He is of medium height," Maupassant described him, "a bit heavy, good-natured and obstinate. His head, very similar to what one finds in many old Italian paintings, without being handsome shows both strength and intelligence. . . . The lower part of this heavy but energetic face is covered with a carefully manicured beard. His look is dark, myopic, penetrating, investigative, often ironic. . . ." Almost always the last one to arrive was Edmond de Goncourt, "dressed as a gentleman, with a fine and nervous air of the well-bred."

Maupassant also seized Flaubert at this moment: "With broad gestures that made him seem to take off, going from one guest to another with a stride that covered the room, his long dressing gown puffed out behind him . . . full of excitement, indignation, vehement flame, resounding eloquence, he amused us with his violence, charmed us with his good nature, often stupefied us with his prodigious erudition. . . ." Then the friends would leave, one after the other, and Flaubert would sleep for an hour on his sofa before going to Princess Mathilde's regular Sunday evening.[16]

Zola noted the absence of trimmings; the only luxury was the cretonne that covered the walls, the only decorative pieces an Arab saddle and a gilt Buddha (Zola remembered it as being of cardboard, not wood).[17] On the desk, recalled still another visitor, the paperweight was a section of a ship mast, which Flaubert insisted his father had extracted from a sailor's posterior.[18] Flaubert was no longer attractive by the time Paris really got to know him, this visitor said. He still had eyes "of an extraordinary kindness . . . , blue, candid, and good," but the rest of his face had been invested with an acne that later degenerated into a veritable eczema, and that led Théophile Gautier to compare him to "a cherry in brandy that has fallen into the fire."[19]

Wearing a long dressing gown did not protect Flaubert from the ravages of winter. In March he was still ill; he told Turgenev, for example, that he was not ready to read him *The Temptation of Saint Anthony*, "and it's not the will that is lacking, since at present you are the only human being for whom I have respect, the only literary person who exists, the only friend who remains. But my throat is too battered to be able to shout properly for several consecutive hours." To George Sand, however, he let on that his indisposition was more one of the mind. "What has been wrong with me for the past four months, what anguish troubles the depths of my soul? I do not know. What is certain is that I have been quite ill, in a vague way. But at the moment I am better, I am even beginning not to think about

Michel Lévy all the time. . . . I'm not quite free of it, but the thought of that miserable person no longer makes my heart beat faster with anger and indignation."

At the beginning of spring he was ready to transfer his literary salon from Rue Murillo to Nohant. He had long promised to visit Sand with Turgenev, but the Russian kept putting him off. Finally Flaubert decided to make the journey alone, and to let Turgenev join them when he could. He arrived during dinner on Saturday, April 12; that night the group played dominoes. (He played well, but "it suffocates him," observed Sand.) The next day after dinner he put on a skirt and danced a fandango. "He is quite funny, but he is out of breath after five minutes. He is much older than I am," said she, although he did seem less overweight, less tired-looking than she had found him in the past. She concluded: "Still too lively in the brain, to the detriment of the body." He read *Saint Anthony* to the family circle — from three to six in the afternoon, and from nine to midnight — and she found it splendid.

Turgenev missed that. He arrived late on April 16. There was time for talk, for family-style merrymaking. After a dinner of truffled turkey on April 17, Sand wrote: ". . . We jump about, we dance, we sing, we shout, we exasperate Flaubert, who always wants to stop everything to talk literature. He is overwhelmed. Turgenev likes noise and merriment; he is as much of a child as we are. He dances, he waltzes. What a good and pleasant man of genius!" Was she taking sides? See what she said to her diary the next day: "Conversation of Flaubert quite lively and funny, but it is all himself; Turgenev, who is much more interesting, finds it hard to get in a word." She summed it up on their departure day, Saturday, April 19: "One *lives* with character more than with intelligence and grandeur. I am tired, aching tired, of my dear Flaubert. I love him all the same, and he is a fine person, but too overwhelming. He kills us." Turgenev she loved less, but he was so much easier to live with!

Then she was in Paris, and it was Flaubert's turn to play host. On Saturday, May 3, she was invited to dinner by him, along with Turgenev and Goncourt. They were to meet at the Magny. She was on time but found no one there; then Turgenev arrived. After more time passed, Goncourt showed up to tell them: "We're not dining here. Flaubert is waiting for you at the Frères Provençaux restaurant." "Why?" "He says he suffocates here, that the rooms are too small . . . , that he's tired." "I too am tired," Sand replied, as she later told the story to her son. "Bawl him out," said Goncourt, "he's a badly behaved child; but do come." "No, I'm dying of hunger, I'm staying; let's have dinner here." They all laughed, but Goncourt warned that Flaubert would be furious. So they got a carriage to take them across the river to the Palais-Royal gardens, only to find Flaubert asleep on a sofa in the restaurant. Sand called him a pig, and he begged her forgiveness, even got down on his knees. "Finally we had a bad dinner," Sand was to tell her son, "in a room much smaller than the one at Magny." Flaubert explained that he was exhausted because he had read a play by Bouilhet to a theater director; it had been accepted, but he would have to spend six months rewriting it. He talked of nothing else, and neither Turgenev nor Goncourt could get a word in. Sand left early, and told Flaubert that she was leaving Paris on Monday, three days earlier than she actually did. "I'm fed up with my little comrade," she explained to her son. "I love him, but he drives me mad. He doesn't like noise, but the noise he makes doesn't bother him."[20]

We can blame some of this on Sand's own irascibility, for Goncourt's version is somewhat less one-sided. Far from being silent, Turgenev spoke up that evening, "and we listened to the giant with a soft voice, with stories made tender by moving and delicate touches." Indeed, an anecdote told by Flaubert about a play he had written in school led Turgenev to tell stories of his own childhood; to accept Goncourt's account of their soirée is to see the evening as all Turgenev's.

Goncourt had his own score to settle with Flaubert: "The older Flaubert gets, the more provincial he becomes." For according to him, if one forgot Flaubert as a beast of burden, "the maker of books at one word per hour," one was left with a quite ordinary talent, lacking originality. Flaubert sought to conceal his quite ordinary bourgeois mind through brutal language, concluded Goncourt, but did he really fool anyone? He claimed to be passionate but had little interest in women. He claimed to be reckless about money but spent nothing. Goncourt did not feel that Flaubert was insincere in his pronouncements; rather, through the very violence of his language, "my friend Flaubert succeeds in convincing himself of the untruths he sells us."[21]

Before returning to Croisset, Flaubert obtained a written promise from a theater director that *Le Sexe faible* would go on the stage that autumn, and a verbal assurance that it would make money. So he put aside *Bouvard and Pécuchet*. He was trying to write "natural conversation," he told his niece — not a simple thing when he also wanted to produce a language with firmness and rhythm. "It has been a long time (it will soon be a year) since I wrote anything, and making phrases seems sweet to me."

His optimism was broadly distributed, for he was spending money to redecorate Croisset, buying curtains, towels, sheets, and kitchen equipment. "Really, it's not a matter of luxury," he assured the Commanvilles, who were not being very forthcoming with his funds. In any case he would use the thousand francs promised by his new publisher Alphonse Lemerre for a reprinting of *Madame Bovary*. "At least something will remain of my works," he told Caroline, "and this something will be used for the house of our poor old lady!"[22]

CHAPTER THIRTY-NINE

"THE CANDIDATE"

I'M WORKING like a madman on *Le Sexe faible* — a wretched piece of work, in fact," he wrote Turgenev on May 29. "Yet I think that I shall be able to make something of it."[1] His shortest day so far had been fourteen hours, he told Mathilde, and there had been one of eighteen. In this abominable weather there was little else to do.[2]

He took time out, all the same, for a visit from Georges Charpentier. Perhaps, as Maupassant observed, this publisher tended to put off young authors, but he was not above traveling all the way up to Croisset to sign up a writer who really interested him. He, too, was to do a new edition of *Madame Bovary*, with an appendix that would reproduce the text of the courtroom proceedings, and he was also going to reissue *Salammbô*. And then it was the turn of the theater director Carvalho, whose name was actually Léon Carvaille; at forty-eight, he was one of the country's best-known theatrical men. He came to hear Flaubert read *Le Sexe faible*, now totally revised, and he still seemed to like it, still thought it would be a success.[3]

As it has come down to us, the Bouilhet-Flaubert play is an account of domestic squabbles and a domineering mother-in-law. A young civil servant woos and wins a charming girl who, once married, turns out to be a shrew. The husband takes the maid as his mistress, but when he loses her to his godfather, he decides that he had better conform to the letter of married life. Men are the *sexe faible*, the "weak sex." The play is hardly a demolition of bourgeois society; in theme, plot, and dialogue it is hardly worthy of Gustave Flaubert.

Finishing this little play exhausted him. But he seemed to have caught the theatrical bug. As he explained it to George Sand, he had gotten into the habit of seeing things dramatically, of thinking in dialogue, and so he had begun to draft a scenario of still another play. It would be called *Le Candidat*. He wrote twenty pages of his outline and then put it in a drawer until he could read it to someone.[4]

Then he turned to more pressing chores. He had proofs to go through for Charpentier and Lemerre (both, as has been said, were doing new editions of *Madame Bovary*, the latter in a very special small format that would make his reputation). He was also reading for his novel-in-progress, *Bouvard and Pécuchet*, calculating that in the past year he had made notes on 194 volumes.[5]

On August 9 he was back in Paris, where he found the theater man Carvalho all smiles. The Bouilhet play would go on stage early in the following year, leaving the autumn free for *Bouvard and Pécuchet*. Flaubert spent the rest of the month in town, going to the theater as often as he could to size up actors and actresses, since he would be choosing the cast with Carvalho. He also read the scenario of his own creation, *Le Candidat*, to the theater manager, who was so enthusiastic that he wanted to mention it to the press immediately — but Flaubert said no, flatly refused.

Before returning to Croisset he undertook what he described to his niece as an "epic" day. Looking for a region in which to place the country home of his copy clerks, he traveled to Rambouillet by rail and hired a carriage to go to Houdan, seventeen miles away, and then another for the sixteen miles separating Houdan from Mantes, where he caught the Rouen train, arriving home at midnight in a torrential rain. He had spent eighty-three francs that day, "for it costs money to make conscientious literature." He did think he had found the perfect house for Bouvard and Pécuchet in Houdan, but before making a final decision he wished to inspect still more countryside.[6]

He resumed his reading. But each evening he did some writing on his own play, *Le Candidat*, encouraged by Carvalho's enthusiasm. He also felt that the manager's eagerness for this play was the best guarantee that *Le Sexe faible*, too, would see production. "Carvalho, until now, has been charming," he told George Sand. "His enthusiasm is indeed so strong that I worry about it; we must remember the good Frenchmen who shouted 'To Berlin!' and received such a pretty thrashing."[7] Clearly he was delighted with what he was doing. He knew there was plenty to revise, but he enjoyed the writing, and enjoyed his solitary existence, he told Caroline — "with no one to bother me, pursuing the same idea from morning to evening, and sometimes all night long." At times he became *too* exalted and had to calm himself down. But he painted a different self-portrait for Mathilde. He was resigned to his life in Croisset. "When I have walked a bit in my garden, escorted by my greyhound, who leaps about, and when I have agitated the dead leaves under my feet and a lot of memories in my old head, I shake off the sadness that has been creeping up on me and I go upstairs to my work table."[8]

Turgenev exasperated him. For most of their years as friends Flaubert had been waiting for something from the Moscovite, as he called him affectionately: waiting for confirmation of a visit, or for a reply to a question about a visit. "I am sure that he wants to come," Flaubert told Caroline, "but the Viardots drag him somewhere else, and he doesn't dare risk their anger. . . ." Then at last, at the end of September, the Moscovite came to life, announcing his arrival on October 2. He kept this promise, and once again Flaubert was captivated. "You cannot imagine all that he knows!" he reported to his niece. "I think he is familiar with *all* literatures down to their depths!" They made one excursion, to the ruins for the Jumièges abbey, but all the rest of the time, over a three-day visit, they talked of books. Flaubert took advantage of his captive audience to read *Le Sexe faible*, *Le Château des Coeurs*, and the first act of *Le Candidat*. Turgenev liked the unfinished play best of all.[9]

On October 20 Flaubert was in Paris. This time there was a surprise, for Carvalho now demanded considerable revisions in *Le Sexe faible*. Flaubert resisted. What Carvalho really wanted was to put off the Bouilhet play in order to produce Flaubert's *Le Candidat* first; Gustave gave in, and even resolved to finish writing it by the first of the year.[10] "Then when it is finished, revised and corrected, he probably won't want it any longer," a disabused Flaubert wrote George Sand. "In any case I don't care, so much do I want to return to my novel, which is going to occupy me for several years. And then theatrical style is beginning to get on my nerves. These short little sentences, this continual bubbling, irritates me, the way seltzer pleases you at first and then just seems like stale water."[11] But he did go to work on his play on his return to Normandy, and finished writing it on November 22, ahead of the schedule he had set for himself. "It was time I stopped," he wrote his niece. "The floors of the rooms were beginning to pitch under me as on the bridge of a ship, and I was under a constant strain of anxiety. . . ."

Carvalho returned to Croisset at the end of that month. He arrived on a Saturday at four in the afternoon, and by ten to five Flaubert was reading *Le Candidat* to him. The theater manager interrupted him with praise. They dined at eight and talked until two. The next day the serious work began. Flaubert found his guest's criticism judicious, but he was exasperated all the same, for he hardly felt like reworking the material now. They talked all day Sunday, breaking only for dinner with the Lapierres. When Carvalho left, it was with a promise that rehearsals would begin by Christmas. The revisions turned out to be less difficult than Flaubert had feared. He had drawn the line at one thing: he refused to insert the Flaubertian tirades that Carvalho was hoping for, which would have given the play more of an air of scandal. That would have been too facile.[12]

On December 5 at seven P.M., a messenger arrived at Croisset with a telegram from Carvalho: "Have you finished? Come. We begin rehearsals immediately." Flaubert went upstairs to pack and was in Paris the following day. It was decided that a cast would be convened within a week for a full reading of the play by its author. On the appointed day, Flaubert prepared by eating a dozen oysters and a large steak with a half bottle of Chambertin wine, followed by a glass of brandy and another of chartreuse liqueur. The reading itself took place on the stage of the Vaudeville theater, lighted by two oil lamps, before the twenty-six actors and actresses who had been selected. The first act was appreciated, and the second a little less so, but during the third the laughing never stopped, and they loved the fourth and final act. Carvalho did have some further suggestions, and Flaubert found them reasonable, for they were similar to what he had heard from Charles d'Osmoy and from Turgenev.

He returned to Rue Murillo thinking of how to make the second act flow more smoothly; that occupied him the next day, his birthday. He also made a decision: he would release *The Temptation of Saint Anthony* to his new publisher Charpentier.[13]

He was happy. His exuberance was a little too much for Edmond de Goncourt, who was a fellow guest at Mathilde's a few nights later. "He had a good dinner," Goncourt tells us. "He is childishly swelled up by his reading at the Vaudeville Theater. He is vulgarly happy, and practically lying on top of me, with finger jabs in my chest that feel like blows from a fencing foil. . . ." Flaubert, who in the diarist's view was always trying to prove that he had done more and suffered more than anyone else, now explained to his friends that no one had been so much in love as he had been. As an adolescent he had risked his life on a cliff in order to kiss a Newfoundland dog on the very spot where the dog's mistress had kissed it. This love affair lasted, Goncourt heard Flaubert say, until he was thirty-two years old.

Goncourt summed up: "Flaubert emits so much nervosity, so much pugnacious violence, that the groups in which he finds himself soon become stormy, and everyone begins to be aggressive."[14]

Flaubert spent Christmas rewriting the first two acts of Le Candidat, working all of Christmas day and the day after. If he was not entirely pleased with the results, he was content, he told George Sand, with his own energy.[15] For the first time he was occupied with a play wholly of his own making; obviously he was no less assiduous than he had been with Bouilhet's work. And then in January 1874 he joined the rehearsals, which lasted from noon until five each day, and afterward worked on the proofs of Saint Anthony. He had his Wednesdays at Mathilde's and his Sundays at home, with little more socializing than that during the six-week period of rehearsals.[16]

February was feverish, part of it in his head, for he had another of his fierce winter colds. "While spitting and coughing at my fireside, I ruminate on my youth," he wrote to George Sand. "Is it because of too much activity for the past eight months or because of the total absence of the feminine element in my life that I feel more abandoned than ever before?" He thought of Sand and her house filled with children, her granddaughters. "Why don't I have that! I was born with all the tender instincts all the same!" He concluded: "I was a coward when I was a young man. I was afraid of life!"[17]

Then Carvalho left the Vaudeville to take over another theater, and Flaubert had to learn to work with his successor. He began to regret having let the censors interfere with his script, for some of his dialogue mocking the arch-conservatives had been removed, throwing the play off balance, he thought. When Le Candidat was actually to be performed for the censors, he enlisted the moral support of Edgar Raoul-Duval, though he was to tell Edma Roger des Genettes that it was the censors' fear of his own shouting that saved the play.[18]

Flaubert's candidate is a provincial bourgeois called Rousselin. A local committee has persuaded him to run for the assembly, but a friend warns him that the owner of the castle, a count, hopes to win Rousselin's daughter for his son and so augment the family fortunes; the candidacy is only a lure. And indeed, when Rousselin rejects the count's son as a suitor, the count threatens to run against him. Meanwhile, a simple bourgeois whose suit for Rousselin's daughter has also been turned down decides to frighten the candidate into seeking his help; he induces yet another man to enter his candidacy. Now there are three candidates, with Rousselin claiming to be the most republican of them all. Then the count withdraws and offers to ally himself with Rousselin; Rousselin now sees himself as conservative, but revises his platform when he suspects he can win over the socialists. The formal presentation of his candidacy becomes a clash of private interests and ends in disorder. The remaining rival offers to give up his candidacy if Rousselin will forgive a debt. A falsely favorable account of Rousselin's electoral meeting is distributed, composed by a journalist who covets his wife. Voters come to the candidate asking for money or for promises on their way to the polls. Our candidate is elected, but he is also cuckolded, for his wife has spent the afternoon in a small hotel with the journalist.

The play opened on March 11 to a total absence of enthusiasm. Once again Goncourt painted the scene with a master's touch and little heart. At the start there was "this theater fired with sympathy . . . waiting to hear sublime tirades, overwhelming dashes of wit, words that are battle cries, and finding itself in the face of nothing, nothing." The first reaction was "pitying sadness," but after being restrained out of respect for Flaubert, "the disappointed audience took its revenge in a kind of facetious hushing, a playful mocking of all the pathos of this thing." The play's humor was gross; there were failures of taste, tact, invention. The public looked for Flaubert but did not find him in this play.[19] "You would have been upset, as we all were," a friend without Goncourt's critical judgment but with more charity, Raoul-Duval, wrote another friend, Charles Lapierre. "The public was not hostile, it was glum and regretfully astonished: the tirades followed one another and fell flat. Our Flau, although visibly hurt, stood up proudly before this failure."[20]

Zola found Flaubert's reaction "very fine, very brave." Flaubert had known as early as the previous day's dress rehearsal that his work was doomed, and his friends knew it, too. It was snowing as they left the theater. Zola found Flaubert smoking a cigar outdoors; other friends joined them and they talked about it all as they walked each other home.[21] "The public was as well composed as it could be, sympathetic to the author, prepared to be indulgent, asking only to applaud," reported one reviewer, "and the four acts went by without an event, a scene, a tirade, a word that would give them the opportunity."[22]

"It's a flop if ever there was one," Flaubert confessed to George

Sand. He did not believe the flatterers who said that *Le Candidat* would find its audience. He was aware of the play's faults and could have corrected them if he had not been harassed by Carvalho during the rehearsals. He admitted that he could have used the money he would have made had the play been a success. "But since my failure is a matter neither of art nor of sentiment, I do not feel concerned."

After the second night, when he saw his leading man return to the wings with tears in his eyes, he decided to withdraw the play, for he did not wish his actors to be booed.[23]

The trouble with *Le Candidat,* as another reviewer observed, was that playwriting was not what its author did best: "Six lines of *Madame Bovary,* chosen at random, are worth more than the whole of *Le Candidat.*"[24] In an interview prior to the opening, Flaubert had talked about another of his works, *The Temptation of Saint Anthony,* which at long last was to be published. He reminded the journalist, a fellow Norman, of the annual Saint Romain Fair in Rouen, during which a performance of the *Temptation* was a regular feature. Flaubert's was a mystery play, "a heroic, philosophical, and archaeological re-creation of the fourth century, of the milieu in which the saint lived with his real temptations. . . ." Would it be a pendant to *Salammbô?* Worse, Flaubert told the interviewer, for distracted readers would look for another *Madame Bovary,* another *Sentimental Education,* and they were bound to be disconcerted.[25]

The book appeared on April 1, with a dedication to Alfred Le Poittevin, who had died more than a quarter of a century earlier. As was his practice, Flaubert autographed countless copies for friends, admirers, and critics. One went to Juliet Herbert, from "her old Gustave" (he called it the "first copy").[26] Another he sent to a woman closer at hand, Léonie Brainne. "You lost something in not coming to see me in recent days," she wrote back in appreciation. "One never knows how far admiration can lead. . . ."[27]

CHAPTER FORTY

AUGUST 1:
BOUVARD AND PÉCUCHET

MY LITTLE BOOK is going well," Flaubert wrote Léonie. Two thousand copies had left the publisher between April 1, 1874, a Wednesday, and the following Monday. There was a second printing before the end of that month, and paper was being acquired for a third.[1] There would always be buyers for a new work by Gustave Flaubert, though his books did not necessarily make the author (or his publisher) rich. There would always be exemplary readers.

George Sand was one. She had not admired *Le Candidat* and told the author that. It was hard to write for the theater, she warned; unless one were Molière, one failed eighteen times out of twenty. But *Saint Anthony* . . . Flaubert had heard that Sand thought his new book detestable. "Those who say that I do not find *Saint Anthony* fine and excellent have lied," she declared.[2] "The insults accumulate," he wrote her on May 1. "I have been vilified from *Le Figaro* to *La Revue des Deux Mondes,* and in passing by *La Gazette de France* and *Le Constitutionnel.*" Even those critics from whom he would have expected better were merciless.[3] In *Le Constitutionnel* his old adversary Barbey d'Aurevilly began by making fun of the advance publicity put forth by Flaubert's coterie. "To deliver their friend of his intellectual pregnancy, they make noise around the book he is carrying all through his laborious gestation, believing that they can thus excite him and give him the energy to push it along and finally to lay it. . . ." Barbey thought this book "could represent the definitive suicide of Flaubert"; it was "so incomprehensible that one perceives neither the initial theme nor even the intention."[4]

Despite all of this, Flaubert was going to write another book that would cause trouble, and he would do it before he returned to the traditional novel. He would begin after he had gotten some rest in Switzerland. Doctor's orders, he told Edma Roger des Genettes; indeed, the doctor had characterized him as "a hysterical old woman," and he had replied, "Doctor, you're on the right track."[5] There was also to be another field trip, for he still had not found the house in the country that he needed for his copy clerks. Now he knew that Bouvard and Pécuchet, after retirement, would move to Normandy, specifically to the dairy region of Flaubert's mother's family. "I need a silly place in the middle of some attractive landscape," he wrote Edma Roger des Genettes, "a place where one can carry out geological and archaeological excursions." Lest she think he was indulging himself, he went on, "Ah! What a book! It has exhausted me in advance; I feel overcome by the difficulties of this work, for which I have already read and summed up 294 volumes!"[6]

Still, he had a charming voyage. With his neighbor from down the Seine, Edmond Laporte, he set out on June 18, to roam the Orne and Calvados districts. They rode in broken-down carriages, dined and slept in country inns; he introduced Laporte to cider brandy — what is now called calvados — and found the younger man a helpful traveling mate. In the end he decided to locate Bouvard and Pécuchet's home between the valleys of the Orne and the Auge, "on a stupid plateau" between Caen and Falaise.[7]

On June 25 he was in Paris, en route to Switzerland. He had some unfinished business to attend to, such as delivering a copy of *Le Sexe faible* to a new theater, the Cluny, since there was no longer any hope for it at the Vaudeville, the scene of his rout. He saw Emile Zola, who listened to his description of his new book. Afterward Zola sat down to write their mutual friend Turgenev. "It is quite unfortunate that none of his friends dares steer him away from the book he is about to begin. I fear he is in for real trouble."[8]

A mountain standing alone, its peak fifty-nine hundred feet above the surrounding lakes, Rigi, in the Swiss-German Alps, has always been a tourist attraction. It is amply endowed with hotels, many of them clustered near the summit, at Rigi-Kaltbad. "It is supposed that the barometric pressure, being lower, will relieve my congestion in making the blood flow toward the lower organs. That is the theory." And the forced rest would not hurt him.

It is certain that he anticipated no pleasure. "I begin by declaring that the beauties of Nature bore me profoundly" — this was his first word to his niece. The idea that he would be spending three weeks in this place appalled him. Surely he lacked the poetic imagination, for he preferred a library, a theater, or a museum to "all the glaciers of Switzerland." He slept during the day as well as at night; he stuffed himself with food; he smoked. "Besides, the Alps are out of proportion with our beings," he explained to Turgenev, who was then in Moscow. "They are too big to be useful to us." By the end of the first week, a week that seemed to last three centuries, he was close to depression. "If I continued such a life for long," he warned Caroline, "I would become absolutely hypochondriacal." Although he had been hiking for two or three hours each afternoon, he had soon *lost* his appetite. "That's how exercise is good for me."[9]

He had brought no books with him, no manuscript, and so could explore new subjects for books; one was a long novel to be called "Under Napoleon III."[10] The notebook in which he did this exploring survives. A pocket sketchbook suitable for mountain walks, it bears the date July 4, 1874. The notes for "Under Napoleon III" read thus:

> a girl who moves up
> she comes from a brothel — rises to business
> and even politics   can obtain medals for people

Was he thinking of Jeanne de Tourbey? For this was how the Goncourts saw her.

He then turned the sketchbook over and began writing on the other side, this time making notes for the story that was to become "The Legend of Saint Julian the Hospitaler."[11]

Flaubert left Rigi-Kaltbad on July 19, a couple of days earlier than originally scheduled. In Paris, after an overnight train ride, he rushed off to the Cluny theater, where the manager, Emile Weinschenk, confirmed that the Bouilhet play *Le Sexe faible* would be performed in November, following a play by Zola. After stopping in Croisset to leave his luggage and to pick up some clean shirts, he went on to Dieppe to visit Caroline. To Turgenev he announced his return to Croisset on the last day of July — "and, on Saturday, August 1, I begin *Bouvard and Pécuchet* at last. I have sworn that to myself! There is no retreating!" But he admitted that the project inspired fear in him. "I feel that I am going to embark for a very long journey toward unknown regions, and that I shall not return."

He respected Turgenev's critical talents. But he could not go along with a suggestion made by Turgenev (and by Zola) that he treat the theme of his new book project lightly. If he did that, he argued, his subject would lose significance; it had to be "something serious and even frightening."[12]

Once again he dramatized the moment of his taking up a new work. We have it in a letter to Ernest Commanville, dated that very August 1, 1874: "Yesterday I finished up all my little affairs, this morning I sharpened some feather pens, and a while ago, at four, after a whole afternoon of torture, I finally produced the first sentence of *B. and P.*, which I am sending Caro[line], as promised."[13] But this was all he would tell Caroline, and it would be all for a long time to come, he warned her. "I flounder, I cross out, I become desperate. Last night [August 5] I had a violent stomachache. But it will work; it *has* to work. In any case the difficulties of this book are frightful. The job might kill me. . . ."[14] This prediction was as chillingly prophetic as his description to Turgenev of a long journey with no return.

Jean-Paul Sartre called *Bouvard and Pécuchet* "a colossal and grotesque work" whose roots were deep in Flaubert's "alienated childhood": in it Flaubert set out to destroy science — that is, to carry out "the murder of the father."[15] One can also see this book as a challenge to the whole nineteenth century, with its rationalism; more than one critic has called it France's *Don Quixote*.[16] Bouvard and Pécuchet, the copy clerks, meet on Boulevard Bourdon in Paris while taking the air on a stifling summer day. They like each other at once and find that they share ideals, so when Bouvard inherits some money and Pécuchet retires, they go off together to a house in the country. There they experiment with agriculture and light industry, chemistry and medicine, archaeology and human relations, and discover the flaws in everything written about each of them. Then they compile (or Flaubert would compile for them) an encyclopedia of the flawed wisdom.

At the outset, in early references Flaubert made to the scheme at the beginning of the 1850s, he planned to include a humorous "Dictionnaire des Idées Reçues" whose preface would be an ironic defense of all that was commonplace. The novel we know as *Bouvard and Pécuchet* eventually replaced that preface. As first conceived, the scenario suggests that Flaubert's protagonists are as stupid as the "learned" books they study. But the copy clerks as Flaubert eventually depicted them were to learn to draw the line at further stupidities. "At this time a complicating faculty developed itself in their minds, that of perceiving stupidity and not being able to tolerate it any longer." But this happens in the eighth of ten chapters.

"What beautiful weather! my darling," he wrote to Caroline in the middle of that first month of work. "How calm it is around me, and how alone I am!" His little characters were continuing "their little road."[17] But before he could go much further, there was a treat: Juliet Herbert was coming to France for a visit, and he was to meet her in Paris. He would also see Turgenev and Princess Mathilde. Once again the virtue of the English governess was to be protected. We know — and this is all we know — that he spent twenty days in his paradise. "Your giant has been gigantesque," he bragged to Edmond Laporte, who called him that.[18] He also concerned himself with the planned production of Le Sexe faible at the Cluny theater, and, as ever, gathered material for his novel. In this strenuous three-week visit (and even leaving his exploits with Juliet out of it) he discovered that his stay in the Swiss Alps had been helpful after all. "I climb stairs without becoming out of breath, and I'm much less red-faced and less nervous," he reported to his niece.[19]

Then it was back to Croisset, his copy clerks, and some bad days. "For a while I thought I could not go on," he complained to Edma Roger des Genettes. "Carrying out this work is a horror! And then I am alone now, absolutely alone, without advice or encouragement, not the slightest help, nothing!"[20]

He confessed to George Sand that his friends were criticizing him for his having given Bouilhet's play to a hole-in-the-wall of a theater. But since no one else had wanted the play and he wished Bouilhet's heir to obtain a little money, he had had no choice.[21] For his own funds he continued to depend on Commanville. He would write to remind his niece that her husband was to send the usual amount, one thousand francs; he would appeal to them to pay those bills, such as household expenses or taxes, that were clearly their responsibility as owners of Croisset. "I should very much like [Commanville] to give me an accounting so that I will know, for once, what I possess, and not have to ask for money continually," he insisted to his niece. "I should like to have a regular schedule for payments."[22]

Soon he was off to Paris for the opening of a play by Emile Zola, Les Héritiers Rabourdin, at the Cluny. On the eve of the opening Flaubert joked to Zola: "Tomorrow you will be a great novelist." And indeed the critics, when faced with Zola's play, suddenly found virtues in his books that they hadn't noticed before. Still, the lack of success of this play meant that the stage would be free that much sooner for Bouilhet's. The theater manager discussed the casting with Flaubert, and it was decided that he would read the play to the assembled actors on November 19.[23]

But his friends had been right about the hole-in-the-wall theater. For when Flaubert found himself face-to-face with his cast — who were "hatefully stupid," he was to tell George Sand — he made a quick decision to withdraw the play. "It would have had a pitiful performance," he explained to Edmond Laporte, "and I should have had a phenomenal failure." One of the problems was that the actors had to bring their own costumes, and they were not successful enough to be able to afford proper ones.[24]

Edmond de Goncourt, at the Wednesday dinner given by Princess Mathilde, declared that Flaubert had made the right decision. "When one has had a failure, as both of us have had, one must be sure, for revenge, to be played by real actors the next time." Flaubert seemed embarrassed by this statement, so Goncourt noted, and confessed that he had now submitted *Le Sexe faible* to another second-echelon theater. He added: "There are five dresses in my play, and at that theater the women can afford to buy them." Goncourt found it incredible that the great Gustave Flaubert could say, "There are five dresses in my play."[25]

Flaubert aired his mood in this last month of 1874 in a letter to George Sand. He told her of his turtle's pace on *Bouvard and Pécuchet.* "Besides the difficulties of execution, which are appalling, I have to learn so many things of which I am totally ignorant." He was, as usual, dissatisfied with the world around him: "You have to be here, in Paris, to have an idea of the universal decline. . . . When I am not torturing myself about my project, I moan about myself. . . . In my free time I do nothing but think about those who have left us. And I am going to say something pretentious: no one understands me."[26]

THE CRASH

So it should be clear that Flaubert was already steeped in gloom before the financial debacle of his nephew Ernest Commanville. He was not only morally ill; a persistent flu all but kept him out of circulation that winter. We know, thanks to the meticulous Edmond de Goncourt, that he even missed the second of the "Flaubert Dinners," also known as the "Hissed Authors' Dinners" or the "Company of Five" (the five being Flaubert, Goncourt, Turgenev, Zola, and Alphonse Daudet) — dinners, Daudet was to say later, at which this select group "cursed the indifference of the era toward literature, the public fear of anything really new." (Daudet felt embarrassed when a book of his sold well.)[1]

Thanks again to Goncourt, we know what Flaubert's friends were thinking. "Leaving Flaubert's," he jotted down on April 18, after one of their regular Sunday afternoon visits, "Zola and I talked about the condition of our friend — a condition, he admitted, that after a period of deep melancholy finishes with tears. And while discussing the literary reasons that are responsible for this condition and are killing us all, we expressed surprise at the *lack of radiance* around this famous man. He is famous, he has talent, he is a good soul, and he is a good host; why then, with the exception of Turgenev, Daudet, Zola, and myself, is there no one at these Sundays that are open to everybody? Why?"[2]

Flaubert himself formed part of the crowd at one event. His "little Guy" had written a pornographic play, *A La Feuille de Rose* ("At the Rose Petal"), which was to be performed in a painter's studio on April 19. "Admission only to men over twenty and women already deflowered," Maupassant informed a guest.[3] In the play a provincial couple find themselves in a Paris brothel, believing it to be a proper hotel in which the harem of the Turkish ambassador happens to reside. The farce was heavy, and the costumes outrageous — giant phalluses and exaggerated, painted-on vaginas. Flaubert, after watching a rehearsal, assured Turgenev: "You'll find it enormously amusing." Goncourt assures us that *he* found it revolting.[4]

It was as if Flaubert's anxiety had been a premonition. Before he left Paris for Croisset, the Commanvilles announced to him that this time there was no hope for Ernest's business. He had been unable to raise sufficient funds to save his sawmill in Dieppe; the decline in the price of timber had wiped him out. Caroline retained her capital; indeed, she could not simply hand it over to her husband even if she wished to, under a marriage law that was designed to protect a family's patrimony. But Gustave could help, and immediately said that he would; he was going to save his nephew for his niece's sake, and save Croisset. As he later summed it up for Goncourt, in the end Commanville owed him a million francs.[5]

He made another decision. There were rooms free in the building the Commanvilles were moving into in Paris, and on the same floor, on Rue du Faubourg Saint Honoré; he took them. "For I cannot stand being alone anymore," he wrote to George Sand.[6]

All the same, he returned to Croisset early in May 1875. "I should prefer to be happy, that would be simpler," he wrote Caroline from there. "Still, if your husband managed to get out of his difficulties, if I saw him making money and confident in the future, as before, if I could earn ten thousand francs' rent from the Deauville farm . . . and if *Bouvard and Pécuchet* satisfied me, I think that I should no longer have anything to complain about."[7] To George Sand he catalogued his ills: "A roving gout, pains that show up here and there, an *invincible* melancholy, the feeling of 'the world's uselessness,' and considerable doubt about the book I'm writing, that's what's wrong with me, dear and brave master. Add to that problems involving money, and the permanent desire to be dead . . . this is my present condition."

Sand had told him how sad she felt at the death of "this poor Michel" — for her publisher, once Flaubert's as well, had died on May 5. She was sure that Flaubert was a good person, if a grumpy one, and would not rejoice at Lévy's death. "For me it is a great loss in every sense," she said, "for he was absolutely devoted to me and proved it to me all the time by his constant concern and help." But Flaubert could not go along with that. Lévy's death had been sudden and without pain, he said, and "I don't think he deserved that." Lévy had done him much evil.[8] Which of course was not what Sand had meant.

Henceforth his thoughts centered on the Commanvilles. Could they save their business, and save themselves and Flaubert from ruin? While awaiting the outcome he could do little work, he informed Caroline on July 8. Her reply contained some reassuring news, which he needed, for he was barely sleeping. Still, her language alarmed him: "Harden our hearts to the view of a tree, an apartment, a favorite object whose disappearance seems to remove the best of us." How could he think that way, having spent his life depriving himself, leading "a hard-working and austere existence"? He now looked at Croisset with the eye of a mother watching over a sick child, wondering, "How much longer will it last?" But what concerned him most was *Caroline's* ruin.[9]

His letters indicate that he knew what was going on, and knew who the investors were, family friends included, that were supporting Commanville, or at least not adding to his difficulties by calling in their debts. Much seemed to depend on some Swedish investors — once Commanville's suppliers, now his creditors.[10] But even if they were willing to let him postpone payment, how would Ernest get his sawmill rolling again without more timber?[11]

"I had thought until now that Death was the worst of evils," he wrote Léonie Brainne. "Well, no! The most painful thing is to see the humiliation of those one loves. My poor niece is wrenching my heart, precisely because she is very brave, very noble. She is giving up everything she can. . . ."[12]

He tried to work. Sometimes he could; there were moments when he felt hope. And then his courage would fail him again. One day he forced himself to write, was stopped by a fierce headache, and burst into tears.[13] This time it was he who had to ask Turgenev to postpone a visit to Croisset, not wanting his friend to see them (for Caroline was with him now) in their anguish. "And God knows that an embrace from my good old Turgenev would relieve my heart!"[14]

Whatever humiliation his nephew's bankruptcy represented for him, it cannot be said that Flaubert sought to conceal the truth from his friends. His letter to Goncourt on August 2, 1875, begins: "Well, my friend, I must tell you the truth: my nephew Commanville is completely ruined and close to bankruptcy." He even requested that Goncourt inform Mathilde.[15] Then he asked Turgenev to tell George Sand what he knew.[16] In sending Flaubert's letter on to Sand, Turgenev commented: "I know that in everything Flaubert says there is the involuntary exaggeration of the sensitive and nervous man accustomed to a free and easy existence, yet I feel he has been hit hard, harder than he himself may realize."[17]

To Sand, who wrote him a solicitous letter as soon as Turgenev informed her of his plight, Flaubert replied: "Since my earliest years I have sacrificed everything for tranquillity of the mind. It is now lost forever." If only he had an idea for a book that excited him; but he had lost his faith. What he needed now was a lucrative job, he said, but he was fifty-four, and one couldn't change one's life at that age. All the same, on receiving his letter Sand wrote a well-placed official — perhaps Agénor Bardoux, an acquaintance of Flaubert's who was then under-secretary of justice — to see if something could be done for her friend.[18] In any event, we know that Bardoux and Edgar Raoul-Duval were soon looking for a solution. Raoul-Duval told Flaubert what they were doing, but on August 29 Flaubert protested to Bardoux: "The disaster that has struck me has nothing to do with the public. It is for me to manage my affairs better, and I feel that it is not up to the national treasury to nourish me. Remember that if I receive a government pension, that fact will be published, and perhaps attacked by the press and in Parliament. . . . Nevertheless, since my life is going to be restricted, if you can find a library job for me paying three or four thousand francs with free lodging (as one has at the Mazarine or Arsenal libraries), I think that would be good for me!" He also turned to Raoul-Duval for another kind of help. Commanville owed fifty thousand francs to a banker in Rouen. The good Edmond Laporte had guaranteed half that sum, and now they required a guarantee from Raoul-Duval for the remaining twenty-five thousand. His niece Caroline would be responsible for these payments, as soon as she received authorization from the civil courts to remove that much property from her dowry. If permission was refused, she could still make the sum available out of her annual income. Raoul-Duval agreed.

For his part, Flaubert took a momentous step. His single significant asset was Deauville, the farm he had inherited with his parents' legacy. At the end of August he made a quick trip to Deauville to obtain the particulars of offers that had been made for the property. Soon he was able to announce that he had found a buyer willing to pay two hundred thousand francs, "which allows me to save my poor nephew," he told Laporte.[19] (Later Baron Henri de Rothschild was to acquire the Flaubert farm, where he put up a house that became a local landmark. In the 1920s it was sold for eight million francs to Ralph Beaver Strassburger, a successful Pennsylvania businessman; his son Peter left the estate to the town of Deauville, which in our own time has made a conference center and tourist attraction out of it.)[20]

Flaubert returned to Deauville on September 13 to complete the sale. Once again Commanville became his banker, using the proceeds of the sale and paying Flaubert interest, which became the latter's chief source of income.[21] Just before leaving Croisset Flaubert had read a letter from Agénor Bardoux, who had been looking into the possibility of a government appointment for him. "Don't hurry," Flaubert begged him now. "For I am afraid that I'll act badly to you later on. If the job I am offered is at the National Library, where the work is atrocious, and if it requires my presence in Paris all year long or if the stipend is less than three or four thousand francs a year, I should make no money by accepting. . . . This required presence in Paris all year would cost me money, and I should in fact earn nothing." He was frank: "In a word, dear friend, what I need is a sinecure, or something close to one."[22]

From Deauville he proceeded to Concarneau, a lively fishing port on the south coast of Brittany, for a long-promised and much-needed holiday in the company of an intelligent friend. Georges Pouchet, twelve years his junior, was the son of the eminent scientist Félix-Archimède Pouchet, a student of Flaubert's father's who had gone on to become the director of Rouen's Museum of Natural History. Like his father, Georges was both a medical doctor and a naturalist. He was the director of a laboratory of marine zoology that carried out observations at Concarneau.

Flaubert was given an attractive room on the old harbor from which he could look out on the ancient fortifications, and a quay lined with small boats for sardine fishing. Although he had arrived on a Thursday, he could not even write a letter until Saturday. "I tremble more and more," he explained to his niece. "I find it hard to write, materially, and the sobbing suffocates me." But he could go bathing. All told, it was a charming place: "What a marvelous vacation I would have here if I had nothing to worry about." He let slip out to Caroline: "Ah! Your poor husband wasn't born to make me happy."

All the same, he began to write. He was beginning the first piece in a book of three remarkable short stories, the last work to be published during his lifetime. This first was based on the legend of Saint Julian the Hospitaler, and had been inspired, he told Caroline, by a reproduction by E.-H. Langlois of a stained glass window in the cathedral of Rouen.[23]

At the beginning of October there was an encouraging telegram from Commanville: his creditors had accepted a liquidation. The family's troubles were not yet over, but they would be able to use their assets to settle their debts, without having to declare bankruptcy. It would be hard to live, with all of their income committed to debt retirement, but they had hopes of surviving. "Honor will be preserved, but nothing else," Flaubert told Léonie Brainne.[24]

He took the time to write George Sand about the status of the Commanville liquidation. "Perhaps [Caroline] will be forced to sell Croisset?" he wondered.

In Sand's reply, sent from Nohant on October 8, she addressed this matter frankly. "If it were not beyond my means, I would buy it, and you would keep it for the rest of your life. I don't have the money, but I'll try to liquidate some small capital I do have." He wept when he read those lines, and then he tried to explain the problem to her in more detail. His nephew had eaten up half of Flaubert's own capital, so Flaubert was utilizing the remaining half to take over one of Commanville's obligations; after the liquidation of assets, the money ought to come back to him. As for the family home at Croisset, it was worth a hundred thousand francs, but it earned nothing, for the upkeep was expensive, and the income from the farm was counterbalanced by the gardener's wages and repairs. In order to live, Flaubert needed six or seven thousand francs a year, *and* Croisset.[25]

THREE TALES

FLAUBERT'S NEW FLAT in Paris, at 240 Rue du Faubourg Saint Honoré, was slightly larger than his previous one on Rue Murillo, "but the windows looked out on a sea of roofs bristling with chimneys," remembered Zola. "Flaubert did not even bother to decorate it. He kept the same wall tapestry and placed his Buddha on the fireplace, and his afternoon receptions began, in a white and gold drawing room in which one felt the emptiness, a temporary installation, a kind of campsite." Yet soon their host seemed his old self again. His circle of friends grew, with younger people now included. Sometimes as many as twenty guests crowded the flat on Sundays.[1]

One of the younger men who turned up that first winter on Faubourg Saint Honoré was Henry James, then thirty-two years old. He had arrived in Paris in November, intending to settle for a while, and had been writing articles on France for the *New York Tribune*. He called on Ivan Turgenev, who escorted him to one of Flaubert's Sundays. When they walked up the five flights and entered Flaubert's apartment, James thought (as he was to write a friend in French): "I am launched in the middle of Mount Olympus." With his mottled complexion and his long tawny mustache, his host seemed a weather-beaten old soldier, despite the fact that he wore what James called "a long colloquial dressing gown." The guests that day (among them Zola, Goncourt, and Georges Charpentier) were clustered in a smallish, high-ceilinged room that, except for the gilt Buddha, seemed "bare and provisional." James felt that he was listening to real conversation for the first time.[2] He reported to his father that he had taken "a mighty fancy to Flaubert," who was "not at all what his books led me to suspect." He was, as Turgenev had said he was, a naïf, "a great, stout, handsome, simple, kindly, elderly fellow, rather embarrassed at having a stranger presented to him."[3]

A year earlier, in *The Nation*, James had reviewed *The Temptation of Saint Anthony*, a book that came as a surprise, he wrote, for "M. Flaubert's strong side has not been hitherto the portrayal of resistance to temptation. . . ." He argued that after the triumph of *Madame Bovary*, Flaubert had been "at extraordinary pains" to undermine his own success; *Salammbô* and then *A Sentimental Education* were less sympathetic and less credible.[4] Later James would baptize Flaubert "the novelist's novelist."[5] Writing to his mother, he called the Flaubert circle "a queer lot, and intellectually very remote from my own sympathies." He would sum up Flaubert for his brother William: "So much talent, and so much naïveté and honesty, and yet so much dryness and coldness."[6]

Yet friends did come to see him, and on Wednesdays Flaubert was part of the crowd at Mathilde's; he was back in the world, and the world found him looking well, to which he could only say "Amen!" On the eve of his fifty-fourth birthday he found room for a bit of optimism. Their business problems seemed to be "taking a rather good turn," he wrote Edmond Laporte.[7] He spelled this out to George Sand: the liquidator was offering a settlement to the creditors. All Commanville needed was a respected citizen to take charge of a stock issue. Sand replied with the name of a banker she knew; in fact, he had once been her lover.

This time the two friends' exchange included a literary quarrel. To Sand, who was now over seventy, it was a disservice to readers to paint life without explaining it; she wished to render her readers less miserable. "I cannot forget that my personal victory over despair was the product of my own will power," she argued; Flaubert's school — for she saw Flaubert and his friends as that — dealt with surfaces and failed to get inside their characters. But he assured her that he did not paint "desolation" for his amusement. Nor was he lacking in convictions. "But in the ideal I have of art," he wrote, "I believe that one must not show one's convictions, and that the artist should not appear in his work any more than God does in nature." He knew that this discipline was not easy to respect; it would be easier to say what he felt. As for his having a school, he did all he could not to have one. His friends did not write as he did; they sought facts, and he beauty. "Goncourt, for example, is very happy when he picks up in the street a word he can stick into a book. And I am quite satisfied when I have written a page without assonances or repetitions."[8]

Before the troubled year of 1875 was over, Flaubert saw print again. Catulle Mendès, a young poet and critic who for a time was married to Théophile Gautier's daughter Judith, launched a new magazine called *La République des Lettres;* its purpose, as announced in the first issue, dated December 20, was "to gather around some illustrious personalities . . . new talents already well known, and still-unknown talents. . . ." There were contributions by Stéphane Mallarmé, Charles Swinburne, and Leconte de Lisle, as well as an excerpt from *Le Château des Coeurs.* A second excerpt from Flaubert's play appeared in the issue of March 20, 1876, together with a piece of verse called "Au Bord de l'Eau" ("At the Water's Edge"), by Guy de Maupassant but signed with the pen name he adopted for his first publications, Guy de Valmont. In this long narrative poem Flaubert's young disciple had a pair of lovers consummate their passion under the reader's eyes.

Meanwhile, Flaubert was pursuing the writing of "The Legend of Saint Julian the Hospitaler." He was almost done, in fact, and he was already thinking about when and where to publish it — not, he hoped, during the spring session of Parliament, when literature would be lost in the political tumult.[9] On a Saturday night in February, the twelfth, he announced to Edma Roger des Genettes, "I have only one more paragraph to find. . . ." Soon he was finished and about to begin another story, for he wished to have a "small volume" ready for publication in August.[10] After that, he told George Sand, he would return to *Bouvard and Pécuchet.* "But the difficulties of that book frighten me," he confessed. "And yet I do not want to die before having done it. For in the end, it is my last will and testament."[11]

"Saint Julian" was a jewel of a tale. Born of noble parents, Julian is raised to hunt and adores the kill. Coming upon a large herd of deer, he commits a veritable massacre, and after his attack on a fawn and its mother, the father deer warns him: "One day, ferocious heart, you will murder your father and mother!" Julian gives up hunting, but while practicing with a javelin tosses it at what he thinks is a bird, almost killing his mother. He runs away, saves an emperor, and marries the emperor's daughter. His parents find his castle, and Julian's wife takes them in and puts them to bed. Mistaking his father for an intruder and his mother for his own wife, Julian kills them both. When he discovers that he has indeed slain his parents, he abandons everything to beg, then befriends a leper and goes to Heaven. "And that is the story of Saint Julian the Hospitaler," concludes this tale, "more or less as one finds it, on a stained glass window, in my land."

"The outline of my second little story is finished," he announced at the beginning of March 1876 to Edmond Laporte. He would have to visit Pont-l'Evêque and Honfleur now.[12] For he was about to begin "A Simple Heart," a remarkable story that some see as his masterpiece — or that and *Madame Bovary*. Like Emma's tale, it goes over ground he knew well, and describes people with whom he grew up. As he was to outline the plot to a friend, it describes "a poor country girl" who "loves in turn a man, the children of her mistress, a nephew, an old man whom she is taking care of, and then her parrot; when the parrot dies, she has it stuffed, and when she herself is dying, she confuses the parrot with the Holy Ghost."[13]

He was ready to leave for Pont-l'Evêque on March 8, but reports of flooded roads and rivers discouraged him.[14] It happened that Louise Colet died that day. He was moved, he confessed, even if the events of the past year had made him more stoic. "I trampled on so many things in order to be able to live!" (This to Edma Roger des Genettes.)

He took an afternoon off for these thoughts, and then dived back into his notebook. He worked sixteen hours the first day and all day long the second, and finally finished the first page of "A Simple Heart."[15] Then an attack of shingles brought him down, but he decided to make his trip all the same. "Happy are those who are not afflicted by the folly of Perfection!" he wrote George Sand, laughing at himself. "I understand all the vanity of it, but I cannot cure myself."[16] We can follow his trip through his notebook, which he filled with what he needed to know about roads, views, and old costumes. Predictably, this voyage set off another bout of sadness, "a bath of souvenirs," he called it in a letter to Edma Roger des Genettes. He also told her about his plan for a third short story, this one about Saint John the Baptist. "If I do it, that will give me three stories, enough to publish a rather amusing book next fall."[17]

No one could say he was working slowly now. He was "only" a third of the way through the writing by the beginning of May, but for him that was speed.[18] Then he stopped writing in order to read about Saint John the Baptist, for he had begun to dream about the feast of Herodias, during which Salomé is presented with the head of John as a reward for her dancing. But it was "A Simple Heart," he assured George Sand, that had benefited from her influence. "I think that the moral tendency, or rather the human side, of this little work will please you! Adieu, dear good master," he closed. "I kiss you with tenderness." She received the kiss but was not destined to read the story that showed his change of heart. By the time his letter of May 29 reached Nohant, she was desperately ill, suffering from an obstruction of the bowels that could not be treated.[19] She died on June 8; the following night Flaubert was on the train, along with Ernest Renan and Prince Napoleon, to attend the simplest of village funerals. (Despite Sand's convictions and her son's objection, there was a religious ceremony.)[20] "Poor dear Madame Sand," Turgenev wrote from Russia, "she loved us both, especially you, and that was natural; what a heart of gold she had. What an absence of all petty, nasty, false sentiments; what a splendid man she was, and what a woman!"[21]

Flaubert went back to Croisset immediately after that, and on the following day was back at his desk, the manuscript of "A Simple Heart" before him. He was hoping for a long period of tranquillity, and was delighted to be home, he confided to Edma Roger des Genettes, "like a petit bourgeois, in *my* chairs, in the middle of *my* books, in *my* office, looking out at *my* garden." Not that the writing came easily; in fact, it became harder, he told Turgenev: "It seems to me that French prose can attain a beauty we cannot imagine." Once again he was being uncannily perspicacious about his work-in-progress. Readers even now marvel at the language of this short story.[22]

On July 8 he wrote Léonie Brainne: "I work a great deal, I swim every day, I receive no one, read no paper, and rather often I watch the sun rise (as just now), for I pursue my labors well into the night, with the windows open, in shirt sleeves and shouting away like a demon in the silence of my study."

If Léonie saw Georges Pouchet in Paris, added Flaubert, he wished her to remind Pouchet that he was waiting for information on the diseases of parrots.[23] He also wrote to Georges Pennetier at the Museum of Natural History in Rouen, for he wanted to drop in on Saturday to look at parrots and to learn something about their habits and diseases.[24] Most likely the Saturday he mentioned was the fifteenth of July, for the museum register has survived, with a note on that date: "Loaned to Mr. Gustave Flaubert: one mounted amazon parrot."[25]

Now he was working like a true demon. "At night," he told Caroline, "the phrases that race through my brain, like the chariots of Roman emperors, wake me with a jump. . . ." At first, he explained, he had become involved with overlong descriptions. He was removing "charming" ones, for "literature is the art of sacrifice. . . ." Or again: "Do you imagine that my ordinary nights do not exceed five or six hours at the most?" Also: "I continue to scream in the silence of my study, and even today [August 7] I have a pain in my back, or rather in my lungs, that has no other cause." And then: "My fervor in this task comes close to mental derangement. The day before yesterday [August 8] I did an eighteen-hour day! Very often now I work before lunch; or rather I do not stop; even while swimming I turn my phrases, despite myself." [26]

He took a moment off, all the same, to reassure Léonie Brainne, who was in Marienbad to lose weight, that he liked her the way she was. "At this moment I am thinking of your shoulders, of your legs in red stockings, of your roguish large and lovely eyes, and I feel like eating you up, that's the truth! I should like to be the bathtub that envelopes you!" [27]

It was time to be done with his tale, he declared to Edmond Laporte on August 9. "My headache never goes away, for lack of sleep. Last night I slept four hours." [28] And then, during another night's work — on August 16, an hour after midnight — he was finished. The next day he felt the exhaustion that had been accumulating, as well as the oppressive mid-August heat. But he intended to go right on to the third of his tales, "Hérodias." Already, so he told Caroline, he perceived "the surface of the Dead Sea sparkling in the sun. . . . I am impatient to get going and to work hard this autumn. . . ." He would stay on in Croisset until the story was completed, and never mind the Paris season. [29]

But he did go to Paris. We cannot prove it, but it has been suggested that he went there to be with Juliet Herbert, for once again he was evasive about where he actually was, and he did forward a letter from Juliet to Caroline! [30] And he confided to Edmond Laporte that though he was supposed, "for common mortals," to be at Mathilde's in Saint Gratien, he was actually in Paris "taking the rust off my sword." [31]

Then he returned to Croisset, and with Turgenev in tow, for a long-promised working holiday. But after forty-eight hours that "evanescent man" was gone, and Flaubert sat down to his reading for the third of his tales. This research would take him a month, but it was not really work, he told Léonie Brainne, only "debauchery"; the real work was to come. "You will learn with stupefaction that I am doing exercise!" he confessed to her, admitting that this was the beginning of decadence. He had gone to Rouen three times on foot, walking along the river and admiring nature.[32]

And then, at the beginning of November, he began to write. It would not be easy, he explained to Turgenev, "because of the explanations the French reader will need."[33] But had it ever been easy for Flaubert?

A LATE SEASON

HE STAYED ON in Croisset, missing his winter season in Paris. He did see his friends and neighbors, including Laporte and the young Dr. Fortin. He read little, except for the classics — La Bruyère, Montaigne. He told his niece that he was so much out of the world that he had been the last to hear that the government had fallen. If he continued the way he was going, he would have "Hérodias" finished by the end of February, he reported to Turgenev. He had an urgent question for Turgenev: could all three of his new stories appear in Russian (in *Vestnik Evropy*) by April, so he could publish them in Paris in May? It would help him deal with pressing money problems. He was staying on in Croisset to finish in time.[1] Turgenev assured him that he would translate all three of the stories into Russian, and quickly.[2]

Indeed, Flaubert was living frugally. He had twenty francs on hand, hardly enough for New Year's gifts and for living expenses through January. "For the next four years," he explained to Goncourt, "life will be quite difficult, unless my nephew finds some money. But the main thing is that whatever happens, I won't leave Croisset, which I like more and more. If necessary, I would give up my Paris lodgings instead, but we haven't reached that point."[3]

"Well, my friend, what has become of you?" Emile Zola wrote him on January 3, 1877. "You know that you are making us all unhappy. We need you. . . . Our Sundays are mortal. . . . The worst of it is that we don't even see each other, for you are not there to bring us together."[4] Flaubert assured the younger man that he missed him,

too. He would be in Paris in a month, though he would not have
finished the last of his short stories by then.[5] Savage though he was,
he did bend to his sister-in-law's imploring, and dined on New Year's
day at the Hôtel-Dieu. Now it was his brother who seemed a savage;
Achille did not open his mouth, and appeared sad and irritable. Gustave decided that he was seriously ill. (In truth, he was.) On another
visit to Rouen Gustave climbed up to the cemetery, carrying fifty francs
with him ("my whole fortune") to pay the caretaker of the family
tombs. But the bill, covering several years, came to 135 francs. He
reproached his niece, gently, for letting that happen.[6]

His money problems gnawed at him. First there were the small
sums he needed for his daily existence, for the cook, for the purchase
of wood and other supplies; their farmer did not even give him veg-
etables. And it now seemed clear that Ernest was going to have to
sell the sawmill after all. Not only could he not return Edmond Laporte's loan, but he was ready to borrow more. Laporte's concern
about how matters were going angered Caroline, as if it were none of
his business.

In fact Laporte now seemed necessary to Flaubert. If he lacked
Bouilhet's literary talent, he was even more dependable, more ready
to come when called than Bouilhet had been. The sorrow was that
the Commanvilles' financial stress and Laporte's willingness to help
were creating a situation with which neither friend would know how
to deal.

In mid-January, in near panic, Flaubert appealed to his nephew for
funds, and immediately regretted his tone of urgency. But he had
never, never, since his days as a student, been so poor. Imagine: he
had not even been able to send his servant to Rouen, lacking the price
of a steamboat ticket. Commanville came through with one hundred
francs and news of further reverses. He was going to be able to sell
his plant, but there would be no material gain from the sale because
of mortgages.[7]

Flaubert stepped up the pace, hoping to complete "Hérodias" before going to Paris. But in Paris, he warned Caroline, he intended to
relax. "I demand fine wines, pretty liqueurs, friendly company, pocket
money, smiling faces, and merry talk."[8] Caroline asked who she should
invite for dinner on Sunday, the day after his arrival, and he replied
(so he informed Turgenev), Turgenev.[9] Soon he added to the guest
list "my pupil Guy the Bald." And Madame Régnier — this was Marie
Régnier, a writer twenty years his junior who used the pseudonym

Daniel Darc for her fictions; he was encouraging her efforts, for reasons we really do not know but can nonetheless guess.[10]

He finished the last of the three tales on February 1, 1877, and was off to Paris. After all those sleepless nights, his appearance was frightening. Invited to the Charpentiers', he was overcome by the heat and drowsiness and left while the party was in full swing. When he was fully rested, he told Edma Roger des Genettes, he would return to *Bouvard and Pécuchet*, about which he had thought a great deal that winter. He now saw the book in a way that would be "more lively and less artificial."[11]

One evening he read "Hérodias" aloud at Mathilde's salon. Goncourt was present, and though he wished his friend all the success that his morale and health demanded, he found this story lacking. "So many music-hall tricks, small modern notions planted in this gaudy mosaic of archaic detail!" But that was only for his diary.[12] Flaubert was back in the world, in any case. We get an idea of this world in a letter he wrote Edmond Laporte, inviting him to dinner: "As fellow guests you will have the obscene Guy and a pretty colleague of mine, Madame Régnier." Another day he organized the "Flaubert Dinner," the "Hissed Authors' Dinner." In inviting his publisher Charpentier to join the group, Flaubert pointed out that Alphonse Daudet was no longer worthy of them, since his last play had been a success.[13]

Thanks to Goncourt, we have an account of a dramatic moment at this dinner. Flaubert spoke disparagingly of the naturalist prefaces and manifestos that Zola utilized to promote his works. Zola in turn made the point that Flaubert had unearned income, while he had to depend on his writing for his livelihood. And the public needed a certain amount of ritual to comprehend that something new was being offered, he said.[14] It was true that the two friends were worlds apart, Zola seeking to reproduce stark reality, Flaubert beginning with language. After Flaubert's death the younger writer summed up his reservations: for him, from *Madame Bovary* to *Bouvard and Pécuchet* Flaubert showed himself increasingly preoccupied with form, at the expense of the humanity of his characters. Zola tried to express this to him when there was still time, but he got nowhere.[15]

Once again Flaubert proved an effective salesman of his own work. The first publication of all three stories comprising his new book was promised to a Russian magazine, and the volume itself, *Three Tales*, was to be issued in France by Charpentier; now Flaubert could also place the stories in French magazines. He quickly sold "A Simple Heart" and "Hérodias" to *Le Moniteur,* and "Saint Julian the Hospitaler" to *Le Bien Public.* "Russia pays me close to two francs a line and France a little more than one franc, which is an extravagant sum! So let people say that I don't know anything about money matters!" exclaimed a satisfied Flaubert to Léonie Brainne.[16]

"I lead a dumb and stupidly active life," he wrote Laporte early in March 1877. "Too many errands, too many cabs, too many dinners." One of those he was seeing was the irrepressible Guy de Maupassant, who had submitted to his master another lascivious play of his making, this one entitled *69.* On the serious side, Flaubert was to intervene with his friend Agénor Bardoux, now the minister of education, to obtain an easy desk job for his protégé.[17]

Meanwhile, an event of another kind, no less significant, had occurred in the life of Guy de Maupassant. At the dawn of his career as an author he had acquired his first serious venereal infection, perhaps the syphilis that was to attack his nervous system and destroy his brain at the age of forty-two. Or as Maupassant explained it to a friend, on the very day he gave his naughty *69* to his master: "I've got the pox! finally! the real one!! . . . the one that killed François I. And I'm proud, damn it! and I thumb my nose at the bourgeoisie. Hallelujah! I have the pox — therefore I no longer fear that I'll catch it!"[18]

Emile Hamard died. Flaubert did not feel that the death of his sister's husband, the father of his niece Caroline, was a great loss. He had already mourned Hamard twenty-five years earlier when "his head fell off," so he put it in a letter to Léonie Brainne.

The same letter contained news of his social life. He had, for instance, called on Sarah Bernhardt, who had declared that she found him handsome and "full of character"; she was thinking of sculpting his portrait. Flaubert had no illusions, and confided to Léonie that he reminded himself of an old ham actor or a retired butcher. But his heart was still young. In this very letter he confesses to Léonie "a crazy desire to eat your marble shoulders."[19]

Then the proofs began to come in. Publication of *Three Tales* was scheduled for late April 1877. He was also doing more research on *Bouvard and Pécuchet,* hoping to get as much as possible done before he settled down to writing in Croisset. When he could dispose of the manuscript of *Three Tales,* he had it bound in leather and shipped to Normandy with a dedication to Laporte. "For the past two years, old man," he wrote to his friend, "your visits have been my only distraction, or better say my only consolation." Then there were the usual frantic preparations for publication. As usual, the author was concerned about the domestic political situation and its probable effect on reader interest. At the time, the cabinet was feuding with President Mac-Mahon; it was to end with his dismissing them.[20]

Flaubert shied away from social obligations. "The stories I invent so as not to make visits and to refuse dinners in town are prodigious," he admitted to Edma Roger des Genettes. He was even using the excuse that he was mourning Emile Hamard.[21] But one social event could not be missed. The younger generation, "the youth of realist and naturalist literature," as Goncourt called them, invited their elders — Flaubert, Goncourt, and Zola — to dinner. The hosts were Maupassant, J.-K. Huysmans, Henry Céard, Léon Hennique, Paul Alexis, and Octave Mirbeau; the place was their regular meeting room, the Trapp restaurant near Gare Saint Lazare, the date April 16. The young hosts consecrated their guests as "the three masters of the present hour," noted Goncourt, "in a most cordial and lively dinner." He in turn anointed them "the new army now in the process of formation."[22]

Three Tales was well received, but nothing ever satisfies an author, and we have Du Camp's word that Flaubert actually believed that the government crisis was a plot aimed at undermining him. He quotes a letter from Flaubert: "The war of 1870 killed *A Sentimental Education,* and now comes a domestic coup d'Etat to paralyze *Three Tales;* this is really pushing hatred of literature quite far."[23]

Flaubert needn't have worried. The respected Théodore de Banville hailed the stories as "three absolute and perfect masterpieces created with the power of a poet sure of his art, and of which one must speak only with the respectful admiration owed to genius."[24]

PART IX

RETURN TO
BOUVARD AND PÉCUCHET

FLAUBERT'S STORIES may have been acknowledged as master-pieces, but masterpieces are not always best-sellers. "It's curious how lack of success diminishes people, makes them say idiotic things," murmured Goncourt in his diary. "This observation is inspired today by Flaubert."[1] Was he that bitter? He certainly could have used an unquestioned success.

In Paris that spring he pursued his research for the next chapter of *Bouvard and Pécuchet*, in which he was to expose the follies of modern science. "For that," he told Edma Roger des Genettes, "I am making notes on physiology and therapeutics from the comic point of view, which is no small job. Then I will have to make them understood and render them plastic." He added: "I don't think that anyone has yet explored the comic element of ideas. It is possible that I will drown in it, but if I succeed, the terrestrial globe won't be worthy of bearing me."[2]

His last recorded outing in Paris was for another performance of his disciple's naughty *A La Feuille de Rose*, this time in a studio on Rue de Fleurus on May 31. Goncourt was shocked once again, and he admitted to his diary that this might seem a strange reaction on the part of the author of the frank *La Fille Elisa*, whose heroine was a prostitute. He was disturbed by the simulated sexual action on stage, and by the presence of the author's father, Gustave de Maupassant, in the audience. Among the few women present was the extravagant Suzanne Lagier, and even she walked out before the play was over. Finally, Goncourt was shocked by Flaubert's enthusiasm. "It's so fresh!" he heard Flaubert say. "Fresh, for this piece of filth," complained Edmond de Goncourt to his diary. "That is truly a discovery."[3]

Soon after that, Flaubert left for Croisset, and was delighted to be back there. "I walk in the garden, which is splendid now," he told Caroline. "I contemplate the greenness and the flowers and listen to the little birds sing." He decided that he could finish his medical chapter in three months if no other business got in the way. Once again the dependable Laporte offered to assist him, reading and annotating books on subjects Flaubert intended to cover. But the books just were not available. "You would have to have a whole idiotic library for me," muttered the author.

He continued to be optimistic about the resolution of the Commanville crisis, and continued to do his part. His letters to his nephew were filled with the names of prospective investors. His niece announced that Commanville was raising 150,000 francs on his own; Flaubert in turn was able to report that Raoul-Duval had offered to help raise funds for the new enterprise Commanville was planning to launch. "See if you can do something," he appealed, even to Edma. "Of the four hundred thousand francs needed, we have nearly 150,000. In a few days another promise of a hundred thousand francs will probably be signed, but this is not yet certain." He did not conceal the effect all this was having upon him: "What degradation!"[4]

There was some good news concerning the Bouilhet monument. The Rouen municipal council had taken up the matter again, and this time Flaubert had an ally in Amédée Le Plé, who was both a councilman and a doctor. Le Plé was to deliver the report of a committee set up to re-examine the affair, and he showed it to Flaubert first so he could make suggestions. Flaubert warned Le Plé not to irritate the council by mentioning the name of Flaubert too often.[5] This time the council voted to accept.[6]

"*Bouvard and Pécuchet* moves ahead slowly, but it moves ahead," Flaubert informed Turgenev on July 12. When he finished his chapter he began the next one, an exposé of geology. "What a book!" he sighed to Turgenev. "What kind of abyss (wasp's nest or latrine) have I fallen into! It's too late to back out." This in a letter thanking the Russian for a magnificent bathrobe from Bukhara that he had brought back to France with him and had shipped up to Croisset.[7]

Caroline came to stay with him in the country, and to paint. For she was now making a serious effort to be a serious painter, perhaps even to earn money thereby. For a while she worked in the studio of a minor academic, Léon Bonnat; but as she later remembered it, this painter saw how much she needed his help and took advantage of that — that is, he sought to take advantage of *her*. And she, deciding that this was lust and not love, slipped out of his hands.[8]

As for Flaubert, he described himself to Léonie as living the life of a monk. Yet he continued his cerebral flirtation, courting her from a distance. "Since we are far from each other, for want of caresses I will pay you compliments. . . . Well then, I find you beautiful, good, intelligent, witty, sensitive." He liked her eyes, her laugh, and her pretty legs. He would like to . . . here there is baby talk for something more serious. When her letter was delivered that afternoon, he confessed, he had just awakened, and had probably felt her presence, for he was in a state . . . very possible to describe.[9] "My life is of a continuous platitude," he wrote Maxime Du Camp's mistress Adèle Husson. "I see no one and feel fine that way, having become completely invisible. I make conversation with my dog. . . . As for the ladies, nothing. I content myself with dreaming about them. . . ." But he told Adèle that from the middle of August to the second week of September he planned to be a "vagabond," and by now we are able to guess what this meant, especially at that particular season of the year.

He took the opportunity of having Adèle's ear to talk about the Commanville affair. His nephew was still finding it difficult to raise the second half of the sum he needed to stay afloat. "No one wants to make the trip from Paris to Dieppe to see his factory and the profits that could be made there," he complained, and yet there *was* money to be made from a sawmill, considering that the world's fair was then being prepared. (The 1878 Exposition in Paris would involve considerable construction.) "It's a matter of lending two hundred thousand francs on guarantees," he assured her.[10]

He prepared for his vagabondage with care. To Princess Mathilde he promised a visit at the end of August, before which he planned to go up to Dieppe, perhaps to see Prince Napoleon; then there were to be "different excursions in the vicinity, and I will be resting my weary mind. . . ." He did find his way to Saint Gratien, and wrote his niece from there.[11] But it is difficult to follow his movements in early September. In Paris, for example, he received a letter from Léonie, who was also in Paris. Did he rush to join her? No; he told her that he was doing errands and then had to return to Saint Gratien. "I am *supposed* to be in Saint Gratien," he whispered in a letter to Edmond Laporte on September 6, adding that he was actually in Paris, "where

I . . . . !" The censors did not let the balance of that sentence come down to us, but we can guess that he was hiding out with Juliet Herbert, for this was the time of year when he usually . . . . with the English governess. "Don't be astonished by my long stay in the capital," he was to write Turgenev. "Between us, I am retained Veneris causa!!!" [12]

Then it was time to be off; surely Juliet's holiday was over. As for Flaubert, he alerted Laporte to be ready. They were to make another field trip in search of geological and archaeological sites for the expeditions of Bouvard and Pécuchet. First to the Calvados district — Caen, Bayeux, the Channel coast — then south to the region of Falaise, "Bouvard and Pécuchet's country," as Flaubert called it. They rose at six each morning and were in bed by nine at night, driving all day, usually in small open carriages. "We are quite well," he assured Caroline from Bayeux, "and do not waste our time. The only debauchery at table is for fish and oysters." [13] Then, at the end of October, what he called "the demands of literature" took him to the rocky cliffs of the Channel coast northeast of Le Havre. But his climbing came to naught; he could not find what he was seeking. So he had recourse to Maupassant, a native of this stretch of coast. "I need a cliff that frightens my two little chaps," he said, for a scene in which Bouvard and Pécuchet speculate on the end of the world, which would be brought on by a cataclysm. A few rocks slide by, and they flee in terror. . . . [14]

Maupassant produced a detailed description of the area, with sketches and a map, all from Paris and from memory; but now Flaubert felt he had *too* much detail. He explained that this episode was to fill only three pages, two of which would be dialogue and "psychology." So Maupassant tried again, but the new information only increased Flaubert's perplexity. [15] In the end his little chaps would have their fright on the cliff above Fécamp.

On the morning of Saturday, November 10, Flaubert uttered a loud sigh of relief, as he announced to Edma Roger des Genettes. His "science chapter" was done. Now his mind was freed to wander. Were he younger, had he the money, he would return to the Middle East to study what he called "the modern Orient, the Isthmus of Suez Orient," and to write the great novel of which he dreamed. "I want to show a civilized person who becomes barbaric and a barbarian who becomes civilized, and to develop this contrast of two worlds that end by joining. But it's too late, just as it is for my 'Battle of Thermopylae.' When will I write it? And 'Monsieur the Prefect'! and so many other books." He was embarked on "an abominable book," he declared to Léonie, which would require at least another three years of labor.[16] It was an accurate prediction.

He took a brief respite from writing in the middle of November, but only long enough to allow him to prepare the next chapter, on archaeology, in the Rouen library. Then he plunged in, having not a minute to lose, as he had resolved to finish this chapter by New Year's Day. He was quite all right, he reassured Turgenev, even if he was not sleeping; but he suffered violent headaches at the end of each day. It rained, rained without cease, he added in this letter of early December. "But as I don't go out, I don't care, and then I have your bathrobe. Twice a day I bless you for this gift: in the morning when getting out of bed, and toward five or six in the afternoon when I wrap myself in it to nap on the sofa."[17]

On Christmas Day he announced his imminent arrival in Paris. But there was a desk in Paris, too, and after a New Year's party with his niece he was back to *Bouvard and Pécuchet*, preparing chapters on history and prehistory. He took up his social life, and on January 12, 1878, was patently pleased to be able to inform a friend that he had been invited to dinner at the Charpentiers' with Léon Gambetta, the fiery leader of the republicans, and the future president of the Chamber and prime minister.[18] He lost no time in describing his success to Laporte. "We had a private talk. Three more of the same and we'll use *tu* to each other!" He was trying to obtain a government job for Laporte, whose livelihood had been placed in jeopardy by the death of the owner of the factory where he worked as manager.[19]

Once again we have a less sympathetic version of the same scene from Goncourt. He watched as Flaubert took Gambetta aside and led him into an adjacent salon, closing the door behind them. "It's astonishing, the effect on Flaubert of a famous person, the need he has to get close to him, to rub against him, to violate his intimacy!"[20]

Flaubert had yet another encounter with history just then. Victor Hugo was publishing his version of the events that had brought Napoleon III to power, and had given it the forthright title *Histoire d'un crime* ("History of a Crime"). In it he would tell how Prince Napoleon had called on him in November 1851 to warn of the planned coup by which his cousin intended to overthrow the republic. Prince Napoleon was alarmed that his name and his role were to be revealed in Hugo's book, and he tapped Flaubert as his intermediary. Flaubert obtained a copy of the offending chapter for the Prince, who was able to suggest changes and of course to secure the omission of his name. Hugo complied, but in his own way. He went ahead and published this chapter with its detailed account of the midnight visit of the Prince, but simply left out the name of "this important and distinguished man." But he did indicate that his mysterious visitor had the right to say, when referring to the Bonapartes, "my family." In the published version the visitor calls himself "the red prince."

The red prince thanked Flaubert for his help, adding, "All's well that ends well."[21]

In Paris Flaubert found himself more involved than ever with his spiritual son. Maupassant felt that his job at the Naval Ministry was beneath him. He thought that Flaubert, whose friend Agénor Bardoux was the minister of education, could help him obtain an "agreeable job" in the Fine Arts department of that ministry.

But Maupassant did not approach Flaubert directly on this; he asked his mother to do it. "To stimulate him a little," Maupassant suggested to Laure de Maupassant, "write him a pathetic letter thanking him for what he has promised to do for me. My situation here is far from being easy; blacken it still more, pity me, etc., etc." Two days later his mother had a letter in the mail to Flaubert: "Since you call Guy your adopted son, you will pardon me, dear Gustave, if I speak to you quite naturally about him." She felt that Flaubert's "declaration of tenderness" toward Guy gave the older man a "quasi-paternal" responsibility for him.

For his part, Maupassant did not always enjoy his reciprocal *filial* responsibilities. He complained to his mother that social obligations were taking up valuable time, time he needed for writing. His Sundays, for example: "My day with Flaubert robs me of the tranquillity necessary for my work." He also felt that Flaubert went about helping him in an awkward way. "As soon as practical matters are involved," he wrote his mother, "my dear Master does not know what to do; he makes requests platonically and never effectively, does not insist sufficiently, and above all does not seize opportunities."[22]

In a letter to Turgenev at the end of January 1878, Flaubert complained: "This little book is a burden. Will I have enough strength to continue it? I must be crazy to have begun it. All the same . . ."[23] If the author was uncertain about where this "little book" was taking him, can it be any surprise that his friends continued to feel a similar anxiety on his behalf? A remarkable letter from Hippolyte Taine confronted Turgenev with the problem: "This letter concerns our friend Flaubert; I beg you to destroy it after reading it; you will see that the subject is delicate." The historian had read, or had heard Flaubert read, draft chapters of the novel, and had promised to mention this to no one except Turgenev. "My impression is that the book, even if carried out as well as possible, cannot be good." Taine felt that the comic element in it would surely fall flat; since the heroes were stupid, their experience could not be of interest; the subject was worth a hundred pages, no more. "If Flaubert had not yet written any part of his book, I should have spoken to him at once, and frankly," Taine went on. "But he has been working on it for two or three years. . . ." On the other hand, he would continue to work on it for another three. "Wouldn't it be cruel, if he is making a mistake, to allow him to throw so much more time into this pit?"[24]

Turgenev did not destroy Taine's letter; it was later found among the Viardot papers. His reply was found in Taine's papers: "Without being entirely in agreement with you, I feel that at bottom you are right, that you have brought to light thoughts I had kept in a state of latency, and that the very friendship we feel for F. imposes duties on us, perhaps painful ones."[25]

FLAUBERT AT FIFTY-SEVEN

I N LONDON's *Fortnightly Review* on the first of April 1878, the young
critic George Saintsbury published a long essay on this French-
man in his late fifties who had written so relatively little. "One thing
that distinguishes M. Flaubert in these days of easy writing is his
determined and conscientious patience of workmanship." He acknowledged that Flaubert was not easy to take: both *Madame Bovary*
and *Salammbô* were likely to irritate, and *A Sentimental Education*,
"with its unbroken presentment of meanness, feebleness, irresolution,
vice without glamour, and virtue without charm, is open to the same
charge. . . ." No, Flaubert was not a popular writer, but he deserved
to be read — "twice and thrice before he can be fully enjoyed."[1]

That month, this unpopular writer finished another chapter of *Bouvard and Pécuchet*, this one containing his dissection of history and
historians. Now his little chaps were to attack literature, and he knew
it would be difficult to make that interesting. "I am not writing," he
told Laporte. "I read, I read! I read!" In the same letter he promised
Laporte that he would keep trying to talk to Minister Bardoux about
a government appointment for him. But he admitted that this friendly
minister was an unreliable friend.[2] Maupassant, who was also waiting
for Flaubert to get him a job, was then writing his mother: "I think
Bardoux doesn't give a hoot about Flaubert."[3] "Guy de Maupassant
has come to see me, delighted by your promises," Flaubert wrote
Bardoux at the beginning of May. "I thank you for this, and I beg
you, I beseech you to follow through. Since I see a great literary career for him, he must have two things: money to live on and time to

write."[4] Maupassant was brought in to Bardoux's secretariat the following January, which seemed a long wait to the young poet.

Home in Croisset at the end of May, Flaubert picked up his work-
in-progress, hoping to finish another chapter before the end of July.
He slept little, worked "violently," and saw no one except his dog,
Julio, as he informed Mathilde. It happened that he was also seeing
Caroline and her husband, and the Lapierres, and his neighbor Dr.
Fortin, and always the good Laporte, who, like Bouilhet before him,
would sometimes stay the night.[5] For the detailed information and
misinformation he was using in his novel, he depended more and
more on his mobile and willing friend. He gave Laporte the task of
copying passages — the more absurd and ridiculous the better — from
works of so-called erudition, this compendium to be published as a
companion volume to *Bouvard and Pécuchet*.[6]

Writing to Turgenev that summer, Flaubert said the same thing
Turgenev might have said to him: "It's the very concept of the book
that worries me."[7] "My book seems more and more difficult to me,"
he wrote Zola — another friend concerned about the folly of his enterprise. "Will it at least be readable?"[8]

There was an uninterrupted barrage of lamentations from his spiritual son Guy. He was ill now, suffering from stomach pains and irreg-
ular heartbeats, and was losing his hair. He could not work, but was
flirting furiously, and disabusedly. "Women's asses are as monotonous as men's minds," Maupassant summed up his melancholy.[9] If
women's asses were monotonous, replied Flaubert, "there is a simple
remedy, which is not to touch them." He felt that Maupassant could
be using his time more profitably — with less whoring, less exercise,
even, and more work. "Civilized men don't need as much motion as
our doctors say. You were born to make verses, so make them!"[10]

He wrote Léonie Brainne on August 15. The heat was unbearable,
and he was in a "black melancholy" — with money worries, notably.
But then he let himself drift into daydream. He and Léonie were in
a huge Moorish bath, she was naked, and they were swimming side
by side. Not for very long, for there was a divan in a corner, and they
moved to it, "and to the sound of the spouting of water," they spent
a pleasant quarter of an hour. Holy God, he wondered, why didn't
these things happen?[11]

They didn't happen, for one thing, because Flaubert had another
woman in mind. There was to be another clandestine meeting in Paris,
again in September; his excuse this time, in addition to a visit to

Mathilde, was the world's fair of 1878, and he really did visit it, telling Caroline about the day he spent "lost in reveries before antique statuary."[12] He signed one of his notes to Laporte "Your Giant who is fucking like a donkey."[13] Clearly the act of love with Juliet Herbert, a woman who was now forty-nine to his nearly fifty-seven, brought out the best in him, morally and physically.

The tryst did not keep him from his chores. He had Minister Bardoux to dinner, and Bardoux not only promised to find a job for Laporte but said he would get a stage for Flaubert's fairy play.[14] (Gustave even asked the minister for an official purchase of a painting by his niece Caroline.)[15]

Leaving for Saint Gratien, he wrote his niece: "Now I know everything I wanted to know about the Exposition, in depth. . . ."[16] Indeed.

And so to Croisset, to *Bouvard and Pécuchet*, to the creditors who would not leave Commanville in peace. Worse, Flaubert now understood that his appeal to friends for financial support was leading to disastrous consequences, especially for Laporte, who could hardly afford to be a banker. Laporte had accepted the notes he had been asked to sign without hesitation, but now there was to be a reckoning. Imagine, a banker in Rouen wanted his money back! "That he is brutal with Commanville, he has reasons for that, really," Flaubert wrote Laporte, concerning this creditor who wished to be paid, "but with you he will be very polite, and even cordial, for you are somebody: a district councilman, a friend of the prefect, etc." But the creditor still wanted his money. Laporte could sleep in peace, Flaubert assured his friend; Commanville would give him what he needed to satisfy the banker.[17]

Maupassant came up to Croisset, arriving late on a Saturday and talking half through the night.[18] Perhaps it was now that the younger man seized the impressions that he would transmit to posterity of the master at work, dressed as always "in large trousers held up by a silk band at the waist, and with an immense dressing gown that fell to the ground." Flaubert stood at a window of his vast work room and watched the ships go by, or he faced "the thousand steeples of Rouen" in one direction and "the thousand factory smokestacks of Saint Sever" in another. He could also look out at "meadows covered with reddish cows and white cows" or, through still another window, at "a forest on a slope closing the horizon where the wide river swept, covered with islands planted with trees, as it descended toward the sea and disappeared in a far-off curve of the enormous valley."

And what was more, Flaubert could be seen. "The bourgeoisie of

Rouen, going to La Bouille for lunch on Sunday, would come home disappointed when they could not see, from the bridge of their steamboat, this character named Flaubert standing at his window."[19] If the reader doubts Maupassant's claim that before the end of his life Flaubert had become a tourist attraction, perhaps another kind of evidence will be accepted. The present writer found an old guidebook to Normandy that, on a page describing the steamboat service from Rouen to La Bouille, reads:

> The first village at which one stops after the church [of Canteleu] is Croisset. The landing stage is just opposite the estate of Mr. Gustave Flaubert, the famous author of *Salambô* [sic] and *Madame Bovary*. What lovely poplar trees! What rich vegetation![20]

And if the tourists could have seen Flaubert now? He was suffering from "a little jaundice and a lot of sadness," he told Laporte. "My life is not amusing," he complained to Turgenev. "Business matters are not being resolved; on the contrary. I have reached the point of resignation, but at times I forget myself, and then I think of the past with bitterness and dream of dying. Then I get back to work."[21] At the end of November 1878 he learned that the periodical to which his fairy play had been submitted was rejecting it. "That's where I am at my age (fifty-seven in twelve days), and after having produced what I have produced," he wrote to another friend.

What was on his mind as he approached this birthday comes through in a letter he wrote to Caroline early in December. He was working in absolute solitude, and working hard; he wondered if anyone else had ever labored and lived as he did. He announced his intention to stay on in Croisset until March 1879, with only a brief visit to Paris in February to see friends. He even had a plan for the more distant future: to travel with Georges Pouchet to Thermopylae, the site of the legendary stand of the Spartans against the Persians. "But in eighteen months won't I be too old to accomplish that?" There is a moving passage of this letter, in which he thinks of Caroline alone in her studio, sacrificing all else to art, just as he had done. "And for what, or better, for whom?" For his niece, of course.[22]

For his niece indeed. Even Goncourt knew that. "Heartbreaking details on poor Flaubert," he recorded at the date of December 10. "He is said to be totally ruined now, and the people for whom he gave up everything out of affection begrudge him the cigars he smokes; his niece is supposed to have said: 'He's a curious man, my uncle is, he doesn't know how to support adversity.'"[23] Did Maupassant tell him this? Flaubert wrote Léonie Brainne: "Let me inform you that we are now at the bottom of the pit, and without hope. Commanville's sawmill will be sold in a deplorable way! And then, afterwards? God knows what will happen to us!"

He would be fifty-seven years old the next day, and he wished he were eighty so the end would be closer. Yet he still intended to "spit barrels of bile on the heads of the bourgeoisie."[24]

While Flaubert celebrated his lonely birthday in Normandy, Edmond de Goncourt dined at the Charpentiers' in Paris, and was a privileged observer, so he informed Princess Mathilde, when Marguerite Charpentier took their illustrious guest of honor, Gambetta, into a corner to tell him of Flaubert's ruin, and to see if a job could be found for him. Gambetta replied that he was prepared to give him the first available position.[25] The Princess now took up the case, beginning with a cautious letter to sound out Flaubert himself.[26]

He, meanwhile, worked. His chapter on love was coming to a close. "Pécuchet has just lost his maidenhead, in his cellar!" he reported to Maupassant, who would appreciate the information. His copy clerk would now get a lovely pox, and then both of his little chaps would moralize about women.[27] So chapter seven was done; three more to go. At the end of the year Flaubert revealed his secret intention to Léonie: "to shock the reader to the point of madness. But my goal will not be achieved, because the reader will not read me; he'll fall asleep at the beginning."[28]

HUMILIATIONS

IF 1879 RESEMBLES 1878," Flaubert wrote Goncourt at the start of the new year, "I won't see 1880." He spoke freely of his anxieties, yet he solicited no help. What had Goncourt meant, he wished to know, by writing that he had been working for him "with appropriate discretion"? For Mathilde had also hinted at a position worthy of him. He was grateful, but he wished she would not bother. "It's as useless as her attempts to nominate me to the French Academy."

He knew something about what his friends had in mind for him. Hippolyte Taine told him that Silvestre de Sacy, the curator of the Mazarine Library, was dying; his job, worth three thousand francs a year and an apartment, would be given to Flaubert by Minister Bardoux if Flaubert wished it. He did not wish it. His duties would require that he live in Paris eight months out of the year, and with those three thousand francs he would be poorer than ever; life was cheaper in the country. The free apartment tempted him, but "I would die of hunger." And then, too, he felt a "stupid but invincible aversion" to a government appointment of any kind.[1] Moreover, the cabinet in which Bardoux was a minister was likely to fall, and even Maupassant feared for his new job. Zola, who had been waiting for the Legion of Honor award, failed to get it, apparently because of a wicked essay he published in Le Figaro that contained an attack on "idealist" writers, among them two academicians. Flaubert approved of Zola and told his friends so. "Seriously, I regret having the medal," he wrote Maupassant. "What saves me is that I don't wear it."[2]

All this while he remained in Croisset, very much alone. It snowed in January, and then heavy rains flooded the grounds. Then came a thaw, and a fog that shut down the steamboat service. He told Caroline how he had waded about in Rouen in the rain, books under his arm, looking for a coach. In turn she informed him that the Commanville sawmill was at last to be liquidated; that kept him awake at night. (Dr. Fortin did not want to give him opium, fearing that this would cause a congestion.)[3]

On Saturday, January 25, he stepped outside his door to greet his lunch guests — Georges Pouchet and Georges Pennetier — and slipped and fell on the ice; it seemed as if he had sprained his leg, and he was helped to bed. Both men were doctors, but neither diagnosed the fracture: a break in the fibula behind his right knee. He waited forty-eight hours before Dr. Fortin could examine him; in the meantime the good Laporte was there, and he even moved into the house to be more helpful. Flaubert painted a picture of himself reading and smoking in bed, and begged his niece not to waste money on a visit. "My accident is the least of my worries. . . ."[4]

Still, this accident was a national event. Even the austere *Journal des Débats* found space to report that "Mr. Gustave Flaubert, the learned novelist, broke his leg on his Croisset estate while going to the door to greet friends." The learned novelist was bombarded with mail; he counted sixty-three letters before the end of the first week in February. And he would have to reply to all these well-wishers. "What an expense of stamps!" he worried to Caroline.[5]

Turgenev showed up, and with a mission. Marguerite Charpentier, the publisher's wife, was prepared to wrest a library appointment from Gambetta if Flaubert would promise to accept it. He did not refuse, but he wanted to know what kind of salary to expect. From Paris Turgenev sent him a telegram on February 5: he thought that it was a matter of six thousand francs. Flaubert wired back and followed up with a letter: "I've put my idiotic pride aside, and I accept. For above all one ought not to die of hunger." But could he really count on this appointment? He feared that the new education minister, Jules Ferry, would have his own protégés, and that if news got out that Flaubert was a candidate for a job, his competitors would jump on him.[6]

Now that he had been persuaded to accept the principle of a library appointment, however, he was ready to fight to get one. To Turgenev, who was postponing his return to Russia in order to help settle the matter, he wrote: "More than ever, I am determined not to sacrifice myself for that excellent Mr. Baudry. So let our friends get to work!"[7] Baudry was Frédéric Baudry, an old Rouen acquaintance who was then the deputy curator of the Arsenal Library and a candidate for the same appointment as Flaubert.

Georges Charpentier tried to see Gambetta but could not get to him; his wife told Zola that it was now Turgenev's turn to do what he could.[8] The curator of the Mazarine Library died on February 14, but Turgenev had already sent a telegram to Flaubert the previous day: "Forget it; definitive refusal." The Russian also gave the sad news to Caroline: Gambetta had informed him that he had another candidate for the vacant post. Flaubert took it well, and even asked Turgenev to believe that he was not upset by his failure to get the job.[9]

Then the worst thing that could happen did happen. On the front page of the daily Le Figaro on February 15, an ironic headline, "The Athenian Republic," introduced the story of Flaubert's upset. "It is known that Mr. Gustave Flaubert, the author of Madame Bovary, lost most of his fortune in a business venture in which he was engaged to help one of his relatives": this was the promising beginning. Le Figaro went on to describe the campaign of Flaubert's friends to obtain the post about to be vacated by the dying Silvestre de Sacy, and recounted how Turgenev had gone to see "a great lady of the republic whose salon is the meeting place of all the influential personalities." (This was Juliette Adam.) She had invited the Russian to a soirée where the president of the Chamber, Léon Gambetta, was also a guest. Turgenev found himself in the presence of Gambetta, who was at that moment digesting, spread out on a sofa with a whole general staff of civil servants and members of Parliament standing nearby. When Turgenev was introduced, said Le Figaro, Gambetta scarcely bothered to look at him; he would not budge for so little. Despite Turgenev's entreaty and the endorsement of their hostess, Gambetta replied in a dry and haughty tone: "No, that won't happen. I don't want it." The report tells us as much about the attitude of the monarchist-inclined Le Figaro toward the republican Gambetta as it does about what actually took place at Madame Adam's home. "This is how we are governed," the paper concluded.[10]

Flaubert still wasn't up and walking on the day the Figaro story appeared. He could not even go down to the dining room, so his maid Suzanne had to carry his food up to him. He was made to wear a boot of dextrin, a gummy substance poured over a bandage that hardened as it dried, but it was too tight and had to be cut open along the side and then held together by another bandage. He was itching all over his body but had no visible rash — it was nerves, Dr. Fortin told him. But the irritation was enough to keep him from sleeping, and when he lay awake he thought of the Commanville crash.

Then he was able to walk again, and dragged himself around with the help of a chair. He could read and make notes. "As for writing," he told Princess Mathilde, "one would have to be more vigorous than I am. A month will pass before I can go downstairs, and I'll limp for a long time to come." Laporte continued to serve him. One day he left Croisset for his home at eleven in the morning, planning to return on the six-thirty steamer. When he found the roads flooded at Couronne, he had to remove his trousers and walk barefoot to the boat landing.[11]

By letter Flaubert sought to convince Georges Charpentier to reissue "The Legend of Saint Julian the Hospitaler" in a deluxe edition, illustrated with a drawing of the stained glass window in Rouen that portrayed that saint; the illustration pleased him precisely because it was not an illustration but a "historical document." He also addressed himself to the publisher's desire to reprint *Madame Bovary*. Flaubert was tired of hearing about that book, which continued to overshadow everything else he had written. "I assure you that if I were not in need, I would see to it that the book was no longer kept in print." The work he did hope to see reprinted was *A Sentimental Education*.[12]

In a letter sent on February 17 Zola apologized, on behalf of all his Paris friends, for the clumsy way they had gone about seeking a library job for him. "You had nothing to do with all of that," Zola reassured him, "and tomorrow, if you consent, everything can be repaired."[13] What did Zola mean by that? Flaubert wondered. "You could not play the mean role of a job-seeker," came the reply, "but if you are offered a position worthy of you, without your having asked for it, you will show yourself to be wise, and superior to all the stupidities that have taken place, by accepting it."[14]

He was hardly in a position to refuse. If he allowed his friends to pursue their efforts, he told his niece, it was in order to be less of a burden to the Commanvilles.[15] The appointment of Frédéric Baudry to the Mazarine became official, and Flaubert learned from Guy de Maupassant that Baudry was angry that he had sought to obtain an appointment Baudry had been trying to get for twenty years. At the same time, Baudry wrote Flaubert to tell him that his friends were trying to win him an appointment as an *honorary* curator at the Mazarine; this would give him an apartment and a literary pension, which would amount to more money than a curator's salary.[16]

The idea of a pension "disgusts me horribly," Flaubert confided to Laporte. "I feel like refusing." And what if the whole business was a scheme of Baudry's to compromise Flaubert and to justify his own behavior? He replied to Baudry: "My family brought me to ruin. So it is for my family to feed me, and not the government."[17]

Yet the news from that family continued to be bad. Flaubert learned, for example, that although the sawmill was appraised at six hundred thousand francs, it would bring only a third of that amount in a sale, and in that case Flaubert, the principal creditor, would receive nothing at all. "Ernest must have been under an illusion again?" This was his mild comment when his niece broke the news to him. "What does he do with his time?" Flaubert was resigned to giving up Paris; he would live alone on what he could earn, on what the Commanvilles could give him, and if necessary on what he could get from his affluent brother. "It will be a great humiliation for me to ask him for something, but I prefer to be helped by him than by the public." He thought of those friends of his who had let themselves be persuaded to lend money to Commanville, out of affection for him: Laporte, Raoul-Duval. Would they be paid back? As for himself, he now realized how badly *he* had been treated. For if his friends had received guarantees, he had not; if as the principal creditor he was to obtain nothing at all, it meant that there was already a considerable mortgage on the sawmill — say, up to two hundred thousand francs' worth. "Then I was not told the truth?"[18]

Maupassant let him know that his minister — the education minister, Jules Ferry — was drawing up a decree for an honorary appointment, which would include a pension to be considered wages attached to the title; Flaubert was to accept it as "a homage rendered by the government and not as a pension for men of letters." There would be no duties, no required residence in Paris. Flaubert asked only that the pension be kept confidential. He told Maupassant that its divulgation would be awkward — and he would be quite humiliated if word got out. Furthermore, he planned to reimburse this pension, and so wished it to be considered merely a loan. Maupassant thought that his master could very well expect the government to be discreet about the pension, but he felt it would be unwise for Flaubert to say that he hoped to pay the money back. As it was, this would be the first time the government had granted a pension without having been asked for it![19]

Spring arrived, but Flaubert was still unable to walk. Five or six steps in his office were the limit, and at the end of the day his leg muscles swelled. He had now made all the notes that he could for his chapter on philosophy, and in fact had even indexed them.[20] Caroline had some good news: she was working conscientiously at her painting. He assured her that her career was the only hope he saw for the future. He was guiding her entrance into the Salon, the annual Paris art show, and once again he proved to be a tireless publicist. He sought out the eminent painters who served on the jury that decided on the admissibility of works, and he did not hesitate to appeal to Mathilde for help on this score. He wrote Louis Viardot, Pauline's husband and Turgenev's eternal host, to explain that Caroline had submitted a portrait of Dr. Jules Cloquet; would this critic give her a helping hand? Caroline's work not only was accepted for showing at the Salon but had the promise of being hung in a "distinguished place."[21]

Even before the Salon opened at the beginning of May, Flaubert was organizing the claque. He had his niece go through the papers to note the names of all of the art critics, so that he could get in touch with each of them. "At the beginning, promotion helps considerably," he explained to Caroline.[22]

"I am beginning my eighth chapter tonight," Flaubert informed Edmond Laporte on April 7. Laporte was to visit the following evening for another session of work. He arrived with bad news: he had not obtained the government job Flaubert had been seeking for him; he was coming to the end of his resources and would not even be able to pay the cost of a mortgage if the bankers who were after Commanville insisted that he take out one on his house. Flaubert was shaken; thinking of what they had done to Laporte did not help him with his writing. . . .[23] But he went ahead all the same. "Not a sound on the quay, not a boat in the river, nothing, absolute silence, and no letter to write!" as he described his Easter weekend to his niece. "So I was able to work until two in the morning. Result: one page and the preparation of two more. This is what I need: removal from all exterior activity and, I dare to say, from all human relations." He was less and less in a hurry to go to Paris. Besides, his leg continued to swell whenever he tried to walk.[24]

Among his minor vexations was the procrastination of his Russian friend. "What do you think of Turgenev," he wrote Laporte, "who again did not keep his word today? He was supposed to come last Sunday, then Tuesday, then Friday, and now it's next Sunday!" "No, I won't bawl you out," he assured Turgenev on April 27, "but if you knew the nervous harm you were doing me, you would feel remorse." Turgenev had said that he would arrive with Zola, Goncourt, and

Daudet, but Flaubert explained that since he only had one servant, his friends could not all come at once.[25] He complained of Turgenev to Caroline: he had disturbed and troubled Flaubert over a period of two weeks, and had hurt him in the end. "Is it my fault for still naively believing in the affection of whores? Let us not speak of it. But it is a *death*. I forget neither good things nor bad, and this one is irreparable."[26]

But he came at last, the Moscovite did, on the first Sunday in May, and he stayed until Tuesday morning, listening to Flaubert reading from his work-in-progress and appearing to like what he heard. Still, after seeing him off Flaubert wrote his niece: "Whatever I do, melancholy overwhelms me; the necessity of stiffening myself constantly exhausts me." What was demolishing his morale, he made it clear, was anxiety about their debts, and the constant dunning by their creditors. "When will it be finished? If it goes on much longer, I will be finished first."[27]

He had not even heard from the Education Ministry! It was likely, or so Maupassant thought, that Flaubert would be given an annual pension of five thousand francs. The fact was that six hundred men of letters received pensions, and many did not even need them. Yet Flaubert continued to feel "an invincible loathing" toward such charity. But if both the honorary title and the details of the pension that accompanied it could be kept secret, he would accept it, temporarily, and then give it up as soon as he could. The death of an old aunt of Caroline's, on the Hamard side, would make that possible.[28]

Finally it came: an offer of appointment as deputy curator of the Mazarine Library, accompanied by an annual stipend of three thousand francs but without an official apartment. And he would have no duties. Flaubert wondered whether the higher figure — five thousand francs — was no longer being considered, and asked Maupassant for clarification.[29] Maupassant explained that since the ministry could not easily find five thousand francs for a pension, the idea of an *appointment* at three thousand francs had been conceived; later it would be possible to add a two-thousand-franc *pension* to that.[30]

Flaubert decided to go to Paris himself to see Minister Ferry. He also had a useful, if painful, encounter with his brother. Achille readily promised him an annual payment of three thousand francs, but was Achille in possession of his faculties? Flaubert found his brother prematurely senile and deteriorating rapidly. A specialist he had consulted in Paris gave him a year to live.

There was also a decision concerning Edmond Laporte. At last

Flaubert's connections had obtained something for him: an appointment as factory inspector, though his assignment would be in Nevers, far from Paris and even farther from Rouen and Croisset.[31]

The first certain news of Flaubert's own appointment came from Juliette Adam, the great lady of Le Figaro's revelatory article; she wrote to congratulate him. Flaubert was convinced that she had been the true instigator of the library appointment for him, and in her memoirs she confessed that this was the case. Soon he was to hear more from Madame Adam, born Juliette Lamber; this premodern feminist had met Flaubert for the first time in the fall of 1867, when George Sand had brought her along to one of the Magny dinners.[32] Now she was about to launch her own magazine, and she hoped Flaubert would contribute to it. He authorized her to place his name on the cover; he could give her nothing to publish just then, but he was able to assure her that he was not committed to any other publication.[33]

Flaubert still had not received any direct word from the government about his appointment. Maupassant was not helpful; three successive letters from Flaubert went without a reply. Flaubert "trembled like a thief"; at times he could not hold his hand steady to write. Dr. Fortin prescribed the sedatives valerian and potassium bromide.[34] And then Maupassant did write, on May 27, 1879: "Your nomination is signed. You will receive the official notice very soon. . . . You can therefore draw 750 francs [the first quarterly payment] on arriving here."[35] Flaubert wrote to his "dear friend" Frédéric Baudry (who of course had gotten the job Flaubert had wanted at the Mazarine): "It's done. I finally yielded to a small group of friends who wished me to be your deputy. . . . My 'uncompromising pride' had resisted until now. But, old man, I'm close to starvation, or almost." He understood that he would have no duties to perform, but he was prepared to help if called upon.

Then he went to Paris to pick up the first payment.[36]

CHAPTER FORTY-SEVEN

THE GOOD LAPORTE

FLAUBERT ARRIVED in Paris on the evening of Sunday, June 1, 1879, and by Monday he had filled up a week's calendar with dinners. It did not help that he caught cold, and he was soon exhausted from dashing about, even though he was utilizing carriages for which he was spending "crazy amounts of money"; though he tried to keep off his bad leg, it was swelling up again. All the same, he could not miss the year's great Universal Exhibition, for which the Eiffel Tower had been built.

Each day at noon he sat himself down in the National Library, reading for his chapter on religion. "Stupid things," as he summed it up for Edma Roger des Genettes. "When one wants to *prove* God, it's then that idiocy begins." He was also trying to promote his beloved niece as a painter, lining up favorable reviews for her debut at the Salon. He was looking for a theater for *Le Château des Coeurs*, his fairy play, and once again discussing the possibility of an operatic version of *Salammbô* — this time with Ernest Reyer, the composer who would actually see it to the stage, albeit a decade after Flaubert's death.[1]

Before he opened his door to friends that first Sunday, he lunched with Edmond de Goncourt, and again sat, unwittingly, for his portrait. "He is more brick-red-colored, more like a Jordaens painting than ever," the diarist told his diary, "and a lock of his abundant hair at the back of his neck, pushed forward onto the bare crown, makes one think of his redskin ancestry."[2] When his friends arrived — that day they included the art critic Philippe Burty and the poet José Maria de Heredia — they expressed enthusiasm for a study of a nude woman by Caroline Commanville that hung in the apartment, Goncourt suggesting that now she ought to paint Salammbô.[3] Before the end of his three-week stay, Flaubert was complaining that everyone he met had to make a comment on his broken leg. "How you must have suffered!" It had become a refrain, like the constant praise for *Madame Bovary* — whose very title now exasperated him, as he complained to Edma Roger des Genettes. "As if I had done nothing else!"[4]

He called on Jules Ferry at the Ministry of Education to thank him.[5] But in a letter to Caroline, he asked whether his old comrade Alfred Baudry, the younger brother of Frédéric, was still involved in one of Commanville's investments. For he wished to be able to tell the elder Baudry, his ostensible superior at the Mazarine Library, what he really thought of him — without jeopardizing the Commanvilles' credit.[6] (We now know something that Flaubert may not have known: Alfred Baudry lost something like forty thousand francs for believing in Commanville.)[7]

And all the while he worked. He was writing as well as reading. And as he wrote, dreaming. "Do you know what *obsesses* me now?" he asked his niece in a letter dated June 19. "The desire to write the battle of Thermopylae."[8] He finished his readings at the National Library on June 20 and was home in Croisset on the twenty-fifth.[9]

In July he was deep in his chapter on metaphysics. It was going to work, but the effort exhausted him. "Ah! How I'll need to sleep for three months in the sun on a Mediterranean beach," he sighed to Laporte. "For I've been leading this rude, laborious life for too many years." And as he moved forward with *Bouvard and Pécuchet,* he was seeing two of his earlier novels into new editions. Alphonse Lemerre had sent him proofs of the small-format version of *Salammbô* while Charpentier was setting *A Sentimental Education* in type, ready to place it on sale in August when the Michel Lévy contract expired. These new editions were really new. Before giving Lemerre a copy of *Salammbô* for his printer, for example, the author did some serious editing, removing certain phrases he felt were stilted as well as some of the *but*'s, *for*'s, and *meanwhile*'s — his usual worries.[10] As for *A Sentimental Education,* one scholar later counted 495 changes in this new edition, 420 of them cuts. Among the words omitted were 125 *but*'s, thirty-nine *then*'s, thirty-one *for*'s, and twenty-three *meanwhile*'s.[11]

He gave Charpentier the green light to publish his fairy play, for once again a theater had disappointed him. He also accepted the idea of including illustrations, since actual stage sets were lacking. He expected that there would be twelve sketches in the book, one for each scene.[12]

In a letter of August 9 to Turgenev, he reported progress on *Bouvard and Pécuchet:* four more pages to go on chapter eight, and then on to the final two chapters. This, he guessed, should take him to March or April of 1880, after which he would attack volume two of the novel, which was to consist of extracts from the idiotic texts he was finding in treatises and manuals. This meant that he would still be "in harness" a year from then. At that point in his summer a patch of blue sky appeared on the horizon — his financial horizon, as he put it. Commanville seemed to have managed to set up a new business, a sawmill in Rouen that was to handle oak trees from the Caucasus.[13]

Then the chapter was done. "I am exhausted," he told Léonie Brainne, "my brain is a porridge, I cannot stand on my feet." It did not help that Normandy had succumbed to summer heat. He sat at his desk as undressed as could be, sweating all the same.[14] By the end of August he was in Paris again. This time he had a new port of call, the office of the magazine Juliette Adam was about to launch, appropriately titled *La Nouvelle Revue,* conceived to challenge the stodgy *Revue des Deux Mondes.* He was prepared to give Juliette Adam *Bouvard and Pécuchet* for publication in installments, though this would depend, said Flaubert in an aside to Caroline, on how much she was willing to pay.[15] In a meeting with Charpentier he arranged for the appearance of his fairy play — illustrated, and also in installments — in the publisher's own *La Vie Moderne,* making sure that the magazine would commission a drawing from a certain Madame Commanville. He planned to be home in Croisset in time for dinner on Sunday, September 21.[16]

Indeed, Flaubert was once again reasonably specific about the beginning of a Paris visit, and about the very end. But we become lost if we try to follow his movements between those dates. We can surmise that he was having another late-summer rendezvous with Juliet Herbert; it was to be their final one. For these were Juliet's usual vacation dates, and this was Flaubert's customary evasiveness — the use of Mathilde's Saint Gratien country house as a foil, for instance — and then there is a boastful remark to his one confidant, Laporte, in the same vein as the boasts concerning previous trysts with the English governess. (He had a busy prick; he had been cop-

ulating a lot over the past fortnight; this was what he did in Paris, he
told Laporte, instead of writing. "Frankly, I write enough all year
long to have the right to rest a little.")[17]

"Flaubert, while closing his trunk, speaks to me of his literary projects," noted Goncourt on Saturday, September 20, Flaubert's last day
in Paris. He had two more chapters to write; the first would be finished in January, the second by the end of March or April. Then the
appendix volume, and he would be ready to publish in 1881. After
that he wished to do another volume of short stories; he was "tormented" by two or three ideas that would suit that format. And then,
Goncourt heard him say, he was thinking of something particularly
original. "I want to take two or three Rouen families from before the
Revolution to our own times." He mentioned an important businessman in Rouen whose ancestor had worked in a weaving mill. And
there was also his ambitious novel on the Second Empire. "But before anything else, I have to get rid of something that obsesses me,
yes, damn well obsesses me; it's my 'Battle of Thermopylae'." He
would travel to Greece for that, he would write it in simple language;
he saw the book as a "Marseillaise" for all the peoples of the world.[18]
A fascinating last monologue of Gustave Flaubert to one of the few
peers he respected, a perception of what his writing would have been
in the next decade.

They had tried to stave it off. But the moment of reckoning was
bound to come for some of those who had entrusted their names and
fortunes to the Commanvilles for Flaubert's sake. Edmond Laporte,
the good Laporte, had signed the guarantees that had been asked of
him, believing Flaubert's assurances that he would be protected. But
Laporte was the one who had to face the creditors — in this case a
Rouen banker — and then hope that Commanville would follow
through with periodic payments on the loan. Flaubert's nephew had
been meeting these obligations, all the while demanding postpone-
ments of repayment of capital. But this required renewed guarantees
from Laporte, and from others, such as Raoul-Duval, who had agreed
to help Flaubert save his niece's husband. Now, in September 1879,
Laporte was being asked to allow another creditor to take over the
Rouen banker's note, which would give Commanville more time and
(said Flaubert) would cost Laporte nothing save his signature. Still,
Laporte was not convinced. "In any case, whatever you decide, good
man, nothing will change between the two of us," Flaubert wrote him
on September 28, "but before deciding, I beg you to reflect seri-

ously." "This is what I was afraid of, my good giant," replied Laporte. "They are involving you in a discussion in which you should
have no part. I cannot accept you as judge in a matter in which your
nephew on one side and a friend on the other have differing opinions." Laporte pleaded with his friend: "Let me discuss this matter
with Commanville alone." He closed with the promise: "Remember,
my good giant, that I will always love you with all my heart."[19]

But Ernest and Caroline would not have it that way. Henceforth
Laporte was an enemy, one who stood in the way of Commanville's
survival, of his future prosperity. And without a true voice in the matter, especially without the will to stand up to a niece who he believed
could do no wrong, Flaubert let it go that way. "A man whom I considered an *intimate* friend has showed himself to be flatly selfish to
me," Flaubert unburdened himself to Edma Roger des Genettes. "This
treason has caused me suffering."[20]

And while the uncertainty continued — what *would* Laporte do with
the creditors? — Flaubert confessed that he could not work. He did
not dare go to Rouen, he told Caroline, for fear of meeting Laporte;
he would not know how to look at him, or what to say.[21] His niece
solved the problem of what posterity would say — or she thought she
solved it — by censoring all references to the crisis in Flaubert's correspondence destined for publication. For the break with Laporte would
never be mended.

When Turgenev wrote, early in November, remarking how old he
was feeling, Flaubert replied: "I too sometimes feel quite old, quite
tired, worn out to the marrow. Never mind! I carry on, and I do not
want to collapse before having poured a few more buckets of shit over
the heads of my fellows."[22]

Caroline came to see him that autumn, and after she left he settled
in for a winter of solitude, "with no other company than my doggy
and my cook," as he painted the picture for Maxime Du Camp. Days
went by with no visits. He began hoping for them — for one from
Turgenev, for example, though he begged the Moscovite not to promise, but simply to let him know a day ahead and then to come. Cold
weather arrived, and snow. He had an invitation to dine with the
Lapierres in Rouen, but didn't go because the evening return in a
carriage would be too "lugubrious," as he told Caroline. His neighbor Charles Fortin came by from time to time. "As long as I am
working, everything is fine, but the moments of rest, the intermissions
of literature are not always joyous days" — this to Caroline. "What
weather! what snow! what solitude! what silence! what cold!" He con-

fided: "I often think of my former friend Laporte. That's a story I haven't digested easily."[23]

One of the bright moments in that final December was to be a visit from Turgenev, and on Flaubert's fifty-eighth birthday, December 12, 1879. Turgenev had promised, but "Will he come?" wondered Flaubert. On December 8 it was so cold, he wrote Mathilde, that he could not set foot outdoors. He wrote Turgenev that day: "It is understood, agreed on, sworn to, and don't forget me, for God's sake! You'll commit a bad deed. . . ." And this time "the great Turgenev" kept his word, staying a whole day and a half and encouraging him on *Bouvard and Pécuchet* before going back to Paris, en route to Russia. "Your departure left me quite sad," Flaubert wrote him on December 18, thanking him for the caviar and salmon Turgenev had shipped him from Paris. "I feel deeply affected. My life has too few pleasures." To Caroline he complained that his poor brain could not take it any longer. "I've got to rest!" He had been working without respite for so many years now![24]

Yet he warned her, on December 21, not to visit with Ernest just then; it was simply too cold. On December 23 he repeated his warning; in any case, he said, one couldn't even get from Rouen to Croisset — now there was a thick fog besides. "Despite my great age, I've never seen such a winter." So Christmas was hardly merry. But he was working well, and that helped. Indeed, this life of a cave bear, as he described it to Mathilde, advanced his book considerably.[25] "Let 1880 be joyous for you, dear girl!" he greeted Caroline on New Year's Eve. "Good health, a triumph at the Salon, success in business! For me in particular I add: to finish *Bouvard and Pécuchet*! For frankly, I cannot go on. There are days like today when I weep with fatigue (really), and I barely have the strength to hold a pen! I should rest. But how, where, and with what?"[26]

One of the letters of New Year's greetings he received was from his former friend and neighbor Edmond Laporte, or Monsieur Laporte, as Flaubert now called him. "My old friend," this letter began. "Whatever feelings others may have led you to have concerning me, I don't want the new year to come without offering you all my tenderness and good wishes. Accept them without fear: perhaps it is the best of all your friends who sends them." Flaubert assured his niece: "I won't reply, of course."[27]

To each his proper wish. "Health, laurels, and coin of the realm, this is what I wish you," he wrote Goncourt, in a letter that also complained of the publicity *Bouvard and Pécuchet* was getting: "Everyone has his weakness, and this one is excessive with me." "Let 1880 treat you well, my beloved disciple," he wrote Maupassant. "Above all, no more heart problems; health to your dear mother; a good subject for a play that will earn a hundred thousand francs. Wishes concerning the genital organs come in last place, since you handle that quite well yourself."[28] In fact Maupassant was now working on "Boule de Suif" ("Ball of Fat"), and hastened to explain that it was to appear in a volume of stories by Zola and the younger naturalists, each of whom would treat an incident of the war of 1870. When Flaubert first heard what Maupassant's subject was — a prostitute who proves better than her betters — he told Léonie Brainne: "Since his planned story is intended to ridicule our compatriots, I approve it! The hatred of the people of Rouen is the beginning of taste."[29]

The new year had not changed him much. He confessed that "work makes one unsociable." Thus, when he had to go to the Lapierres' for lunch, for days before it he was tormented by the disruption it would cause to his routine. "Can you imagine that I haven't been in Rouen since the beginning of November! I should like to be back home already!" Moreover, the postal service was persecuting him: a letter Caroline had sent from Paris Saturday morning arrived in Croisset only on Monday morning, while in Croisset itself the letter box was emptied every hour. The news from Caroline, when it finally arrived, was good. She had rented a studio to enable her to do her painting in more convenient surroundings.[30] On January 11 he offered her a progress report: his ninth chapter was finished, and he had spent ten hours recopying it; today he was correcting it again before re-recopying it. On each new reading he discovered errors. "It has to be *perfect*. This is the only way to be sure the contents will be accepted."[31]

He took the time to read the three-volume translation of Leo Tolstoy's *War and Peace* that Turgenev had sent him. "The two first volumes are *sublime*," he wrote his Russian friend, "but the third falls apart frightfully. He repeats himself and philosophizes. Finally one sees the gentleman, the author, the Russian, while until then one sees only Nature and Humanity. . . . Tell me about this author. Is it his first book?"[32]

Much of his time, Flaubert complained to his niece, was taken up in reading the work of younger writers. He felt the obligation to read them through and to reply with analytical comments, and when he did not have the time to do this he had to write to the authors to explain why. He told Léonie early in February that he received an average of three such books a week that winter, and had up to six letters to write each day.[33] To date he had read more than fifteen hundred books for *Bouvard and Pécuchet,* he informed Edma Roger des Genettes. His pile of notes was eight inches high.[34]

And he was hard at work outlining that "devil of a chapter" in which he would have to find a way to bring so many abstract ideas to life, he told Caroline — this on the twenty-eighth of January 1880. "Perhaps I won't have finished before the end of May! Never mind! Goodnight!"[35]

EXHAUSTION

THE JANUARY 24, 1880, issue of *La Vie Moderne* published the first installment of *Le Château des Coeurs*. Three pages were taken up with sketches of Croisset by Caroline Commanville, one of them showing "The House of Flaubert," and there was a preface by the editor Emile Bergerat, who ventured to say that if the Comédie Française performed fairy plays, Flaubert's would be worthy of that stage. "Genius breathes over every page."[1]

"You cannot imagine how lovely the weather is today, how the Seine looked this afternoon!" Flaubert wrote his niece on January 28. He had some good news: at long last, and thanks to his stubbornness, the plans for the Bouilhet fountain were to be carried out.[2] The next day, indeed, he signed an authorization for the sculptor to begin working. The minutes of the fund-raising committee indicate that Bouilhet's friends had collected some thirteen thousand francs, while the monument would not cost more than twelve thousand.[3]

He was now at work on his final chapter, as usual seeking help from everywhere. "You who are (or better, were) a rustic, have you watched animals making love?" he asked Maupassant, in a letter praising Maupassant's short story "Boule de Suif," which he had just read in proofs. ("This little tale will *last*, be sure of that!" was Flaubert's keen judgment.)[4]

On February 3 he was awakened by another dunning note. "Under such conditions one must be quite a philosopher not to want to die as quickly as possible, because it is becoming a form of torture," he declared to Caroline at noon that day.

Then the inevitable happened. Laporte initiated proceedings to get his funds back, and not only did Commanville's name appear on the process server's writ, but so did Flaubert's.[5] Commanville was to say of Laporte: "If I sink, he sinks with me. If he helped me with his signature, it was purely out of vanity, to become even more initimate with Flaubert."[6]

Flaubert had some diversion in the second week of February, for Guy de Maupassant came up to see him for Mardi Gras.[7] And soon Guy would provide another distraction. Legal proceedings had been initiated against a magazine called the *Revue Moderne et Naturaliste*, for it had published a poem by Maupassant and a story called "Adnia" by a young American using the pseudonym Defenthy Wright — a story in which a former slave on a Southern plantation tells of an African girl's pubescent sexual adventures with a monkey.[8] The poem by Maupassant was here called "Une Fille," but in fact it was the poem originally called "Au Bord de l'Eau," which he had already published in 1876 in *La République des Lettres* under the pseudonym Guy de Valmont (and despite what has been said since by writers who did not bother to look up these old magazines, the later version is not more lascivious). In it the poet spies a young woman washing clothes, and when she sees him she boldly opens her blouse to reveal full breasts. She also suggests a rendezvous, and the action that follows is described in considerable detail. (An example: "She lay back, moaning under my caress.") They make love again and again, over a period of months.

Maupassant himself found it amusing that a prosecutor could attack a poem that Flaubert had once considered worthy of submission to Agénor Bardoux, then the minister of education, as an argument to convince him to appoint its author to his secretariat. But soon the poet was less sanguine. He was being indicted on a charge of outrage to morality. Once again he needed help from his master, this time in the form of a "paternal" letter that would make the point that writers acquitted after such trials were often subsequently decorated, Flaubert himself being a good example. This letter would be published in the daily *Le Gaulois* and would contribute to Maupassant's defense; in fact it was his lawyer who had suggested it.[9]

Flaubert hesitated. He felt it would be unwise to publish such a letter. What Maupassant should do instead was to use his influence and get the prosecution suspended; to this end, Flaubert gave him a list of important people to see. Yet he did write the letter Maupassant was asking for, and did not forget to mention his own prosecution for *Madame Bovary:* "A trial that represented a gigantic promotion and to which I attribute three quarters of my success." He mocked the involvement of the government with morality. "What is beautiful is moral, and that's that. . . ." If they suppressed Maupassant's poem, they should also have to suppress all of the Greek and Roman classics, without exception, and then Shakespeare, Goethe, Byron, Cervantes, Rabelais, and Corneille. Flaubert told Caroline that he had taken fourteen hours away from his novel in order to write this, together with the letters of recommendation Maupassant also required for his defense.[10]

Yet he remained convinced that the publication of his letter was unnecessary, for Raoul-Duval would surely prevent the proceedings from going further. But if Maupassant still felt that he had to place the letter in *Le Gaulois*, then Flaubert wished to read it again so he could touch it up.[11] We are asked to believe, by Maupassant, that he rushed off to the newspaper, whose editor had the text copied so Maupassant could send it to Flaubert; before Flaubert could do anything with his text, however, the newspaper went ahead with publication, on February 21. The editor himself was to explain to Maupassant, Maupassant claimed, that Raoul-Duval himself had requested that the letter be published in haste. Surely it was this, along with Flaubert's private interventions, that saved Maupassant; the case ended in dismissal.[12]

And as if this were not enough to convince the cave bear that publishing was perilous, he discovered that his fairy play was being illustrated in Charpentier's magazine with what he felt were "infantile" sketches. (The reader curious enough to see for himself may indeed find these little drawings — which are in the spirit of nineteenth-century boulevard caricature — out of place in a Flaubert work, even if they were suited to a play designed for a boulevard theater.) "Not *one* of these stupidities can be utilized in the volume!" Flaubert warned Charpentier, for of course the publisher had contracted to bring out the play in book form as well. "Of all the affronts suffered by *Le Château des Coeurs*, this last is not the least, and I sincerely regret having yielded on my principles this one time."[13]

Writing to Charpentier more soberly — and asking for money — he provided the information that he was now, on February 15, 1880, beginning his final chapter. It might take him until midsummer, after which he would need six months to complete the second volume of the novel. To Caroline he added: "My chapter will certainly take four months, for it must be the longest. . . . This will take me until the middle of June. Still, if I don't want to break with civilization, I have to go to Paris this year. I have to go for my research, and if I want to see publication in 1881, I shall even have to hire a secretary for a while. . . ." He does not add that until recently Edmond Laporte had served in that role, copying out texts from so-called scientific treatises for use in the absurd encyclopedia that the second volume of *Bouvard and Pécuchet* was to be.[14]

Incredibly, the financial adventures of the Commanvilles continued. "The fate of my nephew, and thus mine, to be decided in a week" — this was his principal preoccupation, he announced on February 22 to Edma Roger des Genettes. To Caroline he confessed that he continued to think of Laporte as well as of their creditors. "My head is muddied with so many unworthy things."[15] There was sad news from Turgenev. Home in Russia, he was kept in bed by an acute sciatica; the Viardots were concerned not only for his health but for his safety, in a Russia then shaken by political agitation. Would the government prevent him from leaving? Would the threat come from his old friends the nihilists? Pauline Viardot hoped Flaubert would write to him, and of course he did. By this time Flaubert was well into his final chapter, but when it would be finished, he said, "God knows." He was also able to say that on that very day, March 4, his nephew was to open his sawmill in Rouen, for he now had the money. Afterward, Commanville was to go off to Odessa to acquire timber; as it happened, Turgenev was seeking a lawyer in Russia whom Commanville could consult.[16]

Things did seem to be looking up, and it was high time. Flaubert began to plan his own Paris stay. And then in the middle of this planning, another dunning notice arrived. "This kind of document is beginning to annoy me, set upon my desk as if someone had just served me a plate of excrement." Soon a more threatening notice arrived — of property seizure. Flaubert discovered that he had borrowed fifty thousand francs — or rather, of course, his nephew had, in his name.[17]

Despite all of this, he was preparing for a party. His surviving literary club was coming up to Croisset. There would be Goncourt, of course, and Zola and Daudet; he asked his publisher Charpentier to join them, despite his "crimes." (One of these was the appearance of those infamous illustrations alongside his fairy play; another was his publication of Zola's new novel, *Nana*, which had shocked many people with its portrayal of vice under the Second Empire. Here Flaubert was joking, of course.) Flaubert also invited Maupassant; as he had only four beds to offer, the young man would sleep in the room of

the absent chambermaid. Flaubert wanted his disciple, then quite ill
(the diagnosis was paralysis of the right eye, attributed to a lesion in
the nervous system), to be examined by his neighbor Charles Fortin,
"a simple public health officer whom I consider very competent." While
waiting for his friends, Flaubert pursued his writing. "What a book!"
he exclaimed to his niece. "I've run out of expressions, words, and
effects. Only the idea of coming to the end of this book sustains me,
but there are days when I weep with exhaustion. . . ."[18]

His guests showed up on Easter Sunday, which fell on March 28.
Once again we have an eyewitness report from Edmond de Goncourt,
who left nothing out, beginning with the train ride from Paris to Rouen
with Daudet, Zola, and Charpentier — all of them manifestly delighted with this country escapade, though Zola was concerned that
there might not be enough time to urinate during their brief stops at
Mantes and Vernon. "The number of times that the author of *Nana*
pees or at least tries to pee is unimaginable." Maupassant, who had
arrived in Croisset earlier, picked them up at the Rouen station, and
in Croisset they found Flaubert wearing a Calabrian hat, with "his
fat behind in pleated trousers and his good and affectionate face."
The dinner was delicious, turbot in a marvel of a cream sauce, with
a variety of wines. They told naughty stories that made their host
chuckle. He refused to read from his novel-in-progress, pleading fatigue, and they went upstairs to cold rooms filled with busts of family
members. Next morning the friends slept late, then remained indoors
talking, Flaubert having made it clear that for him walking was a
useless occupation. As they left — Zola remembered this — they
promised to meet again when Flaubert came to Paris early in May.[19]

So he was alone again with his manuscript, and with the constant
fatigue that plagued him now. He remembered a remark James Pradier had made while working on the sculpture at the Invalides mau-
soleum in 1848: "The Emperor's tomb will become mine." Now
Flaubert could say that it was time for his book to end, for otherwise
it would be *his* end. "I am afraid," he wrote Turgenev, "that the effect won't justify the effort, and I feel so exhausted that the result
may well be anemic and a failure. In addition to that, I don't understand anything anymore, and I ache all over, with stomach cramps,
for I hardly sleep. . . ." He wrote this, as far as we know, on April 7.
His plan was still to go to Paris around May 8 or 10, to stay there for
a couple of months, and then to return to Croisset to prepare his
second volume.[20]

He did not mention his financial concerns to Turgenev, but they had not gone away. Commanville returned from Russia content with what he had accomplished, but the bills kept coming in, and money continued to be short. If his niece and her husband could not meet their current expenses, could not pay their Paris rent on time, how would Flaubert be able to live in Paris that summer? Caroline came up for a visit. Preparing for it, she asked her uncle what clothing of hers remained in her closet. He found two nightdresses, three blouses, and thirty-four pairs of stockings. "I repeat: *34* pairs of stockings!!!" And one pair of black silk.[21]

After Caroline left, the harassment continued. On April 18 there was another writ. "If this is a wager to make me die of fury," he wrote his niece, "it's practically won. I don't ask for any explanation, but in the name of God, let them leave me in peace! Let them leave me alone, and let this persecution end!"[22]

Then it was time to think about Paris: "Thank heavens, and at long last, I'm going to see you again soon," he announced to Mathilde. He picked up speed, expecting to have finished all but the last two scenes before leaving Croisset.[23] He took time out for dinner in Rouen at the Lapierres', a dinner scheduled for the feast day of Saint Poly-carpe on April 27; the publisher-printer Charles Lapierre had invita-tions made, with the saint's image and the plaint attributed to him: "My God! My God! in what era have you made me live!!!" At dessert, so one of the guests recalled, a child placed a crown on Flaubert's head, but it slipped off, causing him to murmur, so the legend has it, "I feel like a tomb."[24]

He told all of this to his niece, and then he described his anxieties concerning his writing schedule; if he wanted to publish his book the following winter, he didn't have a moment to lose. "But there are times when I feel as if I'm melting down like an old camembert cheese, so tired am I!"[25]

PART X

DEATH OF A HERMIT

Flaubert interrupted his writing in order to get a complaint off his chest to Georges Charpentier. He had not wished to spoil their Easter holiday by bringing up the matter, he said, but now he had in hand the May 1 issue of Charpentier's magazine, in which a section of his fairy play was interrupted by an article on sports. This, declared Flaubert, was a "foul trick you played on me, and it isn't a nice thing coming from a friend." It was the worst of all the affronts he had suffered with this play. "They rejected my manuscript, they didn't shit on it!" He warned his publisher: "Expect to find me in a bad mood next week." He had agreed that the book version of *Le Château des Coeurs* could be illustrated, but Charpentier would have to commission a totally different set of drawings, and they would have to be appropriate to the text.

Reminding Caroline of his forthcoming visit to Paris, he noted that it was then nine on Sunday morning, and he had been up since seven-thirty. "I should like to have arrived at the heart of the next-to-the-last scene by next Saturday [May 8]. So I don't have a minute to lose." [1]

He received a copy of Maupassant's first collection of poems, titled simply *Des Vers* ("Some Poems"). His disciple also announced the success of *Les Soirées de Médan,* the collection of stories by naturalists that included his "Boule de Suif." There had already been eight printings of the book; Flaubert's own *Three Tales* had only had four, and he was jealous, he told the younger man good-humoredly. Flaubert intended to see to it that Maupassant's poems got favorable reviews, and he began by asking Théodore de Banville for "a bit of trumpeting." Banville replied in a letter of May 5 that he would not have to do Flaubert any favor, for Maupassant's book stood on its own merits; he had read nothing so original in twenty years.[2] Flaubert now knew that his disciple had a place of his own in the literary life.

On May 8, 1880, on the day he might have left for his long-awaited, long-postponed trip to Paris, Flaubert suffered a stroke; soon after that, he was dead. The best diagnosis we have — considering that no qualified physician, no reliable witness, was at his side — is apoplexy, caused by the blocking or rupture of a blood vessel in the brain (a cerebral hemorrhage). This seems likely because of what is known of Flaubert's medical history, of his life-style. He *might* have had a coronary thrombosis, which would also have been consistent with his diet and behavior, but he had no record of previous heart problems.[3]

The absence of authoritative medical data, as well as the ambiguities and even the mysteries of Flaubert's life as seen from the outside, obviously invited some speculation about more fanciful causes of death. It has been suggested that he committed suicide, the main evidence for that being the uncertainty concerning his final hours.[4] A more pleasant notion, which has come down through oral tradition, has it that he died while engaged in his (regular) pastime of making love with his young servant Suzanne.[5]

Guy de Maupassant, whose surest talent was his rendition of detail, was one of the first to arrive in Croisset. He had first been informed of the death of his patron by a telegram sent by Commanville, who was also in Paris that day; it bore the time 3:55 on the afternoon of May 8, and read:

> FLAUBERT STRICKEN APOPLEXY WITHOUT HOPE
> WE LEAVE 6 O'CLOCK COME IF POSSIBLE

This may suggest that Flaubert was not dead when the Commanvilles received their own telegram from Croisset.[6] Maupassant did manage to get to the station in time to join the Commanvilles on the six P.M. train. In Croisset they found Flaubert lying in bed, looking the way he always did, Maupassant was to tell Turgenev, "except that the apoplexy had swollen his neck with a black blood color." They obtained more information from Dr. Fortin, who had not been present that morning, and from Suzanne, who had.

Flaubert had seemed well enough, even merry. He had planned to leave for Paris on the following day, Sunday, May 9, and was expecting to enjoy himself — this he must have confided to Fortin — since he had stashed away a bit of money, a small sum earned from his writing. On Friday he spent the evening with Fortin, declaiming Corneille; he slept until eight the next morning, took a long bath, dressed, and read his mail. "It was then that he called his maid," Maupassant told Turgenev, "feeling a little indisposed; as she did not come upstairs quickly enough, he shouted from the window for her to go to look for Fortin, who in fact had just left on the boat. When the maid reached him he was standing up, rather dizzy but seemingly unworried. He told her: 'I think I'm going to have a kind of fainting fit; it's a good thing that it's happening today, for it would have been quite annoying tomorrow on the train.'" He opened a bottle of eau de cologne, continued Maupassant (who surely had this from the maid), rubbed some on his temples, and spread himself out on the sofa, murmuring, "Rouen . . . we're not far from Rouen. . . . Hellot . . . I know the Hellots. . . ." And then he fell back, hands contracted, face swollen with blood — he was dead. The press reports got his last words wrong, suggesting that Flaubert had mentioned the Avenue d'Eylau in Paris, where Hugo lived. But Maupassant understood "Hellot" as being a reference to a Rouen doctor.[7]

In the absence of Charles Fortin, the servant had in fact found another village doctor, Jules Tourneux, who had set up his practice in Croisset in January 1878 and knew both his colleague Fortin and Flaubert. He remembered that Flaubert's maid rushed in to see him at eleven-thirty that morning, "Come quickly; I don't know what's wrong with Mr. Gustave, he frightens us." He hurried over and found Flaubert on the sofa in his study, his face bloated, congested. He no longer seemed to be breathing, though there were still some weak heartbeats. There was no foam at the mouth, and there were no contractions. He also noted that a full pipe, still warm, sat on the fireplace mantel.

Tourneux heated a hammer with boiling water and placed it on Flaubert's stomach, obtaining no reaction. The heart ceased to beat. The doctor concluded that it had not been an epileptic attack; Flaubert's apoplectic appearance, moreover, led him to conclude that a blood vessel had ruptured.[8]

Maxime Du Camp was the first to make public the hypothesis that Flaubert had died of or after an attack of epilepsy that he tried to fight off with ether. When he came out of it, Du Camp postulated, his "yellow vision" persisted and he remained dizzy; then his mouth contorted, and he turned his head away and died.[9] But Du Camp had witnessed his friend's attacks years before; he had not been present this time. During Flaubert's funeral, Georges Pouchet took Goncourt aside to whisper: "He died not of apoplexy but of an attack of epilepsy. . . . Yes, all the symptoms, foam at the mouth. . . . In fact, his niece wanted a cast of his hand, but they couldn't do it, for it was so badly contracted. . . ."[10] "I see yellow," Flaubert was supposed to have told his servant. (This was passed on by Charles Lapierre, who arrived on the scene at noon.)[11]

Against these witnesses, there is the testimony of Tourneux and the inquiry by the observant Maupassant that night. The fact that Flaubert suffered from epilepsy early in his life does not necessarily mean that he died of it. In our own time the best specialists in this disease dismiss the "imaginary descriptions" of Du Camp and Goncourt.[12] One might add that at the time Flaubert was born, male children had an average life expectancy of thirty-eight years; those who made it to age twenty could expect to live for another forty. To die at fifty-eight of "natural" causes was not so strange.[13]

A death mask was made. The papers scattered over the writing table were carefully collected; they included notes for further readings for *Bouvard and Pécuchet*, and some press clippings. One of these was an article from a paper called *Phare de la Loire* about the publication of the Lemerre editions of *Madame Bovary* and *Salammbô*; it contained these lines: "While his sparse production gives him a place apart in contemporary literature, he is no less for that one of the uncontested masters of the contemporary novel, perhaps the only one who owes nothing to anyone, and whom everyone else has more or less imitated." And then another, from *Voltaire*, dated December 20, 1879, and headed "Major literary news." It reported: "We are going to have a new novel from the author of *Madame Bovary*. Title: B . . . . . and P . . . . . Discretion prevents us from saying more."[14]

CHAPTER FIFTY

MONUMENTS

With Charles Fortin and Georges Pouchet, Maupassant prepared his mentor's body for burial. Visits to the funeral chamber could begin. It is said that one of those who came was Edmond Laporte, who wished to see his giant for the last time; Maupassant reportedly refused to allow him in.[1]

Someone had just asked Goncourt if he was going to call at Flaubert's apartment in Paris the next day, for the first of his Sunday receptions, when the two-word telegram arrived from Maupassant: "Flaubert dead." For a time he was stunned. "I felt that a link, at times loose, and yet inextricably knotted, secretly attached us to each other," he told his diary. He also remembered having seen a tear in Flaubert's eye as they had embraced at the door at the end of his Easter visit to Croisset. "At bottom we were the two old champions of the new school, and I find myself very much alone today."[2] He was to survive that other old champion by sixteen years.

Zola had received his two-word telegram at his country house in Médan. He caught the local train to Mantes and then the express to Rouen, arriving just in time to join the funeral procession on May 11. "Ah my friend!" he wrote Henry Céard before leaving, "it would be better if we all passed on. . . . Decidedly, there is nothing but sadness, and nothing is worth living for."[3] When he boarded the train in Mantes, Zola found Alphonse Daudet, coming from Paris. Goncourt and Charpentier, their other companions at the final Easter reunion, had gone up to Normandy the previous evening. Zola and Daudet found a carriage at the Rouen station and met the funeral procession en route. "The hearse was richly decorated, with silver shields bearing the initials of the deceased," a journalist reported. "Large floral wreaths were attached to its four corners." The reporter counted forty rented carriages parked in the village.[4] "What is exasperating at these funerals is the presence of all that reportorial population," grumbled Goncourt, "with their little papers in the palm of their hands, on which they dash off names of people and places that they then get wrong. . . ."[5]

First in the procession came the Commanvilles, Caroline in a carriage with Léonie Brainne and Charles Lapierre's wife — two of the "three angels" — followed by Maupassant, Lapierre, and some local officials. Achille Flaubert was incapacitated and could not be present. One reporter jotted down on his little paper in the palm of his hand the names of the Parisians he could identify, who included (in addition to Flaubert's inner circle of friends) Emile Bergerat, Catulle Mendès, and Théodore de Banville. He also thought it interesting to mention those contemporaries of Flaubert's who were not present, such as Dumas, Taine, and Renan. This particular reporter, from Le Gaulois, had written earlier about the local indifference displayed toward Rouen's best-known author, and the townspeople had not appreciated that. "The way to prove that I was wrong was quite simple," he told his readers the day after the funeral. "They only had to come to Croisset or, more economically, to follow in town, in close ranks, the hearse on its way to the cemetery." If there were people along the way, along the five miles that separated the church at Canteleu from the Monumental Cemetery above Rouen, they were there to see the Parisians, to see Zola — and to see a handsome hearse.[6]

From the Flaubert residence on the river the procession had taken the steep road up to Canteleu, arriving at the Romanesque church as four local farmers tugged at the church bell. The coffin was so heavy that its bearers were doubled over; the service seemed, to Zola at least, routine and without feeling.[7] Another witness remembered exchanging an observation with fellow Parisians in the church: "It's Emma Bovary's funeral!"[8] On the way to the cemetery Goncourt overheard some fellow mourners preparing for the amusements to follow, and there was talk of duckling with oranges; someone pronounced the word brothel.[9]

A scene out of Bovary indeed. Caroline Commanville later confessed — but only to her private memoir, never to be published — that her flirtation with the handsome José Maria de Heredia had blossomed at that hour; it was this charmer of a poet, and not Ernest Commanville, who stood beside her. Later Heredia admitted that he had fallen in love with her as she stood all in black at the edge of the grave. Their love was to bud but not to flower; once again she believed, she said, that "a slightly amorous friendship" could exist between a man and a woman.[10]

As the procession crossed the city — three hundred persons in all, Zola estimated; while he understood why some of the dead man's older colleagues might have hesitated to make the voyage from Paris, he found it harder to comprehend why the people of Rouen were not there — Flaubert's friends took turns holding the ceremonial tassels on the coffin. At the gates of the city they were joined by a platoon of soldiers, a customary tribute paid to a deceased knight of the Legion of Honor. Along the waterfront, "some groups of bourgeois looked on with curiosity." Many seemed not to know who Gustave Flaubert was, though they knew of his father and brother. Up in the cemetery, a single plot already held the mortal remains of three Flauberts, Gustave's father and mother and his beloved sister. (Just below, in a separate plot, Gustave's brother, Achille, was to be laid to rest in January 1882). The tombs of Achille-Cléophas and Anne Justine Caroline were of simple stone, without religious symbols; Gustave's smaller white stone tomb was to be topped with a cross (surely Caroline's doing).

There were prayers, and then Charles Lapierre spoke briefly. Flaubert had told friends that he opposed graveside speeches, and, Lapierre said, "His desire will be respected." When they began to lower it into the grave, they discovered that the coffin was too large — it was "a giant's coffin," noted Zola. For several minutes the gravediggers tried to make it fit. "It was atrocious; the niece whom Flaubert had loved so much sobbed at the edge of the pit." Voices were heard: "Enough, enough. . . ." Zola walked off, his heart in shreds. But the reporter from Le Gaulois stayed behind, and saw the coffin descend at last. Friends sprinkled holy water on it; the ceremony was over by four.[11] Perhaps no one there that day had also been present thirty-four years earlier, when the coffin of Flaubert's sister had failed to fit into the grave dug for it.

Goncourt took Zola and Daudet down to his hotel on the river. "In a cabaret," observed Zola, "a tableful of famished reporters and poets ordered themselves sole Norman-style."[12] The old friends resolved to leave for Paris then and there, refusing to get involved with the revelry in preparation.[13]

"The death of your uncle was one of the greatest sorrows I have had in my life," Turgenev, from Russia, wrote Caroline, "and I cannot get used to the thought that I won't ever see him again."[14] Maxime Du Camp had been kept away from the funeral by illness — a kidney attack that even prevented him from writing to Caroline until a week after the funeral, at which time he told her how he mourned "this man I loved so much, who was the companion of my life and who takes my fondest memories away with him." [15]

Inevitably, the monument. There was a fund-raising campaign of a kind Flaubert himself might have undertaken. Friends managed to collect a total of 8,650 francs, and in 1882 the district council voted to add a thousand francs more to that, but the total was still insufficient. An anonymous donor, so the story goes, made up the difference. A bas-relief was commissioned from the sculptor Henri Chapu. It is of a nude woman representing Truth; she sits under a tree with a quill pen in her hand, a medallion of Flaubert just overhead. It is all in turn-of-century flourishes, belonging neither to Flaubert's time nor to our own, and now stands in the garden of the Hôtel-Dieu, just outside the Flaubert Museum.

The inauguration of this monument was scheduled for November 23, 1890, a decade after the author's death. On a nasty Sunday morning Goncourt met Zola, Maupassant, and other committee members at the Gare Saint Lazare for the trip to Rouen. At the ceremony Goncourt noted what he described as an "indifferent" audience. Some twenty Parisians were present, all of them well-known literary or newspaper personalities, along with some local officials and a band — just as at the agricultural fair in *Madame Bovary*, Goncourt told himself. He found the Chapu statue to be a "pretty bas-relief in sugar," and observed that "Truth seems to be relieving itself in the well." [16]

CHAPTER FIFTY-ONE

WORKS

THE TRUE MONUMENT, of course, had to be *Bouvard and Pécuchet*. But there was no danger that *this* monument would be delayed, for its publication would bring in money, and the Commanvilles intended to earn as much as they could from their uncle's manuscripts. It goes without saying that the book found in Flaubert's office is not the one he would have published; no work of his published during his lifetime was not subjected to conscientious revision. More important still, Flaubert never separated this first volume, the story of his copy clerks, from the compilation of "stupidities" that was to form the second volume. Today the dossier he compiled is available, and it has even been possible to assemble and to publish a "second volume." [1]

As for the first volume — the novel — it existed in draft, with an outline of the final pages. By the very end of the book Flaubert's protagonists have lost interest in the active life, and they decide to return to their copy desks; they will, of course, copy out the stupidities to be published as the second volume. But Flaubert's niece, in preparing the novel for an early publication, changed "copy" to "copy as they used to do," indicating that the disappointed clerks would return to the same mindless work they had performed before retiring to the country. [2] This substitution certainly allowed Caroline Commanville and her publisher to suggest that in publishing the story of Bouvard and Pécuchet they were giving the reader a complete work.

The trials of *Bouvard and Pécuchet* did not end there. Flaubert's heirs demanded twelve thousand francs for the magazine rights from Juliette Adam's *Nouvelle Revue*, finally settling for eight thousand, as Caroline was to remember it. [3] On December 15, 1880, just seven months after the death of the author, *La Nouvelle Revue* published the first installment of the novel; the text was censored, notably in those passages with sexual references, such as the seduction of Pécuchet by his chambermaid. Of course Maxime Du Camp, an earlier censor of Flaubert, remarked this posthumous treason, and surely enjoyed the irony.[4] When Alphonse Lemerre published the first edition of *Bouvard and Pécuchet* as a book in 1881, one of the reviews was written by a long-time literary enemy of Flaubert's, Jules Barbey d'Aurevilly. "The jackals of posthumous literature continue their sad labors," began his report in *Le Constitutionnel* on May 10, 1881, "which consist of picking up the remains of dead lions and feeding on them." So Flaubert had been a lion after all? The author — here Barbey seemed to be correcting himself — had been "a literary worker who had the integrity of his trade, rather than an inspired artist." *Bouvard and Pécuchet* represented a piece of "innocent mumbling," and it could have been placed on the author's grave like a cross. "For it will be one for his memory!"[5]

Were the Commanvilles to be, in Barbey d'Aurevilly's phrase, "jackals of posthumous literature"? Flaubert's niece kept all of her uncle's manuscripts and notebooks, and published some of them; she also collected Flaubert's letters, and published many of these. The manner in which she did this, both her motives and her methods, deserves to be looked into. On Flaubert's death his heirs were his niece Caroline and his brother, Achille, but the latter quickly waived his claim to a share of the estate. The inventory of Flaubert's property included furniture worth 6,925 francs and cash on hand amounting to 2,515 francs; importantly, the money received from the sale of his Deauville farm in 1875 — two hundred thousand francs — was counted as part of his estate, since Flaubert had simply turned it over to Commanville to bank for him. As a final item, Flaubert's works, his unpublished manuscripts, received an evaluation of two thousand francs — a curious figure, for it was easy to guess that *Bouvard and Pécuchet* alone was worth many times that. Presumably it made sense to undervalue the legacy, for there was a 6.5 percent tax to be paid on it. As declared by Ernest Commanville, the sum total of Flaubert's property and capital upon his death amounted to 221,045.50 francs, which included the two hundred thousand francs in the hands of his "banker."[6]

The house and land at Croisset, we know, already belonged to Caroline. Within months of her uncle's death she sold it to an industrial concern. The house was demolished, the trees were cut down, and a distillery was built in what had been the garden, with storerooms occupying the rest of the grounds. Soon the plant was producing alcohol from corn, "enough to inebriate a city," noted a reporter in 1885, or enough "to buy a whole generation of voters." [7]

Only the summer house, a simple, stone, one-room structure with slate roof in Louis XV style, was left standing on its site near the river. It was acquired by admirers of Flaubert early in the twentieth century and became a museum as well as the headquarters of a group of Friends of Flaubert.[8] During the Second World War a pro-German newspaper in Paris described an air attack on the port of Rouen that damaged the pavilion and demolished the caretaker's house; the headline was: "The Anglo-Americans Go Out after Flaubert."[9] All is in order today. The humble summer house holds up well alongside the smokestacks of what is now a paper mill; inside can be found Flaubert's parrot, or one of them.

The question of Flaubert's niece Caroline remains. In his diary, at the time of Flaubert's death, Goncourt expressed concern: "Commanville constantly speaks of the money that can be made from the dead man's work, and keeps going back so curiously to my poor friend's love letters that he gives the idea that he would be capable of blackmailing the surviving women concerned." Goncourt had also observed the graveside flirtation of Caroline with José Maria de Heredia, and Heredia himself was to admit to having felt that had he made a move, she would have thrown herself into his arms. Goncourt even wondered if this were not simply an act, intended to win this "honest and young soul" over to the Commanvilles' intrigues.[10] A year later, when Princess Mathilde asked that her letters to Flaubert be returned, and they were, Goncourt wrote her: "One is always happy to find a man less crooked than his reputation, and I was really afraid that Commanville would be tempted to make money from your private feelings. . . ."[11] But in 1884, four years after Flaubert's death, when Goncourt was invited to dine in Paris by the Commanvilles, "the luxury of their town house and the heavy silk covering the walls and the quiet and satisfied wealth of the hosts made me a little sad and led me to remember the final years of poor Flaubert, completely ruined by this rich couple. . . ."[12]

Unkind critics did portray Caroline as avid, exploiting her late uncle's works in order to live well.[13] We must be grateful to her all the same, for it was she who acquired the extraordinary letters Flaubert wrote to Louise Colet; their contract gave both Caroline and Colet's daughter the right to censor them.[14]

This question of censorship was to trouble scholars and readers from that time until our own. Many of those who turned over their letters expurgated them first, or destroyed selected ones. Thus family tradition has it that Flaubert's childhood friend Ernest Chevalier went through a voluminous dossier, rereading each letter before deciding whether or not to save it, and putting the doubtful ones in the fire. In truth, these letters seem to have survived, but with lines crossed out, presumably by Chevalier himself.[15] When the well-known art dealer Ambroise Vollard decided to publish an edition of *The Temptation of Saint Anthony* with illustrations by Odilon Redon, Flaubert's niece feared that there would be too much nudity in Redon's conception of the temptations and insisted that she be allowed by contract to approve Redon's work.[16]

Ernest Commanville died in March 1890. Three years later his widow, then forty-seven, moved with her Flaubert manuscripts to Antibes, where her Villa Tanit became something of a shrine. (Tanit was the holy temple in Carthage, described in *Salammbô*.) In 1900 Caroline married a childhood friend, Dr. Franklin Grout, the son of a student of Achille-Cléophas Flaubert's. (He and his sister Frankline had both been named for Benjamin Franklin.) We have it on family authority that Caroline did the proposing; she was convinced that Franklin Grout had never married in part because he secretly loved her.[17] He died in 1921. The Villa Tanit, "an aristocratic residence," a frequent visitor was to say, appeared "of sober elegance, surrounded by a park encumbered with exotic plants and dominating one of the world's most beautiful panoramas: in the foreground the sea, and beyond that, as if poised on the horizon, the snow-covered Alps." This house, in the first decades of this century, held "one of the finest literary treasures of France," the Flaubert archives.[18]

The American writer Willa Cather was to describe a chance meeting with Caroline in August 1930 in Aix-les-Bains. In the course of the writer's stay at that fashionable thermal resort, she found herself talking with an elderly woman (Caroline was then eighty-four) who in passing mentioned that she had known Turgenev, adding, "My uncle also was a man of letters, Gustave Flaubert, you may perhaps know." Madame Franklin-Grout, who impressed Cather with her literary and musical knowledge, promised to send her, as a memento, an original letter from Flaubert to George Sand. When the envelope reached the American writer, however, she found it had been torn, and its contents were missing. She wrote Flaubert's niece to tell her this, but shortly thereafter she learned that Madame Franklin-Grout had died.[19]

On the death of Flaubert's niece in 1931, and by the terms of her will, all of those literary treasures were dispersed. The most important manuscripts were bequeathed to institutions; the lesser ones were given to her friends. And then, soon after her death, an extraordinary auction of the remaining papers was held on the grounds of the Villa Tanit; a second sale took place in Paris later that same year.[20] We are told by Caroline's niece and apologist that "it did not displease her to see the remaining papers in the hands of passionate collectors, or even to have them show up at auction rooms, which could only contribute to keeping the memory of Flaubert alive. . . ."[21] Papers sold in Antibes and Paris are still turning up at auctions, to be fought over by collectors, speculators, and sometimes libraries, from all over the world.

As for Flaubert's reputation, there was only a brief purgatory, perhaps exacerbated by the publication of Maxime Du Camp's memoirs. Flaubert's old friend made a point of revealing what he saw as his character defects, as well as the truth about his attacks of epilepsy; it was the first time such things appeared in print, and some of their mutual friends were shocked. (Théodore de Banville told Goncourt that he would not write his own memoirs, for he did not wish to write about "the epilepsy of my friends.")[22] Maupassant retaliated: in an essay about his master, he published the outrageous letter Du Camp had written in 1856 to urge Flaubert to accept his censorship of *Madame Bovary*. When Du Camp indicated that he was going to sue over the unauthorized reproduction of this letter, it was pointed out that Du Camp had not hesitated to use Flaubert's correspondence in his own memoirs.[23]

Flaubert survived that nineteeth century better than most of his immediate peers, and in our time his reputation has been in constant ascent. Having made a priesthood of literature, he became an object of cult worship by others, including Franz Kafka, for whom good writing also meant sacrifice. In France at midcentury Flaubert's admirers were reinforced by a new avant-garde; in America and Britain every modern writer stood behind him; and more recently, a whole generation of Latin American writers has demonstrated that with Flaubert as a guide, one could move in a number of different directions. Closer to our own day, Flaubert returned to fashion when it became clear that the last productive years of a contemporary cultural hero, Jean-Paul Sartre, had been devoted to writing about him. It almost doesn't matter that Sartre's book was condemned from the start by flawed research; thousands of controversial pages have thereby been added to the Flaubert bibliography. Let us hope that Sartre's readers will come away from them with renewed curiosity about Flaubert's true life and works.

ACKNOWLEDGMENTS

THIS BOOK owes an incalculable debt to the scholars who in recent years have made their findings accessible. Professor Jean Bruneau, who is now engaged in editing Flaubert's letters and whose published books and articles contain a wealth of reliable information and insights, has kindly answered questions and offered advice. I am also grateful to Jacques Suffel, the curator of the Spoelberch de Lovenjoul collection of the Institut de France during the time I worked with the Flaubert correspondence, and to Roger Pierrot, who was then in charge of the Bibliothèque Nationale manuscript department and continued to be of assistance thereafter. I have had cordial cooperation from others who make their institutions excellent places in which to work: Marie-Françoise Rose of Rouen's richly endowed Bibliothèque Municipale; Catherine Blondel of the Archives Départementales de la Seine-Maritime in Rouen; Jacques Neefs and Odile de Guidis of the Equipe Flaubert in the Institut des Textes et Manuscripts Modernes. Special thanks also to Thierry Bodin, a dealer in manuscripts who is also a scholar generous with his time, and to André Dubuc, the tireless president of Les Amis de Flaubert. And to Professor Henri Gastaut; Dr. Germain Galérant; Jean-Yves Mollier; Hermia Oliver; Daniel Sickles; and Dr. Benjamin G. Zifkin.

APPENDIX

FLAUBERT'S FRANCS

THERE IS no sure, easy, and universally acceptable way to convert nineteenth-century francs into their twentieth-century equivalents, and the problem is complicated by the sixty-year span of events covered in this book, as well as by the possibility that some readers may not pick it up until long after its publication. Depending upon which yardstick is used — the cost of living, for example, or the value of gold — there are wide variations in the results obtained.

With the help of the Conservatoire National des Arts et Métiers in Paris, and with particular thanks to Dr. Jacqueline Fourastié, we can utilize a very approximate conversion based on official price indexes and pre–World War I indexes drawn up by the Laboratoire d'Econométrie of the Conservatoire. Thus:

1840 francs		17.95	
1850 francs		17.63	
1860 francs	multiply by	16.52	for 1986 equivalent
1870 francs		15.17	
1880 francs		15.09	

As an indication, the assets of Dr. and Mrs. Flaubert at the time of Flaubert's father's death in 1846 were valued at 207,389.38 francs; multiply by the 1846 coefficient of 16.82 to obtain the 1986 equivalent of some three and a half million francs. For years after 1986, one can multiply this result by the cumulative cost-of-living increase in France. For the ten thousand francs Flaubert received in 1862 for *Salammbô*, multiply by that year's coefficient, 16.88, to obtain some 170,000 francs in 1986. For the two hundred thousand francs re-

ceived for the Deauville farm in 1875, multiply by that year's coefficient, 16.22, or some three million francs in 1986.

As a more reliable and less variable and subjective measure of the
value of Flaubert's francs, Dr. Fourastié recommends reference to the
average hourly wage in francs of an unskilled laborer, which amounted
to the following in the period that concerns us:

1840	.19
1846	.185
1850	.195
1860	.205
1862	.210
1870	.220
1875	.225

Thus the ten thousand francs Flaubert received for *Salammbô* represented nearly forty-eight thousand working hours (10,000 divided
by .210), or more than fourteen years' work for an unskilled laborer
employed eleven hours a day for three hundred days a year.

NOTES

ALTHOUGH the original manuscripts of Flaubert's letters are in many cases available for study, a published source is given whenever possible to facilitate consultation. Quotations from books by Flaubert are identified by chapter but not by page, since the reader may not be using the same edition as the author. All translations are my own.

Citations from the *Journal* of the Goncourt brothers are taken from a four-volume edition that is subdivided as follows: 1: 1851–1863; 2: 1864–1878; 3: 1879–1890; 4: 1891–1896. Volume 4 is cited only once in the present work.

The following abbreviations are used:

AF	*Les Amis de Flaubert* (bulletin, published in Croisset)
Bib. I	Bibliothèque de l'Institut de France
BSL	Bibliothèque de l'Institut, Spoelberch de Lovenjoul collection
CC	Flaubert, *Correspondance*, Conard edition, Paris, 1926–1933
CS	Flaubert, *Correspondance*, supplementary volumes published by Conard in 1954
GFGS	Flaubert-Sand, *Correspondance*, published by Flammarion, Paris, in 1981
GP 1	Flaubert, *Correspondance*, published by Gallimard-Pléiade, Paris, volume 1
GP 2	Flaubert, *Correspondance*, published by Gallimard-Pléiade, Paris, volume 2
OC (CHH)	Flaubert, *Oeuvres complètes*, published by Club de l'Honnête Homme, Paris
OC (S)	Flaubert, *Oeuvres complètes*, published by Editions du Seuil, Paris

Full bibliographic references are given at the first citation of each source.

PROLOGUE

1. Gustave Flaubert, *Correspondance*, vol. 2 (Paris: Gallimard-Pléiade, 1980), 657f.
2. Ibid., 659f.

CHAPTER ONE: CHAMPAGNE AND NORMANDY

1. [Emile] Gérard-Gailly, *Flaubert et "les fantômes de Trouville"* (Paris: Le Renaissance du Livre, 1930), 12f.
2. M. G. Reibel, *Les Flaubert, vétérinaires champenois* (Troyes: Frémont, 1913).
3. René Vigo, "Présence de Flaubert à Nogent-sur-Seine," *Les Amis de Flaubert* 13 (1958).
4. Ibid.; Claude Chevreuil, "Nogent-sur-Seine dans la vie et l'oeuvre de Flaubert," *AF* 28 (1966).
5. J. Chevron, "A propos des ancêtres champenois de Gustave Flaubert au XVIIIe siècle," *Revue historique de la révolution française*, October–December 1923.
6. René Dumesnil, *Gustave Flaubert, l'homme et l'oeuvre* (Paris: Nizet, 1943), 18f.
7. Edmond et Jules de Goncourt, *Journal*, vol. 1 (Paris: Fasquelle-Flammarion, 1956), 1221.
8. Flaubert to George Sand, in Gustave Flaubert–George Sand, *Correspondance*, ed. Alphonse Jacobs (Paris: Flammarion, 1981), 184.
9. Caroline Franklin-Grout, "Heures d'autrefois," manuscript courtesy of Jean Bruneau.
10. Gilles Henry, "Les ancêtres de la mère de Gustave Flaubert," *AF*, December 1975, 16, 20.
11. Gustave Flaubert, *Correspondance*, vol. 4 (Paris: Conard, 1927), 457.
12. Caroline Franklin-Grout, "Souvenirs intimes," in Gustave Flaubert, *Correspondance*, vol. 1 (Paris: Conard, 1926), xv; Henry, "Les ancêtres de la mère."
13. Alphonse Védie, *Notice biographique sur M. Flaubert* (Rouen: Brière, 1847).
14. Bibliothèque Municipale de Rouen, 92N2 Flaubert. Also see Gaston Bosquet, "Un Document sur Achille-Cléophas Flaubert père," *AF* 6 (1955).
15. André Dubuc, "La Nomination du père de Flaubert," *AF*, May 1964.
16. Védie, *Notice biographique*.
17. A.-C. Flaubert, *Dissertation*, Bibliothèque Nationale, Paris.
18. Franklin-Grout, "Souvenirs intimes," xv.
19. *Album Flaubert* (Paris: Gallimard, 1972).
20. Bibliothèque Municipale de Rouen, 92N2 Flaubert.
21. Franklin-Grout, "Souvenirs intimes," xvi; Lucien Andrieu, "Les Maisons de la famille Flaubert," *AF*, May 1967.
22. Germain Galérant, "Le Docteur A.-C. Flaubert," *AF* 7 (1955); Lucien Andrieu-André Dubuc, "La Nomination du père de Flaubert," *AF*, May 1967.

CHAPTER TWO: THE HÔTEL-DIEU

1. Andrieu, "Les Maisons de la famille Flaubert," 10.
2. Charles Terrasse, "L'Hôtel-Dieu de Rouen," *Echanges-Actualités*, April 1984; Jean Hossard, "Le Musée Flaubert et d'Histoire de la Médecine," (brochure) (Rouen, n.d.).
3. *Album Flaubert*, 17.
4. Gilles Henry, *L'Histoire du monde c'est une farce* (Condé-sur-Noireau, Calvados: Corlet, 1980), 18, 96f.

5. Gustave Flaubert, *Correspondance*, vol. 1 (Paris: Gallimard-Pléiade, 1973), 844f. (note by Jean Bruneau).

6. *Almanach de Rouen* (Rouen: Periaux, 1834), 43.

7. Théodore Licquet, *Rouen, son histoire* (Rouen: Frère, 1839), 225.

8. *Almanach de Rouen*, 43.

9. Lucien Andrieu, "Les Domestiques de la famille Flaubert," *AF*, May 1974.

10. Franklin-Grout, "Souvenirs intimes," x ff.

11. Georges Mignot, "Le Père Mignot," *AF* 14 (1959); letter from Georges Mignot, 1958, in Bibliothèque Municipale de Rouen, 92N4a Flaubert. Mignot warns that references to *père* Mignot may apply either to the old farmer or to his son Amédée.

12. Franklin-Grout, "Souvenirs intimes," xi.

13. GP 2: 321.

14. GP 1: 660.

15. GP 2: 376.

16. René Dumesnil, *Flaubert: Son Hérédité, son milieu, sa méthode* (Paris, 1906; Geneva: Slatkine Reprints, 1977).

17. Jean-Paul Sartre, *L'Idiot de la famille*, vol. 1 (Paris: Gallimard, 1971), 137ff., 240ff.

18. Gustave Flaubert, *Oeuvres complètes*, vol. 1 (Paris: Seuil, 1964), 230f.

19. Sartre, *L'Idiot* 1: 80ff., 98, 381ff.

20. Gustave Flaubert, *Souvenirs, notes et pensées intimes* (Paris: Buchet-Chastel, 1965), 52.

21. Edmond et Jules de Goncourt, *Journal*, vol. 2 (Paris: Fasquelle-Flammarion, 1956), 964.

22. Quoted in Gustave Flaubert, *Madame Bovary* (Paris: Conard, 1930), 540. When Maupassant asked for information for an article, Caroline Commanville informed him in November 1883 that Flaubert learned to read "only several months before entering the *lycée;* he was nine years old." Daniel Sickles Collection, courtesy of Thierry Bodin.

23. GP 1: 317.

24. Ibid., 110.

25. Ibid., 3ff.

CHAPTER THREE: DR. FLAUBERT

1. Védie, *Notice biographique*, 12ff.

2. Letter to the author from Dr. Germain Galérant.

3. Georges Dubosc, *Trois Normands* (Rouen: Defontaine, 1917), 102.

4. GP 2: 964.

5. Dr. Germain Galérant, "Le Docteur Flaubert," in *Les Rouennais et la famille Flaubert* (Rouen: Amis de Flaubert, 1980), 27.

6. Archives Départementales de la Seine-Maritime, Notariat Bidault, 1872, 4: Liquidation, December 1872.

7. Jean-Pierre Chaline, *Les Bourgeois de Rouen* (Paris: Presses de la Fondation nationale des Sciences Politiques, 1982), 123; ———, *Rouen sur la monarchie de Juillet* (Rouen, Centre de documentation pedagogique, 1971); ———, "A la recherche de la bourgeoisie rouennaise du XIXe siècle," *AF*, December 1969.

8. Georges Dubosc, "La Maison de Gustave Flaubert à Déville," *Bulletin,*

Les Amis de Monuments Rouennais, 1900 (Rouen: Lecerf, 1901).

9. For much basic data, I have relied on the notes of Jean Bruneau in his edition of Flaubert's letters. In this case: GP 1: 837.

10. *OC* (S) 1: 256.

11. Ibid., 236.

CHAPTER FOUR: THE YOUNG WRITER

1. Jean-Pierre Chaline, "Le Milieu culturel rouennais au temps de Flaubert," in *Flaubert et Maupassant, ecrivains normands* (Paris: Presses Universitaires de France, 1981), 21ff.

2. Franklin-Grout, "Souvenirs intimes," xiii.

3. GP 1: 5ff.; Jean Bruneau, *Les Débuts littéraires de Gustave Flaubert* (Paris: A. Colin, 1962), 12.

4. GP 1: 8.

5. *Album Flaubert.*

6. GP 1: 374f.

7. François-Valentin Bouquet, *Souvenirs du Collège de Rouen par un élève de pension (1829–1835)* (Rouen: Cagniard, 1895).

8. Ibid., 68ff.

9. Pierre Labracherie, "L'Elève Flaubert," *AF* 10 (1957).

10. *OC* (S) 1: 760; GP 2: 756f.

11. Académie de Rouen, *Distribution générale des prix faite au Collège Royal* (Rouen: Brière, 1833).

12. GP 1: 295.

13. Ibid., 9ff.

14. Archives Nationales F17 20864.

15. Letter to the author from Jacques Neefs. Also see Claude Mouchard and Jacques Neefs, *Flaubert* (Paris: Balland, 1986).

16. *OC* (S) 1: 42.

17. Bruneau, *Les Débuts*, 44.

18. GP 1: 16ff.

19. Martyn Lyons, *Le Triomphe du livre* (Paris: Promodis, 1987), 86.

20. Bruneau, *Les Débuts*, 52ff.

CHAPTER FIVE: ELISA

1. Bouquet, *Souvenirs du Collège*, 74ff.; Labracherie, "L'Elève Flaubert," 4f.

2. Bruneau, *Les Débuts*, 162ff., 167.

3. Victor Brombert, *Flaubert* (Paris: Seuil, 1971), 33ff.

4. Bibliothèque Nationale, manuscript NAF 18244.

5. André Dubuc, "La Bibliothèque générale du père de Flaubert," in *Les Rouennais et la famille Flaubert;* Franklin-Grout, "Souvenirs intimes," xxxix.

6. *OC* (S): 240ff.; Lucien Andrieu, "Un Amour inconnu de Gustave Flaubert," *AF*, April 1963.

7. Andrieu, "Un Amour inconnu."

8. GP 2: 637.

9. G. Tenon, "Un Amour de Flaubert: Elisa Foucault, une vernonnaise," *Les Cahiers Vernonnais*, April 1974.

10. *OC* (S) 1: 236ff.

11. Gérard-Gailly, *Flaubert et "les fantômes de Trouville,"* 59ff.
12. Maxime Du Camp, *Souvenirs littéraires*, vol. 2 (Paris: Hachette, 1906), 336ff.
13. GP 1: 279.
14. Gérard-Gailly, *Flaubert et "les fantômes de Trouville,"* 91ff.
15. [Emile] Gérard-Gailly, *L'Unique Passion de Flaubert* (Paris: Le Divan, 1932), 31ff.
16. [Emile] Gérard-Gailly, *Le Grand Amour de Flaubert* (Paris: Aubier, 1944), 49.
17. Dr. Germain Galérant was told the story by Emile Gérard-Gailly, who apparently obtained this version of events only after publishing his books on Flaubert. Letter from Dr. Galérant to the author.

CHAPTER SIX: REVOLT

1. *OC* (S) 1: 78ff.; Bruneau, *Les Débuts*, 168ff.
2. Edouard Maynial, *La Jeunesse de Flaubert* (Paris, Mercure de France, 1913), 123ff.
3. GP 1: 22.
4. *OC* (S) 1: 101ff.
5. Bruneau, *Les Débuts*, 189ff.; GP 1: 850f.; Rémy Villand, "Paul Le Poittevin," *AF*, December 1976, 19ff.
6. Alfred Le Poittevin, *Oeuvres inédites* (Paris: Librairie des Amateurs, 1909), 53.
7. GP 1: 26f.
8. Dubosc, *Trois Normands*, 106; Etienne Frère, *Louis Bouilhet* (Paris: Soc. Française d'Imprimerie et de Librairie, 1908), 29ff.
9. GP 1: 676, 864, 1111.
10. *OC* (S) 1: 250.
11. GP 1: 24.
12. Georges Dubosc, "Une composition d'histoire et de géographie par Gustave Flaubert," *Notre Vieux Lycée* (Rouen), September 1913, 114f.
13. R. Deliencourt and J. Chennebenoist, *La Propriété Strassburger* (Deauville: Ville de Deauville, 1981).
14. *OC* (S) 1: 104ff.
15. Bruneau, *Les Débuts*, 129f.
16. Ibid., 131ff.; *OC* (S) 1: 113ff.
17. *OC* (S) 1: 124ff.
18. GP 1: 27f.
19. *OC* (S) 1: 180ff.
20. GP 1: 28ff., 246.
21. Ibid., 32f.; GP 2: 289f. Also see GP 1: 860.
22. GP 1: 34f., 38ff.
23. Bruneau, *Les Débuts*, 202ff., 216.
24. Ibid., 240ff.; Albert Thibaudet, *Gustave Flaubert* (Paris: Gallimard, 1935), 24.
25. GP 1: 36ff.
26. Ibid., 47.
27. Jean-Paul Sartre, *L'Idiot de la famille*, vol. 2 (Paris: Gallimard, 1971), 1472ff.

28. Flaubert, *Souvenirs*, 46.
29. GP 1: 51; Bruneau, *Les Débuts*, 187.
30. Archives Nationales F 17 8011; Labracherie, "L'Elève Flaubert."
31. André Dubuc, "Le Baccalauréat au temps de Flaubert," *AF*, December 1984.
32. GP 1: 58.

CHAPTER SEVEN: EULALIE

1. GP 1: 60f.
2. Flaubert, *Souvenirs*, 57.
3. Ibid., 58.
4. GP 1: 63f.
5. Ibid., 64f.
6. Certificate reproduced in *Les Rouennais et la famille Flaubert*. Also see Dubuc, "Le Baccalauréat," 38ff.
7. *Dictionnaire de biographie française*, vol. 9 (Paris: Letouzey, 1961); Jules Cloquet, *Notice analytique des travaux scientifiques* (Paris: Rignoux, 1854); ———, *Souvenirs sur la vie privée du Général Lafayette* (Paris: Galignani, 1836).
8. Flaubert, *Souvenirs*, 81.
9. Second part, chapter 1.
10. GP 1: 66, 68.
11. Ibid., 71f.
12. Goncourt, *Journal* 1: 709.
13. Ibid.
14. *OC* (S) 1: 242.
15. Ibid., 455.
16. GP 1, 225.
17. *OC* (S) 1: 259ff.
18. GP 1: 279.
19. Unpublished. From an auction, Paris, December 12, 1985, courtesy of Thierry Bodin. The letters had been published in part at the time of an earlier sale. See the following note.
20. Maurice Monda, "L'Eulalie de Flaubert," *Le Figaro*, November 14, 1931.
21. Flaubert, *Souvenirs*, 99.
22. Unpublished. See note 19 above.
23. Monda, "L'Eulalie."
24. Unpublished. See note 19 above.
25. Monda, "L'Eulalie."
26. GP 1: 75ff.
27. Flaubert, *Souvenirs*, 86.
28. GP 1: 83f.
29. J. Bruneau and J. Suffel, "Autour de Gustave Flaubert: lettres inédites," *Bulletin du Bibliophile* 3, 1980, 391.
30. GP 1: 87ff.
31. Ibid., 92.
32. Ibid., 93f.

CHAPTER EIGHT: PARIS

1. GP 1: 95ff.
2. Ibid., 104.
3. Bibliothèque Municipale de Rouen, 92N3 Flaubert.
4. First part, chapter III.
5. GP 1: 120.
6. GP 1: 831.
7. GP 2: 388.
8. GP 1: 107ff.
9. Ibid., 124.
10. Ibid., 114.
11. Philip Spencer, "New Light on Flaubert's Youth," *French Studies*, April 1954, 97ff.
12. Gustave Flaubert, *Oeuvres complètes*, vol. 2 (Paris: Seuil, 1964), 548.
13. *OC* (S) 1: 273ff.
14. GP 1: 126f.
15. Ibid., 127ff.
16. Jean Bruneau and Jacques Suffel, "Pour l'amour de Flaubert," *Nouvel Observateur*, May 5, 1980, 90.
17. GP 1: 134ff.
18. Ibid., 141ff.
19. Bibliothèque Nationale, manuscript NAF 23825.
20. GP 1: 832.
21. Goncourt, *Journal* 1: 1350.
22. GP 1: 489.
23. GP 1: 86, 169f.
24. Goncourt, *Journal* 1: 729f.
25. *OC* (S) 1: 358f.

CHAPTER NINE: THE FALL

1. Letter to Louise Colet, January 16, 1852, GP 2: 29f.
2. Henri Heine, *Lutèce* (Paris: Michel Lévy, 1855), 306f., 321.
3. Richard Wagner, *Ma Vie*, vol. 1 (Paris: Plon, 1911), 292, 310ff., 318ff.
4. Gérard-Gailly, *Flaubert et "les fantômes de Trouville,"* 59ff.
5. Spencer, "New Light on Flaubert's Youth," 105.
6. GP 1: 150, 220f.
7. Quoted in GP 2: 1457.
8. Maxime Du Camp, *Souvenirs littéraires*, vol. 1 (Paris: Hachette, 1906), 160f., 164f.
9. Ibid., 163ff., 170ff., 174, 186. For a descriptive bibliography of Du Camp's early work: note by Jean Bruneau in GP 1: 918.
10. GP 1: 158, 160.
11. Bruneau-Suffel, "Autour de Flaubert" 3: 395.
12. GP 1: 170ff.
13. Bibliothèque Nationale, manuscript NAF 23825.
14. GP 1: 184, 1165.
15. Ibid., 185f.
16. First part, chapter V. See Du Camp, *Souvenirs littéraires* 1: 174.

17. Du Camp, *Souvenirs littéraires* 1: 175.
18. GP 1: 189ff.
19. Arsène Houssaye, *Les Confessions*, vol. 1 (Paris: Dentu, 1885), 404f.
20. GP 1: 195ff.
21. GP 2: 423.

CHAPTER TEN: CONSEQUENCES

1. Du Camp, *Souvenirs littéraires* 1: 180ff.
2. H. and Y. Gastaut, "La Maladie de Gustave Flaubert," *Revue Neurologique* 6–7 (1982), 467ff. In technical language, neonatal atrophy or vascular malformation of the occipitotemporal cortex. For a summary of the evidence: Germain Galérant, "Flaubert vu par les médecins d'aujourd'hui," *Europe*, September–October 1969, 107ff. Dr. Benjamin G. Zifkin, of New York, in correspondence with the author, argues that the condition would have affected Flaubert's personality and behavior in the years preceding the first overt attack.
3. Dr. Félix Regnault in *La Chronique Médicale*, November 1, 1900; Charles Binet-Sanglé in the same journal, January 15, 1901. Letter from Prof. Henri Gastaut to the author.
4. GP 2: 716.
5. Bruneau-Suffel, "Autour de Flaubert" 3.
6. Ibid.
7. GP 1: 202; Du Camp, *Souvenirs littéraires* 1: 180.
8. GP 1: 203f.
9. Maxime Du Camp, *Lettres inédites à Gustave Flaubert* (Messina: EDAS, 1978), 39, 63, 98.
10. Letter from Prof. Henri Gastaut to the author.
11. Du Camp, *Souvenirs littéraires* 1: 178ff.
12. GP 1: 206.
13. Ibid., 207f.
14. Ibid., 214.
15. Ibid., 136.
16. Flaubert, *Souvenirs*, 63.
17. BSL, Correspondence Flaubert, B VIII.
18. Preface by François-Régis Bastide, in Gustave Flaubert, *La Première Education sentimentale* (Paris: Seuil, 1963); Bruneau, *Les Débuts*.
19. GP 1: 220f.
20. Bibliothèque Nationale, manuscript NAF 23825.
21. GP 1: 359f. It is not excluded that the visit took place on Flaubert's return from Italy in June, for at that time he wrote in his travel notes of a visit to the Colliers: "I saw there the defect in the armor of my soul. . . ." *OC* (S) 2: 472.
22. GP 1: 222f.
23. Ibid., 223f.
24. Ibid., 464ff. The painting is now in the Palazzo Odescalchi, Rome. For a reproduction: *Album Flaubert*, 52f.
25. GP 1: 230.
26. GP 1: 225ff.

CHAPTER ELEVEN: CROISSET

1. GP 1: 237ff.
2. Ibid., 240f.
3. Letter from Caroline Flaubert to François Parain, BSL, Correspondence Flaubert, B VII f. 87.
4. GP 1: 241.
5. Ibid., 247f.; note by J. Bruneau, 965.
6. BSL, Correspondence Flaubert, B VII f. 83, 84, 87; Bruneau-Suffel, "Autour de Flaubert" 3: 473f.
7. Védie, *Notice biographique.*
8. Bruneau-Suffel, "Autour de Flaubert" 3: 475; GP 1: 253f.
9. GP 1: 259.
10. *Le Journal de Rouen,* January 18, 1846, quoted in André Dubuc, "L'Enterrement du père de Gustave Flaubert," *AF,* December 1970.
11. GP 1: 255; GP 2: 257.
12. GP 1: 269.
13. Ibid., 257ff., 431.
14. Franklin-Grout, "Heures d'autrefois." Also see Lucien Andrieu, "Emile Hamard," in *Les Rouennais et la famille Flaubert,* 38ff.
15. GP 2: 101.
16. GP 1: 260, 262.
17. Andrieu, "Les Maisons de la famille Flaubert," 11.
18. GP 1: 263.
19. Archives Départementales de la Seine-Maritime, Notariat Boulen, July 4, 1846; Déclaration de succession, July 4, 1846, in Chaline, *Rouen sous la monarchie.*
20. Archives Départementales de la Seine-Maritime, Notariat Bidault, 1872, 4; Liquidation of December 23, 1872.
21. GP 1: 264ff., 268ff.
22. Ibid., 303.
23. Du Camp, *Souvenirs littéraires* 2: 8.
24. Guy de Maupassant, *Correspondance,* vol. 2, in *Oeuvres complètes* (Geneva: Edito-Service, 1973), 16f.
25. Du Camp, *Souvenirs littéraires* 1: 238f.
26. GP 1: 537, 567, 632.
27. Enid Starkie, *Flaubert: The Making of the Master* (London: Penguin, 1971), xii f.
28. Sartre, *L'Idiot* 1: 686f.
29. Gustave Flaubert, *Oeuvres complètes,* vol. 14 (Paris: Club de l'Honnête Homme, 1975), 48.
30. December 1845. Bibliothèque Nationale, manuscript NAF 23825.
31. *OC* (CHH) 14: 42.
32. August 1847. Du Camp, *Lettres inédites,* 109ff.

CHAPTER TWELVE: LOUISE

1. *Statues de chair: Sculptures de James Pradier* (catalogue) (Paris: Editions de la Réunion des musées nationaux, 1986): articles by Jacques de Caso, Guillaume Garnier, and Douglas Siler.
2. Du Camp, *Souvenirs littéraires* 2: 263.

3. GP 1: 275, 299.
4. Memento, June 14, 1845, in GP 1: 807f.
5. *Album Flaubert*, 66, 94.
6. GP 1: 285.
7. Reconstructed from Colet's diary in GP 1: 808.
8. Goncourt, *Journal* 1: 1183.
9. GP 1: 299f., 308.
10. Ibid., 280f.
11. Ibid., 306.
12. Ibid., 280 ff., 289, 303.
13. Jean Bruneau, in GP 1: 979ff.; Joseph C. Jackson, *Louise Colet et ses amis littéraires* (New Haven: Yale University Press, 1937), 4ff., 88ff.
14. GP 2: 1063. We know this because Colet said it in her private diary.
15. GP 1: 285, 287, 297, 301f.
16. Ibid., 303ff.
17. Ibid., 307.
18. Ibid., 308ff.
19. Ibid., 311f.
20. Ibid., 324ff.
21. *Guide du voyager sur le chemin de fer de Paris à Rouen* (Paris: Havard, 1843), 8f.
22. GP 1: 333f.
23. André Dubuc, "Un Poème méconnu de Louise Colet," *AF*, May 1967, 19ff. It can be found in the Carnets de lecture at the Bibliothèque Historique de la Ville de Paris.
24. GP 1: 333f.
25. Ibid., 342f.
26. Ibid., 347ff.
27. Ibid., 361f.
28. Ibid., 355, 374.
29. Ibid., 377ff.
30. Ibid., 394f., 399f., 401ff.

CHAPTER THIRTEEN: WESTWARD WITH DU CAMP

1. GP 1: 404ff., 412ff.
2. Du Camp, *Souvenirs littéraires* 2: 263.
3. GP 1: 346ff.
4. Ibid., 424ff.
5. Ibid., 438ff., 824ff.
6. Ibid., 447ff.
7. Ibid., 439f.
8. Du Camp, *Souvenirs littéraires* 1: 241f.
9. Bibliothèque Municipale de Rouen, 92N7 Flaubert.
10. Du Camp, *Souvenirs littéraires* 1: 256f.
11. Bib. I, MS 1287.
12. *OC* (S) 2: 474ff.
13. Du Camp, *Souvenirs littéraires* 1: 257ff.; *OC* (S) 2: 515f.; GP 1: 457.
14. *OC* (S) 2: 535f.; GP 1: 459ff.

15. GP 1: 462f.
16. Ibid., 463ff.
17. Ibid., 470ff., 478.
18. Ibid., 482ff., 488f.
19. Ibid., 491f.
20. Maxime Du Camp, *Souvenirs de l'année 1848* (Paris: Hachette, 1876), 51ff., 75ff., 104ff.
21. GP 1: 492f.
22. Du Camp, *Souvenirs de . . . 1848*, 10; ——, *Souvenirs littéraires* 1: 269f.
23. GP 1: 493, 1043.
24. Ibid., 493ff.
25. Ibid., 496.
26. Du Camp, *Souvenirs littéraires* 1: 277; ——, *Lettres inédites*, 135f.; BSL, Correspondence Flaubert, B I: letter from Louis de Cormenin, June 1848.
27. GP 1: 499f.
28. Du Camp, *Souvenirs littéraires* 1: 281f.

CHAPTER FOURTEEN: EASTWARD WITH DU CAMP

1. GP 2: 71.
2. Gustave Flaubert, *Oeuvres complètes*, vol. 8 (Paris: Club de l'Honnête Homme, 1973), 279.
3. Brombert, *Flaubert*, 124.
4. Notice, in Gustave Flaubert, *La Tentation de Saint Antoine* (Paris: Conard, 1924), 664ff.
5. Du Camp, *Souvenirs littéraires* 1: 297ff.
6. GP 1: 1166, from Marie-Jeanne Durry, *Flaubert et ses projets inédits* (Paris: Nizet, 1950), 403f.
7. GP 1: 511f.
8. Du Camp, *Souvenirs littéraires* 1: 315ff.
9. Bruneau, *Les Débuts*, 516f.; GP 1: 1071f.
10. GP 1: 809.
11. Du Camp, *Lettres inédites*, 152ff.
12. Antoine Youssef Naaman, *Les Lettres d'Egypte de Gustave Flaubert* (Paris: Nizet, 1965), 29.
13. *OC* (S) 2: 550.
14. GP 1: 514.
15. *OC* (S) 2: 552.
16. Flaubert, *Souvenirs*, 85.
17. Jean Bruneau, *Le "Conte Oriental" de Flaubert* (Paris: Denoël, 1973), 9, 14f., 19f., 37f., 49ff., 91ff., 121, 128f., 186ff.
18. Bib. I, Du Camp Papers, 3720, I.
19. Ibid.
20. Archives Nationales, F 17 2957.
21. Du Camp, *Lettres inédites*, 153.
22. Archives Nationales, F12 2593B.
23. *OC* (S) 2: 555f.
24. GP 1: 532.
25. Du Camp, *Souvenirs littéraires* 1: 352.

26. Ibid., 321f., 351. See also Maynial, *La Jeunesse de Flaubert*, 193ff.; Benjamin F. Bart, "Is Maxime Du Camp a Reliable Witness?," *The Modern Language Review*, January 1953.
27. *OC* (S) 2: 561.
28. GP 1: 537, 543.
29. Du Camp, *Souvenirs littéraires* 1: 352.
30. *OC* (S) 2: 565.
31. Ibid., 566.
32. Eyal Onne, *Jerusalem: Profile of a Changing City* (Jerusalem: Miskenot Sha'ananim, 1985); Nineteenth- and Twentieth-Century Photographs (catalogue) (London: Christie's, 1986); Roger Pierrot, "Flaubert en Orient: Maxime Du Camp, photographe de Jerusalem," *Bull. de la Bibliothèque Nationale*, December 1980, 167ff.
33. Onne, *Jerusalem*, 57f.
34. Du Camp, *Souvenirs littéraires* 1: 310.
35. Maxime Du Camp, *Egypte, Nubie et Palestine, dessins photographiques recueillis pendant les années 1849, 1850, et 1851* (Paris: Gide et Baudry, 1852), pl. 3.
36. GP 1: 556ff.
37. Ibid., 567ff., 638.
38. Ibid., 580.
39. Ibid., 587ff., 590ff.
40. Ibid., 581, 594.
41. Ibid., 600.
42. *OC* (S) 2: 573; GP 1: 607.
43. Maxime Du Camp, *Voyage en Orient (1849–1851)* (Messina: Peloritana, 1972), 71.
44. GP 1: 607; *OC* (S) 2: 575.

CHAPTER FIFTEEN: HOMESICK AND HOME

1. GP 1: 601f.
2. Ibid., 618ff.
3. Ibid., 626ff.
4. Ibid., 646ff.
5. Ibid., 668.
6. Ibid., 661f.
7. Ibid., 660.
8. *OC* (S) 2: 609.
9. GP 1: 673.
10. Ibid., 677ff.
11. Bib. I, Du Camp Papers, MS 3720, II.
12. GP 1: 707, 729, 732.
13. Dr. Germain Galérant, talk with the author.
14. Philippe Ricord, *Traité pratique des maladies vénériennes* (Paris: Rouvier et Le Bouvier, 1838); ———, *Lettres sur la syphilis* (Paris: L'Union Médicale, 1851).
15. *OC* (S) 2: 646f.
16. GP 1: 708f., with note by J. Bruneau, 1121. See also Bruneau, *Les Débuts*, 516f.

17. Du Camp, *Souvenirs littéraires* 1: 373.
18. GP 1: 719f.
19. Ibid., 734ff.
20. Ibid., 772ff.
21. *OC* (S) 2: 697f.
22. Gérard-Gailly, *L'Unique Passion*, 67ff.; GP 1: 783.
23. Franklin-Grout, "Heures d'autrefois."
24. Du Camp, *Lettres inédites*, 173.
25. Bruneau, *Les Débuts*, 546f.
26. GP 1: 781f., 784, 811ff.
27. GP 1: 877; GP 2: 3ff.
28. Du Camp, *Lettres inédites*, 177.
29. GP 2: 877f.
30. Ibid., 5.

CHAPTER SIXTEEN: HESITATIONS

1. GP 2: 5f.
2. Jean Seznec, *Flaubert à l'Exposition de 1851* (Oxford: Clarendon Press, 1951).
3. GP 2: 18f.
4. Ibid., 7, 18f.
5. Ibid., 879.
6. Du Camp, *Souvenirs littéraires* 2: 9.
7. Ibid., 14ff.
8. GP 2: 879f.
9. Ibid., 8ff.
10. Ibid., 12f.
11. Ibid., 14f.
12. Ibid., 863ff.
13. Ibid., 17, 881f. Flaubert immediately wrote to Harriet Collier requesting that she sell or return the album.
14. Ibid., 19f., 28.
15. Ibid., 882f.
16. Ibid., 33ff.
17. Ibid., 27ff.
18. Ibid., 36ff., 39f.
19. Ibid., 884.
20. Ibid., 42ff., 46, 52f.
21. Ibid., 54f.
22. Ibid., 884, 1052f.
23. Starkie, *Flaubert: The Making*, 234.
24. Marie-Claire Bancquart, *Lettres de Louis Bouilhet à Louise Colet* (Rouen: Publications de l'Université de Rouen, 1967), 70.
25. GP 2: 884, 57.

CHAPTER SEVENTEEN: *MADAME BOVARY*

1. Claudine Gothot-Mersch, *La Genèse de Madame Bovary* (Geneva: Slatkine Reprints, 1980), 26f., 35f.; André Dubuc, "Les Époux Delamare et *Madame Bovary*," in *Les Rouennais et la famille Flaubert*, 105ff.

2. Notes by Douglas Siler in *Statues de chair*, 360f.; Douglas Siler, *Flaubert et Louise Pradier: Mémoires de Madame Ludovica* (Paris: Archives des Lettres Modernes, 1973), 4f., 20ff.; *Catalogue des manuscrits de Gustave Flaubert* (auction catalogue), Paris, November 1931.

3. GP 2: 697. Also see GP 1: 708.

4. "L'Écriture de Madame Bovary," in notes, Flaubert, *Madame Bovary* (Conard), 486ff.; Gabrielle Leleu, Madame Bovary, *Ebauches et fragments inédites* (Paris: Conard, 1936).

5. Bibliothèque Municipale de Rouen, Manuscript g 221.

6. Bancquart, *Lettres de Bouilhet*, 154.

7. Du Camp, *Souvenirs littéraires* 1: 183f.

8. Dr. Jean Fretet, "Flaubert: L'Epilepsie et le style," *Europe*, April 15, 1939, 462ff.

9. Dr. P. Voivenel, in *Le Progrès Médical*, November 3, 1917.

10. One specialist observes, however, that epileptics can be prolific letter writers, and thus Flaubert's painstaking craftsmanship would be the conscious slowing down of a hypergraphic style. Letter to the author from Dr. Benjamin Zifkin.

11. GP 2: 70ff., 75ff.

12. Preface to *Portrait of a Lady*, in Henry James, *The Art of the Novel: Critical Prefaces* (New York: Scribner's, 1934), 50.

13. GP 2: 85, 218. See E. W. Fischer, "Un Inédit de Gustave Flaubert: La Spirale," *La Table Ronde*, April 1958, 96ff.; Bruneau, *Le "Conte Oriental*," 200; Katherine Singer Kovács, *Le Rêve et la Vie: A Theatrical Experiment by Gustave Flaubert* (Cambridge, Mass.: Department of Romance Languages and Literatures of Harvard University, 1981), 22.

14. GP 2: 88ff., 133.

15. Ibid., 93, 102ff.

16. Ibid., 113ff., 120ff.

17. Du Camp, *Lettres inédites*, 201f.

18. Jean-Yves Mollier, *Michel et Calmann Lévy* (Paris: Calmann-Lévy, 1984), 90.

CHAPTER EIGHTEEN: LOUISE TAKES A RIDE

1. GP 2: 886f., 58ff., 117.

2. Ibid., 888f.

3. Ibid., 126f.

4. Attributed to Flaubert by a sometime writer friend, Amélie Bosquet: see Bruneau, *Les Débuts*, 479.

5. GP 2: 126ff., 889f.

6. Ibid., 891.

7. Ibid., 134.

8. Ibid., 139f.

9. Ibid., 892ff.

10. Ibid., 148f., 1448.

11. Ibid., 155f., 159, 172.

12. Ibid., 173ff.

13. Ibid., 174, 249; Victor Hugo and Louise Colet, "Lettres inédites," *La Revue de France*, May 15, 1926, 210f.

14. GP 2: 179.

15. Ibid., 199ff., 205.
16. Ibid., 207ff.
17. Ibid., 218ff.
18. Ibid., 336f., 342.
19. BSL, Correspondence Flaubert, B IV f. 12–57. Also see Victor Hugo, *Correspondance*, vol. 2 (Paris: Albin Michel, 1950), 181f.

CHAPTER NINETEEN: GUSTAVE AND LOUISE

1. GP 2: 898f., 229, 234.
2. Ibid., 238f.
3. Ibid., 246ff.
4. Ibid., 275, 287.
5. Ibid., 315ff.
6. Ibid., 901.
7. Ibid., 325f., 338, 344.
8. Ibid., 353.
9. Bancquart, *Lettres à Bouilhet*, 146.
10. GP 2: 388ff.
11. Ibid., 402ff., 411f., 416.
12. Ibid., 422ff., 426ff.
13. Ibid., 386.
14. Ibid., 449.
15. Ibid., 450, 455f., 459.
16. Ibid., 483, 497.
17. Ibid., 500f., 505f., 523, 537.
18. Ibid., 525f., 528, 532f.
19. Ibid., 537, 540, 543ff.
20. Ibid., 548, 557f.
21. Jules Troubat, *Notes et pensées* (Paris: Sauvaitre, 1888), 128f.
22. Goncourt, *Journal* 1: 1022; ———, *Journal* 2: 487.

CHAPTER TWENTY: LAST CHAPTERS

1. GP 2: 560f.
2. Frère, *Bouilhet*, 80f.
3. GP 2: 902f., 498, 1264.
4. Ibid., 340.
5. Ibid., 562ff.
6. Goncourt, *Journal* 2: 238.
7. GP 2: 567f.
8. GP 2: 569f.
9. GP 2: 572.
10. Ibid., 1270.
11. Ibid., 573.
12. Ibid.
13. Hermia Oliver, *Flaubert and an English Governess: The Quest for Juliet Herbert* (Oxford: Clarendon Press, 1980).
14. GP 2: 576.
15. Ibid., 577ff.
16. Ibid., 594.

17. Ibid., 596ff.
18. Franklin-Grout, "Souvenirs intimes," xxxi f.
19. Jackson, *Colet*, 225.
20. Ibid., 228ff.
21. GP 2: 611, 1302.
22. Ibid., 613.

CHAPTER TWENTY-ONE: PUBLISHING *MADAME BOVARY*

1. GP 2: 613ff.
2. Du Camp, *Lettres inédites*, 205.
3. GP 2: 619ff., 623f.
4. Du Camp, *Lettres inédites*, 207.
5. GP 2: 629ff.
6. Du Camp, *Lettres inédites*, 209.
7. GP 2: 633f., 640.
8. Du Camp, *Souvenirs littéraires* 2: 54.
9. GP 2: 639ff.
10. Ibid., 634, 636ff.
11. Du Camp, *Souvenirs littéraires* 2: 135.
12. GP 2: 645.
13. Ibid.
14. Gustave Flaubert, *Correspondance, supplément (1877–1880)* (Paris: Conard, 1954), Complément, 13.
15. Du Camp, *Souvenirs littéraires* 2: 141f., 144f.; ———, *Lettres inédites*, 215.
16. Quoted by J. Bruneau in GP 2: 1462f.
17. Ibid., 649ff.; note by Bruneau, 1329.
18. Du Camp, *Souvenirs littéraires* 2: 148.
19. GP 2: 655.
20. Ibid., 655ff. J. Bruneau says that there is no evidence that Achille Treilhard, the son of a count of the Empire, was Jewish. Ibid., 1336.
21. Ibid., 659ff.
22. Ibid., 666f., 670, 673f.

CHAPTER TWENTY-TWO: FAME

1. GP 2: 672, 1343f.; see also the court decision in Flaubert, *Madame Bovary* (Conard), 628.
2. GP 2: 676f.
3. Flaubert, *Madame Bovary* (Conard), 558ff. (the prosecution argument).
4. Max Brière, "Des Amitiés rouennaises de Flaubert, les frères Baudry," *Etudes normandes* 1 (1981): 41f.
5. Flaubert, *Madame Bovary* (Conard), 579ff.
6. Ibid., 628ff.
7. Du Camp, *Souvenirs littéraires* 2: 156ff.; GP 2: 1347, 1463.
8. GP 2: 678ff.
9. Du Camp, *Lettres inédites*, 212f.; GP 2: 643.
10. Mollier, *Michel Lévy*, 17ff.
11. Ibid., 321ff., 342; Du Camp, *Lettres inédites*, 212.
12. Goncourt, *Journal* 1: 910.

13. Mollier, *Michel Lévy*, 342.
14. Calmann-Lévy archives, courtesy of Jean-Yves Mollier.
15. Mollier, *Michel Lévy*, 180ff.
16. Bibliothèque Municipale de Rouen, manuscript g 222.
17. Mollier, *Michel Lévy*, 267ff.
18. Gustave Flaubert, *Lettres inédites à son éditeur Michel Lévy* (Paris: Calmann-Lévy, 1965), 43.
19. "Les Exemplaires en grand papier de Madame Bovary," *AF* 13 (1958): 23ff.
20. Flaubert, *Lettres à Michel Lévy*, 35.
21. C.-A. Sainte-Beuve, *Causeries de lundi*, vol. 13 (Paris: Garnier, 1858), 283ff.
22. Flaubert, *Madame Bovary* (Conard), 527ff.
23. GP 2: 740.
24. In *Le Courrier de Paris*, reprinted in George Sand, *Questions d'art et de littérature* (Paris: Calmann Lévy, 1878), 287ff.
25. *L'Artiste*, October 18, 1857, in Charles Baudelaire, *Oeuvres complètes* (Paris: Seuil, 1968), 257f.
26. GP 2: 794, 981, 1412ff.
27. BSL, Correspondence Flaubert, B V, f. 51.
28. Ibid., B VII, f. 113.
29. GP 2: 654.
30. Ibid., 1332; Hermia Oliver, "Nouveaux aperçus sur Marie-Sophie Leroyer de Chantepie," *AF*, December 1962, 4ff.
31. GP 2: 696, 691f.
32. Ibid., 691.
33. Ibid., 701.
34. Ibid., 412.
35. Ibid., 497.
36. Du Camp, *Souvenirs littéraires* 2: 152.

CHAPTER TWENTY-THREE: CARTHAGE

1. Morgan Library (New York), Heineman Collection, MS 83.
2. GP 2: 720, 726.
3. Ibid., 721f.
4. Mollier, *Michel Lévy*, 343; note by J. Bruneau in GP 2: 1386.
5. GP 2: 733f.
6. Flaubert, *Lettres à Michel Lévy*, 36.
7. *AF* 9 (1956): 37.
8. GP 2: 725ff., 735.
9. Ibid., 747, 978.
10. Ibid., 750, 762f.
11. Ibid., 764, 767.
12. Ibid., 778f., 982, 990.
13. Ibid., 781ff.
14. Ibid., 786.
15. Ibid., 795.
16. Ibid., 797.
17. Goncourt, *Journal* 1: 908.

18. Gustave Flaubert, *Oeuvres complètes*, vol. 16 (Paris: Club de l'honnête homme, 1975), 387.
19. Charles Baudelaire, *Correspondance*, vol. 1 (Paris: Gallimard-Pléiade, 1973), 458.
20. GP 2: 795.
21. Ibid., 795, 804, 807.
22. *OC* (S) 2: 708, 710; GP 2: 809.
23. *OC* (S) 2: 711ff.; GP 2: 810f.
24. Quoted in Antoine Albalat, *Gustave Flaubert et ses amis* (Paris: Plon, 1927), 16.
25. Morgan Library, Heineman Collection, MS 96.
26. Jean Bruneau and Jacques Suffel, "Autour de Gustave Flaubert," *Bulletin du bibliophile* 4 (1980): 478f.
27. First part, chapter VI.

CHAPTER TWENTY-FOUR: "HIM"

1. GP 2: 817ff.
2. Ibid., 830f., 836f.
3. Ibid., 840, 846.
4. Ibid., 845.
5. Goncourt, *Journal* 1: 308.
6. André Billy, *Les Frères Goncourt* (Paris: Flammarion, 1954), 216ff.
7. Ibid., 243f.
8. Goncourt, *Journal* 1: 602f.
9. Edmond and Jules de Goncourt, *Charles Demailly* (Paris: Charpentier, 1876), 161f. First published as *Les Hommes de lettres* (Paris: Dentu, 1860).
10. Claude Tricotel, *Comme deux troubadours* (Paris: Société d'Edition d'Enseignement Supérieur, 1978), 19, 52.
11. Marie Caro Elme, quoted in Tricotel, *Comme deux troubadours*. See also Joseph Barry, *Infamous Woman: The Life of George Sand* (New York: Doubleday, 1977).
12. BSL, Correspondence Flaubert, July 24 and 29, August 13, 1859, letters from Bouilhet to Flaubert. Copies obtained through the courtesy of Jean Bruneau. See also Oliver, *Flaubert and an English Governess*, 67f.
13. *CC* 4: 325f.
14. [Emile] Gérard-Gailly, *Les Véhémences de Louise Colet* (Paris: Mercure de France, 1934), 65ff.
15. *CC* 4: 343ff.
16. An English translation appeared in 1987: *Lui: A View of Him* (Athens, Georgia: University of Georgia Press).
17. Du Camp, *Lettres inédites*, 223.
18. October 8, 1859. From Jean Bruneau.
19. *OC* (CHH) 16: 369.
20. November 12, 1859. From Jean Bruneau.
21. Goncourt, *Journal* 1: 649f.
22. *CC* 4: 348.
23. Goncourt, *Journal* 1: 683ff.
24. Letters to Jeanne de Tourbey. See catalogue for Laurin-Guilloux auction, Paris, July 1, 1986.
25. "Une Lettre d'Achille Flaubert," *AF* 7 (1955).

CHAPTER TWENTY-FIVE: SOMETHING PURPLE

1. *OC* (CHH) 14: 24.
2. Goncourt, *Journal* 1: 695f, 711, 722.
3. *CC* 4: 370f.
4. Bibliothèque Historique de la Ville de Paris: Carnet 7. Reprinted in *OC* (CHH) 8: 312ff.
5. *OC* (CHH) 14: 28.
6. Goncourt, *Journal* 1: 726.
7. *CC* 4: 380, 382f.
8. July 14, 21, 28, 1860. From Jean Bruneau.
9. *CC* 4: 401.
10. Franklin-Grout, "Heures d'autrefois."
11. *CC* 4: 405f.
12. November 15–20, 1860. From Jean Bruneau.
13. Goncourt, *Journal* 1: 847.
14. *Le Moniteur Universel*, December 10, 1860.
15. *CC* 4: 410f.
16. Ibid., 419.
17. January 6 (?), 1861. From Jean Bruneau; *CS* 1830–1863: 266f.
18. Goncourt, *Journal* 1: 888f.
19. Ibid., 894, 898ff., 903f.
20. *CC* 4: 427.
21. Goncourt, *Journal* 1: 911ff.
22. *CC* 4: 433, 440.
23. September 7, 1861. From Jean Bruneau.
24. Bouilhet to Flaubert, August 9 and 13, 1861. From Jean Bruneau.
25. Gustave Flaubert, *Correspondance, supplément (1830 1863)* (Paris: Conard, 1954), 273f.
26. *CC* 4: 452ff.

CHAPTER TWENTY-SIX: TEN THOUSAND FRANCS

1. Gustave Flaubert, *Correspondance*, vol. 5 (Paris: Conard, 1929), 1, 3f., 7.
2. Ibid., 14.
3. Bouilhet to Flaubert, February 1 and 7, 1862. From Jean Bruneau.
4. Goncourt, *Journal* 1: 1021, 1031f., 1034, 1041.
5. Hippolyte Taine, *Essais de critique et d'histoire* (Paris: Hachette, 1858), i f.
6. Hippolyte Taine, *Sa vie et sa correspondance*, vol. 2 (Paris: Hachette, 1904), 229ff.
7. March 26, 1862. From Jean Bruneau.
8. Goncourt, *Journal* 1: 1047f.
9. *CC* 5: 16ff.
10. Bouilhet to Flaubert, May 23 (?), 1862. From Jean Bruneau.
11. Flaubert, *Lettres à Michel Lévy*, 47ff., 67f.
12. Ibid., 56ff.; BSL, Correspondence Flaubert, B III, f. 3.
13. *CC* 5: 20ff., 23f.
14. E. Duplan to Flaubert, BSL, Correspondence Flaubert, B III f. 5.
15. Ibid., f. 3.

16. *CS* 1830–1863: 289.
17. Jean-Paul Sartre, *L'Idiot de la famille*, vol. 3 (Paris: Gallimard, 1972), 571.
18. Armand Lanoux, *Maupassant le Bel-Ami* (Paris: Livre de Poche, 1967), 335ff., 348.
19. Second part, chapter 5.
20. First part, chapter IV.
21. Chapter IX.
22. GP 2: 111.
23. Mollier, *Michel Lévy*, 366f.
24. September 14, 1860. From Jean Bruneau.
25. Kovács, *Le Rêve et la Vie*, 27f.
26. Bouilhet to Flaubert, November 9 and 16, 1861. From Jean Bruneau.
27. Goncourt, *Journal* 1: 1024.
28. *CS* 1830–1863: 286; *CC* 5:21.
29. *CC* 5: 30, 34ff.
30. *CS* 1830–1863: 289ff.
31. Ibid., 294.
32. Paris, Germer-Ballière, 1863; see Armand Wallon, "Flaubert à Vichy," *AF*, May 1980, 37f.
33. August 12, 1862. From Jean Bruneau.
34. August 15, 1862.
35. BSL, Correspondence Flaubert, B III, f. 11.
36. *CC* 5: 38.
37. BSL, Correspondence Flaubert, B IV, f. 244.
38. Flaubert, *Lettres à Michel Lévy*, 72.
39. *CC* 5: 45f.
40. Ibid., 49, 52f.
41. Flaubert, *Lettres à Michel Lévy*, 78ff.
42. Albalat, *Flaubert et ses amis*, 183.
43. Goncourt, *Journal* 1: 1143.

CHAPTER TWENTY-SEVEN: THE EMPRESS'S GOWN

1. Goncourt, *Journal* 2: 1173.
2. *OC* (CHH) 14: 138.
3. C.-A. Sainte-Beuve, *Lettres à la Princesse* (Paris: Michel Lévy, 1873), 23ff.
4. Goncourt, *Journal* 1: 1179, 1182f.
5. *Le Figaro*, December 4, 1862.
6. Goncourt, *Journal* 1: 1180.
7. C.-A. Sainte-Beuve, *Nouveaux Lundis*, vol. 4 (Paris: Michel Lévy, 1865), 31ff.
8. Théophile Gautier, *L'Orient*, vol. 2 (Paris: Charpentier, 1881), 281ff.
9. Sainte-Beuve, *Lettres à la Princesse*, 30.
10. *CC* 5: 55ff.; BSL, Correspondence Flaubert, A VI, f. 327ff. (for the original draft).
11. Sainte-Beuve, *Lettres à la Princesse*, 37f.
12. Flaubert, *Lettres à Michel Lévy*, 105, 119f., 129, 132f.
13. Goncourt, *Journal* 1: 1197; *CS* 1830–1863: 316.
14. Goncourt, *Journal* 1: 1197.

15. *CS* 1830–1863: 315f.; BSL, Correspondence Flaubert, B I, f. 206ff.
16. C.-A. Sainte-Beuve, *Correspondance générale*, vol. 13 (Paris: Privat-Didier, 1963), 76f.; *Album Flaubert*, 130f.
17. *Album Flaubert*, 131f.
18. Hector Berlioz, *Lettres intimes* (Paris: Calmann Lévy, 1882), 254; Albalat, *Flaubert et ses amis*, 142f.
19. Du Camp, *Souvenirs littéraires* 2: 343; Bouilhet to Flaubert, January 9, 1863, from Jean Bruneau.
20. Sand, *Questions d'art*, 305ff.
21. Juliette Adam, *Mes Premières Armes littéraires et politiques* (Paris: Lemerre, 1904), 383.
22. GFGS, 53.
23. *OC* (CHH) 8: 275.
24. Ca. December 15, 1862, from Jean Bruneau. See Jean Bruneau, "Sur la genèse de l'*Education sentimentale*," in *Flaubert e il pensiero del sue secolo* (Messina: Facoltà di Lettere e filosophia, 1985), 238f.
25. February 6, 1863, from Jean Bruneau.
26. Goncourt, *Journal* 1: 1229; Bruneau, "Sur la genèse," 240.
27. Goncourt, *Journal* 1: 1237ff.
28. Reproduced in Jacques de La Faye, *La Princesse Mathilde* (Paris: Emile-Paul, 1929).
29. Ibid., 94ff., 122f., 127.
30. "Flaubert," by Princess Mathilde, in Marcello Spaziani, *Gli Amici della principessa Matilda* (Rome: Edizioni di Storia e Letteratura, 1960), 97.

CHAPTER TWENTY-EIGHT: COMMANVILLE

1. Durry, *Flaubert et ses projets*, 24f. See Gustave Flaubert, *Carnets de travail*, critical edition by Pierre-Marc de Biasi (Paris: Balland, 1988) for a new reading of the surviving notes.
2. March 7–14, 1863, from Jean Bruneau.
3. *CC* 5: 90.
4. Flaubert, *Lettres à Michel Lévy*, 132.
5. *CS* 1830–1863: 323f.; *CC* 5: 90.
6. *CC* 5: 92.
7. *OC* (CHH) 14:170ff. I am indebted to Jean Bruneau for a corrected chronology of the Vichy visit.
8. Franklin-Grout, "Souvenirs intimes," xxxiii.
9. Du Camp, *Lettres inédites*, 257.
10. Bouilhet to Flaubert, August 2 and 28 and September 1, 1863, from Jean Bruneau; *CS* 1830–1863: 329; *CC* 5: 107.
11. *OC* (CHH) 14: 177.
12. *CC* 5: 113ff.
13. Goncourt, *Journal* 1: 1345ff.
14. *CC* 5: 116ff.
15. Franklin-Grout, "Heures d'autrefois."
16. *CC* 5: 122ff.
17. Bruneau and Suffel, "Autour de Flaubert" 4: 485.
18. Bib. I, Du Camp Papers, MS 3751.
19. Franklin-Grout, "Heures d'autrefois."

20. *CC* 5: 127f.
21. Ibid., 129ff.
22. Goncourt, *Journal* 2: 12f.
23. Du Camp, *Lettres inédites*, 269.
24. Franklin-Grout, "Heures d'autrefois."
25. *CC* 5: 135.
26. Ibid., 141ff.
27. June 25, 1864, from Jean Bruneau.
28. *CC* 5: 151, 156f.; Gustave Flaubert, *Correspondance, supplement* (1864–1871) (Paris: Conard, 1954): 12.
29. *CC* 5: 158.
30. *CS* 1864–1871: 14f.
31. Bouilhet to Flaubert, November 5, 1864, from Jean Bruneau.
32. *CS* 1864–1871: 16; *CC* 5: 162.
33. *CS* 1864–1871: 21; Franklin-Grout, "Heures d'autrefois." The identification of the "Mr. X" whom Caroline Franklin-Grout speaks of in her unpublished memoir with Ernest Le Roy (or Leroy), born in June 1810 and thus fifty-five years old when Caroline was nineteen, was made by Lucie Chevalley-Sabatier in *Gustave Flaubert et sa nièce Caroline* (Paris: Pensée Universelle, 1971), and is based on family tradition. Some authorities have expressed doubts because of the difference of ages. But Leroy's death on July 5, 1872, coincides with the revelation of Flaubert's niece that month.

CHAPTER TWENTY-NINE: THE LEGION OF HONOR

1. *CC* 5: 164.
2. February 18, 1865, from Jean Bruneau.
3. February 10 and March 7, 1865. Bib. I, Du Camp Papers, MS 3751.
4. Bruneau and Suffel, "Autour de Flaubert" 4: 480f.
5. *CS* 1864–1871: 24f.; Bib. I, Du Camp Papers, MS 3751.
6. *CC* 5: 167ff.
7. Ibid., 165, 167, 202 (this last reference is a year later); Franklin-Grout, "Heures d'autrefois"; Chevalley-Sabatier, *Flaubert et sa nièce*, 63ff.
8. Goncourt, *Journal* 2: 152.
9. Ibid., 156f.; cf. *Journal* 1: 179.
10. Spaziani, *Gli Amici*, 69.
11. *CC* 5: 172f.
12. *CS* 1864–1871: 31; Oliver, *Flaubert and an English Governess*, 70ff.
13. BSL, Correspondence Flaubert, B VI, f. 33, 35, 37.
14. Gérard-Gailly, *Flaubert et "les fantômes de Trouville,"* 164ff.
15. Bouilhet to Flaubert, September 9, 1865, from Jean Bruneau.
16. *CS* 1864–1871: 38f.; *CC* 5: 177f.
17. Goncourt, *Journal* 2: 185, 193f.
18. Ibid., 220f.
19. Durry, *Flaubert et ses projets*, 137f. See Flaubert, *Carnets de travail* (Biasi), for the complete text of this scenario.
20. Bruneau, *Les Débuts*, 542ff.
21. Jean Vidalenc, "Gustave Flaubert, historien de la révolution de 1848," *Europe*, September–November 1969, 51ff.

22. Jacques Suffel, "Sur les manuscrits de 'L'Education sentimentale,' " *Europe*, September–November 1969, 10f.
23. Goncourt, *Journal* 2: 236.
24. *CC* 5: 201f.
25. Quoted in GFGS, 59f.
26. *CC* 5: 183.
27. *CS* 1864–1871: 51ff.
28. *CC* 5: 206ff., 210f., 213; Bouilhet to Flaubert, April 27, 1866, from Jean Bruneau.
29. *CC* 5: 213f.
30. GFGS, 62f.
31. Goncourt, *Journal* 2: 262.
32. *CC* 5: 226.
33. *OC* (CHH) 14: 278.
34. Bouilhet to Flaubert, May 26, 1866, from Jean Bruneau.
35. June 30, 1866.
36. *CS* 1864–1871: 62f.; Oliver, *Flaubert and an English Governess*, 92f.
37. Archives Nationales 114 AP 1; cf. C.-A. Sainte-Beuve, *Correspondance générale*, vol. 15 (Paris: Privat-Didier, 1966), 253.
38. *CC* 5: 223ff. On August 13, 1866, Minister Duruy informed Mathilde that the Emperor had just signed Flaubert's nomination. "I am happy to have been able to respond to the wishes of Your Imperial Highness. . . ." Spaziani, *Gli Amici*, 93.

CHAPTER THIRTY: GEORGE SAND

1. *CS* 1864–1871: 65.
2. GFGS, 71.
3. Ibid., 75ff.
4. *CS* 1864–1871: 69ff.
5. Ibid., 70ff., 83ff.
6. GFGS, 85f.
7. Goncourt, *Journal* 2: 295f.
8. Du Camp, *Lettres inédites*, 295.
9. GFGS, 87f.
10. *CC* 5: 246.
11. GFGS, 90ff.
12. Ibid., 106f.
13. *CC* 5: 259.
14. *OC* (CHH) 14: 323f.
15. GFGS, 118.
16. Bouilhet to Flaubert, January 5 and 22, 1867, from Jean Bruneau.
17. Jean Bruneau, "Sur l'avant-dernier chapitre de 'L'Education Sentimentale,' " *Revue d'Histoire Littéraire de la France*, May–June 1983, 412ff. Bruneau points to the many times Flaubert could have seen Elisa and did not, and suggests that they did not even meet in 1867. Later Flaubert told Edmond de Goncourt that at the very moment his long-desired love seemed ready to yield, "he felt like relieving himself," and that ended the matter. Goncourt, *Journal* 2: 956.
18. *CS* 1864–1871: 98ff.

19. *CC* 5: 280f., 288.
20. Ibid., 281, 289.
21. GFGS, 130f.
22. *CS* 1864–1871: 104.
23. C.-A. Sainte-Beuve, *Correspondance générale*, vol. 16 (Paris: Privat-Didier, 1970), 157; B. F. Bart, "Lettres inédites de Flaubert à Sainte-Beuve," *Revue d'Histoire Littéraire de la France*, July–September 1964, 433.
24. *CC* 5: 293.
25. *CS* 1864–1871: 109ff.; Bouilhet to Flaubert, May 4, 1867, from Jean Bruneau; GFGS, 138.
26. *CS* 1864–1871: 113; Bouilhet to Flaubert, April 26, 1867, from J. Bruneau.
27. Bouilhet to Flaubert, June 3, 1867, from J. Bruneau.
28. Michel Cabaud, *Paris et les parisiens sous le Second Empire* (Paris: Pierre Belfond, 1982), 256ff.; *CC* 5: 305ff., 308, 313; *CS* 1864–1871: 114f.
29. GFGS, 148.
30. Gustave Flaubert, *Correspondance*, vol. 4 (Paris: Conard, 1930), 59f. (incorrectly dated here, but properly dated in Oliver, *Flaubert and an English Governess*, 94); *CC* 6: 63 (also improperly dated). See GFGS, 150; *CC* 5: 319; Spaziani, *Gli Amici:* letter of September (?) 1867.
31. GFGS, 153, 159; *CC* 5: 341, 345.

CHAPTER THIRTY-ONE: TURGENEV

1. Tricotel, *Comme deux troubadours*, 83; GFGS, 171.
2. Bruneau and Suffel, "Autour de Flaubert" 4: 482.
3. *CC* 5: 366.
4. Ibid., 359.
5. Dr. Chaume, "Comment se documentait Flaubert," *La Chronique Médicale*, December 15, 1900.
6. *OC* (CHH) 14: 376.
7. Goncourt, *Journal* 2: 416.
8. GFGS, 178; *CC* 5: 372ff.
9. *CC* 5: 374.
10. GFGS, 178, 180f.
11. *CS* 1864–1871: 146ff.
12. Goncourt, *Journal* 2: 450ff.
13. *CC* 5: 398.
14. Ibid., 400; GFGS, 190.
15. *CS* 1864–1871: 153f.
16. GFGS, 199f.
17. *CC* 5: 416.
18. GFGS, 203.
19. André Maurois, *Tourguéniev* (Paris: Tallandier, 1952); Henri Troyat, *Tourgeniev* (Paris: Flammarion, 1985).
20. *Le Gaulois* (Paris), September 5, 1883; see also Guy de Maupassant, "Gustave Flaubert," in *Lettres de Gustave Flaubert à Georges Sand* (Paris: Charpentier, 1889), lxxviii.
21. *CS* 1830–1863: 318.
22. E. Halpérine-Kaminsky, *Ivan Tourguéneff d'après sa correspondance avec ses amis français* (Paris: Charpentier-Fasquelle, 1901), 47f.

23. Ibid.
24. *CS* 1864–1871: 149f.
25. *CC* 5: 422.
26. Halpérine-Kaminsky, *Tourguéneff*, 52.
27. GFGS, 204.
28. December 2, 1868, from J. Bruneau.

CHAPTER THIRTY-TWO: BOUILHET

1. Flaubert, *Lettres à Michel Lévy*, 151f.
2. GFGS, 211.
3. *CC* 6: 6f.
4. *CS* 1864–1871: 167.
5. Bouilhet to Flaubert, February 12, 18, 27, 1869, from J. Bruneau.
6. *OC* (CHH) 14: 473.
7. *CC* 6: 19.
8. GFGS, 228.
9. Goncourt, *Journal* 2: 522.
10. GFGS, 228ff.
11. *CC* 6: 20f., 25. ·
12. Goncourt, *Journal* 2: 524f.
13. See manuscript pages reproduced in, among other publications, *L'Education sentimentale: Images et documents*, P. M. Wetherill, ed. (Paris: Garnier, 1985).
14. *CC* 6: 20ff.; Du Camp, *Lettres inédites*, 312.
15. *CS* 1864–1871: 185.
16. June 2, 1869, from J. Bruneau.
17. *CC* 6: 29.
18. Du Camp, *Souvenirs littéraires* 2: 340; ———, *Lettres inédites,* 313ff., 320ff.
19. BSL, Correspondence Flaubert, B IV, f. 76. Published in Jacques Suffel and Jean Ziegler, "Gustave Flaubert, Maxime Du Camp et Adèle Husson," *Bulletin du Bibliophile* 3 (1978): 392f.
20. GFGS, 233; *CS* 1864–1871: 186.
21. GFGS, 235; *CC* 6: 35f.
22. Georges A. Le Roy, "Quelques souvenirs sur Louis Bouilhet," *Mercure de France*, August 16, 1919.
23. *CC* 6: 40ff.
24. Quoted in Frère, *Bouilhet*, 13f.
25. GFGS, 239.
26. *CC* 6: 53, 56f.
27. Ibid., 65.
28. Ibid., 64ff.
29. Flaubert, *Lettres à Michel Lévy*, 145f., 158ff.
30. Quoted in Tricotel, *Comme deux troubadours*, 111.
31. GFGS, 252.
32. *CC* 6: 90.
33. Gustave Flaubert, *Lettres inédites à Raoul-Duval* (Paris: Albin Michel, 1950), 9ff., 21, 104ff.
34. GFGS, 252.

CHAPTER THIRTY-THREE: FAILURE

1. GFGS, 254ff.
2. Ibid.
3. Sand, *Questions d'art*, 415ff.
4. *CS* 1864–1871: 208.
5. Gustave Flaubert, *Correspondance*, vol. 8 (Paris: Conard, 1930), 309; Bruneau, *Les Débuts*, 548.
6. Mollier, *Michel Lévy*, 401; Flaubert, *Lettres à Michel Lévy*, 146ff.; *CS* 1864–1871: 205f.
7. GFGS, 262ff.
8. Ibid., 267ff.
9. *OC* (CHH) 14: 543.
10. Louise Colet, *Les Pays lumineux* (Paris: Dentu, 1879), 204ff.
11. Halpérine-Kaminsky, *Tourguéneff*, 53f., 55; *CS* 1864–1871: 219f.
12. GFGS, 274ff.
13. Ibid., 282ff.
14. Ibid., 287.
15. *OC* (CHH) 8: 438f.
16. GFGS, 288ff.
17. *CS* 1864–1871: 231f.
18. Goncourt, *Journal* 2: 539.
19. GFGS, 296f.
20. *CS* 1864–1871: 234f.
21. BSL, Correspondence Flaubert, B III, f. 272.
22. *CC* 6: 122f.
23. Preface to Louis Bouilhet, *Dernières Chansons*.

CHAPTER THIRTY-FOUR: DEFEAT

1. *CC* 6: 128ff.
2. GFGS, 300f.
3. *CC* 6: 133f.
4. GFGS, 303f.
5. *CC* 6: 136.
6. *CS* 1864–1871: 238f.
7. *CC* 6: 140.
8. GFGS, 309ff.
9. *CS* 1864–1871: 242.
10. *CC* 6: 143.
11. *AF*, 1955, 7, 45.
12. *CC* 6: 145.
13. GFGS, 311.
14. La Faye, *Princesse Mathilde*, 248ff.
15. Franklin-Grout, "Heures d'autrefois"; Oliver, *Flaubert and an English Governess*, 111. See note 33 for chapter 28.
16. *CC* 6: 157ff.
17. GFGS, 314.
18. *CC* 6: 165f., 168, 171f.
19. Ibid., 173f.; *CS* 1864–1871: 246.

20. *CC* 6: 185f., 182; GFGS, 320.
21. *CC* 6: 187ff.
22. Charles Lapierre, *Esquisse sur Flaubert intime* (Evreux: Herissey, 1898), 17f.
23. *CC* 6: 195f.
24. Ibid., 193f. (misdated); *CS* 1864–1871: 252f.
25. *CC* 6: 197.
26. *CS* 1864–1871: 258f., 260f.

CHAPTER THIRTY-FIVE: *SAINT ANTHONY*

1. GFGS, 324.
2. *CS* 1864–1871: 249 (misdated), 264ff.; *CC* 6: 205f.
3. *OC* (CHH) 14: 628ff. In a letter to Sand, Flaubert specifically said that he would go from Brussels back to Paris: GFGS, 326.
4. Archives Départementales de la Seine-Maritime, Notariat Bidault, 1872.
5. GFGS, 327f.
6. Ibid., 329ff.; *CC* 6: 219f.
7. *CC* 6: 233f., 235f.
8. Ibid., 245f. (misdated).
9. GFGS, 335f.
10. Goncourt, *Journal* 2: 821f.
11. *CS* 1864–1871: 273f.
12. GFGS, 341.
13. *CS* 1864–1871: 281f.
14. *CC* 6: 267ff., 273.
15. *CS* 1864–1871: 284.
16. *CC* 6: 277f.
17. GFGS, 342ff., 350f.
18. *CC* 6: 290ff.; *CS* 1864–1871: 294.
19. Goncourt, *Journal* 2: 839.
20. *CC* 6: 299ff., 302, 304f.
21. Franklin-Grout, "Heures d'autrefois."
22. GFGS, 359.
23. Goncourt, *Journal* 2: 844f. (misdated).
24. *CC* 6: 313, 303, 318f., 331.

CHAPTER THIRTY-SIX: MADAME FLAUBERT

1. *CC* 6: 323f., 326ff.
2. BSL, Correspondence Flaubert, B I, f. 32; André Dubuc, "Les dessous de la lettre de Flaubert," *AF*, December 1973, 17ff.
3. *CC* 6: 331ff., 349.
4. Flaubert, *Lettres à Raoul-Duval*, 147ff.
5. *CS* 1864–1871: 302ff.
6. *CC* 6: 349.
7. Flaubert, *Lettres à Michel Lévy*, 223.
8. Louis Bouilhet, *Mademoiselle Aïssé* (Paris: Michel Lévy, 1872), 141ff.
9. *CC* 6: 341.
10. Flaubert, *Lettres à Michel Lévy*, 222.
11. GFGS, 366ff.

12. Gustave Flaubert, *Correspondance, supplément* (1872–1877) (Paris: Conard, 1954), 9f.
13. Emile Zola, *Correspondance*, vol. 3 (Montreal-Paris: Presses de l'Université de Montréal – Editions du CNRS, 1980), 312.
14. Emile Zola, *Les Romanciers naturalistes* (Paris: Charpentier, 1881), 125f.
15. Ibid., 187f.
16. *CC* 6: 314f.
17. *CS* 1872–1877: 13f., 15, 18.
18. GFGS, 373f.; *CS* 1872–1877: 18.
19. *CC* 6: 359.
20. Flaubert, *Lettres à Michel Lévy*, 211f., 217ff., 237f.; *CC* 6: 359; *CS* 1872–1877: 21f. See also Mollier, *Michel Lévy*, 409f.
21. *CC* 6: 360f.
22. *CS* 1872–1877: 24f.
23. *CC* 6: 366.
24. Archives Départementales de la Seine-Maritime, Notariat Bidault, 1872, 4.
25. *CS* 1872–1877: 27f.
26. See note 24 above.
27. *CC* 6: 369.
28. GFGS, 383f.
29. *CC* 6: 371f., 373ff.
30. Bibliothèque Municipale de Rouen, 92N Laporte: *Le Journal de Rouen*, March 9, 1933; 92 N4a Flaubert.
31. Goncourt, *Journal* 2: 902f.

CHAPTER THIRTY-SEVEN: VENTING SPLEEN

1. Gustave Flaubert, *Oeuvres complètes*, vol. 15 (Paris: Club de l'Honnête Homme, 1975), 138.
2. GFGS, 391.
3. Ibid., 390.
4. *CS* 1872–1877: 38f.
5. Ibid., 41 (misdated); Archives Départementales de la Seine-Maritime, Notariat Bidault, 1872, 4: Liquidation of December 23, 1872.
6. GFGS, 392f.
7. *CC* 6: 395ff.
8. *CS* 1872–1877: 44.
9. *CC* 6: 404.
10. Franklin-Grout, "Heures d'autrefois."
11. *CS* 1872–1877: 45.
12. *CC* 6: 402.
13. *CS* 1872–1877: 49.
14. GFGS, 396.
15. *OC* (CHH) 15: 154.
16. *CS* 1872–1877: 51; *CC* 6: 409.
17. *OC* (CHH) 15: 157ff.
18. *CC* 6: 416.
19. *CS* 1872–1877: 98 (misdated); *CC* 6: 419.
20. *CC* 6: 423ff.

21. Ibid., 427f.
22. Ibid., 430.
23. *CS* 1872–1877: 57; *CC* 6: 431.
24. *CC* 6: 433.
25. GFGS, 399ff., 404.
26. *CS* 1872–1877: 61f., 65.
27. GFGS, 409ff.
28. *CS* 1872–1877: 63f., 71.
29. Archives Départementales de la Seine-Maritime, Notariat Bidault, 1872, 4.

CHAPTER THIRTY-EIGHT: GUY

1. GFGS, 415f.
2. Gustave Flaubert, *Correspondance*, vol. 7 (Paris: Conard, 1930), 3ff.
3. GFGS, 417f.
4. *CS* 1872–1877: 77; GFGS, 417f.
5. Goncourt, *Journal* 2: 927.
6. *CC* 7: 9f.
7. Guy de Maupassant, *Correspondance*, vol. 1 (Geneva: Edito-Service, 1973), 5ff.
8. Ibid., 9ff.
9. Ibid., 27.
10. Franklin-Grout, "Heures d'autrefois."
11. Guy de Maupassant, preface to *Pierre et Jean*.
12. Gustave Flaubert, *Lettres à Maupassant* (Paris: Livre Moderne, 1942), 74ff.; Lanoux, *Maupassant*, 21ff. The contested birth certificates are published in André Dubuc, "Maupassant et son lieu de naissance," *AF*, December 1969, 40f.
13. Edmond et Jules de Goncourt, *Journal*, vol. 4 (1891–1896) (Paris: Fasquelle-Flammarion, 1956), 461ff.
14. Commentary by Marie-Claire Ropars-Zuillemier, in Guy de Maupassant, *Pierre et Jean* (Paris: Livre de Poche, 1984). I am indebted to Prof. Roger Bismut for a summary of the case for filiation.
15. Jacques-Louis Douchin, *La Vie érotique de Flaubert* (Paris: Carrère, 1984), 176.
16. Guy de Maupassant, preface to *Lettres de Gustave Flaubert à Georges Sand*, reprinted in Flaubert, *Madame Bovary* (Conard), 551ff.
17. Zola, *Les Romanciers naturalistes*, 178.
18. Emile Bergerat, *Souvenirs d'un enfant de Paris*, vol. 2 (Paris: Charpentier, 1912), 136ff.
19. Emile Bergerat, *Le Livre de Caliban* (Paris: Lemerre, 1887), 76ff.
20. GFGS, 425ff., 428, 431f.; Tricotel, *Comme deux troubadours*, 196f.
21. Goncourt, *Journal* 2: 930ff.
22. *CC* 7: 16ff.

CHAPTER THIRTY-NINE: "THE CANDIDATE"

1. *CS* 1872–1877: 89ff.
2. *CC* 7: 24f.
3. Ibid., 31, 35.
4. GFGS, 437; *CC* 7: 47.

5. *CC* 7: 46.
6. Ibid., 44ff., 55.
7. Ibid., 57f.; GFGS, 439.
8. *CC* 7: 62, 64.
9. Ibid., 57, 62, 71f.
10. Ibid., 75ff.
11. GFGS, 443f.
12. *CC* 7: 83f., 90, 95, 98.
13. *CS* 1872–1877: 109; *CC* 7: 100ff.
14. Goncourt, *Journal* 2: 955f.
15. GFGS, 447.
16. *CS* 1872–1877: 114.
17. GFGS, 454.
18. Ibid., 452, 454; *CS* 1872–1877: 116f; *CC* 7: 119ff.
19. Goncourt, *Journal* 2: 972f.
20. Lapierre, *Esquisse sur Flaubert*, 36f.
21. Zola, *Les Romanciers naturalistes*, 205.
22. Paul Bourde, "M. Flaubert, auteur dramatique," *Revue de France*, March 31, 1874.
23. GFGS, 457ff.
24. Charles Monselet in *L'Evénement*, quoted in GFGS, 460.
25. André Dubuc, "Un Entretien avec Flaubert en 1874," *AF*, December 1974, 34f.
26. Collection Daniel Sickles, courtesy of Thierry Bodin.
27. BSL, Correspondence Flaubert, B I, f. 266.

CHAPTER FORTY: AUGUST 1: *BOUVARD AND PÉCUCHET*
1. *CS* 1872–1877: 122ff.
2. GFGS, 461, 465f.
3. Ibid., 466f.
4. *Le Constitutionnel*, April 20, 1874, reprinted in J. Barbey d'Aurevilly, *Le Roman contemporain* (Paris: Lemerre, 1902), 106f.
5. GFGS, 467; *CC* 7: 137. The doctor would be Alfred Hardy, professor of internal pathology at the Faculty of Paris.
6. *CS* 1872–1877: 131; *CC* 7: 153.
7. *CC* 7: 154f.
8. Emile Zola, *Correspondance*, vol. 2 (Montreal-Paris: Presses de l'Université de Montréal – Editions du CNRS, 1980), 358.
9. *CC* 7: 153, 158, 164f., 168f.
10. Ibid., 170.
11. Durry, *Flaubert et ses projets*, 366ff.
12. *CC* 7: 176ff., 133.
13. *CS* 1872–1877: 139f.
14. *CC* 7: 184.
15. Sartre, *L'Idiot de la famille* 1: 495.
16. Albalat, *Flaubert et ses amis*, 83.
17. *CC* 7: 187.
18. Ibid., 189ff.; *CS* 1872–1877: 142ff.
19. *CC* 7: 195, 197f.

20. *CS* 1872–1877: 145f.
21. GFGS, 479f.
22. *CC* 7: 208.
23. Zola, *Correspondance* 2: 373ff.; *CC* 7: 217f.
24. *CS* 1872–1877: 159f.; *CC* 7: 220; GFGS, 485.
25. Goncourt, *Journal* 2: 1025.
26. GFGS, 485.

CHAPTER FORTY-ONE: THE CRASH

1. Goncourt, *Journal* 2: 1033; Alphonse Daudet, *Trente ans de Paris* (Paris: Marpon & Flammarion, 1888), 320f.
2. Goncourt, *Journal* 2: 1060.
3. Maupassant, *Correspondance* 2: 76.
4. *CS* 1872–1877: 174f.; Flaubert, *Lettres à Maupassant,* 27ff.
5. Goncourt, *Journal* 2: 1088.
6. GFGS, 496; Franklin-Grout, "Souvenirs intimes," xxxvii.
7. *CC* 7: 241f.
8. GFGS, 495ff.
9. *CC* 7: 246.
10. *CS* 1872–1877: 185f.
11. *CC* 7: 250.
12. *CS* 1872–1877: 185f.
13. *CC* 7: 248f.
14. *CS* 1872–1877: 188f.
15. *OC* (CHH) 15: 395f.
16. *CS* 1872–1877: 190.
17. Halpérine-Kaminsky, *Tourguéneff,* 163.
18. GFGS, 499ff.
19. *CS* 1872–1877: 195ff., 198ff.
20. Deliencourt and Chennebenoist, *La Propriété Strassburger; Le Journal de Rouen,* December 31, 1925: "L'Ancienne Ferme de Flaubert à Deauville."
21. *CS* 1872–1877: 199; Enregistrement hypothécaire (property registration), September 13, 1875, courtesy of Daniel Dousset, Paris.
22. *CS* 1872–1877: 205f.
23. *CC* 7: 257ff.
24. *CS* 1872–1877: 211ff.
25. GFGS, 503ff.

CHAPTER FORTY-TWO: THREE TALES

1. Zola, *Les Romanciers naturalistes,* 179.
2. Leon Edel, *The Life of Henry James,* vol. 1 (London: Penguin, 1977), 443ff.
3. Henry James, *Letters,* vol. 2 (London: Macmillan, 1978), 14ff.
4. Henry James, *Literary Reviews and Essays* (New York: Twayne, 1957), 145f.
5. Henry James, *Notes on Novelists* (London: Dent, 1914), 52ff.
6. James, *Letters,* 2: 26f., 36.
7. *CS* 1872–1877: 229ff., 232.

8. GFGS, 508ff.
9. *CS 1872–1877*: 233ff.
10. Ibid., 238f.
11. GFGS, 523f.
12. *CS 1872–1877*: 244f.
13. *CC* 7: 307.
14. GFGS, 525.
15. *CC* 7: 291f.
16. GFGS, 532.
17. *CC* 7: 295f.
18. *CS 1872–1877*: 249f.
19. GFGS, 533f.
20. *CC* 7: 307f.
21. Halpérine-Kaminsky, *Tourguéneff*, 86.
22. *CC* 7: 300f., 307, 311ff.
23. *CS 1872–1877*: 257f.
24. *CC* 7: 319.
25. Flaubert Museum, Hôtel-Dieu, Rouen. Both this museum and the smaller one in Croisset show parrots that they present as the one Flaubert borrowed (as readers of Julian Barnes's *Flaubert's Parrot* know).
26. *CC* 7: 317f., 334, 336, 338.
27. *CS 1872–1877*: 269f.
28. Ibid., 273f.
29. *CC* 7: 339ff.
30. Hermia Oliver, "Flaubert and Juliet Herbert: A Postscript," *Nineteenth-Century French Studies*, Fall–Winter 1983–1984, 121.
31. *OC* (CHH) 15: 490.
32. *CC* 7: 346ff.; 349f.; *CS 1872–1877*: 286ff., 291.
33. *CC* 7: 356.

CHAPTER FORTY-THREE: A LATE SEASON

1. *CC* 7: 367, 369f.
2. *CS 1872–1877*: 297.
3. *CC* 7: 374, 380, 385f.
4. Zola, *Correspondance* 2: 520.
5. *CC* 8: 1f.
6. *OC* (CHH) 15: 524f.
7. *CS 1872–1877*: 304f.
8. *CC* 8: 10f.
9. *CS 1872–1877*: 308.
10. *CC* 8: 12.
11. *CS 1872–1877*: 315f.; *CC* 8: 15.
12. Goncourt, *Journal* 2: 1171.
13. *CS 1872–1877*: 314, 318.
14. Goncourt, *Journal* 2: 1172.
15. Zola, *Les Romanciers naturalistes*, 212ff.
16. *CS 1872–1877*: 323, 328.
17. Maupassant, *Correspondance* 1: 109ff.; Flaubert, *Lettres à Maupassant*, 56ff.

18. Jacques-Louis Douchin, *La Vie érotique de Maupassant* (Paris: Suger, 1986), 60ff.
19. *CS* 1872–1877: 323f.
20. *CC* 8: 24f., 30ff.; *CS* 1872–1877: 333f.
21. *CC* 8: 24f.
22. Goncourt, *Journal* 2: 1182f.; Henry Céard and Jean de Caldain, "Le Diner Trap [*sic*]," *Revue hebdomadaire*, November 7, 1908, reprinted in *AF*, 1955, 6.
23. Du Camp, *Souvenirs littéraires* 2: 391.
24. Gustave Flaubert, *Trois Contes* (Paris: Conard, 1928), 234.

CHAPTER FORTY-FOUR: RETURN TO *BOUVARD AND PÉCUCHET*

1. Goncourt, *Journal* 2: 1187.
2. *CC* 8: 25f.
3. Goncourt, *Journal* 2: 1189.
4. *CS* 1877–1880: 5.
5. *OC* (CHH) 15: 556.
6. Conseil Municipal de Rouen, Procès-verbal, session of May 4, 1877, 306ff., in Bibliothèque Municipale de Rouen, 92N Bouilhet.
7. *CS* 1877–1880: 3, 9.
8. Franklin-Grout, "Heures d'autrefois."
9. *CS* 1877–1880: 11ff.
10. Ibid., 18ff.
11. *CC* 8: 62ff.
12. *CS* 1877–1880: 27, 29f. See Oliver, "Flaubert and Juliet Herbert," 121.
13. *CC* 8: 75ff.
14. *CS* 1877–1880: 42f.; *OC* (CHH) 15: 615.
15. Maupassant, *Correspondance* 1: 131ff.; *CC* 8: 88ff.
16. *CC* 8: 92ff.; *CS* 1877–1880: 44.
17. *CS* 1877–1880: 45f., 50, 52f.
18. *CC* 8: 108.
19. *CS* 1877–1880: 58.
20. Goncourt, *Journal* 2: 1219f.
21. *OC* (CHH) 16: 33f.; BSL, Correspondence Flaubert, B V, f. 70, 72.
22. Maupassant, *Correspondance* 1: 145ff.; Zola to Bernhardt, January 26, 1878, in catalogue for Laurin-Guilloux auction, Paris, July 1, 1986.
23. *CS* 1877–1880: 59.
24. Claude Digeon, *Le Dernier Visage de Flaubert* (Paris: Aubier, 1946), Digeon dates the letter 1876, but this is an error, for Turgenev's reply can be dated with accuracy.
25. Halpérine-Kaminsky, *Tourguéneff*, 177f.

CHAPTER FORTY-FIVE: FLAUBERT AT FIFTY-SEVEN

1. *The Fortnightly Review*, April 1, 1878, 575ff.
2. *CS* 1877–1880: 62f., 65f.
3. Maupassant, *Correspondance* 1: 158.
4. *CS* 1877–1880: 71f.
5. Ibid., 84ff.; *CC* 8: 120ff.

6. *CS* 1877–1880: 95ff.
7. Ibid., 89.
8. *CC* 8: 132.
9. Maupassant, *Correspondance* 1: 165ff.
10. *CC* 8: 134f.
11. *CS* 1877–1880: 105f.
12. *CC* 8: 134f., 138, 141.
13. Ibid., 145; *CS* 1877–1880: 113ff., 116, 122.
14. *CS* 1877–1880: 114f.
15. *CC* 8: 146.
16. *CS* 1877–1880: 116.
17. Ibid., 110, 127.
18. Maupassant, *Correspondance* 1: 177.
19. Quoted in Flaubert, *Madame Bovary* (Conard), 549f.
20. [H. A. de Conty] *Les Côtes de Normandie* (Paris: Guides Conty, n.d.), 61.
21. *CS* 1877–1880: 134, 130f.
22. *CC* 8: 166ff.
23. Goncourt, *Journal* 2: 1275.
24. *CS* 1877–1880: 135ff.
25. Spaziani, *Gli Amici*, 174.
26. *CC* 8: 170ff.
27. *CS* 1877–1880: 138f.
28. *CC* 8: 174ff.

CHAPTER FORTY-SIX: HUMILIATIONS

1. *CS* 1877–1880: 145ff.
2. *CC* 8: 180f., 184f.; Maupassant, *Correspondance* 1: 197f.
3. *CC* 8: 182f.
4. Ibid., 192ff.
5. Ibid., 196; *CS* 1877–1880: 159; *Journal des Débats*, January 30, 1879.
6. *CS* 1877–1880: 158; Zola, *Correspondance* 3: 289; Halpérine-Kaminsky, *Tourguéneff*, 251.
7. *CS* 1877–1880: 160.
8. Zola, *Correspondance* 3: 290.
9. *CS* 1877–1880: 164f., 166f.; Catalogue, *Autographes et documents historiques*, No. 293, Librairie de l'Abbaye, Paris, [n.d.].
10. A more charitable interpretation is that if Gambetta did not rise to greet Turgenev, it was because he was approached on the side of his glass eye. What Gambetta actually said was that someone else had already been selected. Halpérine-Kaminsky, *Tourguéneff*, 253.
11. *CC* 8: 200f., 203, 205f.; *CS* 1877–1880: 166f.
12. *CC* 8: 207f.
13. Zola, *Correspondance* 3: 295f.
14. Ibid., 298; *CC* 8: 211.
15. *CC* 8: 213.
16. *CS* 1877–1880: 175; Maupassant, *Correspondance* 1: 208; BSL, Correspondence Flaubert, B I, f. 150.
17. *CS* 1877–1880: 181f., 184.
18. Ibid., 175ff., 179, 186.

19. Ibid., 188f.; *CC* 8: 232; Maupassant, *Correspondance* 1: 211ff.
20. *CC* 8: 237f., 239f.
21. Ibid., 239ff., 249; *CS* 1877–1880: 97, 177, 200f., 216; *OC* (CHH) 16: 182.
22. *CC* 8: 245.
23. *OC* (CHH) 16: 187.
24. *CC* 8: 251f.
25. *CS* 1877–1880: 208, 212. See April 26, Turgenev to Flaubert, in Zola, *Correspondance* 3: 317.
26. *CS* 1877–1880: 215f.
27. Ibid., 218f.
28. Maupassant, *Correspondance* 1: 217f.; *CS* 1877–1880: 220f.
29. *CS* 1877–1880: 223f.
30. Maupassant, *Correspondance* 1: 221.
31. *CS* 1877–1880: 227ff., 232.
32. Juliette Adam, *Mes Sentiments et nos idées avant 1870* (Paris: Lemerre, 1905), 162ff.; ———, *Après l'abandon de la revanche* (Paris: Lemerre, 1910), 233; Barry, *Infamous Woman.*
33. *CC* 8: 265f.; Adam, *Après l'abandon,* 321ff.
34. *CS* 1877–1880: 238.
35. Maupassant, *Correspondance* 1: 224.
36. *CS* 1877–1880: 236, 240.

CHAPTER FORTY-SEVEN: THE GOOD LAPORTE

1. *CC* 8: 266f., 269f., 272; *CS* 1877–1880: 241.
2. Edmond and Jules de Goncourt, *Journal,* vol. 3 (Paris: Fasquelle-Flammarion, 1956), 25.
3. *CS* 1877–1880: 243.
4. *CC* 8: 271.
5. Ibid., 270.
6. *CS* 1877–1880: 243f.
7. May 21, 1881, Frédéric Baudry to Maxime Du Camp, in Bib. I, Du Camp Papers, MS 3751.
8. *CC* 8: 275.
9. *CS* 1877–1880: 245.
10. *OC* (CHH) 16: 148, 228f.
11. Note by S. de Sacy in Gustave Flaubert, *L'Education sentimentale* (Paris: Livre de Poche, 1965), 481.
12. *CC* 8: 282ff.; *CS* 1877–1880: 246.
13. *CS* 1877–1880: 251f.
14. Ibid., 254.
15. *CC* 8: 289f.; Adam, *Après l'abandon,* 400f.; Halpérine-Kaminsky, Tourguéneff, 125.
16. *CC* 8: 289f., 295.
17. *CS* 1877–1880: 263f.
18. Goncourt, *Journal* 3: 45f.
19. *CS* 1877–1880: 264ff.
20. *CC* 8: 310.
21. *OC* (CHH) 16: 256.

22. *CS* 1877–1880: 272.
23. Ibid., 271ff., 283f.; *CC* 8: 324, 330.
24. *CC* 8: 330, 332, 334; *CS* 1877–1880: 286, 288f.
25. *CS* 1877–1880: 290f.; *CC* 8: 338f.
26. *CC* 8: 340.
27. *OC* (CHH) 16: 289f.
28. *CC* 8: 344f.
29. *CS* 1877–1880: 280.
30. Ibid., 296f.
31. *CC* 8: 345f.
32. *CS* 1877–1880: 295, 298f.
33. Ibid., 301f., 307.
34. *CC* 8: 355f.
35. *CS* 1877–1880: 302.

CHAPTER FORTY-EIGHT: EXHAUSTION

1. *La Vie Moderne,* January 24, 1880, 50ff.
2. *CS* 1877–1880: 302f.
3. Bibliothèque Municipale de Rouen, 92N4a Flaubert.
4. *CC* 8: 363ff.
5. *CS* 1877–1880: 309f.; *OC* (CHH) 16: 315.
6. Lucien Andrieu, "Un Ami de Flaubert: Edmond Laporte," *AF,* December 1976, 26.
7. *CS* 1877–1880: 310.
8. *L'Evénement,* February 13, 1880, 1.
9. Maupassant, *Correspondance* 1: 261ff.
10. *CC* 8: 392ff., 396ff., 400; *CS* 1877–1880: 313f.
11. *CC* 8: 386, 395.
12. Maupassant, *Correspondance* 1: 266f., 269ff.; Flaubert, *Lettres à Maupassant,* 185.
13. *CC* 8: 384, 403f.; *CS* 1877–1880: 312.
14. *CC* 8: 388ff.
15. *OC* (CHH) 16: 330f.
16. *Cahiers Ivan Tourguénev,* 1980, 4, 75; *CS* 1877–1880: 319f.
17. *CS* 1877–1880: 322f.
18. Gustave Flaubert, *Correspondance,* vol. 9 (Paris: Conard, 1933): 2ff.
19. Goncourt, *Journal* 3: 67ff.; Zola, *Les Romanciers naturalistes,* 164.
20. *CS* 1877–1880: 326ff., 328f.
21. Ibid., 325ff.
22. *OC* (CHH) 16: 353.
23. *CC* 9: 26f.
24. Flaubert, *Lettres à Raoul-Duval,* plate 2; Lapierre, *Esquisse,* 44.
25. *CC* 9: 30f.

CHAPTER FORTY-NINE: DEATH OF A HERMIT

1. *CC* 9: 32, 34.
2. Ibid., 35; *CS* 1877–1880: 332; BSL, Correspondence Flaubert, B I, f. 71.
3. Dr. Germain Galérant, talk with the author.
4. Georges Normandy, in Flaubert, *Lettres à Raoul-Duval,* 260f.

5. Douchin, *La Vie érotique de Flaubert*, 240.
6. Daniel Sickles collection, courtesy of Thierry Bodin.
7. Maupassant, *Correspondance* 1: 283f.
8. Quoted in Dumesnil, *Flaubert: Son Hérédité*, 106ff.
9. Du Camp, *Souvenirs littéraires* 2: 396f.
10. Goncourt, *Journal* 3: 72.
11. Charles Lapierre, "Flaubert à Croisset," in *Les Environs de Rouen* (Rouen: Augé, 1890), 32.
12. Gastaut, "La Maladie de Gustave Flaubert," 476.
13. Marcel Croze, *Tableaux démographiques et sociaux* (Paris: INSEE-INED, 1976), table 96.
14. Bibliothèque Municipale de Rouen, manuscript g 226–7; *CC* 8: 338.

CHAPTER FIFTY: MONUMENTS

1. Maupassant, *Correspondance* 1: 284. The story of Laporte's being denied entry was told by Caroline Franklin-Grout to Pierre Borel: *Lettres inédites de Guy de Maupassant à Gustave Flaubert* (Paris: Editions des Portiques, 1929), 130.
2. Goncourt, *Journal* 3: 71.
3. Zola, *Les Romanciers naturalistes*, 164f.; Zola, *Correspondance* 3: 461.
4. Pierre Giffard, "Les Obsèques de Flaubert," *Le Gaulois*, May 12, 1880.
5. Goncourt, *Journal* 3: 73.
6. Giffard, "Les Obsèques."
7. Zola, *Les Romanciers naturalistes*, 168f.
8. Jules Claretie, *La Vie à Paris, 1880* (Paris: Havard, 1881), 123ff.
9. Goncourt, *Journal* 3: 73.
10. Caroline Franklin-Grout, "Les Hommes célèbres de mon enfance," manuscript, from Jean Bruneau.
11. Zola, *Les Romanciers naturalistes*, 172f.; Giffard, "Les Obsèques"; Claretie, *La Vie à Paris*, 123ff.
12. Zola, *Les Romanciers naturalistes*, 173.
13. Goncourt, *Journal* 3: 73.
14. Halpérine-Kaminsky, *Tourguéneff*, 140f.
15. BSL, Correspondence Flaubert, B VI, f. 399.
16. Goncourt, *Journal* 3: 630ff., 1263ff; Bibliothèque Municipale de Rouen, 92N2 Flaubert.

CHAPTER FIFTY-ONE: WORKS

1. Gustave Flaubert, *Le Second Volume de Bouvard et Pécuchet* (Paris: Les Lettres Nouvelles, 1966).
2. Gustave Flaubert, *Bouvard et Pécuchet* (critical edition edited by Alberto Cento) (Naples: Instituto Universitario Orientale, 1964), lxvii, 13, 124f., 267; also see Bibliothèque Municipale de Rouen, manuscript gg 10; Durry, *Flaubert et ses projets*, 225ff. The addition "Copier comme autrefois" appears in the once-authoritative edition published in 1923 (Paris: Conard), when Flaubert's niece was still alive.
3. Halpérine-Kaminsky, *Tourguéneff*, 143f.; Franklin-Grout, "Les Hommes célèbres de mon enfance."
4. Du Camp, *Souvenirs littéraires* 2: 147.
5. Barbey, *Le Roman contemporain*, 125f., 134f.

6. Archives Départementales de la Seine-Maritime, Bureau de Maronne, May 4, 1881.

7. Flaubert, *Lettres à Raoul-Duval*, 269ff.

8. André Dubuc, preface to *Les Rouennais et la famille Flaubert*, iv.

9. *Je suis partout*, September 24, 1943.

10. Goncourt, *Journal* 3: 74f.

11. Spaziani, *Gli Amici*, 179.

12. Goncourt, *Journal* 3: 310.

13. Jacques-Emile Blanche, *La Pêche aux souvenirs* (Paris: Flammarion, 1949), 63ff.

14. Paul Mariéton papers, Musée Calvet, Avignon, from Jean Bruneau.

15. Bibliothèque Municipale de Rouen, 92N4a Flaubert: letter from Georges Mignot, October 12, 1958. Cf. notes in GP 1.

16. Ambroise Vollard, *Souvenirs d'un marchand de tableaux* (Paris: Albin Michel, 1937), 311.

17. Chevalley-Sabatier, *Flaubert et sa nièce*, 194ff.

18. Pierre Borel in *Lettres inédites de Maupassant*, 7f.; Pierre Borel, cited in Franklin-Grout, "Heures d'autrefois."

19. Willa Cather, "Chance Meeting," *Atlantic Monthly*, February 1933, 154ff.

20. Catalogue, Etude de Me Léon Martelly, April 28–30, 1931, in Bibliothèque Municipale de Rouen, 92N7 Flaubert.

21. Chevalley-Sabatier, *Flaubert et sa nièce*, 203ff.

22. Goncourt, *Journal* 3: 187, 209.

23. *Revue politique et littéraire*, January 19, 1884, 66; *Le Temps*, January 22 and 27, 1884.

INDEX

NOTE: For obvious reasons no entry is provided for Gustave Flaubert, or for Rouen or Paris. Cities and other sites are mentioned only if they figure significantly in Flaubert's life or work.   H. L.

MOTHER AND DAUGHTER
The Letters of Eleanor and Anna Roosevelt
edited by Bernard Asbell

FLAUBERT & TURGENEV
A Friendship in Letters
edited and translated
by Barbara Beaumont

SECRETS OF MARIE ANTOINETTE
A Collection of Letters
edited by Olivier Bernier

TALLEYRAND
A Biography
by Duff Cooper

VIRTUE UNDER FIRE
*How World War II Changed Our
Social and Sexual Attitudes*
by John Costello

PIAF
by Margaret Crosland

CHOURA
The Memoirs of Alexandra Danilova

ONWARD AND UPWARD
A Biography of Katharine S. White
by Linda H. Davis

AMERICAN NOTES
A Journey
by Charles Dickens

FELIX MENDELSSOHN
A Life in Letters
edited by Rudolf Elvers

LETTERS AND DRAWINGS OF
BRUNO SCHULZ
with Selected Prose
edited by Jerzy Ficowski

BEFORE THE DELUGE
A Portrait of Berlin in the 1920's
by Otto Friedrich

THE END OF THE WORLD
A History
by Otto Friedrich

CELL WARS
*The Immune System's Newest
Weapons Against Cancer*
by Marshall Goldberg, M.D.

J. ROBERT OPPENHEIMER
Shatterer of Worlds
by Peter Goodchild

THE ENTHUSIAST
A Life of Thornton Wilder
by Gilbert A. Harrison

THE PARABLE OF THE BLIND
by Gert Hofmann

THE SPECTACLE AT THE TOWER
by Gert Hofmann

INDIAN SUMMER
A Novel
by William Dean Howells

EDITH WHARTON
A Biography
by R.W.B. Lewis

VERDI
A Life in the Theatre
by Charles Osborne

THE CONQUEST OF
MOROCCO
by Douglas Porch

THE CONQUEST OF THE
SAHARA
by Douglas Porch

HENRY VIII
The Politics of Tyranny
by Jasper Ridley

ELIZABETH I
The Shrewdness of Virtue
by Jasper Ridley

LETTERS ON CEZANNE
by Rainer Maria Rilke
edited by Clara Rilke

KENNETH CLARK
A Biography
by Meryle Secrest

THE HERMIT OF PEKING
*The Hidden Life of Sir Edmund
Backhouse*
by Hugh Trevor-Roper

ALEXANDER OF RUSSIA
Napoleon's Conqueror
by Henri Troyat

MARY TODD LINCOLN
Her Life and Letters
edited by Justin G. Turner
and Linda Levitt Turner